Taking Sides:
Clashing Views in
Women's Studies

by Rachel Pienta
Valdosta State University

http://create.mcgraw-hill.com

ISBN-10: 0078139481   ISBN-13: 9780078139482

Contents

i. Preface by Pienta 1
ii. Topic Guide by Pienta 4
iii. Introduction--Women's Studies: What Is It and Why Should We Study It? by Pienta 5

Unit 1 9

1. Women's Rights Are Human Rights: Health and Human Safety by Pienta 10
   1.1. Is Access to Birth Control a Basic Human Right? by Pienta 11
   1.2. Should the Federal Government Adopt a New Legal Definition of Rape? by Pienta 26
   1.3. Are Women More at Risk for Crimes Using Digital Technology? by Pienta 40

Unit 2 51

2. Women's Health, Women's Bodies: Contested Terrain by Pienta 52
   2.1. Is Access to Abortion a Class Issue? by Pienta 53

Unit 3 69

3. Women in the Workplace: She Works Hard for the Money by Pienta 70
   3.1. Should Women Serve in Military Combat Positions? by Pienta 71
   3.2. Can Sex Work Be Empowering? by Pienta 82
   3.3. Have Working Women Destroyed the American Family? by Pienta 97
   3.4. Are Lower Fertility Rates Responsible for Economic Downturns? by Pienta 114

Unit 4 125

4. Gender Equity: Still Unequal After All These Years by Pienta 126
   4.1. Should "Trans" Women Benefit from Gender Equity Policies? by Pienta 127
   4.2. Should Title IX Be Repealed? by Pienta 135
   4.3. Do We Need the Equal Rights Amendment? by Pienta 150

Unit 5 163

5. Feminism in the 21st Century: You've Come a Long Way, Baby by Pienta 164
   5.1. Can a Woman with Conservative Political Views Be a Feminist? by Pienta 165
   5.2. Can Women Be Misogynistic? by Pienta 176
   5.3. Do Women Support the Advancement of Other Women? by Pienta 192

Unit 6 201

6. Double Standards: The Intersection of Sex, Gender, and Culture by Pienta 202
   6.1. Is There Still a Double Standard of Sexuality for Women and Girls? by Pienta 203
   6.2. Should the Word Slut Be Redefined? by Pienta 221

6.3. Are Women "Hard-Wired" to Be Society's Nurturers? by Pienta 230

Unit 7 237

7. Women as Objects: Subject to the Male Gaze by Pienta 238

7.1. Is Pornography for Men Different Than Pornography for Women? by Pienta 239

Preface

Women's Studies is inherently a controversial discipline. The issues studied and the topics discussed in courses generate heated discourse both in academia and in the larger social realm. The field of Women's Studies is not solely focused on studying women but instead encompasses inquiry into how women and men experience the world difference due to social and cultural variations related to sex and gender. One focus of Women's Studies centers on understanding how social stratification and related equality issues impact the life opportunities of women and girls across the world. Underlying questions related to women's historically subordinate role and how changing cultural dynamics have larger implications for social transformation and cultural change form the foundation of what comprises Women's Studies' core focus as an academic field of study.

Taking Sides: Clashing Views in Women's Studies is a tool for stimulating critical analysis. The ultimate goal of the text is to serve as an impetus for further study beyond the classroom walls. The issues examined in the book have implications for public discourse and represented numerous politically charged topics.

This book contains issues that are being widely debated in contemporary scholarly and public discourse on legal and policy issues that involve the status of women. The issues presented in this book are phrased as YES/NO questions. Two opposing perspectives are explained and compared. Each issue is prefaced by an issue introduction that contains background information intended to frame and contextualize the positions. Questions for discussion follow each issue. While no issue is truly binary, the shades of gray that envelop each topic present an opportunity for rich discourse within the classroom setting.

The issues examined within this text provide insights into some of the most controversial topics that drive public discourse in contemporary society. Readers will be challenged to examine their personal gender ideologies from the first to the final chapter. My hope is that students will find new ideas and perspectives that will challenge them to examine their own ideologies and will finish the book as more informed consumers of public discourse on contemporary women's issues.

Rachel Pienta
Valdosta State University

Editor of This Volume

Rachel Sutz Pienta, PhD has taught for the College of Education at Valdosta State University since 2009. She earned her doctorate in Educational Leadership and Policy Studies at Florida State University where she also taught Women's Studies courses from 1999 to 2012.

Dr. Pienta's career has included working as a legislative policy analyst, an independent governmental affairs consultant, and as a classroom teacher. Her research interests include education policy and reform, women and leadership, gender equity, diversity issues, and social justice.

Dr. Pienta speaks and writes frequently on public policy issues. Her writing on women and political advocacy has been featured in numerous publications, included the edited collection The 21st Century Motherhood Movement: Mothers Speak Out on Why We Need to Change the World and How to Do It.

Academic Advisory Board Members

Members of the Academic Advisory Board are instrumental in the final selection of articles for *Taking Sides* ExpressBooks. Their review of the articles for content, level, and appropriateness provides critical direction to the editor(s) and staff. We think that you will find their careful consideration reflected in this ExpressBook.

Mary Beth Ahlum
Nebraska Wesleyan University

Louise Alderson
Front Range Community College

Sine Anahita
University of Alaska Fairbanks

Patricia Andersen
Midwestern State University

Amani Awwad
SUNY Canton

Harriet Bachner
Pittsburg State University

Jill Barris
Houston Community College SW

Cameron Basquiat
College of Southern Nevada

Barbara Baumgartner
Washington University, St. Louis

Josephine Bradley
Clark Atlanta University

Mariana Branda
College of the Canyons

Kristi Branham
Western Kentucky University

Patti Britton
Chicago School of Professional Psychology

Harry Brod
University of Northern Iowa

Kimberly Brown
Ball State University

Diana Bruns
Southeast Missouri State University

Becky Bryant
Texas Woman's University

Laurie Buchanan
Clark State Community College

Kathleen Butterly Nigro
University of Missouri, St. Louis

Mike Calvert
Butler Community College

Joe Camiolo
Rutgers University

Barbara Carl
Pennsylvania State University

JoAnn Carpenter
Florida State College Jacksonville

Kimberly Chandler
Xavier University of Louisiana

H. David Chen
Widener University

Oak Chezar
Front Range Community College

Rose-Marie Chierici
State University of New York-Geneseo

Kurt Choate
Northeastern State University

Margaret Chojnacki
Barry University

Yesudas Choondassery
Berkeley College

Dana Cochran
Radford University

Deborah Cohen
University of Missouri-St. Louis

Sandra Collins
Brown Mackie College

Tara Conant
Westfield State University

Allison Cummings
Southern New Hampshire University

Kevin Cummings
Mercer University

Valerie Davis-LaMastro
Rowan University

Melanie Deffendall
Delgado Community College

Danielle DeMuth
Grand Valley State University

Fabiana Desrosiers
Dominican College

Nancy Lee Donde
Dona Ana Community College

Penelope Dugan
Richard Stockton College of NJ

Lauren Duncan
Smith College

Miriam Ehrenberg
John Jay College—CUNY

Maureen Ellis-Davis
Bergen Community College

Edward Fernandes
Barton College

Danielle Ficco
Carlow University

Johanna Fisher
Canisius College

Allison Foley
Augusta State University

Lori Fox
Art Institute of Las Vegas

Anne Freeman
Rockingham Community College

Michael Gill
University of Connecticut

Jeanne Gillespie
University of Southern Mississippi

Adrienne Gillespie
Weber State University

Stephanie Gray
College of Lake County

Janet Griffin
Howard University

Rachel Griffin
Southern Illinois University, Carbondale

Elizabeth Hackett
Agnes Scott College

Margaret Haefner
North Park University

Misty Haggard-Belford
Rollins College

Davida Harris
Savannah State University

Elizabeth Hegeman
John Jay College—CUNY

Candace Hendershot
University of Findlay

Melissann Herron
San Diego State University

Jodie Hertzog
Wichita State University

Tahereh Alavi Hojjat
DeSales University

Kristin Holster
Dean College

John Howell
Southern Utah University

Jennifer Hudson
Southern Connecticut State University

Fathima Ismail
Union County College

Courtney Jarrett
Ball State University

Susan Jordan
Fisher College

Arnold Kahn
James Madison University

Hilda Kahne
Brandeis University

Debra Kaufman
Northeastern University

Janice Kelly
Purdue University

Barbara Kernan
University of Wisconsin-Eau Claire

Mary Klein
Marian University

Marcia Klotz
Portland State University

Melissa Knight
California State University, Fresno

Elizabeth Kolsky
Villanova University

Charlene Kolupski
Edinboro University of Pennsylvania

Connie Koppelman
SUNY Stony Brook

Holly Korta
Caldwell Community College

Catherine Koziol
University of Missouri, St. Louis

Mary Krueger
Bowling Green State University

Jane Lehr
California Polytechnic State University

Darby Lewes
Lycoming College

Adrianna Lozano
Purdue University

Kristina Lucas
NHTI Concord Community College

Mark Lynch
Saint Francis University

Ed Madden
University of South Carolina

Alison Mandaville
Pacific Lutheran University

Rita Marinho
Towson University

Jennifer Martin
Oakland University

Lisa Martin
University of Michigan-Dearborn

Chandra Massner
University of Pikeville

Krista Mazza
Georgia Highlands College

Mary McGinnis
Columbia College Chicago

Kristen McHenry
University of Massachusetts Dartmouth

Deborah Meadows
Columbia Basin College

Elsie Miranda
Barry University

Rosalinda Moctezuma
Los Angeles Mission College

Celeste Montoya
University of Colorado

Sujata Moorti
Middlebury College

Maureen Morley
Cuyahoga Community College

Bonnie Morris
George Washington University

Annette Morrow
Minnesota State University Moorhead

Kathryn Myers
Saint Mary of the Woods College

Patricia E. Neff
Edinboro University

Jean O'Brien
King's College

Gul Ozyegin
College of William and Mary

Mark Packard
Southeast Community College

Abigail Palko
University of Notre Dame

Gloria Park
Indiana University of Pennsylvania

Debra Sue Pate
Jackson State University

Leandra Preston
University of Central Florida

Karen Rayne
AUSTIN Community College

Doug Rice
California State University - Sacramento

Rebecca Richards
Saint Olaf College

Patricia Rind
Purchase College—SUNY

Nancy Risch
Caldwell Community College

Yosalida C. Rivero-Zaritzky
Mercer University

Carlos Rodriguez
Dominican University of California

Kim Schreck
Oberlin College

Brittney Schrick
Southern Arkansas University

Helena Semerjian
Worcester State University

Hideko Sera
Argosy University

Denise Shaw
University of South Carolina—Union

Sheida Shirvani
Ohio University-Zanesville

Amy Slater
Metropolitan Community College—Blue River

Nicole Smolter
University of Delaware

Sheila Stepp
SUNY Orange

Racheal Stimpson
Alamance Community College

Eva Ludwiga Szalay
Weber State University

Johnnie Terry
Sierra College

Mary Thompson
James Madison University

Silvia Tomaskova
UNC Chapel Hill

Claire Van Ens
Kutztown University of Pennsylvania

Kate Waites
Nova Southeastern University

Martha Walker
Mary Baldwin College

Glenda Warren
University of the Cumberlands

Patricia Wasielewski
University of Redlands

Jacquilyn Weeks
University of Notre Dame

Kristin Wesner
Clarke University

Kathleen Westman
Waubonsee Community College

Mark William Westmoreland
Penn State Brandywine

Vera Whisman
Ithaca College

Joylette Williams Samuels
Nassau Community College-SUNY

Anne-Marie Womack
Texas A & M University

Bonnie Wright
Limestone College

Cigdem Yazici
Koc University

Q. Zeng
Arkansas Tech University

Opportune Zongo
Bowling Green State University

Maliha Zulfacar
California Polytechnic State University

Topic Guide

This topic guide suggests how the selections in this book relate to the subjects covered in your course. All the articles that relate to each topic are listed below the bold-faced term.

Abortion

Is Access to Abortion a Class Issue?

Birth Control

Is Access to Birth Control a Basic Human Right?

Crime

Are Women More at Risk for Crimes Using Digital Technology?

Family

Have Working Women Destroyed the American Family?
Are Women "Hard-Wired" to Be Society's Nurturers?

Feminism

Can a Woman with Conservative Political Views Be a Feminist?
Can Women Be Misogynistic?

Fertility

Are Lower Fertility Rates Responsible for Economic Downturns?

Gender Equity

Should "Trans" Women Benefit from Gender Equity Policies?
Should Title IX Be Repealed?

Gender Roles

Are Women "Hard-Wired" to Be Society's Nurturers?

Harassment

Are Women More at Risk for Crimes Using Digital Technology?

Military

Should Women Serve in Military Combat Positions?

Misogyny

Can Women Be Misogynistic?

Politics

Should the Federal Government Adopt a New Legal Definition of Rape?
Is There a Double Standard for Women Political Candidates?

Population

Are Lower Fertility Rates Responsible for Economic Downturns?

Pornography

Is Pornography for Men Different Than Pornography for Women?

Prostitution

Can Sex Work Be Empowering?

Rape

Should the Federal Government Adopt a New Legal Definition of Rape?

Self-image

Should the Word Slut Be Redefined?

Sexual Consent

Should the Federal Government Adopt a New Legal Definition of Rape?

Work

Do Women Support the Advancement of Other Women?

Introduction

Women's Studies: What Is It and Why Should We Study It?

As this book went to press in 2013, a debate over a "war on women" dominated national political discourse. The academic discipline known as Women's Studies represents the history and philosophy of women as well as the science of gender. The policy and politics of women's lives represent an integral part of Women's Studies—from earning the right to vote in nations across the globe to gaining access to equal legal rights and status as human beings and full citizens wherever women may reside.

Women now enjoy many, if not most, of the same rights and privileges that men do. However, women throughout history have fought battles for rights that most would take for granted today. Historically, we are not far removed from the notion that women should not be educated alongside men, nor even allowed the opportunity to learn to read. Gains in legal status such as the right to own property or to vote are even more recent developments in women's struggle for equality.

Early proponents of women's potential for intellectual development have advocated for female equality for centuries. Mexican nun Sor Juana Inés de la Cruz wrote "Respuesta de la poetisa a la muy ilustre" (1691). "The Reply" was a pro-feminist work that argued for women's intellectual capacity and the equality of their souls. British writer Mary Astell wrote *A Serious Proposal to the Ladies, for the Advancement of Their True and Greatest Interest. By a Lover of Her Sex.* (1694). Like Sor Juana, Astell made an argument in favor of women's capacity for learning.

The seed that inspired Mary Wollstonecraft's 1792 treatise on women's rights, *A Vindication of the Rights of Woman*, was sown in response to Jean-Jacques Rousseau's famous essay, *Emile* (1762), which recommended education stratified according to sex roles. However, Wollstonecraft's work would become the foundation for a women's movement that would span centuries. Her work represented the first time that a woman questioned traditional patriarch thinking and articulated that while women might differ from men, their rights were just as important and worthy of consideration.

In 1848, in the United States, American women convened a women's rights convention in Seneca Falls, New York. It was there that Elizabeth Cady Stanton would read the *Declaration of Sentiments*, a document which called for women to have full and equal standing as citizens.

The first Women's Studies program in the United States was established at San Diego State University in 1970. Cornell University followed suit and began a program that same year. The impetus for the formation of Women's Stud-ies programs across the nation came from the civil rights movement of the 1960s. Efforts to expand education beyond the realm of the traditional white male European canon resulted in multicultural education evolving in primary and secondary schools. At the postsecondary level, programs such as Chicano/a Studies and African American Studies would be followed by Women's Studies.

Women's Studies programs today offer a variety of courses that range from subjects aimed at making women visible in culture and history such as *Women in Western Culture* to classes that focus on sexuality, psychology, anthropology, religion, literature, or gender theory. More specialized courses may focus on specific aspects of public policy, women's health, or particular time periods in history.

The inception of Women's Studies as an academic discipline more than 40 years ago was followed by the landmark 1972 Title IX legislation, which instituted watershed education amendments. Title IX would alter the landscape of American education and create new opportunities for women and girls in the classroom and on the athletic fields.

While the United States has yet to institute an Equal Rights Amendment, women have made strides toward parity in many realms of society. The Lily Ledbetter Act of 2010 brought women closer to achieving pay equity. Although women have enjoyed many firsts since 1970, this nation has yet to inaugurate a female president.

Intersectionality

A discussion of controversial issues in Women's Studies begins with the premise of intersectionality. Women's identities are a complex set of statuses and roles. Variables which include but are not limited to race, class, sexual orientation, ethnicity, age, religion, and education all factor into how women experience their lives. How do different aspects of a woman's identity intersect to influence how she experiences the world in which she lives?

Feminist writers approach the topic of intersectionality from different standpoints. Patricia Hill Collins (1990) articulated a theoretical perspective of intersectionality based on what she termed a "matrix of domination." The premise of her theory was built on an examination of how African American women experience the world through an intersection of race, gender, and class. Collins (1990) characterized the lived experiences and identities of African American women as "an interlocking system of oppression" and described this system as a "matrix of domination."

Examining Viewpoints

In the field of Women's Studies, the study of women's ways of learning and feminist perspectives on teaching and learning influence the scholarly discourse. Belenky et al. (1986) examined differences in how women construct, create, and receive knowledge. In doing so, Belenky et al. developed a theory of "women's way of knowing" that articulated a feminist perspective on communication and learning. The feminist theoretical framework embodied in standpoint epistemology provides further expansion on the idea of women and situated knowledge (Harding, 1993).

In this text, no assumptions—feminist or otherwise—are made about audience receptivity or the learner's perspective. Opposing viewpoints on controversial issues are presented for the reader to examine. Topics are presented in an objective, bias-free manner with care taken to faithfully represent opposing perspectives on the issues.

Tools for Argument Analysis

Readers of this text are tasked with examining two opposing perspectives on a variety of contemporary topics. At times, the perspectives on these issues are diametrically disparate while, in other instances, the opposing viewpoints are highly nuanced and subtle. The issue introductions are intended to provide a framework for analysis and scholarly discourse. Each issue is followed by questions designed to elicit critical thinking and provide direction for debate and discussion.

Philosophical Considerations

The philosophical underpinnings of this text draw on a range of academic perspectives. Historical and theoretical foundations of the women's movement and feminist philosophy provide a framework for this book. The ongoing evolution of women's pursuit of equality and equity, from the earliest feminist writings of the seventeenth century to the arguments on the twenty-first-century multimedia stage of global politics, is chronicled and examined on the following pages.

Power and Control: The Woman Question

The issues contained in this book cover a wide expanse of contested terrain. However, there is common ground to be found. The underlying argument woven into all the topics discussed in the seven units and eighteen issues which comprise this book all share one common denominator—the controversy is rooted in a conflict over the origins of power and the struggle for control regarding concerns ranging from the cultural and social spheres to the economic and political realms. Questions of power and control relative to the lives of women range from disputes over women's roles in the workplace to arguments over medical decisions. Ultimately, questions of power and control and the ongoing debate over women's basic human rights and personal agency drive the inquiry process that serves as the organizing principle for this book.

Issues in This Volume

The examination of critical contemporary issues in Women's Studies is organized into seven units. In Unit 1, women's rights are examined within a global context of human rights. Fundamental assumptions about health and human safety are examined from a feminist perspective, while opposing viewpoints are presented for objective consideration and classroom analysis. In Unit 2, women's health issues and personal body politics are examined. The critical relationship between health, class, and privilege are analyzed from opposing perspectives.

In Unit 3, women's roles as workers in the twenty-first century global economy are examined. The impact of women's increased participation in paid work outside the home is analyzed from opposing viewpoints. The fundamental issue of women's right to self-determination and, by association, the choice to work for compensation as questions of individual agency and personal empowerment are unpacked from multiple perspectives. From participation in the military in combat zones to working in the sex industry, issues of women's rights and access to equal opportunities are presented for critical examination. The role of women as biological mothers is also considered. The larger impact of women's expanded educational and employment opportunities and the corresponding influence on fertility rates and the effect on the workforce over time are also presented for examination.

Unit 4 examines gender equity from multiple perspectives. The concept of gender equity becomes more complex as people can opt to change their biological sex and as our notions of how gender is constructed and determined continue to expand. From the Equal Rights Amendment to Title IX, public policy and the issue of gender equity within the framework of evolving social norms are examined. The challenge of adapting policies to accommodate a shifting cultural landscape is presented for consideration.

In Unit 5, twenty-first century feminist thought and perspectives are explored. The notion of what it means to be a feminist and who can identify with the label is presented for examination. Issues of how women interact with and perceive other women are analyzed from opposing viewpoints. Opposing tropes of sisterhood and competition are compared within a framework of understanding how women's expanded social options have altered what it means to be a feminist in the twenty-first century.

Unit 6 addresses cultural double standards and how race, gender, and class intersect to influence social rules. The concepts of privilege and oppression are examined within a framework of understanding the real and the perceived rules that guide and govern social conduct in contemporary culture. The power of labels and words are analyzed in the context of the 24-hour media culture. The influence of social media and the impact of twenty-first-century technology on public perception and culture change are presented for consideration. Finally, changing perceptions about status and relative social power is considered within the context of traditional constructions of women's cultural roles.

In Unit 7, one more aspect of women and sexuality is considered. The question of women and pornography is examined from opposing perspectives. Pornography is often framed within the context of power and privilege and discussed within a framework of sexual objectification. This unit challenges notions of power, privilege, and subjectivity by presenting women as independent, empowered agents able to act—both literally and figuratively—in ways that suggest the twenty-first-century pornography industry may offer equal economic opportunities for men and women.

Suggestions for Classroom Use

I first addressed using a debate format to teach controversial issues in an article co-written with colleague Jeanne O'Kon in 2004. After using debates as an instructional strategy across multiple disciplines, including Education, English, Sociology, and Women's Studies, I compared pedagogical approaches with my program chair Jeanne O'Kon. She had experienced great success implementing similar approaches in her own Education and Psychology courses. We found that the use of debates helped to create a non-threatening, scholarly environment in which students could safely examine controversial ideas (O'Kon & Sutz, 2004).

Conclusion

Women's Studies scholars find that each day offers new opportunities to engage in critical discourse on the issues that impact women. The barrage of media in all its forms provides constant fodder for intellectual consideration. The scholars' challenge is to sift through the competitive narratives and to separate the hyperbole from the facts in order to focus on the essential questions.

References

Belenky, M.F. (1986). *Women's Ways of Knowing: The Development of Self, Voice, and Mind.* Basic Books: New York.

Collins, P.H. (1990). *Black Feminist Thought: Knowledge, Consciousness, and the Politics of Empowerment* (pp. 221–238). Unwin Hyman: Boston.

Harding, S. (1993). "Rethinking Standpoint Epistemology: What Is 'Strong Objectivity'. In Linda Alcoff and Elizabeth Potter (Eds.), *Feminist Epistemologies*. Routledge.

O'Kon, J. and Sutz, R. (2004). "Using In-Class Debates to Teach Gender Issues in Psychology." In Bryan K. Saville, Tracy Zinn, and Vincent W. Hevern (Eds.), *Essays from Excellence in Teaching: 2004* (vol. 4). ©1999–2012 APA Division 2, Society for the Teaching of Psychology. Retrieved from: http://teachpsych.org/ebooks/eit2004/index.php

Unit 1

UNIT

Women's Rights Are Human Rights: Health and Human Safety

*W*hat constitutes basic human rights? Do women's rights require additional articulation to ensure their health and safety? How can we ensure that biological aspects of sex align with social aspects of gender in ways that are congruent with preserving women's basic human rights? How do changing definitions of crime impact women's human rights? Should laws be reviewed and revised as our definitions expand and evolve? How do changing technologies affect the law? Advances in technology have altered aspects of daily life in myriad ways from the landscape of reproductive rights to the development of legal procedures for conducting evidence collection. New technologies change the way we live and raise legal questions that drive media discourse and influence public policy. This section will explore basic definitions of human rights and examine ways in which women's rights may or may not require expanded definitions to ensure that women receive comparable legal protections relative to men.

Selected, Edited, and with Issue Framing Material by:
Rachel Pienta, *Valdosta State University*

ISSUE

Is Access to Birth Control a Basic Human Right?

YES: **B. Jessie Hill**, from "Law Review Symposium 2010: Reproductive Rights, Human Rights, and the Human Right to Health," *Case Western Reserve Law Review* (vol. 60, no. 4, Summer 2010)

NO: **Pamela Laufer-Ukeles**, from "Reproductive Choices and Informed Consent: Fetal Interests, Women's Identity, and Relational Autonomy," *American Journal of Law & Medicine* (vol. 37, no. 4, December 2011)

Learning Outcomes

As you read the issues, focus on the following points:

- Where do the rights of a woman end and the rights of a potential new life begin?
- Can the rights of a woman and a fetus be reconciled without a human rights violation?

ISSUE SUMMARY

YES: B. Jessie Hill, a professor and associate director of the Center for Social Justice at Case Western Reserve University School of Law, links reproductive rights and the right to health to make a case for the human dignity of women within the context of health and reproductive rights.

NO: Pamela Laufer-Ukeles, an associate professor of law at University of Dayton School of Law, elaborates on the concept of informed consent as a key component in healthcare decision making that expands the discourse to include both the interests of the woman and the fetus.

The relationship between reproductive rights and health care continues to be contested legal terrain. Proponents of reproductive rights argue for women's autonomy and expanded access to reproductive health services. Critics of the reproductive choice movement argue for increased restrictions on access to birth control and expanded limitations on women's access to abortion procedures. Legislative measures to further limit women's autonomy related to reproductive capacity have expanded to include increased scrutiny on lifestyle and stipulations mandating invasive medical tests.

The debate over who is best able to make decisions related to reproduction may begin with the individual but then transitions into medical examining rooms and often ends in courtrooms. The Supreme Court's decision to uphold the Affordable Care Act could be viewed as a great step forward for women's reproductive health. The Act should expand women's access to copay-free preventive health care—including contraception.

The question of what constitutes informed consent and what knowledge should be required to terminate a pregnancy has increasingly dominated both the political

and popular discourse in contemporary American society. Informed consent, once considered a safeguard against the dictates of paternalistic traditional medicine, has now become the heavy hand punitively wielded to impose obstacles on women seeking to exercise reproductive agency.

In the YES and NO selections, two legal perspectives are considered that examine opposing perspectives on human rights, reproductive agency, and where the interests of the state collide with individual autonomy. Hill examines current legal thinking regarding human rights and health care. Laufer-Ukeles deconstructs the double-edged sword of informed consent.

The crux of the argument about human rights relative to reproductive rights rests within conflicting perspectives about health care and, in general, life. At times, these opposing interests create a Hobson's choice when medical emergencies arise. Irish hospital officials faced this issue in 2012 when Savita Halappanavar, a 31-year-old Indian woman who was 17 weeks pregnant, experienced complications from blood poisoning (Pogatchnik, 2012). Halappanavar ultimately died after the fetus she was carrying died. Irish laws against abortion and murky provisions for medical decision making in the event of life-threatening circumstances all seemed to contribute to a legal dilemma that left Halappanavar and her husband with no options. Investigations into the circumstances were still pending at the time this book went to press.

The issue of a women's relational autonomy and her right to personal health remains in question in many nations across the world. Examining the issue within the framework of positive rights relative to negative rights may help to provide perspective for further analysis. Positive rights generally involve the provision of a service, while negative rights tend to refer to protections against government restrictions on personal liberties.

Across the United States, state legislatures annually debate issues of maternal culpability in miscarriages and occasionally seek to limit the medical options of pregnant women. The notion that a pregnant woman cedes all rights to self-determination at the moment of conception remains a controversial issue that, in the United States, tends to divide ideological adversaries along partisan lines. The policy implications for women, reproductive rights, and access to health care continue to dominate discussion and legislative proposals on this issue.

Samantha Burton's experience in March 2009 exemplifies the murky lines between a woman's personhood and fetal rights. Burton, a mother of two who suffered from pregnancy complications, was ordered to involuntary hospital confinement and mandated to undergo treatment by the Circuit Court of Leon County. Forbidden to transfer to another hospital and prevented from seeking a second medical opinion, Burton suffered three days of state-compelled hospitalization. Forced to undergo an involuntary caesarean section, Burton suffered a stillbirth and was subsequently released from the hospital. In 2010, Burton's case was adjudicated and "the Florida District Court of Appeal ruled that the rights of a pregnant woman were violated when she was forced to remain hospitalized against her will after disagreeing with a hospital's recommended treatment" (ACLU, 2010 accessed at www.aclu.org September 2012).

The experiences of Burton and Halappanavar illustrate how poorly defined the rights of women are in cases where the health of a fetus is in question. The flip side of the argument addresses the issue of how and when a fetus can qualify for protection against his or her mother. Paltrow (1999) raised this question relative to "crack moms" and "crack babies." In the 2000s, the treatment of

"meth babies" would become a public health concern. The issue of fetal rights has been playing out in courtrooms for decades. In 1988, the Illinois Supreme Court ruled, in *Stallman v. Youngquist*, that a child did not have the right to sue a mother for alleged abuse during gestation. Alabama enacted a chemical-endangerment law in 2006. Since the law's enactment, more than 60 new mothers have been charged (Calhoun, 2012).

On the opposite end of the spectrum, maternal health advocates have worked to put personal power back into the hands of women across the world. Public health experts like Dr. Allan Rosenfeld have become pioneers in global advocacy for maternal health. Described as a "social entrepreneur in the world of maternal health," Rosenfeld's holistic approach has encompassed expanding contraceptive options in nations like Lagos and Thailand (Kristof, 2009, p. 104). The efforts of early trailblazers like the late Dr. Rosenfeld, who served as dean for Columbia University's School of Public Health, continue to save women's lives in the form of organizations like Averting Maternal Death and Disability (AMDD). While groups such as AMDD work overseas in developing countries, organizations such as Planned Parenthood and Crisis Pregnancy Centers maintain a pitched battle for access to pregnant women.

Laws that permit states to prosecute mothers on behalf of their fetal or newborn children open the door to "fetal personhood" statutes. Legislative bills and state constitutional amendments in favor of establishing "fetal personhood" laws have proliferated in recent years. In the United States, arguments to permit religious-based institutions to deny health care to save the lives of pregnant women when doing so would jeopardize the health of the fetus have resulted in bitter policy arguments. In 2011, H.R. 358, the "Protect Life Act" became known by opponents as the "Let Women Die Act" (Bassett, 2011). In 2013, a New Mexico state legislator filed legislation that would make abortion after rape a felony. The bill language stated, "Tampering with evidence shall include procuring or facilitating an abortion, or compelling or coercing another to obtain an abortion of a fetus that is the result of criminal sexual penetration or incest with the intent to destroy evidence of the crime" (Agence France Presse, 2013). Legislation such as this 2013 measure in New Mexico exemplifies the arguments that continue to be waged over where the rights of women end and the rights of possible or potential lives begin.

YES

B. Jessie Hill

Law Review Symposium 2010: Reproductive Rights, Human Rights, and the Human Right to Health

Introduction

The human right to health, it seems, has finally come of age. First articulated in the human rights context in 1946,[1] the right to health is now sufficiently developed that it can form the basis for recognizing or strengthening other rights, and commentators can debate its complexities and limitations, as in this diverse and timely Symposium. At the same time, advocates, academics, and policymakers have begun to consider reproductive rights in a broader and more global context—one that reaches beyond the narrow confines of the right to privacy in U.S. constitutional jurisprudence to encompass concepts of human rights, reproductive justice, and access to holistic reproductive health care, from the earliest beginnings of the reproductive cycle to its end.[2] And perhaps most importantly, they have begun to connect reproductive rights to the right to health in various productive ways. Yet, the array of contributions to this Symposium demonstrates that as the right to health has matured and our understanding of reproductive rights has become more complex and more global, a dizzying proliferation of new and urgent questions, problems, opportunities, and challenges have presented themselves.

Attempts to achieve judicial enforcement of human rights domestically have long been plagued by resistance resulting from a variety of factors, including the intransigence of the distinction between positive and negative rights in U.S. jurisprudence, with only the latter being considered the proper objects of constitutional protection.[3] Although commentators have long questioned the usefulness and meaningfulness of the distinction itself, it remains alive and well in the U.S.[4] Even setting aside the negative/positive rights distinction, moreover, there are reasons to doubt whether full judicial enforcement of rights such as reproductive rights and the right to health is possible or desirable. One might question, for example, whether judges are competent to engage the complex scientific and policy issues involved in certain right-to-health claims, or whether the task of realizing such socioeconomic rights is better left to legislative bodies, or even non-governmental entities. Notably, several of the authors in this issue have drawn upon comparative analysis both

to critique and to substantiate reproductive rights and right-to-health norms.

A number of the contributors to this Symposium explore the question of how best to enforce reproductive rights in greater depth. Some bring to bear fresh perspectives on judicial competence and role, while others move beyond judicial enforcement to conceive of a more broad-based assumption of human rights duties and enforcement among both state and non-state actors. Andrew Coan, Assistant Professor at the University of Wisconsin Law School, examines the issue of judicial competence in the reproductive rights realm from a fresh perspective in *Assisted Reproductive Equality: An Institutional Analysis*. In particular, Professor Coan considers the problem of the right to access assisted reproductive technologies through the lens of institutional competence. Professor Coan's article, which critiques Professor Radikha Rao's scholarship on this issue, argues for a nuanced comparative approach to institutional analysis. Professor Coan observes that even the most attentive institutional scholarship on reproductive liberty, including Professor Rao's, fails to take fully into account the comparative limitations of the judiciary in distinguishing between the motivations and targets of ART legislation, as well as the comparative limitations of the legislature in terms of its incentives to find facts and to truly reflect the views of an informed public. "The basic point is simply expressed," Professor Coan explains. "Intelligent institutional choice requires a comparison of the plausible institutional alternatives. It is never enough to show that one institution functions well or poorly in the abstract."[5]

Professor Browne Lewis's article, too, gives us reason to doubt the competency of courts to deal with the legal and factual complexities surrounding reproductive health and technologies. Professor Lewis, who is Associate Professor and Director of the Center for Health Law and Policy at Cleveland-Marshall College of Law, describes the patchwork of laws, and substantial areas of remaining uncertainty, concerning the regulation of new reproductive technologies in *Graveside Birthday Parties: The Legal Consequences of Forming Families Posthumously*. Despite the fact that assisted reproductive technologies have been in use for several decades,[6] Professor Lewis shows, through a thoughtful analysis of the difficulties of determining both maternity and paternity of certain children born through assisted reproductive technologies and a broad sketch of the legal issues surrounding posthumous conception with the sperm of deceased men, that the law has yet to catch up with the complexities of modern reproductive science. She also shows that it needs, urgently, to do so.

By contrast, Cynthia Soohoo and Jordan Goldberg, both attorneys with the Center for Reproductive Rights, take a distinctly optimistic tack in *The Full Realization of Our Rights: Social and Economic Rights in State Constitutions*. While recognizing the inherent difficulties involved in judicial enforcement of social and economic rights, Soohoo and Goldberg argue that state courts nonetheless can and should develop a distinct set of standards for reviewing and realizing those rights. Indeed, Soohoo and Goldberg question the importance of the traditional positive/negative rights distinction, as well as the traditional arguments against judicial enforcement of socio-economic rights, drawing on the widely discussed jurisprudence of the South African Constitutional Court for support.[7] Moreover, they note that important differences between state courts and federal courts make state courts a particularly appealing choice for the enforcement of socio-economic rights like the right to health. At a minimum, Soohoo and Goldberg suggest, state courts can enforce a negative right to health. The authors then chart a path for possible enforcement of a positive right to health.

If Soohoo and Goldberg's article gives reason to hope that socio-economic rights can be enforced in domestic courts, Professor Martha Davis's article highlights one reproductive policy domain in which a human rights lens is desperately needed in the United States. Professor Davis's article shows the importance of "bringing human rights home"[8] by applying international human rights norms in population planning policies to domestic child exclusion laws. In *The Child Exclusion in a Global Context*, Professor Davis, who is Associate Dean and Professor of Law at Northeastern University School of Law, persuasively demonstrates that the child exclusion policies in effect in various states in the U.S. are among the harshest and most morally questionable in the world, potentially violating a number of international legal standards. Professor Davis's article brings a keen comparative perspective to bear on the issue of family planning incentives. She notes that the U.S. policies largely comprise coercive or punitive disincentives to childbearing that target distinct and vulnerable populations, including the children themselves. Moreover, those punitive policies are often supported by very little sustained or careful debate or analysis and do not relate to any coherent national policy on population planning. The population measures of the countries examined by Professor Davis—India, China, Ghana, Kenya, and Tunisia—do not exhibit all of these characteristics in combination, as the American policies do.

Moving beyond the problem of enforcement, the goal of identifying new and enforceable human rights also entails the challenge of defining the right's contours and substance. Several of the contributors to this Symposium have taken on the difficult intellectual task of conceptualizing and giving content to new human rights based on the existing right to health and reproductive rights. Wayne State University Law School Professor Lance Gable's article, *Reproductive Health as a Human Right*, persuasively argues for a distinct human right to reproductive health that would transcend the traditional categories of negative and positive rights. Professor Gable trenchantly notes that the right to reproductive health is situated at the intersection of reproductive rights—which are traditionally viewed as negative, decisional rights—and the right to health, which grows out of a tradition of positive, foundational rights and includes recognition of the importance of underlying social determinants of human health. His article thus aspires to sketch a broad but enforceable right to reproductive health by combining the two rights models. Professor Gable recognizes many of the difficulties inherent in the inclusive, positive nature of the right but suggests that the chances of the right's enforcement can be improved through a flexible understanding of government obligations and through exploitation of legal and normative redundancies that support those rights.

In *From the Bottle to the Grave: Realizing a Human Right to Breastfeeding Through Global Health Policy*, Benjamin Mason Meier, Assistant Professor of Global Health Policy at the University of North Carolina at Chapel Hill, and Miriam Labbok, Professor of the Practice of Public Health and Director of the Carolina Global Breastfeeding Institute at the UNC Gillings School of Global Public Health, argue for a human right to breastfeeding, which requires them to identify both a new rights-holder—the mother-child dyad—and new duty-bearers—including state and non-state actors—to take account of the complexities of the globalized public health landscape. Of course, the project of articulating and protecting human rights cannot be a mere academic exercise; rather, Professors Meier and Labbok's article demonstrates that real people's lives are at stake. It thus presents a provocative and eye-opening account of the way in which global health law and policy, by largely succumbing to the will of the powerful transnational formula industry, has failed to protect the health of women and children at the end of the reproductive cycle. Despite the obvious and overwhelming benefits of breastfeeding, particularly in the developing world, Professors Meier and Labbok demonstrate the concrete importance of human rights discourse, showing that the shift away from the human rights framework for encouraging breastfeeding has prevented the issue from gaining both the salience and the enforcement mechanisms that could save the lives of millions of infants every year.

Finally, Professor Reva Siegel's symposium keynote address, *Dignity and Reproductive Rights*, provided a meditation on both the power and the drawbacks of broad, inclusive human rights concepts in vindicating rights on the ground. Professor Siegel, the Nicholas deB. Katzenbach

Professor at Yale University, incisively illuminated the various meanings and uses of the concept of dignity in contemporary political and judicial discourse surrounding abortion. Though not itself recognized as a right, the multifaceted concept of dignity—which may take on the meanings of autonomy, equality, or even respect for bare life itself—grounds various human and constitutional rights. Yet in the reproductive rights context, dignity has repeatedly been used as a basis for restricting as well as expanding abortion rights. Driven in part by this startling recognition, Professor Siegel's address considered the possibilities and limitations of engaging dignity in the service of advancing women's rights, rather than undermining them. Professor Siegel thus explained that dignity can be dangerous, due to its plural and malleable nature; at the same time, dignity has possibilities for bringing together in dialogue members of diverse normative communities about the most fundamental questions concerning not only human rights but also human nature itself. Indeed, it provides a fitting motif for the diversity of scholarly contributions on human rights, reproductive rights, and the right to health that comprise this excellent Symposium. While much work remains to be done in order to realize fully this aspect of human dignity, in the form of robust rights to health and reproductive justice both at home and abroad, these Symposium contributions demonstrate the power of creative, comparative thinking, as well as the vital importance of further thoughtful and nuanced debate.

Notes

1. *See, e.g.,* United Nations High Comm'r for Human Rights & World Health Org., Fact Sheet No. 31, The Right to Health, at 1 (June 2008), *available at* http://www.ohchr.org/Documents/Publications/Factsheet3l.pdf; Lance Gable, *Reproductive Health as a Human Right,* 60 Case W. res. L. Rev. 957,977 & n.95 (2010).
2. The contributions by Andrew Coan and Browne Lewis pertaining to assisted reproductive technologies, for example, speak to the beginning of the reproductive cycle; Benjamin Mason Meier and Miriam Labbok's article in this Symposium on the right to breastfeeding arguably pertains to its end.
3. The term "positive rights" usually refers to rights that require the government to provide something to individuals, such as health care or education, whereas "negative rights" are usually rights against government interference with the individual's liberty to do something, like speaking freely or practicing one's religion. For further discussion of this distinction, see generally B. Jessie Hill, *Reproductive Rights as Health Care Rights,* 18 Colum. J. Gender & L. 501,502–03 (2009).
4. *Id. But see, e.g.,* William E. Forbath, *Social and Economic Rights in the American Grain: Reclaiming Constitutional Political Economy, in* The Constitution in 2020, at 55, 62–63 (Jack M. Balkin & Reva B. Siegel eds., 2009) (arguing that "social and economic rights . . . are not strangers in the province of U.S. constitutional experience").
5. Andrew B. Coan, *Assisted Reproductive Equality: An Institutional Analsyis,* 60 Case W. Res. L. Rev. 1143, 1155 (2010).
6. The first instance of in vitro fertilization dates to 1978, however, commentators have pointed out that the practice of artificial insemination may have begun as early as the 18th century. *See, e.g,* Barry Dunn, Note, *Created After Death: Kentucky Law and Posthumously Conceived Children,* 48 U. Louisville L. Rev. 167, 169 (2009). Nonetheless, the use of reproductive technologies has greatly increased in recent years. *See generally* Jacques de Mouzon et al., *World Collaborative Report on Assisted Reproductive Technology, 2002,* 24 Hum. Reprod. 2310 (2009).
7. For a sample of the extensive U.S. scholarly literature on the socio-economic rights jurisprudence of the South African Constitutional Court, see, for example, Eric C. Christiansen, *Using Constitutional Adjudication to Remedy Socio-Economic Injustice: Comparative Lesson from South Africa,* 13 UCLA J. Int'l L. & Foreign Aff. 369 (2008); Brian Ray, *Policentrisn, Political Mobilization, and the Promise of Socioeconomic Rights,* 45 Stan. J. Int'l L. 151 (2009); Mark Tushnet, *Social Welfare Rights and the Forns of Judicial Review,* 82 Tex. L. Rev. 1895 (2004).
8. Bringing Human Rights Home: A History of Human Rights in the United States (Cynthia Soohoo, Catherine Albisa & Martha F. Davis eds., 2008).

B. Jessie Hill is a professor and associate director of the Center for Social Justice at Case Western Reserve University School of Law.

Pamela Laufer-Ukeles    **NO**

Reproductive Choices and Informed Consent: Fetal Interests, Women's Identity, and Relational Autonomy

· · ·

The Context of Informed Consent and Reproductive Choices

The Narrow Doctrine of Informed Consent

The notion of informed consent, although subject to significant criticism, has revolutionized the medical field. The need to relay appropriate information and then obtain consent from the patient has become the standard for reform of old-world protectionist and paternalistic medicine and the standard for aspiration in improving patients' rights. Although not perfectly implemented, patients' rights, bed-side manner, the need to inform patients of medical alternatives, and the need to obtain patient consent are now common considerations in medical schools, hospitals, clinics, and private practice.

As originally conceived, under the doctrine of informed consent, any doctor who performed a surgery or medical procedure without obtaining proper consent committed a battery or assault. The tort of informed consent has since become a tort sounding in negligence as opposed to battery—not focused on physical touching without any consent, but physical touching without proper consent based on insufficient information. Patients must not only consent to a medical procedure, they have a right to sufficient information to be able to make an informed decision about that procedure. Patients are given the right to refuse treatment proposed by the doctor as well as the right to be informed enough to make rational decisions with the help of the doctor. A doctor is negligent if he does not provide a reasonable amount of information to his patient about the risks, alternatives, and potential side effects of a certain course of treatment and gain her consent thereto. A slight majority of courts have stated that a reasonable amount of information is what reasonable professionals would disclose, although a solid and growing minority demands the provision of information that a reasonable patient would want to know before making a medical decision. There are also minority and majority positions regarding whether causation must be proven for a reasonable patient or that particular patient. The vast majority of courts require proof of physical injury to recover damages, but some courts, in limited circumstances in which the action of the doctors comes closer to battery, have allowed recovery for infringements on dignity alone.

The legal doctrine of informed consent was born of a belief in the fundamental importance of human autonomy: that "[e]very human being of adult years and sound mind has a right to determine what shall be done with his own body . . . ." Informed consent, reflecting the legal shift in healthcare and society more generally in the second half of the 20th century, focuses on individualism." In *Salgo v. Leland Stanford*, the court comments "[t]hat each patient presents a separate problem, that the patient's mental and emotional condition is important . . . to [determining] an informed consent." The doctrine's avowed purpose is to protect the patient's right to his own autonomous "thoroughgoing self-determination." This shift from the focus on medical beneficence in prior medical practice and the Hippocratic Oath, which is silent on the duty of physicians to inform, results from the liberal tradition emphasizing the individualistic right of autonomy and self-determination. The doctrine of informed consent is intended to ensure that patients are not just the objects of medical practice but also free and willing participants. Under the doctrine of informed consent, patients have a right to be left alone to make up their own minds about medical procedures free from doctor coercion.

As the law currently stands, the obligation on the doctor is to provide standard information to all patients with the same condition and not to personalize the information by digging deeper into a patient's personal goals, values, and interests. Although the doctrine aims to treat patients as individuals and not as objects, it is essentially a one-size-fits-all endeavor. There is a requirement that the doctor provide certain information; there is no requirement of discourse with the patient to find out more about the patient's values and preferences. In reality, the doctor views the patient as an individual medical problem, not as a truly individual person with a set of situational and contextual realities. Accordingly, the doctor's obligations relate only to providing information about medical conditions, treatments, alternatives, and risks based on the medical condition. Typically, such information covers only the patient's healthcare alternatives and the side effects of any medical treatments and not dignitary or emotional needs.

It is a process of providing and conveying information, and revealing medical knowledge. Limited cases have required doctors to provide information regarding plans for the use of blood or tissues extracted, and the provision of information pertaining to the doctor's own medical capabilities or practices. For the most part, however, the doctrine of informed consent is a narrow medical doctrine intended to ensure that a patient understands and therefore can give consent to undergoing medical procedures.

Informed consent also has a parallel meaning in bioethics, which frames the informed consent process between patient and doctor as well. It focuses on four elements: (1) competency to make a decision; (2) consenting to a given option; (3) the provision of adequate information; and (4) freedom from explicit coercion such that the decision is voluntary. Informed consent in medical decision making is based on individualistic autonomy through freedom from paternalism and coercion. The informed consent process is intended to ensure that a patient is left alone to make a decision based on a set of medical facts free from direct coercion. The ethical notion of informed consent does not require inquiry into a patient's particular circumstances and contextual pressures. Informed consent concentrates on "the preferences of particular patients . . . . It asks health care providers to ensure that individual patients have the information they need to make rational decisions about their health care, yet it does not ask necessary questions about the circumstances in which such decisions are made." The ethical endeavor is thus one of providing basic information, ensuring competency and freedom from explicit coercion, and obtaining consent. As conceived and applied as an ethical medical doctrine, informed consent does not seriously facilitate the exploration of the circumstances in which such consent is obtained or the broader concerns of the patient giving that consent.

In sum, informed consent is a doctrine born of a liberal, individualized notion of autonomy, focused on allowing individual patients to make up their own minds about medical treatment free from coercion. Moreover, it is a narrow doctrine, requiring that doctors provide information regarding standard medical risks and alternatives to patients without inquiring any deeper into a patient's values, interests, and circumstances.

The Complex Realm of Reproductive Choices

In contrast to the narrow doctrine of informed consent, the realm of reproductive choices has expanded and become more complex at an alarming rate. Reproductive technologies have created an explosion of reproductive options, particularly in the context of reproductive endocrinology. What began with "test-tube babies" has expanded to a host of ART options that push the realm of believability, including extended multi-year courses of fertility treatments, tanks full of frozen embryos, post-menopausal pregnancies, octuplets conceived by implanting numerous embryos into one woman's uterus, babies "conceived" by two men with the use of an egg donor from another country and a surrogate from a third, and babies created without any biological connection at all to the intended mother or father. In obstetrics, technological advances have enabled interventions from increased genetic and ultrasound screening at multiple stages, to elective Caesarean sections ("C-sections"), while opposing forces have maintained the need to protect the choice to use midwifery services and engage in home births. Moreover, reproductive choices are at the center of political, social, and ethical disputes. Debates surrounding the right to choose to abort take center stage in legislative, jurisprudential, and political arenas in a relentless and ever-developing discussion of the proper parameters of a woman's choice to terminate a pregnancy.

To clarify which choices I am referring to as "reproductive choices," every reproductive choice I discuss involves a woman's body—so far, we are still unable to produce babies in incubators. The complexity in the reproductive choices that I explore in this Article surrounds the woman's body and her ability to gestate. Moreover, since the medical doctrine of informed consent is at issue, these are choices that involve medical intervention. For instance, the choice to create a family through sexual intercourse is not part of this inquiry. Similarly, a decision to engage a surrogate mother is a reproductive choice; but, it is not a medical choice and thus does not implicate informed consent. While the choice to become an egg donor or a surrogate is reproductive and involves informed consent for the medical treatments involved, it is not a choice to procreate for oneself and therefore is also not subject to this analysis. A choice to become a reproductive donor involves a whole set of different interests and inquiries, including issues of commodification and exploitation, which are beyond the scope of this Article.

There are three categories of reproductive choices that I consider in this Article: (1) the choice to terminate a pregnancy; (2) the choice to reproduce with the help of a doctor using fertility treatments; and (3) the choice to undergo medical intervention during pregnancy and labor. In this Part, I will describe the parameters of each of these three choices, the legislative and constitutional framework for such choices, and the current hot button, controversial issues that have arisen in these three areas. Although it is my aim to create a framework for considering this broad array of reproductive choices, the distinct contexts in which these choices operate and the unique complexities of each will be delineated and serve as contextual background for my arguments.

The Choice to Terminate a Pregnancy
The choice to terminate a pregnancy is an individual liberty interest protected from state prohibitions by the right to privacy under *Roe v. Wade*. Under the holding of *Roe*, the right to abort is a fundamental right and thus states cannot restrict access to abortion unless there is a

"compelling state interest." Yet, even when the right was first announced it was limited by valid state interests. According to *Roe,* the state's interest in the health of the fetus permits it to prohibit abortion in the third trimester, defined as the point of viability; in the interests of the woman's health, the state can legislate the parameters of abortion beginning in the second trimester.

States have since been allowed to legislate beyond the limits set by *Roe.* In *Planned Parenthood of Southeastern Pennsylvania v. Casey,* based on the state's interest in the fetus, as well as in maternal health, the state is permitted from the onset of pregnancy to dictate which procedures must be undergone and which information must be conveyed before a doctor can perform an abortion, as long as such legislation does not create an "undue burden" on the right to abort. *Casey* upheld a mandatory twenty-four hour waiting period before a doctor can perform an abortion requested by a patient. *Casey* also found that during the waiting period, the woman can be given information intended to dissuade her from aborting as long as the information is "truthful, non-misleading information." Mandatory spousal notification, on the other hand, was found to be too burdensome.

By mandating the provision of certain information intended to make a woman question her choice to abort, states have been allowed to shape the conveyance of information to patients by doctors before that choice is made. *Casey* allows "informed consent" laws that vindicate the state's interest in potential life even if the information given is biased, representing the particular beliefs and ideological perspectives of the state. The information that is deemed permissible in *Casey* is "the nature of the procedure, the health risks of the abortion and of childbirth, the probable gestational age of the unborn child," and the availability of printed materials published by the state describing the fetus and "providing information about medical assistance for childbirth, information about child support from the father, and a list of agencies which provide adoption and other services as alternatives to abortion." ' Such information clearly conveys the state's interest in dissuading a woman from aborting a fetus, and this clear ideological message is explicitly permitted by *Casey.*

Many states have taken *Casey's* lead in adopting "informed consent legislation" that shapes the information conveyed by a doctor to a patient before an abortion is performed. More recent legislation in some states has mandated that women view ultrasounds of the fetus before undergoing an abortion. Furthermore, in *Gonzalez v. Carhart,* the Supreme Court allowed the federal government and, by extension states, to ban a particular kind of abortion procedure, partial-birth abortion, even if the doctor believes using such a procedure to be in the best interest of the woman due to medical concerns.

With the state compelling and directing the conveyance of particular information to the patient, the informed consent process clearly transcends what is required under the narrow legal doctrine of informed consent. This allows for a very impressionable and biased relaying of information coerced upon the doctor and patient by the state. It also creates instability and controversy. For instance, some courts have held that a woman can be told that calling the fetus a "human being" is truthful and not misleading, while others have said the opposite. The informed consent legislation transforms the informed consent process from a platform for promoting autonomy into a forum for political strife.

In response to pro-life influence on the informed consent process, pro-choice activists are focused on freeing women from coercive, protectionist, and one-sided interference from the state. They oppose any intrusion into the individualistic privacy of the patient as discriminatory and problematic. The focus on individuality and privacy for the deciding woman aims at allowing her to make the decision to abort without pressure from the state, but does not focus affirmatively on what information the patient needs to support her decision. Hence, the discourse surrounding what information to give a patient prior to an abortion is no longer about facilitating and informing patient choice and maximizing autonomy. Rather, it is an arena for highly charged political debate, despite the fact that it is still cloaked in informed consent language and justified by the need to provide information. The focus on women and their needs has been surrendered in pursuit of political aims. The law and discourse surrounding abortion decision making should refocus on making sure that the informed consent process provides women with the information they need to make difficult and complex reproductive choices.

The Choice to Undergo Fertility Treatments

Although most reproductive rights are developed in the context of abortion and contraception, there is language and some precedent to suggest a constitutional right to procreate as well. A number of scholars have argued that constitutional precedents regarding reproductive freedoms should include the right to reproduce using ART. But, even if coital reproduction and non-coital reproduction do not mandate the same level of constitutional protection, because ART entails a more complicated set of rights and state interests than spontaneous sexual reproduction, limiting ART does arguably implicate some constitutional and privacy concerns. This is particularly true when third-party donors are not involved.

In fact, the strength and limits of these liberty interests have not been tested, as legislative restrictions on fertility treatments in the United States are limited. Instead, most oversight stems from limited self-regulating medical practice boards. State interests in the health of citizens, interests in the health of the fetus, societal values in the sanctity of life, and the economic burdens on society could justify restrictive legislation. Internationally, many regulations have been enacted limiting access to or banning certain ART choices, or imposing oversight by state or regulatory agencies. Given strong state interests in fetal life in the abortion context, more such legislation is likely to develop in the future, both within the United States and worldwide. In fact, the American Bar Association (ABA) has created a model act governing ART that recommends far-ranging regulations.

In the U.S., there are a number of pieces of legislation that have been enacted governing fertility treatments. One is the Fertility Clinic Success Rate and Certification Act, a federal statute that requires reporting clinic success rates. In addition, there is state legislation in California that created a comprehensive legal infrastructure for embryo transfer. Moreover, some jurisdictions have begun to legislate limits to the use of frozen embryos. For instance, in Louisiana all frozen embryos must be implanted. In Germany and Italy, there is a prohibition on freezing embryos altogether, greatly increasing the number of egg extraction procedures that women must go through. Furthermore, the Bush Administration's opposition to embryonic stem cell research has been accompanied by a one million dollar initiative to promote embryo donation, despite the lack of success experienced in these programs. Overall, however, the U.S. federal and state governments have been hesitant to regulate in the realm of ART. Medical professionals in the United States are largely against such legislation, arguing that legislative rigidity does not comply with serving the best interests of patients. Nevertheless, proposals for regulation are increasing in number and frequency.

In this relatively unregulated context, decision making and informed consent in fertility clinics regarding such diverse choices as the extent and duration of fertility treatments, the use of in vitro fertilization (IVF), multiple implantations, and egg donors are causing legal and ethical predicaments. The problem of multiple births due to aggressive fertility treatments is reaching a level of national, if not international, concern. ART produces forty percent of triplet pregnancies and sixteen percent of twin pregnancies in the United States. Multiple births have an array of negative side effects for the babies that are born and for the mothers, as well as for states that may have to pick up the tab for medical treatment of multiple births. Indeed, multiple births are integrally related to premature birth, which has a myriad of negative health effects: "[a] study released [recently] by the March of Dimes cited fertility treatments as one of the main reasons for a 36 percent increase in prematurity in the last twenty-five years." The cost to society of multiple births and premature babies due to health complications and the need for intensive care is staggering.

Another weighty concern is the problem of disposing of "leftover" frozen embryos that are not implanted in a woman's uterus. Storing frozen embryos reduces the number of times women need to undergo egg retrieval, which is an invasive and potentially painful procedure that entails hormone treatments, sonograms, and intra-vaginal or intra-abdominal procedures, often under general anesthesia. Therefore, many IVF patients retrieve and inseminate many more eggs than they are likely to use. As many as one million embryos are frozen through cryopreservation worldwide and many are stored without any long-term solution for what should be done to dispose of them. The alternatives of implanting the embryos—perhaps risking multiples or conceiving more children than desired, destroying the embryos, donating them to other families in a process that only rarely produces results, donating them to research, or storing them indefinitely—too often results in the gridlock of storing the embryos indefinitely. Moreover, disputes between couples upon the breakdown of marriages are leading to an increasing amount of litigation. Two other concerns are the dangers of the advanced age of the gestating mother and the effects of reproductive technologies and hormone treatments on women.

Thus, arguably, the biggest problem facing ART is that innovations are proceeding without enough control and contemplation regarding their repercussions. Patient choice is producing perhaps too much experimentation. Regulation may be necessary to cure some of the excesses described above in the fertility context. Indeed, maximizing autonomy may include the need for some regulation. As Martha Ertman notes, "[s]cholars continue to explore optimal regulations that would both protect people's freedom to order their affairs and honor human dignity and equality." Yet, there are many reasons to make room for private ordering so as to allow for diversity and individualized needs. Reproductive choices are personal, identity-forming choices and therefore liberty is particularly valued. Moreover, overregulation can not only impede technological advancement, but also impair patient care because individual needs cannot be taken into account. Regulation alone is not the answer. Instead, as I will argue below, regulation mixed with an enhanced system of informed consent that takes into account the complexities of reproductive choices and promotes women's autonomy is necessary. As one commentator explains:

> Elimination of unnecessary procedures by patient choice through informed consent is preferable to intervention by an outside body, such as a national health board or an insurance company. In this way, the decision is driven by the individual and by a policy-making body, which can lose sight of individual needs and idiosyncrasies.

As described below, however, informed consent needs to be improved to better recognize the complexities of these choices.

Medical Treatment During Pregnancy
Medical reproductive choices are also made when women undergo medical treatment during pregnancy, including prenatal testing, prenatal surgery, and medical intervention during the labor and birthing process. Some have argued that the right to use a midwife at birth should be

part of constitutional reproductive liberties, but this argument has never been adopted by a U.S. court.

The contours of the right to refuse suggested or needed medical intervention to save the fetus, either during pregnancy or labor, are ambiguous. The right to abort arguably includes the right to refuse or agree to medical treatment that can harm the fetus, although in some circumstances, this right has been questioned and affirmatively limited. In fact, the state's interest in the fetus has been allowed, in exceptional cases, to be balanced against the mother's autonomy in making medical decisions, and courts have ordered forced C-sections. But, other courts have found that balancing is not allowed when determining whether to force medical treatment on a woman because her rights to autonomy and bodily integrity are too strong.

There are significant regulatory limits on reproductive choices during pregnancy. Regulations surrounding the use of midwives are increasingly restrictive. Moreover, women who want to undergo natural childbirth are increasingly restricted from doing so because of hospital regulations prohibiting natural birth after C-sections, breach births, and other high-risk vaginal deliveries. Home births are increasingly rare as doctors and midwives cannot obtain insurance coverage for attending such births and because of explicit restrictions. The mandatory use of fetal monitoring devices in hospitals is at an all-time high, even when not medically indicated. Thus, women's options for non-interventionist births are increasingly limited.

The ultimate intervention is the C-section—when a fetus is surgically removed through a woman's stomach as opposed to being birthed vaginally. In the United States, the C-section rate has risen 48% since 1996, reaching a level of 31.8% in 2007. For example, a 2008 report found that a full one-third of babies born in Massachusetts in 2006 were delivered by C-section. Yet, the C-section rates in other countries are much lower without affecting mortality rates. For instance, the C-section rate in Holland is around 8% and infant mortality rates are lower. One study into the reasons for emergency C-sections found that 66% occur between the 25% of day-shift hours of 8 AM and 3 PM, and the least between 5 AM and 6 AM, leading the authors to conclude that physician convenience is a leading cause of "emergency Caesareans. Conservative estimates indicate that around 300,000 C-sections are unnecessarily performed in the United States in a given year. The World Health Organization has indicated that no country should have more than a 10-15% C-section rate.

In addition, genetic testing and fetal monitoring are increasingly changing the dynamic of reproductive choices. Prenatal tests and prenatal surgery at all stages are becoming more common and less discretionary as they are routinized. Thus, although intervention in labor and pregnancy has been instrumental in improving infant and maternal mortality rates, it arguably has gone too far. Medical intervention during pregnancy and labor is being done in an elective manner for reasons that extend beyond women's health, in particular, fetal interests as well as medical convenience. Checks are completely lacking to control the extent of such intervention. As the pressure toward intervention grows, the room for free choice is increasingly limited by legislation, regulation, and pressure to act on behalf of the fetus. More is needed to help women make autonomous choices in the face of strong interventionist pressures.

Conclusion

The spectrum of reproductive choices is constantly expanding; they are more frequently made and are garnering increasing attention and concern. In the abortion context, such choices are heavily regulated, but political interests and concerns about the fetus seem to completely overshadow the interest in ensuring that the woman has the opportunity to make an informed and deliberate decision. In the relatively unregulated fertility and pregnancy contexts, technological innovation and medical sophistication have led to remarkable rates of medical intervention, unexpected ethical dilemmas, and new arenas for litigation. On the other hand, the informed consent doctrine remains narrow and limited.

Having described the doctrine of informed consent and the regulatory, technological, and political context in which reproductive choices are made, in the following Part I will examine what makes reproductive choices so unique and how the legal doctrine of informed consent is particularly ineffective in securing autonomy when such choices are made.

The Unique Nature of Reproductive Choices

Reproductive choices are different than other medical choices because the act of gestation, of being pregnant, is unique. The interrelated nature of women and fetus has no equal outside of pregnancy. Reproductive choices are not unilateral, independent, or individual when compared to most medical decisions in which a patient, in consultation with a doctor, makes a decision about treatment with the goal of optimizing her own health or minimizing her own pain. The reproductive choices that the woman makes will also affect the fetus or the potential fetus. The fate of the fetus and mother are entirely intertwined. This unique environment for making choices creates a web of complexity that necessitates particularized attention to whether the goal of patient autonomy is adequately met.

Having stressed the uniqueness of reproductive choice, there are other medical decisions that may be comparable to this standard of relational complexity outside of reproduction, and my analysis may apply to these contexts as well. One example is organ or bone marrow donation to a relative from a living relative or third party. Medical choices concerning conjoined twins may also reach a comparable level of novel complexity. Yet even such complex medical decisions are different from decisions made by pregnant women or women trying to become pregnant. Reproductive decisions are not directly comparable to decisions made by parents about children, even conjoined twins, because such decisions are made by parents for third persons, without physical attachments to themselves. Kidney donors make the decision for themselves and retain autonomy, although they may do it for the sake of another. Making decisions regarding a living being that is intended to grow or is growing inside one's own body creates the framework for a unique set of choices, particularly in a legal system designed to protect the rights of individuals. It is neither personal nor focused on the other—it is both simultaneously.

The intertwined nature of woman and fetus complicates medical decision making in two fundamental ways. The first is the distinctive misalignment of interests among patient, state, and physicians that arises due to the protection of fetal interests—a being other than the woman who is the primary patient. To be clear, in the context of reproductive choices, the state and medical interests are not necessarily aligned or even complementary, but are both potentially misaligned with a woman's interest due to fetal concerns. The second is the identity-forming nature of reproductive choices, as gestation and childbearing are more than medical choices; they reflect social and cultural values. Each of these complications will be discussed in turn in the context of the three arenas of reproductive choices included herein.

Distinctions between the different reproductive choices must also be kept in mind. In the context of abortion, a woman's health or interests are directly opposed to fetal interests. In the other medical situations that I am considering, there may be tensions between competing interests but no direct opposition. Therefore, in the abortion context, the tension in interests is the most striking and compelling. In the other contexts, the tension may be more subtle but is nevertheless a significant factor in how and what information is conveyed to patients.

Choices regarding abortion and pregnancy can be distinguished from fertility choices that occur ex-utero, such as choices regarding the disposition of frozen embryos. In such choices, gestation is still a key factor, as it is ultimately the woman who will gestate the embryos or not. Moreover, it is the woman's reproductive capacities that result in invasive procedures that make such decisions potentially fraught. Thus, despite declarations that such reproductive choices are gender neutral, the woman is still the primary patient. Yet, the issue of whether to allow the intended father's input is different in the ex-utero context than when a woman's bodily integrity is more directly at stake. In labor and abortion decisions, where women's bodies are more directly involved, the choice must be the woman's; the intended father's input should only be with her consent. But, in ex-utero decisions where an intended father's interest

may prevail, for instance regarding disposition of frozen embryos if he later desires not to procreate, the intended father should be encouraged to participate in the decision-making process. In fact, men are arguably too absent from certain fertility and labor choices. The 2007 annual meeting of the American Society for Reproductive Medicine included a course for healthcare professionals titled "Men and ART: The Missing Voice." The fear that husbands will coerce or abuse their wives should be taken into account, but it should not silence intended fathers altogether, especially when reproductive choices occur ex-utero.

Furthermore, in abortion decisions and choices made during pregnancy, a fetus clearly exists. In the context of ART, a fetus may never exist. Thus, the tension is with an intended fetus, which is much more abstract. But the interest of fertility doctors in realizing the goal of creating the fetus can overshadow the interests of the female patient significantly. This tension between maternal and intended fetal interests mirrors the tension in abortion and pregnancy intervention contexts. . . .

Women's Identity Interests

The fact that reproductive choices are deeply value laden, personal, and identity forming further compromises the use of the traditional legal doctrine of informed consent to support women's autonomy. A woman's reproductive choices go beyond considerations of maintaining and optimizing her own health or that of her fetus or intended fetus, by relating to her personal values and self-perception. How and when one reproduces are identity-forming and deeply personal choices.

The choice to terminate a pregnancy, while coveted to protect women's equality and bodily integrity, is a deeply personal and difficult act for many. Fertility treatments are a robust ethical, cultural, and sociological experience—far more so than a medical treatment for a typical health problem. There are serious social pressures on women to become mothers, and women who are not mothers often complain of feeling alienated by society. Moreover, modern technology has made fertility not a condition but a matter of autonomy and choice, which creates a complex dynamic in which a choice not to undergo invasive treatments is tantamount to choosing not to become a mother. It can be crushing for a woman to be told she cannot reproduce. Women have very different attitudes about childbirth and intervention during pregnancy, with some placing a high value on natural vaginal birth and others focusing on minimizing pain and risk. Decisions regarding the process of labor can be personal and ideological, representing the will of a woman to labor in a manner that she desires for reasons other than her own medical health, although not necessarily in contradiction to health concerns. The constitutive nature of these choices is not just hyperbole; this is precisely why reproductive choices are protected liberty interests—they are self-defining and fundamental.

Yet, information and counseling about identity interests are not mandated under the current informed consent doctrine. These interests are largely deemed private and outside the realm of the tort doctrine of informed consent. In part, it is the failure to have these broader conversations that causes the problematic reliance on the stereotypes discussed above. Stereotypes about a woman's relationship to her fetus, about the essential nature of motherhood for a woman, and about her potential for irrationality are quite pervasively used by doctors as well as the state. These stereotypes cannot be broken down unless more individualistic consultations occur.

In the realm of hysterectomies and mastectomies, a woman's personal identity interests, which are not specifically health related, have been tentatively acknowledged. It was perceived by patients' rights groups and documented by government studies that these invasive, extreme procedures were being used too aggressively. The concern was that doctors, who of course elicited consent, were not providing sufficient and appropriate information to patients and were too readily advising them to have mastectomy or hysterectomy procedures that remove body parts associated with being a woman and thus may affect these women's sense of self. Advocates of specific informed consent legislation wanted more balanced information to be provided. New York, for instance, enacted state legislation aimed at informing women about alternative treatments to hysterectomy procedures. The statute calls for a standardized form to be developed by the New York Medical Society and patients, which is to be given to women who are contemplating a hysterectomy. Similarly, mastectomy informed consent statutes were initiated and driven by patient advocates who wanted women to be able to make more holistic choices and to combat doctors who did not view the breast as being important to women, especially older women.

Patient advocates recognized that something was missing from informed consent, but the mandatory provision of pamphlets is a limited solution. While progressive, attempts to improve decision making by mandating certain information have been too formulaic, static, and impersonal. Advances in medicine and treatments develop quickly, while the law and informational pamphlets are much slower to change. In addition, doctors are generally wary of informed consent legislation that mandates relaying certain information and thereby dictates the flow of information that is conveyed. In the hysterectomy context, the information mandated was dictated largely by doctors because only a single patient sat on the drafting committee. The doctors were overly focused on reproduction as opposed to other relevant interests, such as sexuality and feminine identity. For example, the guidelines did not address benefits to avoiding the procedure past child-bearing age. The disappointment with such statutes is felt both by those wary of the legislative goal of increasing patient autonomy and by those who want to do even more to support women's autonomy.

Even more than for women contemplating mastectomies and hysterectomies, women making reproductive choices face significant personal and identity-forming concerns. Reproduction includes many real choices without obvious medical answers. These choices are value-laden, identity-forming, and personal. Moreover, they are very individualistic. Without personal consultation, overbroad stereotypes undermine personal autonomy. Few if any courts have been able to internalize these self-perceptions or identity interests in considering whether a decision was truly informed. While not all women will suffer from the lack of engagement on identity issues, since women are individuals and some or many may resolve such tensions on their own, the identity issues exist and should not be ignored.

Admittedly, other medical procedures can also be personal, identity-forming, and momentous, for example, sex reassignment therapy. Interestingly, however, legally required informed consent procedures for many of these treatments go beyond the physical and require psychological consultations. On the other hand, even in a complex medical procedure such as kidney donation, a man or woman who has donated a kidney is still every bit the same man or woman in terms of self-identity, and cultural and social perception. Other treatments such as hysterectomies and mastectomies may have more comparable effects on identity and informed consent. These procedures should perhaps also consider personal identity issues, as I discuss below. Still, a typical medical decision is not identity-forming and constitutive, and therefore reproductive choices need more support than typical medical decisions.

Conclusion

Misalignment of interests due to fetal concerns and the failure to emphasize the identity interests involved for women undertaking reproductive choices has significantly compromised women's autonomy. This failure most visibly occurs in the context of the termination of pregnancy and occurs significantly in the context of fertility treatment and decisions during pregnancy and labor as well.

Competing interests have led to the provision of information that is often based on overbroad assumptions about women and is biased in its interventionist and pro-life tilt; yet, this information is presented as objective through the voice and with the authority of the medical profession. The full panoply of interests and values that comes into play when such a decision is made is not discussed. Most significantly excluded are women's identity interests, which are left for a woman's own private deliberation.

Indeed, information stemming from biases and viewpoints that favor fetal interests, intervention, and technology all may be part of the information conveyed to women before they make fundamental reproductive choices. Such bias is derived from assumptions regarding a woman's desire to optimize a fetus's health, her desire to create life, and her potential regret in harming that fetus, as well as the state's interest in the life of the fetus. At the same time, it is a woman's own value-laden preferences regarding intervention, the importance of motherhood, fetal health or minimizing fetal pain, and the potential for regret that are left unheeded in the informed consent discussion. It cannot be fairly argued that these latter interests are private and should be left for personal contemplation while the former interests deserve medical attention. Such biased information is authoritative, suggestive, and even coercive, particularly in the abortion context. While individually many women may be able to withstand social pressures and bias in the informed consent process, they should not have to. This method of conveying information creates imbalanced choices and undermines patient autonomy. . . .

Conclusion

There has been too much division and alienation in the context of reproductive choices. The conversation surrounding abortion rights is extremely polarized and has been gradually but readily spilling over into the fertility context, as well as into the context of medical decisions or actions during pregnancy. In addition, advances in technology have created a strong push toward medicalization of reproduction, overshadowing the personal values and identity interests of reproducing women. With the broadening of the scope and public interest in reproductive choices, what has been lost is the focus on optimizing patient autonomy, the central goal of informed consent. Patients making reproductive choices—choices acknowledged as being integral and constitutive—need more from informed consent than the formulaic, one-size-fits-all process, subject to state and medical biases and unresponsive to personal values and goals. Patients need a balanced

informed consent consultation, supported by legal and legislative incentives, that opposes overbroad stereotypes and bias while seeking to promote reproductive autonomy, as opposed to achieving political agendas.

The vision of autonomy I describe is not an isolated individualism embodied in being left alone to choose, nor do I mean to undermine autonomy altogether by advocating for protective legislation. The vision of autonomy I present elevates choice but acknowledges the relational social pressures and interdependencies that affect choice; it is complex and achieved only by degrees. Still, autonomy is a worthy goal and society needs to think seriously about how to promote autonomous choices for women in an era marked by an explosive interaction of reproductive choices, medical intervention, and state involvement.

The discussion surrounding reproductive choices centers on constitutionality and regulation. Most analyses of autonomy in the abortion context consider whether regulation is constitutional and an appropriate infringement on a woman's individual right to choose. In the context of ART, discussions of autonomy focus on the need for more regulation to preserve women's health. In the context of decisions during pregnancy and labor, questions arise about the appropriateness of balancing fetal and maternal interests when providing medical care. In this Article, I argue that promoting autonomy and women's well-being is not only about regulations, constitutionality, and professional medical standards. Rather, supporting autonomy and women's health in reproductive choices should be about recognizing the complexity involved in such choices and providing an appropriate framework for women to make such choices in their own best interests.

PAMELA LAUFER-UKELES is an associate professor of law at the University of Dayton School of Law.

EXPLORING THE ISSUE

Is Access to Birth Control a Basic Human Right?

Critical Thinking and Reflection

1. How do issues of individual personhood and human rights intersect in the question of access to birth control?
2. How is the issue of birth control as much an argument about abortion as it is about preventing conception?
3. How are the rights of women impacted by their potential to become pregnant and carry a fetus during the gestation process?

Is There Common Ground?

Do women have access to affordable, safe contraceptive methods? If a woman is raped, can she make the choice to prevent contraception with the assistance of trained medical staff? When does the right to self-preservation become secondary to the life of an unborn child? How do we examine the human rights of women as autonomous beings relative to their biological ability to become pregnant?

The consideration of women as potential mothers has long been a double-edged sword in human rights' discussions. The question of when we proffer privilege on the status of motherhood and when it becomes a liability that limits a woman's ability to act as a fully enfranchised citizen has been a policy flashpoint for decades. Smith (2005) situated her analysis of these issues within the framework of reproductive justice. When efforts to restrict access to contraceptives or to criminalize abortion intersect with concerns of class or race, equity considerations become part of the conversation.

Additional Resources

Smith, A. (2005). "Beyond Pro-Choice Versus Pro-Life." *NWSA Journal, 17*(1), 119–140.

Agence France Presse. (2013, January 25). "New Mexico Bill Would Make Abortion after Rape a Felony." *Business Insider.* Retrieved from: http://businessinsider.com/new-mexico-bill-would-make-an-abortion-after-rape-a-felony-2013-1

American Civil Liberties Union. (2010). "Florida Court Upholds Right of Pregnant Woman to Determine Medical Care." Retrieved from: http://aclu.org/reproductive-freedom/florida-court-upholds-right-pregnant-woman-determine-medical-care

Bassett, L. (2011, October 13). "Nancy Pelosi: Protect Life Act Would Let Pregnant Women 'Die On The Floor'." *The Huffington Post.* Retrieved from: http://huffingtonpost.com/2011/10/13/nancy-pelosi-protect-life-act_n_1009461.html

Calhoun, A. (2012, April 25). "The Criminalization of Bad Mothers." *The New York Times.* Retrieved from: http://nytimes.com/2012/04/29/magazine/the-criminalization-of-bad-mothers.html?pagewanted=1&_r=2&hp&

Kristof, N. and WuDunn, S. (2009). *Half the Sky: Turning Oppression into Opportunity for Women Worldwide.* Random House: New York.

Pogatchnik, S. (2012, November 5). "Ireland Probes Death of Ill Woman Denied an Abortion." Free Daily News Group, Inc. Retrieved from: http://metronews.ca/news/

Paltrow, L. (1999). "Punishment and Prejudice: Judging Drug-Using Pregnant Women." Article first appeared in *Mother Troubles, Rethinking Contemporary Maternal Dilemmas.* Edited by Julia E. Hanigsberg and Sara Ruddick. (1999, Beacon Press; www.beacon.org, ISBN 0-8070-6787-3). Retrieved from: http://advocatesforpregnantwomen.org/articles/ruddick.htm

Stallman v. Youngquist, 125 Ill.2d 267, 531 N.E.2d 355 (1988).

Create Central

www.mhhe.com/createcentral

Internet References . . .

Our body, Ourselves

http://www.ourbodiesourselves.org/default.asp

National Women's Law Center

http://www.nwlc.org/resource/if-opponents-birth-control-have-their-way-millions-women-would-lose-access-birth-control

Planned Parenthood

http://www.womenarewatching.org/issue/protect-access-to-birth-control

Selected, Edited, and with Issue Framing Material by:
Rachel Pienta, *Valdosta State University*

ISSUE

Should the Federal Government Adopt a New Legal Definition of Rape?

YES: Dan M. Kahan, from "Culture, Cognition, and Consent: Who Perceives What, and Why, in Acquaintance-Rape Cases," *University of Pennsylvania Law Review* (February 2010)

NO: Jennifer L. Broach and Patricia A. Petretic, from "Beyond Traditional Definitions of Assault: Expanding Our Focus to Include Sexually Coercive Experiences," *Journal of Family Violence* (November 2006)

Learning Outcomes

As you read the issue, focus on the following points:

- What is meant by "unwritten rules of sexual conduct?"
- Should a verbal "No" be enough to establish a lack of consent?

ISSUE SUMMARY

YES: Dan M. Kahan examines cultural constructions of sexual consent and how society's understanding determines social interaction and has legal implications in rape cases.

NO: Jennifer L. Broach and Patricia A. Petretic examine social norms that govern sexual consent based on the premise that unwanted sexual contact is not always nonconsensual given unwritten behavior contracts and established sexual scripts between potential partners.

We are told "yes means yes" but what happens when those words are not actually spoken? The rules of sexual consent are murky waters fraught with potential for misunderstandings at best and criminal charges at worst.

Unwritten rules about sexual conduct and persistent social mores governing female sexuality cloud the rhetoric on issues of consent. Debate over what constitutes forcible rape suggests that the law may require an escalated level of refusal beyond a verbal no to establish lack of consent.

In the YES and NO selections, Kahan examines cultural constructs about sexual consent and what constitutes an understood refusal of sexual contact. Broach and Petretic discuss social expectations and norms surrounding sexual intimacy and the distinctions between desire, consent, and coercion.

Kahan, in "Culture, Cognition, and Consent: Who Perceives What, and Why, in Acquaintance-Rape Cases," explores the cultural-cognition aspects of perceived consent. Gender constructs and cultural biases remain an inherent pitfall to achieving a universal understanding of consent. Antioch College somewhat famously developed a consent policy for students at that institution (Hall, 1998). The Antioch College (2012) "Sexual Offense Prevention

Policy" delineates what constitutes consent and how to obtain it:

> "Consent" is defined as the act of willingly and verbally agreeing to engage in specific sexual conduct. Previously agreed upon forms of non-verbal communication are appropriate methods for expressing consent. In order for "consent" to be valid, all parties must have unimpaired judgment and a shared understanding of the nature of the act to which they are consenting, including the use of safer sex practices. The person who initiates sexual conduct is responsible for verbally asking for the "consent" of the individual(s) involved. "Consent" must be obtained with each new level of sexual conduct. The person with whom sexual conduct is initiated must verbally express "consent" or lack of "consent." Silence conveys a lack of consent. If at any time consent is withdrawn, the conduct must stop immediately.

> —(Antioch College, 2012, p. 36)

Discussions of consent and how to define rape became fodder for political sound bites during the months leading up to the 2012 presidential election. Candidates, elected officials, and media pundits all had opinions on rape and the nature of consent. The 2012 election spawned the phrase "legitimate rape," suggesting that not all rapes are actual or "real" rapes. In one instance, Congressman Todd Akin of Missouri famously claimed that in cases of legitimate rape, the female body had "ways of shutting that down" (Kroll, 2012).

In "Beyond Traditional Definitions of Assault: Expanding Our Focus to Include Sexually Coercive Experiences," Broach and Petretic examine the blurred lines between coercion, including consent obtained under duress, and assent that is freely given. The issue of coercion and participation in unwanted sexual activity when one partner feels unable to refuse, for whatever reason, bears more study. Broach and Petretic (2006) found that "this study suggests that the legal criteria for rape are not necessarily adequate predictors of the psychological impact of unwanted sexual experiences (p. 485).

The definition of rape used by the Federal Bureau of Investigation (FBI) narrowly defined rape as forcible penile–vaginal penetration. The law did not recognize the possibility of same sex rape and also left the definition of what "forcible" meant open to widely varying interpretations. The vagueness of the federal law, unchanged since 1929, became a flashpoint on the floor of Congress during a debate in 2011 on health care, abortion, and the definition of "forcible rape."

Dan M. Kahan

Culture, Cognition, and Consent: Who Perceives What, and Why, in Acquaintance-Rape Cases

Introduction

Does "no" always mean "no" to sex? More generally, what standards should the law use to evaluate whether a woman has genuinely consented to sexual intercourse or whether she could reasonably have been understood by a man to have done so? Or more basically still, how should the law define "rape"? These questions have been points of contention within and without the legal academy for over three decades.[1]

The dispute concerns not just the content of the law but also the nature of social norms and the interaction of law and norms. According to critics, the traditional and still dominant common law definition of rape—which requires proof of "force or threat of force" and which excuses a "reasonably mistaken" belief in consent—is founded on antiquated expectations of male sexual aggression and female submission.[2] Defenders of the common law reply that the traditional definition of rape sensibly accommodates contemporary practices and understandings—not only of men but of many women as well. The statement "no," they argue, does *not* invariably mean "no" but rather sometimes means "yes" or at least "maybe." Accordingly, making rape a strict-liability offense, or abolishing the need to show that the defendant used "force or threat of force," would result in the conviction of nonculpable defendants, restrict the sexual autonomy of *women* as well as men, and likely provoke the refusal of prosecutors, judges, and juries to enforce the law.[3]

This article describes original, experimental research pertinent to the "no means . . . ?" debate. In both law journals and law school classrooms, that debate is frequently brought into sharp focus—and sharp contention—by examination of a controversial case, *Commonwealth v. Berkowitz*.[4] In an experimental study, a large and diverse national sample of adults reviewed the key facts in *Berkowitz*, including the uncontested fact that the victim in the case repeatedly said "no" immediately before and during intercourse with the defendant.[5] The subjects then indicated whether they believed the victim consented to sex or could reasonably have been understood to have done so by the defendant. Subjects also indicated how they

believed the case should be decided after being supplied with the common law definition of rape or with one of several reform alternatives. The goal of the study was not merely to generate data on whether people perceive "no" as sometimes meaning "yes" to sex and on how different legal standards affect their willingness to convict a man of rape in a case presenting that question. The study also aimed to connect the "no means . . . ?" debate to a psychologically realistic account of how and why people form such perceptions and make such judgments.

"Cultural cognition" refers to the influence of group values on individuals' perceptions of facts.[6] The law often requires decisionmakers to infer facts they cannot directly observe: states of mind, causal links, risks, and the like. In such circumstances, individuals naturally gravitate toward factual perceptions that reflect their group commitments. People who share formative identities tend to apprehend facts in a similar way in part because they are likely to be drawing on common life experiences when interpreting the significance of various events. But more importantly, such individuals face strong psychological pressure to fit their perceptions of how the world *does* work to their shared appraisals of how the world *should* work: forming beliefs at odds with their core values exposes them to dissonance and risks putting them in conflict with others whose opinions of them affect both their material and emotional well-being.[7] As a result, even when individuals of diverse cultural values are exposed to the same sources of evidence—eyewitness statements, expert opinions, and even videotaped recordings of key events—they can hear and see very different things.[8]

The study found that exactly this dynamic is at work when individuals consider the evidence in a case like *Berkowitz*. The question whether the putative victim in that case effectively conveyed consent or the lack of it depends on the answer to another question—*who* is being asked. Individuals who adhere to a largely traditional cultural style, one that prescribes highly differentiated gender roles and features a commitment to hierarchical forms of authority and social organization more generally, are highly likely to believe that "no" did not mean "no" in *Berkowitz*. In contrast, persons who subscribe to a more egalitarian cultural style that denies the legitimacy of hierarchical forms of social organization, including those founded on gender, are much more likely to perceive that the complainant did not consent and that the defendant knew that. These competing perceptions cohere with opposing sets of norms and related scripts of sexual behavior, conformity to which apportions status within the cultural groups adhering to them.

The influence of culture on individuals' perceptions of fact is much stronger, the study found, than other factors that might be expected to affect the result in a case like *Berkowitz*. One such factor is the legal definition of rape. Subjects who were instructed to apply a standard reflecting one or another "reform" definition of rape were not more likely to convict than were subjects instructed to apply the traditional common law definition—or than those who were not supplied with any definition of rape at all. Subjects who were instructed that rape includes sex when a woman says "no"—regardless of what she might have meant to convey or what the man understood her to be communicating—were slightly more likely to convict. But the size of this increase was relatively small compared to the impact of cultural predispositions on subjects who received this or any other definition of rape.

Gender also mattered much less than culture—or, more accurately, mattered only in conjunction with it. Overall, women were no more or less likely to favor conviction than were men. However, women who subscribed to the hierarchical cultural style—particularly older women who did—were more inclined to form a pro-defendant view of the facts. This result also reflects cultural cognition. Those who subscribe to traditional gender norms conceive of saying "no" but meaning "yes" as a strategy some women use to evade the stigma that these norms visit on women who engage in casual sex. Women who have earned high group status by conspicuously conforming to these norms are the ones most threatened by the prospect that women who use this strategy will escape censure. The former are thus the ones with the greatest psychological motivation to construe facts in a case like *Berkowitz* in a manner that focuses the condemnatory force of the law *against* women who can be depicted as saying "no" while meaning "yes."

The cultural-cognition account of who is likely to see "no" as meaning "yes," and why, does not logically entail a particular resolution to the debate over how the law should define rape. It does, however, cast considerable empirical doubt on the factual premises of certain normative arguments conventionally advanced within that debate.

One such premise is that the traditional common law definition reflects a distinctively "male" point of view. The "no means . . . ?" debate does not pit men against women, but rather pits men *and* women who adhere to one cultural style against men and women who adhere to another. Indeed, those with the greatest stake in preserving the law's attentiveness to the possibility that women who say "no" might be merely feigning lack of consent are women whose cultural identities endow them with resentment of other women whose behavior they regard as deviant and subversive.

At the same time, the cultural-cognition account also weakens the claim that modifying the traditional elements of rape risks unjust punishment of men who reasonably rely on social convention. Because of the strong tendency of individuals to conform their perceptions of fact to their cultural outlooks, legal definitions have relatively little impact on how actual cases are likely to be decided. Accordingly, even in jurisdictions that adopt reforms aimed at making "no" mean "no" without qualification, men who have internalized norms that members of their own communities share are unlikely to be judged differently from what they had reason to expect. The group that is likely to be most aggrieved by such a revision in the law consists of hierarchical women, whose concern is not with the impact that redefining rape law would have on their or anyone else's conduct, but rather with the message that such a redefinition would express about the norms on which their status depends.

For this reason, the primary normative issue posed by the cultural cognition of consent in acquaintance-rape cases is not behavioral but political. As a result of the formative impact of cultural outlooks on their perceptions, people are unlikely to behave differently, and legal decisionmakers to decide cases differently, if a jurisdiction replaces the common law formulation of rape with one or another reform standard. But precisely *because* individuals are conscious of the cultural significance of law, such reform is likely to be strongly advocated by those who want to overthrow traditional, stratified gender norms, and resisted by those who are committed to the same—all of whom will understand the stance the law takes as adjudicating the conflict between their worldviews. In this sense, the "no means . . . ?" debate is akin to numerous other debates that present themselves as empirical in nature (e.g., whether the death penalty deters murder, whether gun-control laws reduce crime, and whether global warming is a serious threat to human health and the environment) but that are at their essence expressive status conflicts between the adherents of competing cultural styles.[9] How to respond to such issues goes to the core of whether the law should strike a posture of liberal neutrality and what doing so would require in light of individuals' psychological disposition to impute harm to behavior that denigrates their visions of the best life and the ideal society.[10] . . .

The "No Means . . . ?" Debate

The Pennsylvania Supreme Court's decision in *Commonwealth v. Berkowitz*[11] furnishes an instructive focus for examining how the law responds to "acquaintance" or "date" rape. The facts not only highlight those aspects of the law that (in the overwhelming majority of jurisdictions) make proof of nonconsensual sexual intercourse with a person who verbally resists—who says "no"—insufficient to convict a man of rape. They also powerfully evoke the array of conflicting responses—perceptual, emotional, moral, and political—that account for the enduring debate over whether those features of the law should be changed. . . .

The Controversy

The topic of "acquaintance" or "date" rape had been a matter of intense political controversy for the better part of two decades by the time *Berkowitz* was decided.[12] Women's rights groups argued that women were being punished for the exercise of sexual autonomy by laws and attitudes that licensed men to impose unwanted sex on women who engaged in supposedly "suggestive" behavior or who had engaged in consensual sexual relations on other occasions with other men.[13] The advocacy efforts of these groups led to legal reforms, including the near-universal adoption of "rape shield" evidentiary provisions, which prohibit rape defendants from introducing evidence of a woman's sexual history.[14] In some states, legislatures amended the definition of rape, although usually in ways that were ambiguous.[15] Such hedging might well have been a deliberate response to the resistance that demands for reform also provoked. Social conservatives dismissed concern over date rape as a species of political correctness aimed at obliterating gender differentiation in social roles; a small group of eclectic feminists also dissented, arguing that the agitation over date rape was conditioning women to accept a disempowering "victimhood" identity[16] Singled out for particular, and particularly effective, ridicule were campus sexual-conduct codes, such as Antioch College's, which required explicit verbal confirmation of consent at each "stage" of sexual activity (kissing, removal of clothing, touching of breasts, contact with genitals, and so forth).[17]

The decision in *Berkowitz* incited a predictable clash between those on both sides of the date-rape divide. Excoriating the "all-male Pennsylvania Supreme Court,"[18] women's rights advocates characterized the ruling as "one of the worst setbacks for the sexual assault movement in the last several years."[19] "What is it about the word 'no' they don't understand?" critics of the decision asked.[20] "Obviously the court has a difficult time comprehending the most unambiguous word in the English language. . . . Almost anyone would agree [the victim] had been raped."[21]

But in truth, not everyone did. Some denied *Berkowitz* was "even remotely about rape."[22] "Oh, please," commented date-rape skeptic Camille Paglia, "she goes into the room of a man who's in bed and sits on the floor with her breasts sticking up: What are we teaching our girls? . . . When you go into a man's room and stretch on the floor, you are sending a signal."[23] Other commentators described *Berkowitz* as representative of a class of "cases where there has been some overreaching, disrespect and abuse, but not

the overwhelming life-threatening violence we think of traditionally in rape cases. . . ."[24]

Notes

1. *See generally* SUSAN CARINGELLA, ADDRESSING RAPE REFORM IN LAW AND PRACTICE 12–27 (2009) (chronicling the development of the rape-reform movement that began in the mid-1970s).

2. *See, e.g.,* JOANNA BOURKE, RAPE: SEX, VIOLENCE, HISTORY 50–82, 389–99 (2007) (discussing the history and cultural understandings of rape, as well as the legal system's current treatment of rape). *See generally* Catharine A. MacKinnon, *Feminism, Marxism, Method, and the State: Toward Feminist Jurisprudence,* 8 SIGNS 635, 651–55 (1983) (discussing the connection between the ideology of male dominance and female subordination and the definition of rape).

3. *See, e.g.,* Douglas N. Husak & George C. Thomas III, *Rapes Without Rapists: Consent and Reasonable Mistake, in* SOCIAL, POLITICAL, AND LEGAL PHILOSOPHY 86, 107–09 (Philosophical Issues vol. 11, Ernest Sosa & Enrique Villanueva eds., 2001).

4. 641 A.2d 1161 (Pa. 1994).

5. *Id.* at 1164.

6. *See generally* Dan M. Kahan & Donald Braman, *Cultural Cognition and Public Policy,* 24 YALE L. & POL'Y REV. 149, 150 (2006) (defining "cultural cognition" as "the psychological disposition of persons to conform their factual beliefs about the instrumental efficacy (or perversity) of law to their cultural evaluations of the activities subject to regulation"); Dan M . Kahan, Paul Slovic, Donald Braman & John Gastil, *Fear of Democracy: A Cultural Evaluation of Sunstein on Risk,* 119 HARV. L. REV. 1071, 1072 (2006) (reviewing and criticizing CASS R. SUNSTEIN, LAWS OF FEAR: BEYOND THE PRECAUTIONARY PRINCIPLE (2005), for its inattention to the phenomenon of cultural cognition).

7. *See* Geoffrey L. Cohen, *Party over Policy: The Dominating Impact of Group Influence on Political Beliefs,* 85 J. PERSONALITY & SOC. PSYCHOL. 808, 821 (2003); Dan M . Kahan, Donald Braman, John Gastil, Paul Slovic & C.K. Mertz, *Culture and Identity-Protective Cognition: Explaining the White-Male Effect in Risk Perception,* 4 J. EMPIRICAL LEGAL STUD. 465, 470 (2007) (introducing the theory of "identity-protective cognition" and arguing that individuals process information in a way that supports the beliefs associated with the groups to which they belong because challenges to such beliefs could hurt the individuals' well-being).

8. *See* Dan M. Kahan, David A. Hoffman & Donald Braman, *Whose Eyes Are You Going to Believe? Scott v. Harris and the Perils of Cognitive Illiberalism,* 122 HARV. L. REV. 837, 838 (2009) (using the varied responses to the online video posted in Scott v. Harris, 550 U.S. 372 (2007), to suggest that people are psychologically inclined

to interpret facts in a manner consistent with their group identity); *see also* Dan M. Kahan & Donald Braman, *The Self-Defensive Cognition of Self-Defense*, 45 Am. Crim. L. Rev 1, 3–5 (2008) (suggesting that the political debate over self-defense should be attributed to individuals' inclination to form beliefs that support their core values and group commitments).

9. For accounts of the nature of symbolic status competition in law, see Joseph R. Gusfield, Symbolic Crusade: Status Politics and the American Temperance Movement 1–24 (2d ed. 1986), and J.M. Balkin, *The Constitution of Status*, 106 Yale L.J. 2313 (1997).

10. *See* Dan M. Kahan, *The Cognitively Illiberal State*, 60 Stan. L. Rev. 115, 116–42 (2007).

11. 641 A.2d 1161 (Pa. 1994).

12. *See generally* Stephen J. Schulhofer, Unwanted Sex: The Culture of Intimidation and the Failure of Law 29–46 (1998) (describing reform efforts and debates from the mid-1970s onward).

13. *See, e.g.*, Vivian Berger, *Man's Trial, Woman's Tribulation: Rape Cases in the Courtroom*, 77 Colum. L. Rev. 1, 22–32 (1977) (reviewing the negative effects of common myths and stereotypes about female sexuality on both social attitudes and judicial treatment of rape victims).

14. *See, e.g.*, Fed. R. Evid. 412.

15. *See* Schulhofer, *supra* note 31, at 30–33 (summarizing reforms aimed at modifying the resistance requirement and at shifting emphasis from consent (a subjective state of mind) to "forcible compulsion" (an objective measure), but concluding that "even when reform statutes seemed to protect women from sex without their consent, force almost always reentered the picture").

16. *See, e.g.*, Camille Paglia, Op-Ed., *Rape and Modern Sex War*, N.Y. Newsday, Jan. 27, 1991, *reprinted in* Sex, Art, and American Culture 49, 49–50 (1992); Katie Roiphe, *The Rape Crisis, or*

"Is Dating Dangerous?", *reprinted in* The Morning After; Sex, Fear, and Feminism on Campus 51, 56–84 (1st ed. 1993); Christina Hoff Sommers, Who Stole Feminism? How Women Have Betrayed Women 242–46 (1994).

17. *See* Mark Cowling, *Rape, Communicative Sexuality and Sex Education* (reproducing and critiquing the Antioch College Sexual Offense Policy), *in* Making Sense of Sexual Consent 17, 19–23 (Mark Cowling & Paul Reynolds eds., 2004).

18. Robin Abcarian, *When a Woman Just Says "No,"* L.A. Times, June 8, 1994, at B10; *see also* Editorial, *Redefine Rape Law So that No Means No*, Hartford Courant, June 5, 1994, at D2, *available at* 1994 WL 4527718 ("In a ruling that can only be called outrageous, the all-male Pennsylvania Supreme Court held unanimously that a woman who merely says 'no' is not a rape victim . . . .").

19. Dale Russakoff, *Where Women Can't Just Say "No,* "Wash. Post, June 3, 1994, at A1 (quoting Cassandra Thomas, President, Nat'l Coal. Against Sexual Assault).

20. Editorial, *When "No" Means Nothing*, St. Louis Post-Dispatch, June 6, 1994, at 6B, *available at* 1994 WLNR 705949 (quoting Deborah Zubow, Women's Int'l League for Peace and Freedom in Phila.).

21. *Id.*

22. Nancy E. Roman, *Scales of Justice Weigh Tiers of Sexual Assault; Slate May Reform Rape Law*, Wash. Times, June 16, 1994, at A8, *available at* 1994 WLNR 231421 (quoting Camille Paglia, Professor, Univ. of the Arts).

23. *Id.*

24. Tamar Lewin, *Courts Struggle over How Much Force It Takes to Be a Rape*, N.Y. Times, June 3, 1994, at B8 (quoting Stephen Schulhofer, Professor, Univ. of Chi. Law Sch.).

Dan M. Kahan is a professor of law at Yale Law School.

Broach and Petretic

Beyond Traditional Definitions of Assault: Expanding Our Focus to Include Sexually Coercive Experiences

Introduction

The substantial psychological and interpersonal consequences of sexual victimization have been widely documented and, given the high prevalence rates of sexual aggression in our culture, are well deserving of continuing attention. The current study sought to expand the scope of this research by examining post-assault symptoms within a group of women who reported coerced sexual intercourse as well as women within more traditionally defined victim groups.

Not all unwanted sexual activity is nonconsensual. In fact, a significant percentage of college students (one quarter of college men and one half of college women) report consensually engaging in unwanted sexual activity in the context of their dating relationships (O'Sullivan & Allgeier, 1998). It has been suggested that many couples follow an unspoken "sexual contract" with the expectation that during discrepancies in the level of sexual desire between partners, the less interested partner will often consent to sexual activity, even feigning sexual desire in order to satisfy their partner, avoid tension in the relationship, or promote intimacy. Others have reported acquiescing to unwanted sexual intercourse in response to various forms of coercion from a partner. This illustrates an entirely different interpersonal dynamic than is typically imagined when researchers ask about "unwanted sexual experiences" (O'Sullivan & Allgeier, 1998). If we consider mutually desired and consensual sexual intercourse at one end of the spectrum, and forcible rape at the other, there is a wide range of sexual interactions falling between these two extremes. In addition to traditionally defined sexual assault groups, this study focused on coerced sexual intercourse and sought to examine the psychological repercussions of such coercion.

Individuals may employ a wide variety of tactics in the processes of sexual negotiation, coercion, or assault. Struckman-Johnson, Struckman-Johnson, & Anderson (2003) point out that behaviors which are normative within consensual sexual activity, such as persistent kissing and touching or removing clothing, become coercive within a context where one partner has already refused sexual activity and these tactics are being employed in an attempt to change the individual's refusal to consent. Other forms of sexual coercion involve verbal pressure or emotional manipulation and lies, such as threats of ending a relationship if a partner will not consent to sex. Impairment due to alcohol or drug intoxication may also provide a context for unwanted sexual activity, with a partner either taking advantage of such a situation, or purposely getting a date intoxicated in order to force or promote sexual activity. Finally, tactics of physical force (forcible rape) represent the most extreme end of the spectrum.

Examination of the most common forms of sexual coercion identified techniques of sexual arousal (persistent kissing and touching) and verbal pressure/emotional manipulation as the most common strategies for obtaining sex from an uninterested partner reported by both men and women. Taking advantage of alcohol consumption was also commonly endorsed, though more commonly used by men than women. Some estimates suggest that up to 70% of college students have been the target of sexual persistence after refusal (Struckman-Johnson, Struckman-Johnson, & Anderson, 2003). The estimates of sexual coercion in this study are considerably lower, reflecting a more conservative definition of sexual coercion. Only those individuals reporting completed sexual intercourse due to coercion and denying any events that could be categorized as rape or childhood sexual abuse were included in the coerced sexual intercourse group. Those who endorsed both coerced sexual intercourse and adult rape or childhood sexual abuse were included in the more "severe" victimization category, contributing to the appearance of lower rates of sexual coercion, but actually reflecting the co-occurrence of sexual coercion with other sexual victimization in many young women.

Testa and Derman (1999) suggest that sexual coercion, rather than representing a less severe form of sexual assault than rape, is better conceptualized as a qualitatively different type of sexually aggressive experience. They found that personality variables, such as low-self esteem, lack of assertiveness, and high sexual alcohol expectancies, were associated with sexual coercion, but not rape. The differential presence of such personality characteristics among assaulted versus coerced groups may suggest that many women who experience sexual coercion are particularly vulnerable to psychological pressure in intimate relationships, causing them to acquiesce to partner demands. The current study sought to assess whether, given the possible qualitative differences in the constructs, women who had experienced coerced sexual intercourse would report post-event symptom levels similar to traditionally defined rape victims, regardless of possible differences in etiology.

The only study the author was able to locate within the literature to include a similar focus on symptomatology following sexual coercion was in a longitudinal investigation following a cohort of female junior high school students through young adulthood (14 year time span) (Zweig, Crockett, Sayer, & Vicary, 1999). Here, the researchers assessed the psychosocial consequences of sexual coercion and sexual victimization, controlling for pre-assault functioning. They classified unwanted sexual experiences into four subtypes, internal psychological pressure, substance-related coercion, external psychological manipulation, and threat or use of violence. They found that external psychological pressure resulted poorer functioning, similar to threat or use of force, and suggested that constructs of self-blame and cognitive interpretations of the event may help to explain their findings. The current study was able to expand this research by allowing comparison of a coerced sexual intercourse group with traditionally defined adult, child, and multiple victimization groups, as well as non-victim controls on a measure specific to symptoms related to interpersonal trauma.

Methods

Participants

Participants in this study included 300 female undergraduate college students. Participants were volunteers recruited from undergraduate psychology classes and received course credit toward a research requirement or extra credit for their participation.

Measures

This study utilized a self-report questionnaire format. All participants were guaranteed of anonymity as informed consent was gathered separately from the questionnaires and no identifying information was included in the questionnaire packet.

Participants were requested to provide minimal personal information including their age, college level, ethnicity, and marital status.

Trauma Symptom Inventory

The *Trauma Symptom Inventory* (TSI; Briere, 1995) was chosen as the preferred instrument for this study because it has been shown useful in the specific assessment of several symptom areas that are prevalent in victims of interpersonal traumas such as sexual assault. The TSI includes 10 clinical subscales assessing different symptom clusters. Scales include Anxious Arousal (AA), Anger/Irritability

(AI), Depression (D), Defensive Avoidance (DA), Dissociation (DIS), Dysfunctional Sexual Behavior (DSB), Intrusive Experiences (IE), Impaired Self-Reference (ISR), Sexual Concerns (SC), and Tension Reduction Behaviors (TRB). In addition, three validity subscales are included: Atypical Responses (ATR), Response Level (RL), and Inconsistent Responses (INC). In a validation study using a college population, and inpatient and outpatient clinical samples, Briere, Elliott, and Smiljanich (1993) reported that the individual scales of the TSI have a mean reliability of .87 with college populations and .90 with clinical populations. Gender differences in TSI responses indicated the need for different norms to be used with males and females and with clinical versus non-clinical populations. In the second phase of the study, Briere and colleagues (1993, cited in Briere, Elliott, Harris, & Cotman, 1993) reported mean reliability of the 10 clinical subscales at .90. The need for separate norms for males and females was also supported in the community sample. As this study included only female participants, the female norms were utilized.

Modified Sexual Experiences Survey

The *Sexual Experiences Survey* (SES; Koss & Oros, 1982) was designed to assess degrees of sexual victimization and aggression. There is a female version (sexual victimization) and a male version (sexual aggression). Only the female version was used in this study. The SES has been reported to yield an internal consistency coefficient of .74 for women (Koss et al., 1987). The SES is reported to have a test-retest reliability coefficient of .93 when test-retest administrations are one week apart (Koss & Gidycz, 1985). A Pearson correlation coefficient of .73 was reported between women's level of victimization according to the SES self-report data and level of victimization based on an interview (Koss, Dinero, Seibel, & Cox, 1988). The wording of some items on the SES was slightly modified and some questions were added to the measure to further identify victim status and perceptions of victimization.

Sexual Contact During Childhood Scale

The Sexual Contact During Childhood Scale (SCDCS) was developed specifically for this study using items from the *Sexual Experiences Survey* (Koss & Oros, 1982) that were modified to be more appropriate for assessing child sexual assault. Items not considered applicable to child sexual abuse were omitted from the questionnaire while other items were rephrased to be more congruent with behaviors categorized as child sexual abuse.

Results

Demographics

Three hundred and three female participants took part in this study. The data from three participants were not included in any analyses due to incomplete surveys. The remaining participants in this study included 300 female undergraduate college students with a mean age of 19.72 years (*SD* = 3.25, Range = 18–47 years). The majority of the participants were freshmen (64%), followed by sophomores (19.7%), juniors (9.3%), and seniors (6.7%). The majority of the participants (79.3%), were Caucasian. African-Americans, the largest represented minority group, composed 11.3% of the sample. The remaining participants included individuals of Hispanic (3.0%), Asian-American (2.3%), Native American (2.0%), and other ethnic origins (2.0%). Of the sample, 69.3% reported current involvement in a relationship. The majority of the participants (93%), were single and had never been married, while 5% were currently married, and 2% were divorced.

Sexual Assault History

Sexual assault group categorization. Sexual assault victimization was determined on the basis of experiences reported by the participants on the SES and SCDCS. Criteria for group inclusion was as follows: Participants included in the Coerced Sexual Intercourse group endorsed at least one item identified as sexually coercive intercourse on the SES but did not endorse any of the adult rape or child sexual abuse items. The coerced sexual intercourse construct was framed as unwanted sexual intercourse due to psychological pressure.

Participants included in the adult rape group endorsed at least one item identified as adult sexual assault on the SES. These items meet legal criteria for rape or attempted rape. Participants included in the adult sexual assault group did not endorse any of the items pertaining to child sexual assault. Rape and attempted rape were collapsed into one adult sexual assault group since only four respondents met the criteria for attempted rape without meeting criteria for completed rape. This inclusion of attempted rape victims in the Adult Sexual Assault group is conceptually sound considering the relevant and common assault variables and the expected similarity of post trauma responses.

Participants included in the Child Sexual Abuse group endorsed at least one item identified as child sexual abuse on the SCDCS, the items of which inquired about unwanted sexual contact before the age of 14. Participants included in the child sexual assault group did not endorse any of the items pertaining to adult sexual assault.

Participants included in the Multiple Victimization group endorsed items for both adult rape and child sexual abuse. It should be noted that participants in the adult rape, child sexual abuse, and multiple victimization groups may also have endorsed coerced sexual intercourse, but were classified in their respective groups based on the most severe criterion endorsed. Participants not meeting any of the above criteria were categorized as non-victims. Group membership was treated as mutually exclusive.

Based on the above criteria for victim group classification, 8.7% (*n* = 26) were classified as having coerced sexual intercourse, 21.0% (*n* = 63) had experienced sexual assault meeting legal criteria for rape or attempted rape as adults, 11.7% (*n* = 35) had experienced sexual abuse as a child, and 6.0% (*n* = 18) had experienced sexual assault both in childhood and as adults. The remaining 52.7% (*n* = 158) of the participants were classified as non-victims.

Trauma Symptom Inventory and Sexual Assault Groups

TSI subscales by victim groups ANOVAS. It was hypothesized that there would be differences in personal problems or symptomatology, as measured by the TSI, between the groups, with the most notable differences expected between the non-victim group and the groups who had experienced some form of sexual victimization. The multiple victimization group was expected to show the greatest severity of trauma-related symptoms. The authors also hypothesized that the coerced sexual intercourse group would demonstrate clinical scale elevations more consistent with the adult rape group than the non-victim group.

ANOVAs were significant for group differences on all clinical subscales of the TSI. A more conservative significance level of $p < .01$ was chosen to correct for the multiple planned ANOVAs.

Tukey post hoc analysis was used to establish significant differences within the five groups. As hypothesized, the distinct trend showed elevated symptom levels in the sexual assault and coercion groups compared to the non-victim group, with the exception of the child sexual abuse group. Means and post hoc analyses supported the hypothesis that the coerced sexual intercourse group would endorse symptoms consistent with adult rape rather than non-victimization and that multiple victimizations (victimization during childhood and as an adult) would result in the highest symptom elevations.

A discriminant function analysis was also performed using the ten clinical subscales of the TSI as predictors of membership in the five victimization groups. Of the 300 subjects, one was dropped from the non-victim group due to incomplete data. Four discriminant functions were calculated, with a Chi-Square (40) = 131.67, $p < .001$. The first and second functions were significant, while the third and fourth did not attain significance after removal of the first two. The first function accounted for 59.8% of the between group variability, showing the largest absolute correlation of the four functions with nine of the ten TSI scales. The second function accounted for an additional 26.4% of the between group variability, summing to a total of 86.2% of the variance. However, the functions classified only 55.3% of the cross-validated grouped cases correctly, with a strong tendency to misclassify members of the victim groups as non-victims. The analysis accurately predicted group membership for over 80% of the non-victim group, approximately 43% of the adult rape group, and 20% of the multiple victimization group, but failed entirely to identify members of the child sexual abuse group, which is consistent with the previously discussed analyses indicating no differences between the CSA and non-victim groups on the TSI clinical scales. The analysis also failed to predict membership in the coerced sexual intercourse group, but was the exception to the predictive bias toward non-victim status, classifying approximately 75% of the coerced sexual intercourse cases in the adult rape group with the remaining 25% predicted as non-victims. This prediction was consistent with the study hypothesis that these individuals would be characterized by trauma symptom patterns similar to those found in more traditionally defined sexual assault victims. As previously noted, the relatively high functioning nature of a college student sample, reflected in the relatively mild scale elevations for many victims, may explain some of the difficulty in adequately classifying the victims.

Discussion

Trauma Symptom Inventory and Sexual Assault Groups

The overall pattern of differences found between the victimization groups on the TSI was indicative of increased distress in the groups identifying sexual victimization in adulthood, specifically the coercive sexual experiences as well as the adult rape and multiple victimization groups, when compared to the non-victim group. One unexpected finding was the relative lack of elevation in symptomatology for the child sexual abuse group. For each of the TSI subscales, the child sexual abuse group failed to differ significantly from the non-victim group, though, it did seem to span the gap between victim and non-victim, in that it was often not significantly different from the other victimization groups either. This finding is inconsistent with other research indicating significant post-traumatic stress-related symptoms in women with childhood sexual abuse histories (Messman-Moore, Long, & Siegfried, 2000). It is possible that this lack of findings reflects the group inclusion criteria, with the identified cases weighted heavily toward less severe acts of victimization, such as fondling rather than intercourse. It is also possible that the lower symptom elevations reflect the greater elapsed time since victimization or the high functioning nature of a college student sample.

As expected, the multiple victimization group evidenced the highest subscale elevations and the greatest proportion of cases falling within a clinically significant range. The multiple victimization group was significantly different from the non-victim group on all clinical subscales and consistently demonstrated the highest scale elevations of all groups. This trend is clear when viewing the group means, though the analysis did not differentiate this group from the other victim groups on many subscales, possibly due to limited power given the relatively small group size ($n = 18$). However, consideration of the percentage of participants in each group obtaining clinically significant subscale scores should clearly illustrate the elevation of symptoms within the multiple victimization group.

As for the main focus of this study, the hypothesis was clearly supported, with the coerced sexual intercourse group showing elevations equivalent to the adult rape group on all clinical subscales. Previous research has shown that coercive psychological strategies, such as being promised or receiving rewards from a perpetrator, predicted greater distress and trauma related symptoms in adult survivors of childhood sexual abuse (Lucenko, Gold, Elhai, Russo, & Swingle, 2000). This has interesting implications when examining coercive sexual dynamics in adult dating relationships. The elevated symptom levels observed in the coerced sexual intercourse group within the current study may reflect a similar etiology, with self-blame and low self-esteem mediating the individual's perceptions of their acquiescence to a partner's unwanted sexual demands.

The coerced sexual intercourse group scored significantly higher than the non-victim group on seven out of ten clinical subscales, with only intrusive experiences, dysfunctional sexual behavior and tension reduction behaviors failing to show significant differences. It should also be noted that the coerced group did not differ significantly from the adult rape group on these scales, with elevations on these subscales falling between the non-victim and rape groups'. Beyond this general interpretation of the observed TSI scale scores, it is interesting to look more closely at the patterns and implications of the groups' scores on the specific subscales.

Though verbal or emotional coercion is rarely equated to the perception of force which defines rape, the findings of this study suggest that the emotional and interpersonal consequences may be similar. As noted above, the coerced sexual intercourse group endorsed symptom levels equivalent to those of the group meeting criteria for rape. In examining the subscale elevations, it is interesting to consider the likely psychological causes or dynamics of the symptoms. Below is a consideration of each subscale and the group elevations observed.

The Anxious Arousal (AA) subscale reflects heightened arousal and anxiety, a common reaction following experiences of trauma that falls clearly into one of the three main symptom clusters for PTSD. Within the adult rape and multiple victimization groups, this may be related to perceptions of danger or feelings of fear continuing after the assaults, with many victims becoming hyper vigilant to potential threats. This increased awareness would theoretically help the victim to predict potential dangers, gaining some sense of control, and avoid the situations or people evoking those cues. However, given the different dynamics of the sexual coercion, this heightened anxiety may reflect instead the anticipation of sexual demands and psychological pressure in intimate relationships and concern regarding one's ability to manage such pressures in the coerced sexual intercourse group. The elevation observed here may be indicative of a heightened degree of caution and expectations of negative interpersonal outcomes within the coerced group.

The Anger/Irritability subscale taps into the anger that many victims feel, anger at their attacker, anger at their helplessness, and anger at the impact the assault has on their normal functioning. Anger may be a sustaining emotion for many victims, giving them the strength to cope with the pain, fear, and frustration associated with the assault. Within the coerced sexual intercourse group, the observed elevation in anger and irritability may reflect similar dynamics, such as anger at the coercive partner or anger at self for acquiescing to unwanted sexual demands. However, additional considerations are raised when the individual is in an ongoing relationship with the coercive partner. In such cases, anger and irritability may also be reflective of overall relationship distress or dissatisfaction and problems with conflict management.

Significant elevations on the Depression subscale were observed in the multiple victimization and coerced sexual intercourse groups in comparison with non-victims, but may reflect different origins and dynamics for the two respective groups. Within the multiple victimization group elevated depression scores would certainly be expected, reflecting the general dysphoria that is often observed when an individual is distressed and struggling with the aftermath of recurrent trauma. As noted before, the multiple victimization group showed the highest symptom elevations across scales with a significant number falling within the clinically significant range. This suggests a degree of distress and dysfunction in which depression may be seen as a reaction to the ongoing problems as well as the initial trauma. In contrast, the elevated depression in the coerced sexual intercourse group may be more likely to manifest in response to unhealthy relationship patterns and perhaps a sense of low self-esteem. This dysphoria may be tied to general relationship dissatisfaction as well as more specific relational issues such as giving in to a partner's coercive or manipulative sexual demands.

Defensive Avoidance (DA) may be seen as relating to escape/avoidance coping behavior in victims. Safety might be expected to be of concern for the adult rape and multiple victimization groups, and the avoidance of potentially traumatic people, places, or events may serve as a more or less effective coping mechanism. However, one might expect a different dynamic with the coerced sexual intercourse group, perhaps reflecting a strategy for avoiding potentially coercive situations due to the anticipation of psychological pressure to engage in unwanted activities, rather than in reaction to safety concerns per se. Endorsement of defensive avoidance items may also reflect a cognitive strategy in which the individual avoids consideration of the coercive event or their own acquiescent behaviors, refusing to acknowledge or look more closely at the effects of this interpersonal dynamic.

Heightened dissociative symptoms in the multiple victimization group suggests a self-protective strategy or coping process developed in response to multiple victimizations, possibly begun during childhood abuse and strengthened in response to adult assault experiences.

There is substantial literature and ideographic clinical cases pointing to dissociation as a response to severe trauma. That the multiple victimization group evidences heightened dissociative symptomtology is consistent with the multiple traumas and interpretation of greatest distress within this group. On the other hand, the coercive sexual experiences group's heightened score on the Dissociation (DIS) subscale may seem somewhat surprising, given the expectation that this group would interpret their experiences as the least traumatic. The elevations observed for the coerced group were in excess of those in the adult rape group, and equivalent to the multiple victimization group. The authors hypothesized that the dissociation endorsed by the coerced sexual intercourse group may reflect a choice of coping mechanisms, with these individuals distancing themselves as a way to cope with their ineffectiveness in exerting control over their sexual involvements. This dissociation may make it possible for those individuals to maintain a more positive evaluation of the coercive process in which they were involved, thereby protecting their sense of control over their own bodies as well as their investment in the relationship with the coercive partner.

Dysfunctional Sexual Behavior (DSB) has distinct interpersonal ramifications. Sexual functioning would be expected to be a salient area affected for all victim groups as well as an area of continuing difficulty in their intimate relationships. Elevations on the DSB subscale for the adult rape and multiple victimization groups suggest continuing difficulties with judgment in sexual or intimate relations. Sexuality may prove one of the most difficult areas to negotiate, particularly within our college student sample, who are largely of an age where maturation into adult sexual roles has been complicated by victimization. The multiple victimization group showed distinct elevations in dysfunctional sexual behavior, scoring significantly higher than the other victim groups as well as the non-victim group. Since this group would theoretically have the poorest model for appropriate or healthy sexual functioning, given their multiple victimizations experiences (in childhood and as adults), it makes sense that they would experience the greatest difficulty in negotiating healthy sexual roles. The temporal relationship between the adult assaults and the assessment of these difficulties may also be reflected within the adult rape and multiple victimization groups, given the young age of the sample.

Intrusive experiences represent a common reaction to trauma, with re-experiencing symptoms being recognized criteria of PTSD. The intrusive re-experiencing of the traumatic event or intrusive thoughts and feelings related to the event underline the victims' continued sense of powerlessness, first over their attacker, then over their own recovery from the events. The unpredictability and threat of the assault is paralleled by their perceived inability to stop these intrusive thoughts and images which reflect their fear and continuing emotional distress. Relationship to perpetrator may present an additional concern, with the majority of the rapes perpetrated by dates or acquaintances, leaving the victims struggling to understand how someone they trusted could have raped them, as well as adding to concerns about safety and the reliability of their judgments about others. One other factor to note when considering the elevations in the adult sexual assault and multiple victimization groups is the temporal significance of a rape experience in a group of this generally young age. Though time since the experience was not assessed, the nature of the sample would suggest that many of the participants' rape experiences occurred within the preceding few years.

Elevations on the Impaired Self-Reference subscale, which is notably highest in the coercive sexual experiences group, reflect disturbances in self-concept. Considering the elevations in the adult rape and multiple victimization groups, a victim must often re-evaluate her views of herself and others following her sexual assault. In this negotiation of what the assault means for her, the victim may have a sense of losing the person she was before the assault occurred, leaving her trying to redefine herself within the context of being a rape victim. Within the coerced sexual intercourse group, the notable elevation on the impaired self-reference scale may actually tap an underlying dynamic which predisposes these individuals to become involved in such coercive relationships. Individuals with deficiencies in self-identity and low self-esteem may be more easily manipulated into roles or activities they would not have chosen for themselves. It may also be that the higher elevation in impaired self-reference within the coerced sexual intercourse group reflects the cognitive interpretations the individuals in this group use in explaining their experiences and behavior in the context of a sexually and emotionally coercive environment. Their lack of understanding regarding their own behaviors or roles may reflect the confusion of trying to reconcile their own needs and wants within their relationships with those behaviors they feel compelled to by others.

Sexual Concerns may be seen as directly related to the intimate, sexual nature of the interpersonal trauma or to the maladaptive interpersonal relationships which the victim groups have experienced. Sexual functioning is an area of concern and emotional distress for many victims. The adult rape and multiple victimization groups may be expected to manifest sexual concerns as they attempt to reconcile their rape with normative sexual functioning within the context of their intimate relationships. The association of the sexual act with feelings of fear, pain, humiliation, or guilt may last long after the rape is over. Interestingly, similar feelings may explain the report of sexual concerns within the coerced sexual intercourse group, with feelings of confusion and shame surrounding sex within a coercive relationship.

The tension reduction behaviors subscale reflects dysfunctional and even harmful behaviors in which some individuals may engage in an attempt to manage psychological distress. The adult rape and multiple

victimization groups show the highest elevations on this scale, which might be expected given the severity of the victimization experience, other symptom elevations, and the temporal relationship of the assaults to the symptom assessment, suggesting perhaps the greatest difficulty in adequately coping with their distress. The elevation is most pronounced in the multiple victimization group when observing the percentage of cases falling within the clinically significant range, suggesting again that repeated trauma inflicts progressively more psychological damage.

The observation of primary interest in the group differences was the tendency for the coerced sexual intercourse group to endorse symptom levels comparable to those of the more traditionally defined sexual victimization groups. This suggested that the sexually coercive, and perhaps emotionally abusive, dynamics of some relationships can contribute to difficulties and symptomatic reactions similar to those observed in rape victims. Research supports a link between coercive sexual behaviors and psychological abuse in relationships. It has also been shown that higher levels of coercive sexual behaviors are associated with more abusive conflict tactics in ongoing relationships (Hines & Saudino, 2003; Katz, Carino & Hilton, 2002; Hogben & Waterson, 2000). This has significant implications for the coerced sexual intercourse group, as scale elevations may reflect an additive effect of sexual coercion and emotional abuse.

These findings beg further research into the dynamics of sexual coercion as well as having implications for the evaluation of relationship based problems. In clinical interventions with clients experiencing relationship difficulties, assessments which carefully attend to abusive and coercive sexual or emotional experiences may provide insights into personal as well as interpersonal distress which may be a focus in treatment. A treatment plan incorporating measures to address the cognitive interpretations of and emotional reactions to such experiences may be of importance in promoting adaptive coping strategies and healthy relationship patterns.

The findings of this study suggest that the legal criteria for rape are not necessarily adequate predictors of the psychological impact of unwanted sexual experiences. More surprisingly, it appears that the provision of consent, if coerced, is likewise not an adequate protection against negative psychological outcomes.

References

Briere, J. (1995). *Professional manual for the trauma symptom inventory.* Odessa, Florida: Psychological Assessment Resources.

Briere, J., Elliot, D., Harris, K., & Cotman, A. (1993). The trauma symptom inventory: *Reliability and validity in a clinical sample.* Unpublished manuscript, University of Southern California School of Medicine, Los Angeles, CA.

Briere, J., Elliot, D., & Smiljanich, K. (1993). The trauma symptom inventory: Reliability and validity in clinical and nonclinical samples. Unpublished manuscript, University of Southern California School of Medicine, Los Angeles, CA.

Hines, D., & Saudino, K. (2003). Gender differences in psychological, physical, and sexual aggression among college students using the Revised Conflict Tactics Scales. *Violence and Victims, 18,* 197–217.

Hogben, M., & Waterman, C. (2000). Patterns of conflict resolution within relationships and coercive sexual behavior of men and women. *Sex Roles, 43,* 341–357.

Katz, J., Carino, A., & Hilton, A. (2002). Perceived verbal conflict behaviors associated with physical aggression and sexual coercion in dating relationships: A gender sensitive analysis. *Violence and Victims, 17,* 93–109.

Koss, M., & Gidycz, C. (1985). Sexual Experiences Survey: Reliability and validity. *Journal of Consulting and Clinical Psychology, 53,* 422–423.

Koss, M., & Oros, C. (1982). Sexual Experiences Survey: A research instrument investigating sexual aggression and victimization. *Journal of Consulting and Clinical Psychology, 50,* 455–457.

Lucenko, B., Gold, S., Elhai, J., Russo, S., & Swingle, J. (2000). Relations between coercive strategies and MMPI-2 scale elevations among women survivors of childhood sexual abuse. *Journal of Traumatic Stress, 13,* 169–177.

Messman-Moore, T., Long, P., & Siegfried, N. (2000). The revictimization of child sexual abuse survivors: An examination of the adjustment of college women with child sexual abuse, adult sexual abuse, and adult physical abuse. *Child Maltreatment, 5,* 18–26.

O'Sullivan, L., & Allgeier, E. (1998). Feigning sexual desire: consenting to unwanted sexual activity in heterosexual dating relationships. *The Journal of Sex Research, 35,* 234–243.

Struckman-Johnson, C., Struckman-Johnson, D., & Anderson, P. (2003). Tactics of sexual coercion: When men and women won't take no for an answer. *The Journal of Sex Research, 40,* 76–86.

Testa, M., & Derman, K. (1999). The differential correlates of sexual coercion and rape. *Journal of Interpersonal Violence, 14,* 548–561.

Zweig, J., Crockett, L., Sayer, A., & Vicary, J. (1999). A longitudinal examination of the consequences of sexual victimization for rural young adult women. *The Journal of Sex Reseach, 36,* 396–409.

JENNIFER L. BROACH is a psychologist at the Lexington VA Medical Center in Lexington, Kentucky.

EXPLORING THE ISSUE

Should the Federal Government Adopt a New Legal Definition of Rape?

Critical Thinking and Reflection

1. How does the recently updated federal definition of rape provide a more accurate, more inclusive way to encompass the broad spectrum of possible sex crimes?
2. Does the new definition fully address all the possible shortfalls in ensuring that all rapes are considered equally under the law? Why or why not?
3. How does the new definition more inclusively address who can be victims of rape?

Is There Common Ground?

For more than a decade, women's advocacy groups asked the U.S. federal government, specifically the Federal Bureau of Investigation (FBI), to change the legal definition of rape (Women's Law Project, 2012). The federal definition of rape, used by the FBI to track rape in the Uniform Crime Report (UCR), had not been updated since 1929. In January 2012, Attorney General Eric Holder announced that the federal government would update the official definition of rape that would be used by the FBI in the UCR:

> The new definition of rape is: "The penetration, no matter how slight, of the vagina or anus with any body part or object, or oral penetration by a sex organ of another person, without the consent of the victim." The definition is used by the FBI to collect information from local law enforcement agencies about reported rapes.
>
> —(U.S. Department of Justice, 2012).

After a congressional health debate put the 1929 definition of rape under a national microscope in 2011, the Department of Justice examined the shortfalls of the 82-year-old policy that narrowly defined rape as unwanted, forcible penile–vaginal penetration. While the issue of how to define and prove consent will likely continue to be adjudicated in courtrooms across the nation, the definition of what the nation considers rape was updated and established in January 2012.

Additional Resources

Antioch College. (2012). "Sexual Offense Prevention Policy." *Student Handbook*. Retrieved from: http://antiochcollege.org/assets/pdf/student-handbook.pdf

Hall, D. (1998, August 10). "Consent for Sexual Behavior in a College Student Population." *Electronic Journal of Human Sexuality, 1*. Retrieved from: www.ejhs.org/volume1/conseapa.htm

Kroll, A. (2012, November 6). "Claire McCaskill Shuts Down Todd 'Legitimate Rape' Akin." *Mother Jones*. Retrieved from: www.motherjones.com/mojo/2012/11/claire-mccaskill-win-missouri-todd-akin-senate

United States Department of Justice. (2012, January 6). "Attorney General Eric Holder Announces Revisions to the Uniform Crime Report's Definition of Rape: Data Reported on Rape Will Better Reflect State Criminal Codes, Victim Experiences." Retrieved from: www.fbi.gov/news/pressrel/press-releases/attorney-general-eric-holder-announces-revisions-to-the-uniform-crime-reports-definition-of-rape

Women's Law Project. (2012). "Rape and Sexual Assault." Retrieved from: www.womenslawproject.org/NewPages/wkVAW_SexualAssault.html

Create Central

www.mhhe.com/createcentral

Internet References . . .

Centers for Disease Control

http://www.cdc.gov/ViolencePrevention/RPE/index.html

Men Can Stop Rape

http://www.mencanstoprape.org/

Selected, Edited, and with Issue Framing Material by:
Rachel Pienta, *Valdosta State University*

ISSUE

Are Women More at Risk for Crimes Using Digital Technology?

YES: Danielle Keats Citron, from "Law's Expressive Value in Combating Cyber Gender Harassment," *Michigan Law Review* (vol. 108, no. 3, 2009)

NO: Rebecca Eckler, from "Finding Out What Men Are Up To: Some Women Pride Themselves on Their Cyber-Sleuth Skills," *Macleans* (September 28, 2009)

Learning Outcomes

As you read the issue, focus on the following points:

- Does online anonymity increase abuse and harassment? Why?
- Is the preservation of anonymity for the sake of the masses worth the cost of abuse to the few?

ISSUE SUMMARY

YES: Professor of law at University of Maryland Law School, Danielle Keats Citron argues that women face higher rates of gender-based cyber harassment and it creates a gender divide online where women are disenfranchised from full participation.

NO: Rebecca Eckler asserts that women are equal opportunity offenders in the realm of digital crime and that women have used online tactics to harass men in increasingly greater numbers.

The online universe of the Internet along with other computer-assisted digital technologies has, for many, opened a virtual "wild west" of criminal opportunities. The relative anonymity of digital interactions in digital and virtual environments creates a fertile environment for abuse and harassment.

While law enforcement agencies report increased incidences of digital stalking and other forms of cyber harassment, research suggests that cyber crime does not divide neatly along gender lines.

In the YES and NO selections, two different perspectives on the gendered patterns of cyber-based behavior are presented. Citron examines the scope of cyber harassment arguing that the prevalence of gender-based online abuse inhibits women's potential participation in digital environments. Eckler presents a counter-narrative in which women have embraced technology as a way to engage in male-focused harassment and stalking behavior.

In "Law's Expressive Value in Combating Cyber Gender Harassment," Citron examines how the bulk of cyber gender harassment is focused on women. This online targeting of women, Citron posits, inhibits women from free and full participation in the Internet world. According to Citron, while cyber gender harassment "encompasses various behaviors," three core features characterize cyber gender harassment and make it a gendered form of abuse that is primarily experienced by women: "(1) its victims are female, (2) the harassment is aimed at particular women, and (3) the abuse invokes the targeted individual's gender in sexually threatening and degrading ways" (p. 378).

In "Finding Out What Men Are Up To: Some Women Pride Themselves on Their Cyber-Sleuth Skills," Eckler examines how women appropriate technology to flip the power narrative in order to cyber-stalk men. The anonymity of new technology and the relative ease of access the technology provides afford opportunities for anyone with the inclination to engage in invasive online activities. Women's online activities allow them to furtively spy on current and former relationships using purloined passwords. Other technological advances allow both men and women to engage in mischief that ranges from prank calls to fake text messages.

YES

Danielle Keats Citron

Law's Expressive Value in Combating Cyber Gender Harassment

Introduction

The harassment of women online is a pernicious and widespread problem.[1] It can be severe, involving threats of sexual violence, doctored photographs of women being suffocated, postings of women's home addresses alongside the suggestion that they should be raped, and technological attacks that shut down feminist blogs and websites.[2] Cyber harassment is a uniquely gendered phenomenon—the majority of targeted individuals are women,[3] and the abuse of female victims invokes gender in threatening and demeaning terms.[4]

Such harassment has a profound effect on targeted women. It discourages them from writing and earning a living online.[5] It interferes with their professional lives. It raises their vulnerability to offline sexual violence. It brands them as incompetent workers and inferior sexual objects. The harassment causes considerable emotional distress.[6] Some women have committed suicide.[7]

To avoid future abuse, women assume gender-neutral pseudonyms or go offline, even if it costs them work opportunities.[8] Others curtail their online activities.[9] For the "digital native"[10] generation, forsaking aspects of the internet means missing innumerable social connections. Although online harassment inflicts the most direct costs on targeted individuals, it harms society as well by entrenching male hierarchy online.

But no matter how serious the harm that cyber gender harassment inflicts, the public tends to trivialize it. Commentators dismiss it as harmless locker-room talk, characterizing perpetrators as juvenile pranksters and targeted individuals as overly sensitive complainers.[11] Others consider cyber gender harassment as an inconvenience that victims can ignore or defeat with counterspeech.[12] Some argue that women who benefit from the internet have assumed the risks of its Wild West norms.[13] Although the arguments differ, their message is the same—women need to tolerate these cyber "pranks" or opt out of life online. This message has the unfortunate consequence of discouraging women from reporting cyber gender harassment and preventing law enforcement from pursuing cyber-harassment complaints.[14]

The trivialization of harms suffered by women is nothing new.[15] Society ignored or downplayed domestic violence's brutality for over 200 years.[16] No term even existed to describe sexual harassment in the workplace until the 1970s, despite the pervasiveness of the practice.[17] In light of this history, the current refusal to take seriously the cyber harassment of women is as unsurprising as it is disappointing.

Due to the internet's relative youth, this is an auspicious time to combat the trivialization of cyber gender harassment before it becomes too entrenched. If it continues unabated, cyber harassment could very well be the central front of struggles against sexual harassment in the coming decades given our increasing dependence on the net. More people make friends, apply for jobs, and discuss policy online than ever before, shifting their social and professional interactions to the net and with it the risk of sexual harassment.[18] As the market leans toward more realistic sensory experiences in virtual worlds and as these sites become more popular, cyber gender harassment may more closely approximate conventional notions of sexual violence. For instance, Second Life users' avatars have reportedly been forced to perform sexually explicit acts after being given malicious code.[19] These developments, and others like them, would further threaten gender equality in our digital age.

Wrestling with the marginalization of cyber sexual harassment is a crucial step in combating its gender-specific harms. Law has a crucial role to play in this effort. Law serves different functions here. It can deter online harassment's harms by raising the costs of noncompliance beyond its expected benefits. Law can also remedy such harm with monetary damages, injunctions, and criminal convictions. My article *Cyber Civil Rights* explored antidiscrimination, criminal, and tort law's role in preventing, punishing, and redressing cyber harassment.[20] In this piece, I explore law's other crucial role: educating the public about women's unique suffering in the wake of cyber harassment and potentially changing societal responses to it. Because law is expressive, it constructs our understanding of harms that are not trivial. The application of a cyber civil rights legal agenda would reveal online harassment for what it truly is—harmful gender discrimination. It would recognize the distinct suffering of women, suffering that men ordinarily do not experience or appreciate as harmful.

Once cyber harassment is understood as gender discrimination and not as a triviality to be ignored, women are more likely to complain about it rather than suffer in silence. Law enforcement could pursue cyber harassment complaints rather than just counseling women to get off their computers and seek help only if their harassers confront them offline. As a result, some perpetrators might curtail their bigoted assaults. Viewing cyber harassment as gender discrimination could become part of our cultural understandings and practices. As with workplace sexual harassment and domestic violence, changing the norms of acceptable conduct may be the most potent force in regulating behavior in cyberspace. An antidiscrimination message is crucial to harness law's moral and coercive power.[21]

. . . [This article] explores the gendered nature of online harassment.[22] It first defines the phenomenon of cyber gender harassment. It then explores the distinct harms that such online abuse inflicts on targeted women and society.

Cyber Harassment Through a Feminist Lens

Online harassment is a problem that has a profound impact on women's lives but is little understood. Just as society ignored sexual harassment until scholars and courts recognized it as sex discrimination, a definition of cyber gender harassment is crucial to understanding and tackling its distinct harms to women. No working definition has been constructed, perhaps because cyber gender harassment has been relegated to the shadows of our thinking. This [article] fills that void and provides an account of the gendered nature of online harassment, highlighting its distinct effect on targeted women and society.

Understanding Cyber Gender Harassment

Although cyber gender harassment encompasses various behaviors, it has a set of core features: (1) its victims are female, (2) the harassment is aimed at particular women, and (3) the abuse invokes the targeted individual's gender in sexually threatening and degrading ways.[23]

While cyber attackers target men, more often their victims are female.[24] The nonprofit organization *Working to Halt Online Abuse* has compiled statistics about individuals harassed online. In 2007, 61% of the individuals reporting online abuse identified themselves as women while 21% identified themselves as men.[25] In 2006, 70% of online harassment complainants identified themselves as women.[26] Overall, from 2000 to 2008, 72.5% of the 2,519 individuals reporting cyber harassment were female and 22% were male.[27] Forty-four percent of the victims were between the ages of 18 and 40,[28] and 49% reportedly had no relationship with their attackers.[29] Similarly, the Stalking Resource Center, a branch of the National Center for Victims of Crimes, reports that approximately 60% of online harassment cases involve male attackers and female targets.[30]

Academic research supports this statistical evidence. The University of Maryland's Electrical Engineering and Computer Department recently studied the threat of attacks associated with the chat medium Internet Relay Chat.[31] Researchers found that users with female names received on average 100 "malicious private messages," which the study defined as "sexually explicit or threatening language," whereas users with male names received only 3.7.[32] According to the study, the "experiment show[ed] that the user gender has a significant impact on one component of the attack thread (i.e., the number of malicious private messages received for which the female bots received more than 25 times more private messages than the male bots . . .)" and "no significant impact on the other components on the attack threat[,]" such as attempts to send files to users and links sent to users.[33] The study explained that attacks came from human chat users who selected their targets, not automated scripts programmed to send attacks to everyone on the channel, and that "male human users specifically targeted female users. . . ."[34]

Distinct Impact on Targeted Women

Cyber gender harassment invokes women's sexuality and gender in ways that interfere with their agency, livelihood, identity, dignity, and well-being. The subsequent injuries are unique to women because men do not typically experience sexual threats and demeaning comments suggesting their inferiority due to their gender.[35]

First, cyber gender harassment undermines women's agency over their own lives. Online threats of sexual violence "literally, albeit not physically, penetrate[]" women's bodies.[36] They expose women's sexuality, conveying the message that attackers control targeted women's physical safety.[37] The rape threats are particularly frightening to women as one in every six women has experienced an attempted or completed rape as a child or adult.[38] Such threats discourage women from pursuing their interests in cyberspace. For instance, women shut down their blogs and websites.[39] They retreat from chat rooms. A 2005 Pew Internet and American Life Project study attributed an 11 percent decline in women's use of chat rooms to menacing comments.[40] Women limit their websites' connectivity to a wider, and potentially threatening, audience by password protecting their sites.[41] They close comments on blog posts, foreclosing positive conversations along with abusive ones.[42] The harassment scares women away from online discourse "by making an example of those females who [do] participate" with "very real threats of rape."[43]

Cyber harassment also affects women's agency in their offline lives. For instance, a woman stopped going to the gym because her anonymous harassers encouraged her law school classmates to take cell phone pictures of her and post them online.[44] After posters warned a female blogger that she needed to watch her back because they knew where she lived, the woman "g[o]t an alarm" and "started [carrying a] bat to and from the car when [she] went to work at night."[45] Kathy Sierra's cyber harassment experience left her fearful to attend speaking engagements and even to leave her yard: "I will never feel the same. I will never *be* the same."[46] Another woman explained: cyber threats had a "major impact on me both online and offline—I removed my name from my Website and my Internet registration. I rented a mailbox to handle all snail mail related to the Website, and I changed my business and home phone numbers . . ."[47] As Ms. Sierra noted, "[h]ow many rape/fantasy threats does it take to make women want to lay low? Not many. . . ."[48]

Online harassment replicates in cyberspace the autonomy erosion that female employees have long experienced in real space. Workplace sexual harassment exposes and exploits a female employees' sexuality. Verbal sexual abuse and displays of pornography make female employees "feel physically vulnerable" to attack.[49] Female employees leave their jobs or seek transfers to escape hostile work environments in much the same way that women shut down income-generating sites or limit access to their blogs to avoid cyber abuse.

Second, cyber gender harassment undermines women's ability to achieve their professional goals. It may impair women's work directly, such as technological attacks designed to shutter feminist websites or postings designed to discourage employees from hiring women.[50] It may take a more indirect form of professional sabotage by discrediting women's competence in their careers.[51] Assertions that "[t]his is why women are TOO STUPID to think critically and intelligently about film; AND business for that matter" and "why don't you make yourself useful and go have a baby"[52] appear designed to generate feelings of inferiority and to discourage women from engaging in professional activities online. Rape threats and sexually menacing comments have a similar effect. This sort of intimidation is unique to women—men are not routinely told that they belong in the kitchen or bedroom instead of earning a living online.

The abuse harms targeted individuals' careers because employers routinely rely on search engines to collect intelligence on job applicants and may discover negative postings about them. Employers may decline to interview or hire targeted women not because they believe the malicious postings but because it is simply easier to hire individuals who don't come with such baggage. Moreover, candidates with impressive online reputations are more attractive to employers than those who lack them. Indeed, an online presence is crucial to obtaining work in certain fields. Noted technology blogger Robert Scoble explains that women who don't blog are "never going to be included in the [technology] industry."[53] This parallels workplace sexual harassment's interference with women's economic opportunities.[54] Demeaning verbal abuse can be so severe that women leave their jobs,[55] just as online intimidation has pushed women out of the blogosphere.[56] It impairs women's work opportunities by making clear to them that they will be viewed and judged by traditional and subordinate female roles,[57] in much the way that cyber gender harassment does.

Third, women sustain harm to their identities *as women*. Women may feel impelled to compromise their female identity by "passing" as men to prevent discrimination.[58] . . .

Fourth, cyber harassment harms women's dignity and sense of equal worth.[59] Online assaults objectify women, reducing them to their body parts.[60] For instance, posters on the message board AutoAdmit described one targeted female student as a "dumbass bitch . . . [who] I wish to rape . . . in the ass"[61] and stated that another has "huge fake titties."[62] Harassers further humiliate women by reducing them to *diseased* body parts. For example, a poster says of one woman, "just don't FUCK her, she has herpes."[63] They make clear that women have worth only as sex objects.

Such objectification injures women by signaling that they are nothing but things to be used by men, not persons with feelings.[64] Online rape threats say to women "[y]ou claim to be a full human being, but you are much less than that. You are a mere thing . . . . [whose] autonomy can be snatched away, your feelings ignored or violated."[65] Women feel rejected and less worthy.[66] A victim explained: "someone who writes 'You're just a cunt!' is not trying to convince me of anything but my own worthlessness."[67] Martha Nussbaum considers the online objectification of women an attempt to "restor[e] the patriarchal world before the advent of sex equality, the world in which women were just tools of male purposes . . . . [and] had no right to be more than tits and cunt."[68]

Sexual harassment in the workplace similarly treats women as moral subordinates and undermines their self-respect.[69] Employers and co-workers who refer to female workers as "nice pieces of ass" or "stupid pair of boobs" cause women to see themselves as less equal and able than men.[70] As Kathryn Abrams develops in her work, sexual inquiries, jokes, and innuendos in the workplace have the effect of reminding women that they are viewed as objects of sexual derision, not colleagues worthy of respect and equal treatment.[71]

Last, cyber harassment inflicts unique harms to women's physical and emotional well-being. Posts providing women's home addresses alongside the suggestion that they have rape fantasies or should be raped have led to offline stalking and rape. Women also fear that online threats of sexual violence will be realized. Women's anxiety may be particularly acute as the posters' anonymity eliminates cues—such as the identity or location of the person who made the threat or a joking tone of voice—that might diminish concerns about the threat. Women's emotional distress often produces physical symptoms, such as anorexia nervosa, depression, and suicide. Women experience similar symptoms in the face of workplace sexual harassment.

This destructive phenomenon not only has profound consequences for individual women, but for society as well, as the next Section demonstrates. . . .

Notes

1. Although its scope is difficult to estimate, one study suggests that approximately 40 percent of female internet users have experienced cyber harassment. Azy Barak. *Sexual Harassment on the Internet,* 23 Soc. Sci. Computer Rev. 77, 81 (2005); *see also* Francesca Philips & Gabrielle Morrissey, *Cyberstalking and Cyber-predators: A Threat to Safe Sexuality on the Internet,* 10 Convergence: Int'l J. Res. into New Media Techs. 66, 72 (2004) (estimating that one-third of female internet users have been harassed online). Any existing statistical evidence surrounding cyber gender harassment is likely to underestimate the phenomenon as women tend to underreport it due to feelings of shame and embarrassment. *See* Att'y Gen. to Vice President, Cyberstalking: A New Challenge for Law Enforcement and Industry (1999), http://www.usdoj.gov/criminal/cybercrime/cyberstalking.htm [hereinafter Rep. on Cyberstalking]. This is unsurprising given women's underreporting of workplace sexual harassment. Louise Fitzgerald et al., *Why Didn't She Just Report Him?,* 51 J. Soc. Issues 117, 119–21 (1995).
2. Danielle Keats Citron, *Cyber Civil Rights,* 89 B.U.L. Rev. 61, 69–75 (2009).
3. L.P. Sheridan & T. Grant, *Is Cyberstalking Different?,* 13 Psychol., Crime & L. 627, 637 (2007) (citing various studies suggesting that the majority of cyber stalking victims were female and their online stalkers were less likely to be ex-partners of the victims).
4. *See* Barak, *supra* note 1, at 78–79.
5. Posting of Louisa Garib to On the Identity Trail, *Blogging White Female, Online Equality and the Law,* http://www.anonequity.org/weblog/archives/2007/08/blogging_while_female_online_i.php (Aug. 21, 2007, 23:59 EST).
6. *See* Ellen Nakashima, *Sexual Threats Stifle Some Female Bloggers,* Wash. Post. Apr. 30, 2007, at A1.
7. *See* B.J. Lee. *When Words Kill: Suicide spurs bid to regulate the net in South Korea,* Newsweek.com, Oct. 15, 2008. http://www.newsweek.com/id/164013.
8. Nakashima, *supra* note 6; *see also, e.g.,* Posting of womensspace to Women's Space, *Blogging White Female. Hacking as Sexual Terrorism,* http://www.womensspace.org/phpBB2/2007/08/06/blogging-while-female-men-win-hacking-as-sexual-terrorism/ (Aug. 6. 2007) (explaining that she shut down her women's issues website due to cyber harassment that included threats of violence, technological attacks, and publication of her home address).
9. *See* Posting of Louisa Garib to On the Identity Trail, *supra* note 5.
10. A digital native is "a person for whom digital technologies already existed when they were born." and who has "grown up with digital technology such as computers, the Internet, mobile phones and MP3s." Wikipedia, Digital Native, http://en.wikipedia.org/wiki/Digital_native (last visited Aug. 29. 2009).
11. Posting of Rev. Billy Bob Gisher to Less People Less Idiots. *Silence of the hams,* http://lessidiots.blogspot.com/2007/04/silence-of-hams.html (Apr. 3, 2007, 16:19 EST) (on file with author).
12. Posting of Markos Moulitsas to Daily Kos, *Death threats and blogging,* http://www.dailykos.com/story/2007/4/l2/22533/9224 (Apr. 11, 2007, 23:45 PDT).
13. Posting of Susannah Breslin to The XX Factor, *Is Blogging While Female Really So "Perilous"?,* Slate, http://www.slate.com/blogs/blogs/xxfactor/archive/2009/03/13/is-blogging-while-female-really-so-perilous.aspx (Mar. 13, 2009. 17:03 EST) (arguing that the web is an equal-opportunity attack forum and thus urging women to "get over yourselves"); Comment of Fistandantalus to Posting of Rev. Billy Bob Gisher to Less People Less Idiots, *Silence of the hams,* http://lessidiots.blogspot.com/2007/04/silence-of-hams.html (on file with author).
14. *See, e.g.,* Paul Bocij, Cyberstalking: Harassment in the Internet Age and How to Protect Your Family 17 (2004).
15. Robin West. Caring for Justice 96 (1997).
16. *Id.*
17. Catharine A. MacKinnon, Sexual Harassment of Working Women: A Case of Sex Discrimination xi (1979).
18. *See, e.g.,* Posting of Danielle Citron to Concurring Opinions, *Zuckerberg's Law on Data Sharing, Not Puffery,* http://www.concurringopinions.com/archives/2009/07/zuckerbergs-law-on-data-sharing-not-puffery.html (July 16, 2009, 12:32 EST) (explaining that as of July 2009, Facebook had 250 million members, up from 150 million in January 2009).
19. Michael Tennesen, *Avatar Acts: When the Matrix Has You, What Laws Apply to Settle Conflicts?,* Sci. Am., July 2009, at 27; *see also* Regina Lynn, *Virtual Rape Is Traumatic, but Is It A Crime?,* Wired.com Comment.—Sex Drive, May 4, 2007, http://www.wired.com/culture/lifestyle/commentary/sexdrive/2007/05/sexdrive_0504; Posting on Tech FAQ, *Second Life virtual rape,* http://www.tech-faq.com/blog/second-life-virtual-rape.html (last visited Aug. 29. 2009) (explaining that a Belgian user of Second Life was forced to perform sexually explicit acts after being given a "voodoo doll," a piece of code that takes the form of a regular object such as a cup or pen but in fact takes control of your avatar).
20. Citron, *supra* note 2.
21. *Cf.* Kimberlé Williams Crenshaw, *Race, Reform, and Retrenchment: Transformation and Legitimation in Antidiscrimination Law,* 101 Harv. L. Rev. 1331, 1335 (1988) (describing the importance of an antidiscrimination message to combat racial subordination).
22. Brian Leiter aptly calls social networking sites that house and encourage such gender

harassment "cyber–cesspools." Brian Leiter, Cleaning Cyber–Cesspools: Google and Free Speech 1 (Nov. 21, 2008) (unpublished manuscript, on file with author).

23. Online harassment is also targeted at gay men—the harassment similarly invokes targeted individuals' gender in a sexually threatening manner. For instance, anonymous posters on the high school gossip site Peoples Dirt noted that named male students were gay and threatened them with violence. A posting under a male student's name asserted "we know your [sic] g@y . . . just come out of the closet . . . and you should choke on a dick and die." Posting of Danielle Citron to Concurring Opinions, *Peoples Dirt, Now Terrorizing High Schoolers Everywhere,* http://www.concurringopinions.com/archives/2009/05/peoples-dirt-now-terrorizing-high-schoolers-everywhere.html (May 18, 2009, 15:05 EST) (alteration in original). Anonymous posters on the Encyclopedia Dramatica site direct sexually threatening taunts to named gay men. Posters accused a man of having an incestuous relationship with his brother and a bestial relationship with his dog. Encyclopedia Dramatica, Chris Cocker, http://www.encyclopediadramatica.com/Chris_Crocker (last visited Aug. 29, 2009).

24. Sheridan & Grant, *supra* note 3, at 67. A 2003 study of 169 individuals who reportedly experienced cyber harassment found that 62.5 percent of the respondents were female. Paul Bocij, *Victims of Cyberstalking: An Exploratory Study of Harassment Perpetrated via the Internet,* FIRST MONDAY, Oct. 6, 2003, http://firstmonday.org/htbin/cgiwrap/bin/ojs/index.php/fm/article/view/1086/1006. The harassment consisted of threatening or abusive email messages, threats or abusive comments via IM messages, threats or abusive comments in chat rooms, the posting of false rumors in chat rooms, impersonation of individuals in e-mail messages to friends, and encouragement of others to harass or threaten the respondent. *Id.*

25. WORKING TO HALT ONLINE ABUSE, 2007 CYBERSTALKING STATISTICS 1, http://www.haltabuse.org/resources/stats/2007Statistics.pdf. Eighteen percent of those reporting cyber harassment did not report their gender. *Id.*

26. WORKING TO HALT ONLINE ABUSE, 2006 CYBERSTALKING STATISTICS 1. http://www.haltabuse.org/resources/stats/2006Statistics.pdf.

27. WORKING TO HALT ONLINE ABUSE, CYBERSTALKING COMPARISON STATISTICS 2000–2008 1. http://www.haltabuse.org/resources/stats/Cumulative2000–2008.pdf. Five and one-half percent of the reporting individuals refused to provide their gender to the organization. *Id.*

28. *Id.*

29. *Id.* at 2.

30. Christine Petrozzo & Sarah Stapp, *To catch a predator: How some cyber–agencies help victims*

fight back against online aggression. DAILY ORANGE (Syracuse. N.Y.), Jan. 24. 2008. http://media.www.dailyorange.eom/media/storage/paper522/news/2008/01/24/News/To.Catch.A.Predator-3165676.shtml#cp_article_tools.

31. *See* Robert Meyer & Michael Cukier, *Assessing the Attack Threat due to IRC Channels, in* PROCEEDINGS OF THE INTERNATIONAL CONFERENCE ON DEPENDABLE SYSTEMS AND NETWORKS 467 (2006), *available at* http://www.enre.umd.edu/content/rmeyer-assessing.pdf. Chat rooms using IRC protocol permit live conversations via the internet, containing as many as several thousand people, whereas other chat programs such as MSN messenger and Yahoo focus on two-person conversations. *Id.* Users can join existing discussions or create new ones. BOCIJ. *supra* note 14, at 126. "Estimates of the number of publicly accessible channels available [on IRC] range from 100,000 to more than 580,000." *Id.* (citation omitted).

32. Meyer & Cukier, *supra* note 31, at 469. The researchers used simulated users with female names Cathy, Elyse, Irene, Melissa, and Stephanie, and simulated users with male names Andy, Brad, Dan, Gregg, and Kevin. *Id.* at 469–70.

33. *Id.* at 470.

34. *Id.* at 471.

35. This statement is particularly true for heterosexual men who are less likely to face sexual intimidation by women or homosexual men, but less true for gay men who confront sexual taunts when others perceive them as effeminate. *See* Jerry Finn, *A Survey of Online Harassment at a University Campus,* 19 J. INTERPERSONAL VIOLENCE 468 (2004).

36. WEST, *supra* note 15, at 102–03 (discussing real space rape) (emphasis omitted).

37. *See* Martha Nussbaum, *Objectification and Ressentiment* 18–20 (Nov. 21–22, 2008) (unpublished manuscript, on file with author).

38. LENORA M. LAPIDUS ET AL., THE RIGHTS OF WOMEN: THE AUTHORITATIVE ACLU GUIDE TO WOMEN'S RIGHTS 180 (4th ed. 2009) (describing incidence of rape in United States). To the extent that we see men experience threats of sexual violence online, the victims are gay men. *See* Posting of Danielle Citron to Concurring Opinions, *supra* note 23.

39. Sheridan & Grant, *supra* note 3, at 637.

40. *See Female Bloggers Face Harassment,* WOMEN IN HIGHER EDUC., June 2007, at 5.

41. Nakashima, *supra* note 6 (explaining that women attacked online by anonymous posters suspend their blogging, turn to private forums, or use gender-neutral pseudonyms).

42. *See* Comment of Alyssa Royse to Posting of Alyssa Royse to BlogHer, *supra* note 71.

43. Comment of C.L. to Posting of Danielle Citron to Concurring Opinions. *Cyber Harassment: Yes, It is a Woman's Thing,* http://www.concurringopinions.com/archives/2009/03/cyber_harassmen.html (March 12, 2009, 22:37 EST).

44. *See* Ellen Nakashima, *Harsh Words Die Hard on the Web; Law Students Feel Lasting Effects of Anonymous Attacks*, Wash. Post, Mar. 7, 2007, at A1.

45. Tracy L.M. Kennedy, *An Exploratory Study of Feminist Experiences In Cyberspace*, 3 Cyberpsychol., & Behav. 707, 716 (2000).

46. Dahlia Lithwick, *Fear of Blogging: Why women shouldn't apologize for being afraid of threats on the Web*. Slate, May 4, 2007. http://www.slate.com/id/2165654 (internal quotation marks omitted).

47. Kennedy, *supra* note 99, at 716.

48. Valenti, *supra* note 35 (internal quotation marks omitted).

49. Kathryn Abrams, *Gender Discrimination and the Transformation of Workplace Norms*, 42 Vand. L. Rev. 1183, 1206 (1989) [hereinafter Abrams, *Transformation*].

50. *See supra* notes 80–81 and accompanying text (describing activities of Anonymous).

51. *See, e.g.*, Posting of Alyssa Royse to BlogHer, *supra* note 38.

52. *Id.*

53. Nakashima. *supra* note 6 (internal quotation marks omitted).

54. *See* Vicki Schultz. *Reconceptualizing Sexual Harassment*, 107 Yale L.J. 1683. 1763–65 (1998) (conceptualizing hostile-work-environment harassment as a means for men to preserve dominance in favored types of work by undermining women's effectiveness on the job through demeaning comments, deliberate sabotage, and refusals to provide women support they need on the job).

55. Kathryn Abrams, *The New Jurisprudence of Sexual Harassment*, 83 Cornell L. Rev. 1169, 1207 (1998) [hereinafter Abrams, *New Jurisprudence*].

56. Posting of John Hawkins to Right Wing News, *Blogging While Female Part 2: Five Women Bloggers Talk About Gender Issues And The Blogosphere*, http://www.rightwingnews.com/mt331/2008/03/blogging_while_female_part_2_5_l.php (Mar. 18, 2008 11:30 EST) (interviewing blogger Ann Althouse).

57. Abrams, *New Jurisprudence, supra* note 109, at 1208.

58. *See* Kenji Yoshino, Covering: The Hidden Assault on Our Civil Rights 22, 144 (2006) [hereinafter Yoshino, Covering]. Discrimination has long forced women to pass as men to gain access to professions or relationships that would otherwise have remained unavailable to them. *See also. e.g.*, Marjorie Garber, Vested Interests: Cross–Dressing & Cultural Anxiety 67–70 (1992). Kenji Yoshino identifies films such as *Yentl* and *Boys Don't Cry* as examples of female passing. Kenji Yoshino, *Covering*, 111 Yale L.J. 769, 926 & n.880 (2002) [hereinafter Yoshino, *Covering*].

59. As Leslie Meitzer elegantly develops in her article *Spheres of Dignity: Conceptions and Functions in Constitutional Law* (on file with author), the term dignity implicates a variety of values, including dignity as equality. I aim to use the term dignity here to refer to the value harmed by conduct that demeans, devalues, and denigrates women due to their gender.

60. Nussbaum, *supra* note 91, at 5–6; *see also* West, *supra* note 15. at 146 (explaining that sexual harassment objectifies women, inflicting a dignitary injury).

61. First Amended Complaint at ¶ 25. Doe v. Ciolli, No. 307CV00909 CFD (D. Conn. Nov. 8. 2007) (internal quotation marks omitted).

62. *Id.* at ¶ 18 (internal quotation marks omitted).

63. *Id.* at ¶ 21 (internal quotation marks omitted).

64. Nussbaum. *supra* note 91, at 3–4.

65. *Id.* at 8 (internal quotation marks omitted).

66. Kennedy, *supra* note 99, at 717.

67. *Id.* at 715 (internal quotation marks omitted).

68. Nussbaum, *supra* note 91, at 19.

69. Abrams, *Transformation, supra* note 103, at 1208. *See generally* Deborah Hellman, When is Discrimination Wrong? (2008) (exploring when and why discrimination is morally wrong).

70. Kathryn Abrams, *Title VII and the Complex Female Subject*, 92 Mich. L. Rev. 2479, 2529–30 (1994).

71. *E.g.*, Abrams, *New Jurisprudence, supra* note 109, at 1207–08.

Danielle Keats Citron is the Lois K. Macht Research Professor of Law at the University of Maryland Francis King Carey School of Law.

Rebecca Eckler

 **NO**

Finding Out What Men Are Up To: Some Women Pride Themselves on Their Cyber-Sleuth Skills

On a recent episode of the reality show *Keeping Up with the Kardashians,* Kourtney Kardashian tells her sister Kim she has her boyfriend's old phone. "Have you gone through it?" Kim asks Kourtney excitedly. What's the point, Kourtney wants to know. "What do you mean what is the point?" Kim asks. "You want to know what your boyfriend is up to." Then, speaking directly to the camera, Kim proudly says, "I can break into any phone, can get any code, can get into any voice mail." She's not the only phone-email snooper out there. One of the main characters on the show *Entourage* just dropped a woman who listened to one of his phone messages when he was in the shower.

Ali Wise, a stunning 32-year-old New Yorker, was arrested in July on felony charges of computer trespass and eavesdropping after allegedly hacking into the voice mail of Nina Freudenberger, an interior designer and socialite. Hacking "isn't the sort of crime that normally comes to mind when you think of a pretty young publicist who attends glam parties on a nightly basis," says Remy Stern, founder of Cityfile, a gossip website that has followed the story. "It was a little more juicy because she wasn't accused of hacking into her boyfriend's voice mail; the victim was another woman . . . who may have been involved with an ex-boyfriend of hers."

Wise used software called SpoofCard to hack into the voice mail. The SpoofCard can be bought online and, according to information on the product's website, "offers the ability to change what someone sees on their caller ID display when they receive a phone call." You simply dial SpoofCard's toll-free number or local access number in your country and then enter your PIN (like a calling card). What comes up on a person's phone is a number that's not yours.

The SpoofCard is meant to be used, mostly it seems, for crank calls and for other times people want to hide their number. But, obviously, it's being misused. The Internet is rife with information about how to break into someone's voice mail using a SpoofCard. "I'll tell you how," writes one snooper. "Call up SpoofCard and when they ask you to enter the number you want to show [up] on the caller ID, you enter your boyfriend's number.

When they ask you to enter the number you want to call, you enter your boyfriend's number again, and, bingo, you'll get into his messages. This works because it tricks the cellphone to think the cell is calling into the voice message system." The deviousness doesn't end there. "Now remember," another writes, "when you get into the voice message, you must quickly change the password so you can always access the voice mail messages."

According to a friend of Wise's, when the police asked her if she had used a SpoofCard, her answer was, "Of course I used a SpoofCard." It was as if they had asked a meat lover if they ate steak.

Wise stepped down from her job at Dolce & Gabbana, and has become fodder for New York gossip rags. But to some women she's become, if not a hero, at least relatable. Movie producers have begged to option her story.

On a recent night out, five women laughed at stories of breaking into men's voice mails. "I would wait until he went into the shower," said one, "and I would manically try and figure out his password." Another admitted that for years she has broken into her boyfriend's, and ex-boyfriend's, email and voice mail accounts. "It's really not that hard. Men are stupid. If you know their Interac password, that's generally their code for all their other PDAs," she said. One woman is so skilled at figuring out passwords, she can hear someone type in the phone digits, and from the tones of the numbers, figure out the code. "I want to see if they're up to no good," she laughs.

Obviously, serial snooping isn't just for the rich and famous. The founder of Toronto-based Blue Star Investigations Inc. International, Allen Brik, has been a private detective for 15 years. He says this kind of invasion of privacy has exploded in the past five years. "It's not always easy, but it's certainly doable." It's strictly illegal, he says, and shouldn't be done, "but people want to know they can trust someone. They're not thinking with their heads about right or wrong."

Brik agrees that men "don't often change their password. They usually use their date of birth or their middle names. Women are more creative." (He hasn't changed any of his passwords in 12 years.) It's not only females who snoop, he says, but the majority are women. "I think it comes down to men cheating more."

A judge could turn Wise's case, due in court in October, into an "example" à la Paris Hilton's jail stint. "I do hope that no prison time is involved," says Stern. "A much better punishment would be to require her to have those godawful orange jumpsuits worn by American prisoners redesigned by Dolce & Gabbana. That might make it all worth it."

REBECCA ECKLER is a Canadian journalist and an author whose work has appeared in *Elle, Maclean's,* and *Mademoiselle*. She is also a columnist for *Post City Magazines* in Toronto.

EXPLORING THE ISSUE

Are Women More at Risk for Crimes Using Digital Technology?

Critical Thinking and Reflection

1. How does the Internet pose greater dangers to women than men?
2. How might technological advances level the playing field in a way that allows women to be online aggressors in greater numbers?

Is There Common Ground?

Schenk (2008) developed the Cyber-Sexual Experiences Questionnaire to study sexual harassment that occurs online via the Internet. While Schenk's study focused on how women experience cyber-sexual harassment, her findings can also help explain how women can become aggressors in the online environment. The Internet can be a power equalizer that serves to empower both men and women to engage in cyber harassment. The "dissociative anonymity" that people experience within the online environment may allow both men and women to engage in behavior on the Internet that seems separate from their day-to-day offline personas (Schenk, 2008, p. 84). Online disinhibition may also occur due to the relative invisibility of easily navigating Internet sites without the need to self-identify. Schenk's (2008) review of the literature additionally noted the "minimization of authority" that occurs in the online world where people are empowered to speak freely without regard to relative social status (p. 84). All of these factors may contribute to a potential leveling of the power field that would permit both men and women to engage in harassment behavior using the Internet.

Cook (2010) reviewed the world of online gossip sites and how their proliferation has impacted campus life at colleges around the nation. The posting of gossip, including photos, has created new challenges for higher education student personnel professionals in combating campus harassment. Officials find that men and women can be equal opportunity offenders as well as harassment targets.

Additional Resources

Cook, S. G. (2010, July). "Gossip on Steroids: Cyber-Bullying, Stalking, Harassing." *Women in Higher Education, 19*(7), 18–19.

Schenk, S. (2008). "Cyber-Sexual Harassment: The Development of the Cyber-Sexual Experiences Questionnaire," *McNair Scholars Journal, 12*(1), Article 8.

Create Central

www.mhhe.com/createcentral

Internet References . . .

Electronic Crime Technology Center of Excellence

http://ectcoe.net/

Unit 2

UNIT

Women's Health, Women's Bodies: Contested Terrain

*T*he war over reproductive rights continues to be a polarizing issue in American culture. Political battles over reproductive health issues such as birth control and abortion are waged annually in state legislatures. Skirmishes related to women's health and funding for medical services frequently erupt in the halls of Congress and play out across the media airwaves. Where does a women's right to her body begin and end? When does the state have an interest in women's health outcomes and when do those interests supersede a woman's right to self-determination? As access to basic health care has become a dividing line between socioeconomic classes in America, so has access to abortion. The battle that waged in the summer of 2012 (Pettus, 2012) over the sole remaining abortion provider in Mississippi exemplifies the access issue at the heart of the abortion debate. Efforts to shut down the one clinic providing affordable abortions to all women in Mississippi illustrated how easily abortion could become an option only available to wealthy Americans.

Pettus, E.W. (2012). "Jackson Women's Health Organization, Mississippi's Sole Abortion Clinic, May Not Survive." *The HuffingtonPost.com.* Retrieved from: www.huffingtonpost.com/2012/07/14/mississippi-abortion-acce_n_1673241 .html

Selected, Edited, and with Issue Framing Material by:
Rachel Pienta, *Valdosta State University*

ISSUE

Is Access to Abortion a Class Issue?

YES: **Karen Weingarten**, from "The Inadvertent Alliance of Anthony Comstock and Margaret Sanger: Abortion, Freedom, and Class in Modern America," *Feminist Formations* (March 20, 2012)

NO: **Laura S. Hussey**, from "Welfare Generosity, Abortion Access, and Abortion Rates: A Comparison of State Policy Tools," *Social Science Quarterly* (vol. 91, no. 1, March 2010)

Learning Outcomes
As you read the issue, focus on the following points:
• Does policy aimed at limiting reproductive rights unfairly target minorities?

ISSUE SUMMARY

YES: Professor Karen Weingarten of Queens College examines the parallel ideologies of Anthony Comstock and Margaret Sanger to illustrate how the public discourse over abortion has an underlying class component. Her article explores how class and privilege play a role in the framing of the abortion debate and in determining the general exercise of reproductive rights across the social spectrum.

NO: Professor Laura S. Hussey of the University of Maryland analyzes how welfare policy relates to abortion access and abortion rates across states. Her article foreshadows and frames the congressional policy debates over Medicaid and tax-funded abortion access that would galvanize the political discourse regarding women, reproductive rights, and healthcare in the months preceding the 2012 presidential election.

The conflict over who controls the reproductive organs and processes of women in the United States is deeply rooted in the nation's history. Control over reproductive issues is ultimately a question of power. While the perceived ability to control the birth process has remained a "symbol and basis of female power," biological status as potential mothers has historically not afforded women commensurate power in society (Gordon, 2002, p. 109).

Efforts to exercise control over women and by association, control reproduction, have ranged from arguments about property rights to issues of morality. The passage of the Federal Comstock Law in 1873 opened the door for states to pass obscenity laws that enabled local and regional restriction of birth control (Meyer, 2004). The Comstock Law, combined with and following the invention of the forceps in the eighteenth century, served to further separate women from self-governance over reproductive issues (Mintz, 2011).

The Comstock Law would be the primary law restricting the promotion, sale, and use of contraceptive methods in the United States until 1971 (Meyer, 2004). Practitioners of the medical profession, in concert with the authority of governing officials, ensured that the reproductive process was highly regulated.

Feminist proponents of the women's rights movement coalesced around the issue of birth control in the late nineteenth century with the slogan "voluntary motherhood" (Gordon, 2002). In 1916, the modern birth control movement began when Margaret Sanger opened a birth control clinic in New York City (Planned Parenthood, 2011). This clinic was soon followed by the formation of a group called the American Birth Control League (Planned Parenthood, 2011; Gordon, 2002).

The politics of reproduction has continued to be a highly polarizing issue in American politics. The shift from midwives to physicians that transpired between the 1700s and 1900s reflected the social values of the time period and cultural notions of who should control fertility (Gordon, 2002). There was also an economic component to physicians' organized efforts to wrest control of childbirth away from midwives. Midwives posed economic competition for physicians who wanted to charge higher prices for their expertise (Mintz, 2011).

For over a century abortion has been one of the most controversial reproductive rights issues in American society, at times dominating both popular and political discourse. In the nineteenth century, abortion was legal and widely available as a procedure to the point that it was advertised in newspapers (Lindsey, 1997). By the early twentieth century, efforts to make abortion illegal were largely successful. Abortion would not become available legally everywhere throughout the United States until the *Roe v. Wade* Supreme Court decision codified a woman's right to choose into federal statute in 1973.

The abortion issue still plays a role in contemporary American politics. Potential political candidates are evaluated by the electorate on a professed public stance about the issue. The battle over reproductive rights also shares political ground with arguments over proposed laws such as the proposed Equal Rights Amendment. The Equal Rights Amendment (ERA), first passed by Congress in 1972, has not yet been ratified although efforts toward this goal remain in progress. Notable among opponents' anti-ERA arguments is the idea that it would "mandate federal funding for abortion" (Paxton & Hughes, 2007, p. 294).

YES

Karen Weingarten

The Inadvertent Alliance of Anthony Comstock and Margaret Sanger: Abortion, Freedom, and Class in Modern America

There's more than one kind of freedom. Freedom to and freedom from. In the days of anarchy, it was freedom to. Now you are being given freedom from. Don't underestimate it.

—Aunt Lydia from Margaret Atwood's, *The Handmaid's Tale* ([1985]1998, 34)

This article seeks to trace a continuum between Anthony Comstock's moralizing jeremiads against "obscene acts" and Margaret Sanger's quest to legalize birth control, by demonstrating the ways in which both used disciplining tactics that condemned abortion. Most important, this article demonstrates how Comstock and Sanger succeeded in criminalizing abortion, thus completing the task begun by the American Medical Association, which by the 1880s had managed to outlaw abortion in every U.S. state. (For more on this history, see Janet Brodie's *Contraception and Abortion in Nineteenth-Century America* [1994], James Mohr's *Abortion in America* [1978], and Leslie J. Regan's *When Abortion Was a Crime* [1997].)

Comstock's contribution to this juridical process worked by lumping abortion with other "sexual crimes" and contributing to the misconception that abortion was primarily used by working-class and poor women. Similarly, Sanger promoted birth control by separating it from the issue of abortion; by emphasizing abortion's pernicious effects, she often portrayed birth control as a means to better the human race, thus paralleling Comstock's construction of abortion as degrading and destructive. While Sanger and Comstock initially appear to be working through different paradigms, the opposition between them is belied by the investment that both activists made in similar constructions of freedom and protection that subtend liberal *and* conservative ideologies.[1] Comstock's opposition to abortion mirrors Sanger's position, because both are invested in constructing laws that interpellate subjects into individualizing and moralizing persons who, if properly trained, *should* be capable of self-control. It is through laws concerned with rights that the emphasis on the individuated life becomes foregrounded; indeed, it is precisely through the emergence of rights-based laws that the concept of an entitled subject capable of self-regulation emerged, as well as the inverse concept of a subject incapable of self-control and therefore legally stripped of "choice."

Using rights-based discourse, or what is sometimes called "the right to choose," as a means to re-enfranchise historically oppressed communities has a prominent though conflicted history in the United States. From Patricia Williams's (1992) work that asserts that rights granted through constitutional law are crucial in the fight to grant African Americans equal status in the United States to Wendy Brown's (1995) critiques of rights as embedded in a liberalism that establishes identity-based politics, the discussion of rights as a tool for remedying civil and social inequality has been heated. Much has also been written about the role of rights in granting women access to abortion and control over their bodies. One of the most well-regarded and thorough texts critiquing the rhetoric of choice in abortion politics is Ricki Solinger's *Beggars and Choosers* (2001). Solinger calls choice a watered-down version of rights, and strongly advocates for a more rights-based abortion politics. On the other hand, Mary Poovey (1992) has argued that giving women the *right* to have an abortion maintains an individualistic attitude toward a procedure that should be based in community decision and with a community's support. In rehearsing rights rhetoric from the U.S. civil rights movement, Kimberle Crenshaw (2000) provides a nuanced picture of the critique of rights that emerged from the movement, but also the necessity for those rights.[2] Crenshaw recites the "Crits" argument, which argues that rights discourse is often legitimated through a "victims" perspective; it focuses not on the reasons why crimes or oppressions are perpetuated, but rather on the ways in which victims' experiences are shaped. Indeed, the argument can be taken a step further: Rights then function as protection and therefore approach every subject as a potential victim that needs the shield of the law.

Thus, we end up with a rights-based system that sounds strikingly like Aunt Lydia's description in *The Handmaid's Tale* (Atwood [1985]1998). In *Roe v. Wade*, while the Supreme Court decided that women had the freedom *to* make their own reproductive choices, because the state granted individual privacy, the court also granted women freedom *from* the potentially undue burden of pregnancy.[3] The slipperiness between freedom *from* and freedom *to* points to a tension in the foundations of U.S. liberalism. Freedom *from* assumes what Crenshaw points to as a victims-based protectionist ideology: The Supreme

Court is "protecting" women who, without laws protecting abortion rights, would fall prey to the potentially difficult conditions of an unwanted pregnancy, even as the same law mandates that the individual woman has a right to control her own body.[4] Freedom to, assumes an individuated private body that should not be subject to government interference. While Sanger and Comstock were both invested in outlawing abortion, the rhetoric they established for anti-abortion arguments mirrors a rights-based pro-abortion law and thus points to how pro-abortion policy in the United States has been so deftly undermined in the years following *Roe v. Wade.*

The House Built on Sand

While much has been documented about Sanger's investment in eugenics and birth control, relatively little has been written about her fluctuating stance on abortion. Sanger's more ambivalent positions are often elided; relatively little attention has been paid to the element of her rhetoric that is compatible with neither contemporary mainstream feminist arguments nor anti-racist nationalisms.[5] Perhaps this has occurred because of polarization over her other views. Her work either elicits stringent criticism for its racism or effusive praise for its efforts in legalizing contraception. Some of Sanger's strongest anti-abortion claims were published in *The Birth Control Review (BCR)*, which began its run in February 1917 as a simply formatted periodical to be used as a political tactic in the quest to legalize birth control. In its first few issues, the journal mainly published polemical essays by known birth-control activists like Havelock Ellis and Elizabeth Stuyvesant, as well as desperate letters from women seeking birth-control help (only as a means to demonstrate the dire situation), but at the start of its second year, it broadened its publication scope to include short stories and poetry, and eventually added disturbing photo essays depicting dysgenic "types" overrun with children.

From the start, the journal was clearly invested in promoting the politics of eugenics; almost every issue mentions eugenics or has an article featuring the topic. Anna Blount (1918), a frequent contributor to the journal, captures its eugenic philosophy best when she writes: "God speed the day when the unwilling mother, with her weak, puny body, her sad, anaemic, unlovely face, and her despondent whine, will be no more. In that day we shall see a race of American thoroughbreds, if not the superman" (3). Essays like Blount's made explicit that *BCR* was invested in a eugenics-like policy that would "improve" the conditions of all Americans, and eventually eliminate "undesirable" citizens through preventing or reducing their ability to reproduce. However, Sanger also distanced herself from eugenicists who argued that woman's first duty is to reproduce for the state. In February 1919, in an article titled "Birth Control and Racial Betterment," she strongly states that if eugenics is to succeed, it must rely on birth control and change its position on volun-

tary motherhood. She writes that birth-control activists contend that woman's first duty is not to the state, as eugenicists believed, but "that her duty to herself is her first duty to the state" (11). Sanger continues to insist that birth control is the necessary foundation for eugenics, and in an elaborate gesture, she ends with a compelling metaphor, arguing: "Eugenics without Birth Control seems to us a house builded upon sands. It is at the mercy of the rising stream of the unfit. It cannot stand against the furious winds of economic pressure" (12). As her metaphor suggests, one of BCR's most strident goals was to irrevocably link the issues of birth control and eugenics through its emphasis on a freedom *from* politics. Here, Sanger stresses that eugenics, and hence the betterment of U.S. citizenry, is doomed to fail unless there is a freedom *from* uncontrolled reproduction. And yet elsewhere, Sanger also insists on the necessity that women have freedom *to* control their reproductive capacities so that they can have freedom *from* abortion.

Sanger's most explicit anti-abortion stance came in an article she wrote early in the journal's run that is starkly titled "Birth Control or Abortion—Which Shall It Be?" (1918). She opens the article by associating abortion with working-class women, arguing that wealthy and middle-class women have discovered how to limit family size and to be voluntary mothers, while more working-class women are denied "the knowledge of the safe, harmless, scientific methods of Birth Control" and thus limit their families "by means of abortion" (3). Sanger's disciplining tone—her juxtaposition of birth control as rational and safe, with abortion as dangerous and volatile—is the main focus of the article. She proceeds with a scientific explanation of conception, clinically describing how pregnancy occurs and then explicitly states: "When scientific means are used to prevent this meeting, and thereby to limit families, one is said to practice Birth Control" (3). She cites a doctor to prove that abortion risks women's health, potentially causing "hemorrhage, retention of an adherent placenta, sepsis, tetanus, perforation of the uterus . . . sterility, anemia, malignant diseases, displacements, neurosis, and endometritis" (4).

And if this long list did not scare readers enough, Sanger also adds that the "hundreds of thousands of abortions performed in America each year are a disgrace to civilization" (4). Birth control, she argues, means "health and happiness—a stronger, better race," while abortion "means disease, suffering, death" (4). She ends by rhetorically asking "*Birth control or abortion—which shall it be?*" (4; emphasis in original), making clear that the division between the two is definitive and complete. Her logic, ultimately, depends on maintaining populations demarcated by class positions that are so well controlled they discipline themselves. . . .

Ellen Chesler (1992) argues that Sanger dissociated abortion from contraception to make her arguments for legalizing birth control more palatable to contemporary legislators, and that Sanger took this position because "[i]n respectable circles, illegal abortion was universally condemned as primitive, dangerous, and disreputable" (271). Following a similar line of argument, Joan Jensen (1981) traces the evolution of Sanger's position in *Family Limitation,* a pamphlet of Sanger's that provided information for women about contraception, sex, and, in the early days of its publication, abortion. Initially printed in 1914, the pamphlet went through several revisions, including one in 1921 that expurgated information about abortion techniques. From its first to ninth editions, Sanger advised women in the early stages of an unwanted pregnancy to take quinine to "restore the menses." However, she warned that this procedure might not work past the first month of gestation, and that women further along should consult a doctor (Sanger 2003, 88–89, 359).

By its tenth edition, Sanger had omitted this advice. Jensen contends that this shift in position is reflective of Sanger's move to more right-wing politics, away from her earlier socialist-inflected stance. As institutionalized support for birth control from radical organizations waned, Sanger strategically approached middle-class suffrage organizations and other liberal feminists for financial and political support. Additionally, *Family Limitation* faced threats from postal censors, who under the 1873 Comstock Act deemed the material obscene and inappropriate for public circulation. Jensen argues that the combination of political changes and personal hardship pushed Sanger to revise the tenth edition of the pamphlet so that no references to abortion, either direct or oblique, were included.[6] Jensen views these edits as purely pragmatic: Sanger needed a new source of funding, and she found one most readily in a more conservative middle class.

Was Sanger's view rooted in sheer pragmatism as Chesler and Jensen suggest? A closer look at Sanger's writings on abortion, including her personal letters to friends and political associates, reveal a more complicated position. These writings evince that her stance on abortion changed as she became more concerned with medical issues, health, and what was then popularly called "dysgenics"—the passing on of negative traits to progeny. In a letter to her friend and activist ally Marie Stopes, one of the leading birth-control activists in early twentieth-century England, Sanger revealed her ambivalent feelings about abortion. She confided that she understood that women resorted to seeking abortion out of desperation, but she also stressed her firm belief that once contraception was legal and accessible, the necessity for abortion would be eliminated (Sanger 2003, 164–66). Thus she justified her condemnation of abortion as a practice that would soon become null if her efforts succeeded.[7]

By the time she started publishing *BCR*, Sanger was intent on putting forth her anti-abortion position, and her tactics were so forceful that it is difficult to consider them merely an attempt to please an anti-abortion public. In November 1917, she wrote a letter to the editor of *Medical World* expressing her dismay that the American Medical Association approved of laws that allowed women access to abortion if continuation of pregnancy would severely impact their health. Sanger angrily wrote that "abortion laws were broad enough to allow in such cases a 'duly licensed physician' to perform an abortion in order to save the life of either the women or the child. It all seemed such a chaotic state to me—that it was perfectly legal to go thru the sufferings of an abortion, but illegal to prevent conception" (Sanger 2003, 199).[8]

This was a position she would put forth in many of her arguments against abortion in *BCR*. Furthermore, she widely publicized stories about the "dangers" of abortifacients; she believed that if a woman did not successfully abort her pregnancy using these drugs, the fetus would be negatively impacted and the woman had a high chance of giving birth to an infant with defects (see Sanger's *Women and the New Race* 1920, 126–27). She continually stressed that her opposition to abortion was based on health factors, citing statistics (miscalculated in the above quotation according to the editors of *The Selected Papers of Margaret Sanger* [Sanger 2003]) about the number of women who died during or after the procedure (Sanger 2003, 381). Thus, she emphasized that if she sought to outlaw abortion, it was only for women's own protection, because she aimed to grant them the freedom *from* the dangerous effects of abortion.

In reading Sanger's work, Lealle Ruhl (2002) points out that Sanger's fight to legalize birth control rests on two separate platforms. On the one hand, she argued that until birth control was accessible, women could not be free and equal citizens; birth control was a feminist issue. Yet, on the other, she also stressed that birth control was necessary to prevent overpopulation, especially since "dysgenic types" tended to produce the most children. Ruhl notes the slipperiness between these two positions: one demands that women have the freedom *to* control their bodies, whereas the other argues for the medical management of "unfit" women and their reproductive functions. Subtending these positions, Ruhl sees Sanger as putting forth an argument about responsibility, stating that women "need to uphold their end of the bargain of reproductive freedom: Contraception in exchange for a guarantee to act 'responsibly' where reproductive decisions are concerned. . . . To act responsibly means *to* conform to an essentially middle-class, educated, and scientifically oriented worldview" (656).

Sanger's contradictory programs point to the slipperiness of the language of rights, choice, and control. Rights and choice are *granted* to individuals when they can prove themselves to be responsible citizens, abiding by certain normative conditions. And as demonstrated most clearly by current federal abortion laws that set age limits on who can responsibly seek an abortion without guardian permission and that force women to view fetal ultrasounds so that decisions can be *responsibly* made, the discourse of self-control itself disciplines subjects into normative categories. In Sanger's writings, abortion comes to represent irresponsible and reckless behavior, meant to highlight how the use of contraception can construct a self-controlled woman, one who can responsibly choose when pregnancy occurs. Sanger was invested in constructing a birth-control discourse that both managed and disciplined bodies. Furthermore, she appealed to class status in her constructions of familial and reproductive norms: Subjects *should* be properly interpellated, and if they refused to be, they were abnormal and needed to be managed or else they posed a threat to the supposedly wellmanaged, properly demarcated American.

Exposing Frauds Through Family Values

Anthony Comstock is perhaps best-known for his anti-prostitution and anti-obscenity reforms. In 1872, the U.S. Congress, after pressure from his organization, the New York Society for the Suppression of Vice (NYSSV), and the Young Men's Christian Association (YMCA), passed what are now known as the Comstock laws, banning all forms of "erotic" material, from the distribution of pornography to the availability of contraception.[9] Even information about how to limit family size was deemed obscene under these laws, and Comstock himself volunteered to sort through the mail at the post office to seize any material that was suspect. Although Comstock never attacked access to abortion specifically, he classified abortion with all the other immoral acts and ideas that he saw corrupting American society. The language of his act concerning abortion reads:

> Every obscene, lewd, or lascivious, and every filthy book, pamphlet, picture, paper, letter, writing, print, or other publication of an indecent character, and every article or thing designed, adapted, or intended for preventing conception or producing abortion, or for any indecent or immoral use; and every article, instrument, substance, drug, medicine, or thing which is advertised or described in a manner calculated to lead another to use or apply it for preventing conception or producing abortion, or for any indecent or immoral purpose; and every description calculated to induce or incite a person to so use or apply any such article, instrument, substance, drug, medicine, or thing—Is declared to be nonmailable matter and shall not be conveyed in the mails or delivered from any post office or by any letter carrier.

> —(18 USC Section 1461)

Comstock, even more than Sanger, was explicitly engaged in a discourse of protection and a concern for freedom from harmful materials and practices. By deeming any abortion-related instruments and information "nonmailable," the law allowed for a breach of privacy, because a postal agent could open any suspect package or letter. Yet, this violation of privacy was justified because it provided a freedom *from* "indecent" materials that could infiltrate innocent lives. . . .

Comstock's encounter with the infamous New York abortionist Madame Restell is another example of his relentless anti-abortion pursuits. Restell's given name was Anne Lohman (sometimes also printed as Caroline Lohman). An immigrant from England, Madame Restell sold pills that claimed to abort fetuses. Her business was so successful, she moved to Fifth Avenue in New York City and worked among the most elite New Yorkers, many of whom were her clients. Comstock initially pursued Restell on a dare that he could not succeed in finding grounds for her arrest, despite the fact that the nature of her practice was an open secret. In 1886, Comstock went to Restell's home disguised as a man seeking to help his pregnant lover obtain an abortion. When Restell agreed to sell him an abortifacient, he arrested and charged her with distributing illegal and obscene material. Before Restell's case came to trial she committed suicide, which stirred much controversy in the New York media. As sociologist Nicola Beisel (1997) documents, most of the circulating newspapers condemned Restell, although the *World* also denounced Comstock for luring the woman to sell him an illegal product. In the words of the newspaper, "[n]o matter what the wretched woman was who took her life with her own hand yesterday, *her death has not freed the world from* the last of detestable characters. Whatever she was *she had her rights*" (47; emphasis added). The *World's* representation of the case again points to an important tension in discourses of freedom. Although the editorial asserted that Restell had rights, which Comstock violated when he tricked her, it also contributed to Comstock's conviction that to rid the world of debased people like Restell was to free us *from* their dangerous influences.

Historian Janet Brodie (1994) notes that Comstock frequently passed moral judgment on women he deemed immodest. As she explains it, Comstock viewed women who put effort into their appearance as seeming "too independent, not 'belonging' to any man" (273). Brodie traces Comstock's involvement in curtailing contraception access to his conflict with Victoria Woodhull, the nineteenth-century feminist and "free love" activist, who was also the first woman to run for President and become a stockbroker on Wall Street. According to Brodie, Comstock felt threatened by Woodhull, because she was precisely the type of woman who refused to belong to any man and insisted on pursuing ambitions that were usually reserved only for men. Comstock had Woodhull arrested on charges of libel, only to face humiliation when the judge dismissed the case. Brodie notes that the case reflected so poorly on Comstock that both the YMCA and his sympathetic biographer made no note of the incident in their records. Soon after this setback, he began his aggressive campaign to outlaw access to abortion and contraception. Brodie argues that the proximity of these two events suggests that Comstock, after his failure in prosecuting Woodhull, became driven to root out the causes that he saw "ruining" women. Implicit in this new quest was Comstock's concern with containing female bodies that could potentially exceed what he viewed as the norm for family, reproduction, and sexuality.

Comstock's construction of these norms was tied to ensuring the hegemony of the middle-class family—a construction that in the late nineteenth century was built on the subservient positions of women and children. His commitment to "respectability" *was* tied to a classed notion of family. For example, in his description of Cora Sammis, he bemoaned the loss of a daughter in "a respectable" family—one that went to church and lived in a "quiet village on the eastern end of Long Island" (Brodie 1994, 417). In other words, this family had all appearances of existing apart from the moral debauchery to which Comstock dedicated his life to eradicating. In this example, as in others, Comstock revealed that he is most intent on protecting the Christian, middle-class family from the seedy elements infiltrating society. Thus, his polemic against open displays of sexuality in general became a technology for regulating and controlling the bodies that posed the greatest danger to hegemonic norms.

Worse yet was when people from a "good, upstanding home" were so polluted by lust and desire that they began to embody the moral degradation of society—a slippage difficult to return from. As Comstock preached: "Lust defiles the body, debauches the imagination, corrupts the mind, deadens the will, destroys the memory, sears the conscience, hardens the heart, and damns the soul. . . . Like a panorama, the imagination seems to keep this hated thing before the mind, until it wears its way deeper and deeper, plunging the victim into practices he loathes" (Brodie 1994, 416). Clearly, Comstock was focused not only on protecting society—and Christian families in particular—from debauchery, but also on protecting individuals from themselves. He did not merely fear evil men (or women) who seduced innocent persons, but he also depicted lust as affectively entering the bodies of the seducers and turning them into something/someone they were not. "The victim," as Comstock wrote, was most often a young man or woman from a "good" middle-class home who became drawn in by more powerful forces to become the immoral debaucher he was never *intended* to be. And what *Frauds Exposed* made clear was that Comstock viewed abortion, or the possibility of abortion, as one of those dangerous moments: Once abortion was inflicted, the subject quite literally aborted her possibility of returning to the respectable positions of her birth. Thus, Comstock's work was bent on preventing women from having access to abortion so that they could be protected and freed from being victims that acted against their own best interests.

Procreative behavior is socialized to interpellate reproducing subjects into an ethic of "responsibilization," so that reproduction can be controlled through generating particularized knowledge about what constitutes responsible behavior.[10] This ideology is precisely what Comstock constructed to regulate sexuality and to tie it to a number of other "perverse" acts and discourses. By lobbying for laws that banned the distribution of obscene materials and the practice of abortion, because innocent women would then be protected, Comstock's anti-abortion measures not only outlawed abortion, but also discursively framed women as potential victims that needed discipline and security.

Comstock differed from Sanger in that he refused to allow for the possibility that women could be self-controlled citizens; for him, the ability to be responsible was tied to masculinity, which was why he only imagined how Sammis's father felt after her death and why women like Woodhull and Restell were so threatening. In Comstock's world, men must be disciplined so that they can protect and rein in women. As Sally Shuttleworth (1990) writes about Victorian body politics:

> Notions of gender differentiation fulfilled the ideological role of allowing the male sex to renew their faith in personal autonomy and control. Unlike women, men were not prey to the forces of the body, the unsteady oscillations of which mirrored the uncertain flux of social circulation; rather they were their own masters—not automatons or mindless parts of the social machinery but self-willed individuals, living incarnations of the rational individualists and self-made men of economic theory. (55)

This worldview aptly describes Comstock's motivation to outlaw abortion: While men should be self-willed, rational, and individualist, women are incapable of attaining these traits because of the more "natural" conditions of their bodies and therefore need to be given freedom *from* the harmful elements in society. Therefore, despite Comstock's critiques of liberals, his ideologies are ultimately embedded in a liberal construction of the state and its societal structures that discipline citizens—albeit only male ones—to be self-controlling individuals. Yet, a key point to understanding Comtock's investment in male autonomy is that the autonomous, self-willed man is also a classed construction that works to discipline middle-class men into seeing themselves according to class. Depicting men as autonomous and self-willed already imagines them as having a certain degree of disposable income or job security; when Comstock imagined the dismay Sammis's father must have felt after learning about his daughter's abortion, he appealed to a middle-class man who had the luxury of constructing a rational and individualist identity because of his class status.[11]

Comstock's writings put forth that abortion, because it is both keenly tied to procreative behavior and presumably control, becomes a linchpin of responsibilization. Anti-abortion laws function not only to prevent the practice, but to construct a knowledge about how subjects should behave according to certain gender norms—through what is defined as "responsible" behavior—as a means of disciplining and controlling the body-as-machine, the individual, and the demarcation of populations so as to deem which bodies and populations are "deserving" of responsibility and which need to be regulated and enclosed. In other words, law functions as judgment, but it also produces subjectivity. For Comstock, a society that allowed abortion was a society in demise, because it demonstrated men's lack of control and women's exposure to lustful forces: It both disallowed men the freedom *to* and it impeded women's freedom *from*. However, more importantly, his texts became technologies of discipline through their distribution of knowledge about the supposed inherent evil of abortion, and their attempts to interpellate middle-class Americans into their disciplinary apparati.

First Encounter: Final Thoughts

Sanger's first encounter with Comstock occurred in 1913, after Sanger had published several columns in *The Call*, a popular New York socialist daily. Her column "What Every Girl Should Know" provided women with information on topics ranging from menstruation to masturbation and was one of the first explicit sex manuals for women written by a woman. Comstock banned its circulation for several weeks, citing it for containing obscene material, although after relentless protests calling for First Amendment rights its publication was resumed (Chesler 1992, 66). Later, Comstock prosecuted Sanger's husband, William, for distributing materials related to birth control; however, during the trial, Comstock fell ill with pneumonia and died eleven days later. In her autobiography, Sanger attributed his death to William's release from jail, writing that "[t]here was a terrific demonstration in Court which made the three judges turn pale & gave Comstock a shock from which he never recovered" (2003, 165). She wrote about his death and her husband's acquittal with triumphant glee, which points to how strongly she perceived Comstock a major opponent in her fight to legalize birth control. And after all, her perception was not inaccurate, because the Comstock laws inscribed some of her major legal constraints. Yet, despite this apparent opposition, this article reveals that, in some ways, Comstock and Sanger depended upon a similar ideology.

Sanger's and Comstock's works, while seeming to profess conflicting political paradigms, actually both share discourses based on individuated freedoms that work to manage bodies and populations. They were committed to outlawing abortion by employing two intertwined ideologies. First, they argued that middle-class values were a foundation for the betterment of the race. In Comstock's logic, if abortion were outlawed, then (middle-class) families, and specifically daughters, would be protected and preserved; whereas in Sanger's logic, if access to abortion were prohibited, then people would see the need for the "cleaner," better-"controlled" form of birth control, which would also ultimately lead to a better human race. And second, both activists appealed to elements of a liberal discourse: Americans had the right to be protected, to

monitor their homes, and to maintain their individualism. Neither asked about the rights of those that presented the threats, that contributed to an "unclean" America, and that destabilized the "house built on sand."

This article covers a rather long span of time, from Comstock's polemics beginning in the 1870s to Sanger's politics in the 1920s and '30s. Still, when their arguments are juxtaposed, similar principles emerge that reveal the limitations of contemporary mainstream abortion politics both on the Right and Left. Abortion debates that are rooted in discourses of rights and individual liberties are inherently limited. The discourses of Comstock and Sanger—and the gaps in them—reveal how problematic it is to support abortion by using the rhetoric of rights and choice, which can so easily be argued in reverse.

Wendy Brown (1995) presents one of the most compelling challenges to contemporary rights-based politics. She begins her speculation on the role of rights in U.S. politics by asking: "What is the emancipatory force of rights claims on behalf of politicized identities in late-twentieth-century North American political life?" (96). Brown is not interested in whether rights actually free subjects from repressive structures, but rather how rights work to shape those subjects into identity-based individuals, thus pointing to the impossibility of the universal claims that many rights-oriented arguments posit. As she astutely argues, in order to be persuasive, those arguments must provide the illusion that they are granting access based on a naturalized and universalized paradigm; however, it is precisely their ahistoricity that works to curtail their potential emancipatory force, because of the power these claims have to foreclose identity and refuse the recognition of those subjects outside its boundaries. Similarly, abortion rights maintained through legal provisions that grant either freedom *from* or freedom *to* always result in a granting of rights that is less than universal. Some populations can be excluded based on arguments that appeal to a lack of self-will, responsibility, or maturity, in much the same way that Comstock and Sanger attempted to free women from abortion for their own protection.

Notes

1. I see the rhetorics of rights and choice as related, because they are both grounded in a liberal and individuated understanding of law: Both assume a universal, ahistoricized subject with no attention to particularities, which often make the access to rights or choice impossible or even more oppressive. There is a rich scholarship critiquing the legalization of abortion through rights and choice. See, for example, Drucilla Cornell's *The Imaginary Domain* (1995) and Ricki Solinger's *Beggars and Choosers* (2001) for a critique of choice, but a defense of rights; Rosalind Petchesky's *Abortion and Woman's Choice* (1990) for a critique of choice that avoids valorizing rights; and Mary Poovey's

"The Abortion Question and the Death of Man" (1992) for a critique of both rights and choice, which the argument made here follows most closely. I will argue here that Comstock's positions, traditionally seen as conservative, contain components of liberal ideology, because they are invested in an individuated and self-controlled (male) subject.

2. Crenshaw begins her article, "Were the Critics Right About Rights? Reassessing the American Debate About Rights in the Post-Reform Era" (2000), by asserting that the era of civil rights is dead. She notes, for example, that whenever "civil rights" are invoked in legislation, the words often signal a reactionary attack on gains made during the civil rights era, such as affirmative action, thus demonstrating the slipperiness of rights language. In tracing the history of critiques of rights, Crenshaw identifies the critics of rights as "Crits"—those that during the civil rights movement opposed the rights-based attempts to overcome U.S. racism.

3. In *Roe v. Wade*, the rhetoric of *freedom to* appears in Justice Blackmum's opinion as follows: "This right of privacy, whether it be founded in the Fourteenth Amendment's concept of personal liberty and restrictions upon state action, as we feel it is, or, as the District Court determined, in the Ninth Amendment's reservation of rights to the people, is broad enough to encompass a woman's decision whether or not to terminate her pregnancy." And *freedom from:* "We repeat, however, that the State does have an important and legitimate interest in preserving and protecting the health of the pregnant woman, whether she be a resident of the State or a nonresident who seeks medical consultation and treatment there, and that it has still another important and legitimate interest in protecting the potentiality of human life."

4. The April 2007 Supreme Court case decision on abortion rights, in *Gonzales v. Carhart,* made this point even more explicit when Justice Kennedy argued that "partial-birth" abortion must be outlawed to protect women from making a harmful decision for themselves.

5. For example, a Google search for "Margaret Sanger" turns up Planned Parenthood sites praising their founder for work to make birth control accessible, as well as feminist organizations exalting Sanger as a role model for women, while also revealing sites that vilify her, accusing Sanger of racial genocide for her involvement in the U.S. eugenics movement.

6. Jensen (1981) acknowledges that her theory is speculative, since the eighth and ninth editions of *Family Limitation* are missing, which perhaps could have provided important clues regarding Sanger's seemingly new position on abortion.

7. The editors of *The Selected Papers of Margaret Sanger* (Sanger 2006) include a different reading in their notes. They argue, "since MS never strongly reprimanded BCCRB [Birth Control Clinical Research Bureau] workers Marjorie Prevost and Anna Lifshiz for referring patients for abortions, her private views may not have changed much since 1914," referring to Sanger's earlier more lenient view of abortion. However, as I demonstrate here, almost all of her writing, including personal letters, suggest that she did view abortion as personally irresponsible behavior, even if she was occasionally forgiving of the circumstances that led women to seek the procedure.

8. Allowing women access to abortion if pregnancies presented health risks (physical or mental) gave rise to "therapeutic abortions," which were legal in the United States until *Roe v. Wade* made all abortions legal.

9. The official title of the law is "An Act for the Suppression of Trade in, and Circulation of, Obscene Literature and Articles of Immoral Use." Comstock objected to the colloquial reference to this law by his name. In *Frauds Exposed* ([1880]1969), he tries to show that he was not responsible for its passing, but that several members of Congress strongly supported anti-obscenity laws and championed their passage. However, with the act's passing into law, Comstock was made a special agent of the U.S. Postal Service, which inextricably associated him with its enforcement. These laws would not be federally overturned until the 1965 Supreme Court case *Griswold v. Connecticut.*

10. The concept of "responsibilization" comes from Michel Foucault's *The History of Sexuality* (1990, 104–05). Foucault also adds that procreative behavior is socialized as one means to construct sexuality, which he writes should "not be thought of as a kind of natural given which power tries to hold in check, or as an obscure domain which knowledge tries to gradually uncover" (105). In other words, there are no normative sexualities such as Comstock and Sanger wanted their audiences to believe; rather, they both constructed sexualities that fit into their political agendas, which were concerned with maintaining a hegemonic status quo.

11. My point here about how autonomous and self-willed men are a middle-class construction is also reflected in Comstock's temperance crusades during the late nineteenth century; see Nicola Beisel's conclusion to *Imperiled Innocents* (1997), where she argues that temperance movements were based in preserving class divisions and maintaining a well-disciplined middle class.

References

Atwood, Margaret. 1985/1998. *The Handmaid's Tale.* New York: Anchor.

Beisel, Nicola. 1997. *Imperiled Innocents: Anthony Comstock and Family Reproduction in Victorian America.* Princeton, NJ: Princeton University Press.

Blount, Anna. 1918. "Large Families and Human Waste." *The Birth Control Review* 2(1): 3.

Brodie, Janet Farrell. 1994. *Contraception and Abortion in Nineteenth-Century America.* Ithaca, NY: Cornell University Press.

Brown, Wendy. 1995. *States of Injury: Power and Freedom in Late Modernity.* Princeton, NJ: Princeton University Press.

Chesler, Ellen. 1992. *Woman of Valor: Margaret Sanger and the Birth Control Movement in America.* New York: Doubleday.

Comstock, Anthony. [1880]1969. *Frauds Exposed; Or, How the People are Deceived and Robbed, and Youth Corrupted.* Reprint. Montclair, NJ: Patterson Smith.

Cornell, Drucilla. 1995. *The Imaginary Domain: Abortion, Pornography, and Sexual Harassment.* New York: Routledge.

Crenshaw, Kimberle. 2000. "Were the Critics Right About Rights? Reassessing the American Debate About Rights in the Post-Reform Era." In *Beyond Rights Talk and Culture Talk: Comparative Essays on the Politics of Rights and Culture,* ed. Mahmood Mamdani, 61–74. New York: St. Martin's Press.

Foucault, Michel. 1990. *The History of Sexuality,* vol. 1: *An Introduction.* Trans. Robert Hurley. New York: Vintage Books.

Jensen, Joan M. 1981. "The Evolution of Margaret Sanger's 'Family Limitation' Pamphlet, 1914–1921." *Signs: Journal of Women in Culture and Society* 6(3): 548–67.

Mohr, James. 1978. *Abortion in America.* New York: Oxford University Press.

Petchesky, Rosalind Pollack. 1990. *Abortion and Woman's Choice: The State, Sexuality, and Reproductive Freedom.* Boston: Northeastern University Press.

Poovey, Mary. 1992. "The Abortion Question and the Death of Man." *Feminists Theorize the Political,* ed. Judith Butler and Joan W. Scott, 239–56. New York: Routledge.

Regan, Leslie J. 1997. *When Abortion Was a Crime.* Berkeley: University of California Press.

Ruhl, Lealle. 2002. "Dilemmas of the Will: Uncertainty, Reproduction, and the Rhetoric of Control." *Signs: Journal of Women in Culture and Society* 27(3): 641–63.

Sanger, Margaret. 2003. *The Selected Papers of Margaret Sanger,* vol. 1: *The Woman Rebel, 1900–1928,* ed. Esther Katz. Urbana: University of Illinois Press.

———. 2006. *The Selected Papers of Margaret Sanger,* vol. 2: *Birth Control Comes of Age, 1928–1939,* ed. Esther Katz. Urbana: University of Illinois Press.

———. 1919. "Birth Control and Racial Betterment." *The Birth Control Review* 3(2): 11–12.

———. 1918. "Birth Control or Abortion—Which Shall It Be?" *The Birth Control Review* 2(11): 3–4.

Shuttleworth, Sally. 1990. "Medical Discourse and Popular Advertising in the Mid-Victorian Era." In *Body/Politics: Women and the Discourses of Science,* ed. Mary Jacobus, Evelyn Fox Keller, and Sally Shuttleworth, 47–68. New York: Routledge.

Solinger, Ricki. 2001. *Beggars and Choosers: How the Politics of Choice Shapes Adoption, Abortion, and Welfare in the United States.* New, York: Hill & Wang.

Williams, Patricia. 1992. *Alchemy of Race and Rights.* Cambridge, MA: Harvard University Press.

KAREN WEINGARTEN is an assistant professor and co-director of First Year Writing at Queens College in New York.

Laura S. Hussey

 **NO**

Welfare Generosity, Abortion Access, and Abortion Rates: A Comparison of State Policy Tools

From time to time, political commentators muse that a goal many Americans want in the abstract—reduced abortions—could be achieved in compromise fashion by expanding child care, health care, and other economic benefits for families, thus enabling more disadvantaged women to carry pregnancies to term. Backing such arguments are findings that low-income women abort at disproportionately high rates and that economic factors heavily influence abortion decisions. Economic theories of abortion demand further posit that demand for the procedure should decrease as the cost of abortion, relative to the cost of childbearing, increases. Governments can raise the cost of abortion by raising barriers to abortion access, and can lower the cost of childbearing by increasing material assistance to families and making employment more compatible with parenthood.

These actions represent alternative policy approaches to the same goal: reduction of abortion among low-income women. Not only would these approaches differ in the political coalitions expected to support them, but they imply different theories of why pregnant women consider abortion in the first place. The second, I suggest, assumes a more dominant role for economic hardship, while the first assumes a more complex mix of preferences and concerns. In practice, the United States employs a little of both approaches, although welfare policy discourse typically does not incorporate the abortion issue.[1]

Social scientists have extensively studied abortion demand and its relationship with abortion access policy, but the literature has paid only marginal attention to welfare generosity, defining it very narrowly when including it at all. Considering a wider array of social policies than have been studied to date, and a more nuanced theory of their effects, this article asks: Is welfare generosity related to abortion rates? In doing so, it empirically examines a relatively untested proposition attractive to those seeking middle ground in abortion politics. More broadly, it assesses the relevance of policy tool choice to policy compliance. Following much of the literature on abortion policy, I employ data from the U.S. states, exploiting changes in welfare generosity and abortion policy over 1987–2000.

I conclude that welfare state expansions may help reduce abortion, but programs' effects are not unambiguously pro-natalist. Estimated impacts of welfare generosity on abortion rates vary by program, and some with abortion policy context.

Theory and Literature

Governments employ various policy tools in their attempts to affect behavior, and some may be more effective than others. Although choice of a tool often boils down to political preferences, different instruments carry different assumptions about the causes of target group behavior and what will motivate change. Employing Schneider and Ingram's framework of policy tools, the welfare policies I consider in this article should operate as "capacity tools." Such tools assume that a lack of resources, information, or skills best explains particular choices. Providing those needed resources, in theory, enables one to make different, presumably preferred, choices.

By definition, capacity tools involve little to no coercion, a characteristic hypothesized to improve policies' political palatability but to decrease their effectiveness. Although a comprehensive review of capacity tools' performance lies outside the scope of this article, the literature includes examples of varying success and failure for the capacity tool aspects of welfare programs. The Women, Infants, and Children nutrition assistance and education program is associated with healthier birth outcomes and more nutritious diets for pregnant women and children, but not with increased breastfeeding. Studies also link child care subsidies to mothers' increased labor force participation, and Medicaid expansions to small improvements in prenatal care usage.

Viewing U.S.-style welfare programs as capacity tools means their effect on low-income women's abortion decisions should be conditional on underlying preferences toward motherhood. For the many women whose reasons for the abortion also involve concerns about changes a baby would bring, unreadiness for parenthood, relationship issues, and reluctance to be a single mother, it is hard to see U.S. assistance programs as mind-changing "incentive tools." They provide a floor, but recipients still struggle to get by and to maintain self-esteem.

Nonetheless, economic need may drive many abortion decisions. In 2000, women with household incomes below 200 percent of the federal poverty line accounted for 57.4 percent of abortion patients, but only 30.3 percent of the female child bearing age population. The abortion rate for these poor and near-poor women was about four times that of women in households earning over 300 percent of the poverty line, and the percentage of their pregnancies ending in abortion was more than twice as large (33 vs. 15 percent). In a large study of abortion patients, 73 percent chose inability to afford a child as a reason for their decision, while 23 percent identified it as the *primary* reason.

In trying to understand variation in abortion's prevalence, most models assume sensitivity to the relative costs of abortion and child rearing. In theory, as states increasingly regulate abortion, the procedure becomes more costly to supply and difficult to access, and therefore less attractive. Abortion laws and a relative scarcity of abortion providers may also carry a "psychic" cost, since they may symbolize a community's disapproval of abortion. With some exceptions, studies find such policies associated with lower abortion rates.

Generosity of social benefits such as health insurance, cash, child care vouchers, or job protected leave time should also decrease abortion's attractiveness by defraying the material and opportunity costs of parenthood instead. Generally, the only welfare measure receiving much consideration has been the Aid to Families with Dependent Children (AFDC) program. One study finds higher AFDC benefits associated with lower state abortion rates, while others find no relationship. Studies of the welfare reform "family caps" adopted by some states—which ended the practice of increasing cash grants upon birth of another child—do not clearly find the anticipated increase in abortion rates, and are sensitive to method. Individual-level studies of adolescents link cash welfare receipt to a greater chance of choosing birth, and benefit generosity to a small decrease in abortion's likelihood, but cannot say how older women would respond.

The rest of the welfare state has been virtually unstudied in relation to abortion. A rare example, a study of three states, concluded that Medicaid expansions reduced abortions among potentially eligible white women. A substantial literature on fertility indicates that policies on maternity leave, child care, cash transfers, and tax credits for families may increase births, but the effect is small and may reflect changes in timing more than numbers. We do not know how much this represents foregone abortions.

Only one study explicitly compares the impact of different policy tools—abortion regulation and welfare—on fertility. Studying Eastern European efforts to increase birth rates after World War II, Legge and Alford find that a policy emphasis on welfare expansion more successfully increased birth rates than a policy emphasis on abortion restrictions. Yet these findings may not translate to abortion rates and the contemporary U.S. context.

Welfare generosity's impact on abortion also may not be straightforwardly pro-natalist and uniform across programs. Depending in part on the wider policy context in which they are situated, policy tools that build some women's capacity to choose childbearing may build other women's capacity to choose abortion. In states where Medicaid funds abortions, expansions in Medicaid eligibility make abortion more affordable. When Medicaid does not fund abortion, higher cash benefits can help poor women pay for desired abortions. More generally, the importance of public assistance to low-income women's pregnancy decision making may increase in environments where obtaining an abortion could entail raising money, involving parents, making two visits to an abortion provider, and facing community disapproval.

Some capacity tools may also indirectly affect abortion rates by boosting target groups' capacity in other areas. Child care constraints, for example, limit women's work hours and reduce expected fertility. Over the longer term, however, policies relieving those constraints may reduce childbearing by strengthening women's labor force attachment and so raising the stakes of parenthood when (another) pregnancy occurs.

It thus remains unclear whether, and how, welfare policies should affect abortion rates. Rather than being an independent alternative to more controversial abortion regulations, welfare policies may interact with abortion policies, affecting the abortion rate in different ways in different abortion policy contexts. Indeed, in studying the welfare family cap, Camasso finds that its estimated impact is conditioned by whether or not Medicaid funds abortions. . . .

Results

A glance at abortion rates and welfare policies in 2000 suggests little crosssectional relation and that, if anything, welfare generosity predicts higher abortion rates. Abortion rates in the 10 most expansive states for cash welfare benefits, child care grant money, and Medicaid eligibility exceed those of the 10 least expansive states by 61, 56, and 21 percent, respectively. Those 12 states whose family leave laws were more expansive than the FMLA recorded abortion rates that were 3 percent higher than those of other states. The expected relationship obtains only with family caps: abortion rates in the 25 states without these laws were 9 percent lower than in those states enforcing family caps. Meanwhile, abortion rates in the 11 states enforcing parental involvement laws, counseling laws, and bans on Medicaid-funded abortions are almost half those of the 14 states enforcing none of these policies.

Abortion attitudes and political ideologies may help explain these patterns. Although state-level abortion opinion data are hard to come by, Norrander's mean abortion legality measure from data pooled over 1988–1992 correlates with cash welfare benefits and family leave laws at a significant −0.60 and −0.39, respectively, meaning that these programs' generosity coincides with more prochoice populations. The other welfare policies are not significantly correlated with abortion attitudes.

Despite these observations, changes in some welfare policies over time may have contributed to changes in abortion rates. Abortion rates declined substantially during the early 1990s and continued to do so more softly the rest of the decade. Meanwhile, the mean COLA income level at which pregnant women and infants were eligible for Medicaid jumped between 1987 and 1990, and then continued to increase thereafter. The average amount of child care grant money that states drew down also soared over 1992–2000. Real cash welfare benefits, however, stagnated. . . .

Access to Medicaid-funded health care is also significantly associated with abortion rates over 1987–2000, but initially it appears that expanded Medicaid access predicts *increases* in the abortion rate. When we allow the effect of Medicaid to vary with abortion access policy, however, a different story suggests itself. In states that do not enforce bans on Medicaid abortion coverage, parental involvement laws, or counseling laws, each additional $1,000 increase in the Medicaid eligibility threshold is associated with a statistically significant 0.4 percent increase in the abortion rate. In a state with the mean abortion rate and number of reproductive-age women, this represents just under 100 abortions. Although most women seeking abortion services would be subject to a different, lower Medicaid eligibility threshold than the pregnancy coverage threshold in my data, greater expansiveness on this measure is likely to signal more expansive eligibility for other categories of applicants. Meanwhile, the negative coefficient on the interaction of Medicaid eligibility and abortion policy suggests that this pattern weakens and then reverses itself as state policy presents more potential barriers to abortion access. Although not significant over the 1987–2000 timeframe, this same coefficient is a little larger and marginally significant over 1992–2000. One-unit ($1,000) increase in the Medicaid eligibility threshold predicts a net abortion rate reduction of just over 0.7 percent for states enforcing all three abortion policies. Applied to the mean state abortion rate, this is about 175 fewer abortions. . . .

State child care spending is associated with abortion rates when its effect is allowed to vary with abortion policy. In states that are not enforcing any of our three key policy barriers to abortion access, each $100 increase in child care spending per child under age five is associated with a significant 2.8 percent increase in the abortion rate. This effect appears to diminish with the number of enforced abortion policies, but the coefficient on the interaction term is smaller and not statistically significant.

Interpreting the impact of abortion policies is complicated. Before allowing them to vary with welfare policy, the relationship between enforced abortion policies and the abortion rate is small and statistically indistinguishable from zero. Methodologically, this is not entirely surprising, since within-state variation in this measure is quite small relative to cross-state variation. . . . The large, positive abortion policy coefficients refer to the nonexistent situation in which all welfare policy variables would

equal zero. Meanwhile, the negative coefficients on the interaction terms suggest that abortion policies' potential for reducing abortion rates may grow with the generosity of welfare. Abortion policies may also indirectly affect abortion rates by influencing abortion provider supply. In my data, ρ for these measures is -0.54 and an increase of one abortion provider per 100,000 state residents is associated with a marginally significant but very large abortion rate increase of about 24 percent. . . .

Unspecified state-specific factors matter more. An empty fixed effects model explains 87 percent of the variation in the abortion rate, and the R^2 rises to 97 percent when adding state-specific time trends. In the full models, many of these coefficients (not shown) are statistically significant. Variables in the model may very well contribute to interstate differences in abortion levels and over-time abortion rate patterns within states, especially since some aspects of state demographic and economic composition, abortion provider markets, and public policies logically predate my study period. They may also help shape the social and cultural contexts in which women make abortion decisions, creating environments that are more or less supportive of particular reproductive decisions. But these contexts are difficult to measure. Further, in guarding against omitted variable bias with unit effects and different ways of handling dynamics, it becomes challenging for a single panel data model to test such theoretically richer accounts; we acknowledge trends and unit differences, without explaining why they exist. Unfortunately, such a richer, historical account is beyond the scope of this article.

Discussion

This study finds little support for a general pro-natalist effect of welfare generosity. The story appears more complicated and, even then, estimates involve considerable uncertainty. Expansions in some social benefits—family leave laws and, to a lesser extent, Medicaid eligibility and child care spending—may have contributed to over-time changes in state abortion rates, but the relatively large standard errors on these coefficients make estimation of their impact on abortion rates somewhat imprecise. Also, as I shall discuss momentarily, the direction of the latter two policies' impact on abortion rates appears to vary with the abortion policy context. There is still less evidence of a relationship with abortion rates for cash welfare benefits and family caps, a finding consistent with some previous research.

Perhaps the most interesting, although somewhat tentative, conclusion is that expansions in Medicaid eligibility and child care spending are not unambiguously pro-natalist. In states that do not enforce any of three key abortion regulations, increases in Medicaid and child care generosity predict increases in the abortion rate. This estimated effect may diminish and reverse itself as states enforce more abortion policies, though only the

Medicaid interaction is significant, and not in both models. Generally, a less restrictive abortion policy environment may make it materially and psychologically easier for low-income women to obtain abortions in times of financial stress. On top of that, while I have measured only Medicaid eligibility for prenatal care and delivery, abortion-funding states that also expanded more general eligibility may have made abortion more affordable for the poor. This could potentially offset the pro-birth effects of expanded delivery coverage. Child care spending also pulls in two ways: reduced costs and improved quality of child care may defray the costs of parenthood, but may also build labor force attachments that discourage additional childbearing. Relatively inexpensive abortion may enable the anti-natalist aspect of this policy, but as policy makes abortion more costly, it may become a less feasible response to economic hardship. Welfare generosity may become more important, enabling those low-income women who wish to do so to carry their pregnancies to term.

These findings seem to point to the broader range of choices that welfare programs arguably make more accessible to poor women, beyond just having a(nother) child. How they use the capacity built by these policy tools may be conditioned not only by the abortion policy environment but, perhaps more importantly, by things that are difficult to observe in existing data, such as the attitudes of women and their social networks toward abortion and childbearing. This seems consistent with Salamon's hypothesis on the lesser effectiveness of low-coercion policy tools, and may generalize to the study of other capacity tools.

More expansive family leave laws are associated with lower abortion rates. Interestingly, of the five policies studied here, family leave is arguably the least relevant to poor women. While the poor may more frequently turn to abortion out of economic need, the relatively limited scope of U.S. social benefits may be too small to meaningfully mitigate their need. However, for financially stretched women who nonetheless have a stable enough job and support system to qualify for and use maternity leave time, those policies may more effectively reduce economic barriers to parenthood. This may help explain the differences in the family leave and child care spending impacts, as states devote the latter disproportionately to the poor and near-poor.

Descriptive data from three individual-level surveys of abortion patients fit well with the emerging story.

Between 1994 and 2001, abortion rates decreased among higher income, more educated women. They increased among less advantaged women, however, reversing the falling abortion rates observed among Medicaid recipients and low-income women between 1987 and 1994. Poor women faced a mix of policy signals over the mid to late 1990s: states continued expanding Medicaid and spent more money on child care, especially for welfare-to-work clients, but welfare reforms made cash welfare more difficult to obtain and keep.

On the political idea introducing this article—that welfare generosity could substitute for more controversial abortion policies and thus unite pro-life and pro-choice Americans—this work also offers limited support. Although I fail to discern a direct statistical relationship between pro-life advocates' policies and abortion rates within states, most welfare policies also fail to yield common-grounders' expected effect. It is hard to imagine that the kinds of conclusions reached here could inspire the enormous political will required for common ground. Further, signs on the coefficients of most welfare/abortion policy interactions suggest that welfare and abortion policies may have interdependent effects on abortion rates.

Expanded access to maternity leave and health care may have prevented abortions among some poor or working-class women, but these findings do not shatter the notion of pregnancy decisions as highly personal, albeit embedded in some larger social context, and difficult for governments to influence with the tools they presently use. We can only speculate whether the adoption of more European-style social policies, such as universal health care, extended paid parental leave, and guaranteed, publicly funded child care, would have a stronger impact on abortion rates. It is also plausible that welfare (and abortion) policies may work more indirectly, by shaping individual attitudes, community norms, economic circumstances, and other factors in pregnancy decision making—but my data are not well equipped to tease out these causal paths, and the paucity of state-level time-series opinion data presents an important obstacle. These are fascinating questions—but must wait for future research.

LAURA S. HUSSEY is an assistant professor of American Public Policy and Administration at the University of Maryland.

EXPLORING THE ISSUE

Is Access to Abortion a Class Issue?

Critical Thinking and Reflection

    1 How do issues of class and race intersect with conflicting cultural beliefs about abortion in the United States?

    2. How do economic and political considerations influence the abortion debate?

    3. How do notions of privilege impact how the discourse on abortion is framed?

Is There Common Ground?

An examination of reproductive issues through a political economy perspective rests on an understanding of the role that power plays in matters related to health and medicine. Kinser (2010) argues that "unequal allocations of power impinge upon women's experiences of parenting and impede their ability to adequately care for their children while living full and purposeful lives" (p. 3). Laws premised on notions of female subordination form the foundation of women's inequality and relative lack of power in society. Traditional gender roles contribute to women's status as members of a group that has historically experienced cultural, economic, legal, and political restrictions on their social roles (Lindsey, 1997). The core challenge in an analysis of reproductive health is how to develop public health policy that will balance considerations regarding "women's capacity for childbearing with a recognition of the economic vulnerability that mothers still face" (Freedman, 2002). The complexity of the issues related to the exercise of power over the reproductive process and related maternal health policies ensures that the struggle for reproductive control will continue to shape the public policy discourse and the field of medicine in the United States.

Additional Resources

Freedman, E. (2002). *No Turning Back: The History of Feminism and the Future of Women*. Ballantine Books: New York.

Gordon, L. (2002). *The Moral Property of Women: A History of Birth Control Politics in America*. University of Illinois Press: Urbana.

Lindsey, L. (1997). *Gender Roles: A Sociological Perspective*. 3rd edition. Prentice Hall: New Jersey.

Kinser, A. (2010). *Motherhood and Feminism*. Seal Press: Berkeley.

Meyer, J. (2004). *Any Friend of the Movement: Networking for Birth Control, 192–1940*. Ohio State University Press: Columbus.

Mintz, J. (2011). "Empowering women to become mothers." In O'Reilly, Andrea, Editor. (2011). *The 21st Century Motherhood Movement: Mothers Speak Out on Why We Need to Change the World and How to Do It*. Demeter Press: Ontario.

Paxton, P. and Hughes, M M. (2007). *Women, Politics, and Power: A Global Perspective*. Pine Forge Press: Los Angeles.

Planned Parenthood Federation of America. (2011). "History and Success." Retrieved from:/www.plannedparenthood.org/about-us/who-we-are/history-and-successes.htm#Sanger

Create Central

www.mhhe.com/createcentral

Internet References . . .

Reproductive Rights

http://reproductiverights.org/

United Nations Population Fund

http://www.unfpa.org/rights/rights.htm

NARAL Pro-Choice America

http://naral.org

Unit 3

UNIT

Women in the Workplace: She Works Hard for the Money

*S*hould women work outside the home? What positions should the military allow women to hold? Is it possible for sex work to be an empowering occupation? How are women's families affected when mothers work outside the home? What impact do working women have on the economy?

The role of women in the workplace continues to be a source of controversy in American culture. Women entered the American workforce in unprecedented numbers during World War II. With men on the frontlines overseas, the factories needed workers and women were called into service. The famous Rosie the Riveter media campaign to encourage women to leave the home and enter the workforce successfully introduced women to the world of wage earning. After the war ended, the government less successfully asked women to return home to make way for the veterans.

In the 1960s, the government would establish the Equal Employment Opportunity Commission. Landmark legislation would guarantee new protections for women entering the workforce. By the late 1960s, employers could no longer post help wanted advertisements that specified a preferred applicant's sex.

Despite the employment gains made by women in the decades since World War II, issues such as wage disparity and discrimination against working mothers continue to pose barriers to women's workplace equity. Women continue to battle for equality in occupations once thought to be solely the province of men. Questions persist over women's role in the military and women are still barred from certain frontline combat roles.

Women's increased presence in the workplace has changed the structure of family life. From delayed childbearing to lower fertility rates, families have been changed by women's expanding social roles. Social scientists continue to study the long term ramifications of women's increased workforce participation on the economy.

Selected, Edited, and with Issue Framing Material by:
Rachel Pienta, *Valdosta State University*

ISSUE

Should Women Serve in Military Combat Positions?

YES: Krystyna M. Cloutier, from "Marching Toward War: Reconnoitering the Use of All Female Platoons," *Connecticut Law Review* (vol. 40, no. 5, July 2008)

NO: George Neumayr, from "Your Mother's Army," *The American Spectator* (vol. 38, no. 4, May 2005)

Learning Outcomes

As you read the issue, focus on the following points:

- Should women be allowed access to any of the military's combat positions?
- Should the military be allowed to informally utilize women as combat troops?

ISSUE SUMMARY

YES: Krystyna M. Cloutier, writing for the *Connecticut Law Review*, examines arguments centering on mounting pressure for the military to adopt gender-neutral policies that will allow women to serve in forward combat positions.

NO: George Neumayr, executive editor of *The American Spectator*, examines the feminization of the military that began during the administration of former President Bill Clinton and continued to expand during the Bush years.

Women have played roles in the American military since the nation's birth. Roles for women, however, have historically and traditionally been limited to medical, clerical, and, more recently, law enforcement work. In the 1990s, women's roles in the military expanded after the passage of the 1992 Defense Reauthorization Act. For the first time in American history, women were assigned to forward combat support rules.

The 1997 movie G.I. Jane featured Demi Moore as a navy topographic analyst who was chosen to serve as a test case for women in the military. The movie chronicled her fictional battle to complete Navy SEAL training and the bureaucratic and personal challenges she faced.

After 2001, women would serve in further expanded roles. In 2003, Lori Ann Piestewa was killed in an ambush near Nasiriyah, Iraq. She was the first woman killed in action in Iraq. Jessica Lynch was captured in the same attack and her subsequent rescue dominated media coverage of the early Iraq conflict. Piestewa, a single mother, along with Lynch would become key names in the debate over women's roles in the military.

As recently as 2009, media reports noted that although women's combat support roles were limited by policy, actual field practices often put women into direct forward combat positions. Military commanders, short

handed in the field in the face of multiple conflicts on different fronts across the globe, have used semantics to utilize women as combat troops. Women can be attached to combat platoons rather than assigned to these positions, a bureaucratic loophole that allows commanders to skirt the current policies.

In recent years, challenges facing women in the military range from sexual harassment to sexual assault. In response, the military has taken steps to implement procedures that recognize potential for further trauma for victims who report. New protocols and procedures such as the Forensic Experiential Trauma Interviews technique recently adopted by the Army provide improved strategies and tools for the contemporary military to handle an acknowledged issue.

In spring 2012, two female army reservists filed suit against the U.S. Military to address current policy that limits women's access to combat assignments. In the suit, the women allege that the current ban on women serving in frontline combat positions, "violates their right to equal protection under the Fifth Amendment—and affects their salaries, promotion and advancement, and future retirement benefits" (Baker, 2012).

In "Marching Toward War: Reconnoitering the Use of All Female Platoons," Krystyna M. Cloutier examines the current debate on the role that women should play in the armed forces and focuses specifically on the prospect of all-female platoons. Framing her analysis within a larger historical context, she suggests that all-female Special Operations Forces may be a unique way to offer women to serve in the military.

In "Your Mother's Army," George Neumayr frames his examination of women's expanding role in the modern military as a feminist experiment that attempts to reconcile gender equity with national security. Neumayr cites men and women lacking suitable training to combat due to gender equity accommodations. The article also suggests that women's expanded roles in the military have social consequences on the home front as well with children of single military mothers experiencing unintended emotional collateral damage due to long separations or, in the worst case scenarios, a mother's death overseas.

YES

Krystyna M. Cloutier

Marching Toward War: Reconnoitering the Use of All Female Platoons

Introduction

Women have always played an active, albeit restricted, role in the United States military. Before the 1990s, women's roles in the military were limited to nursing, secretarial duties, and military police positions. After Operation Desert Storm and Operation Desert Shield in the early 1990s, the issue of whether women should be assigned to direct combat units was brought to the foreground. In 1992, President Clinton signed the 1992 Defense Authorization Act which, for the first time in the nation's history, permitted the assignment of women to combat support positions, combat naval vessels, and aircraft engaged in combat missions. Then, in 2001, the War on Terror again brought the debate concerning women in combat to the attention of Congress and the nation.

Proponents of inclusion argue that women should be allowed in combat because prohibiting women from serving in combat violates the Equal Protection Clause of the Fourteenth Amendment and denies women's rights as full citizens. Opponents argue that in order for the military to focus on winning wars, the military must make decisions that best affect military readiness, cohesion, and morale, and women's physical abilities are not best suited to combat. Recently, proponents of inclusion have suggested that the military adopt physical requirements for each military specialty and assign soldiers to each specialty based on their ability to meet those requirements regardless of gender.

This Note analyzes the possibility of allowing women in combat without jeopardizing the efficiency and success of the United States military through the implementation of all-female special operations forces units.[1] This Note will argue that implementing all-female platoons ensures that women have a real opportunity to participate in combat while also accounting for the fundamental nature of the military and its primary mission, winning wars. . . .

Feminism and Inclusion

Overview

The feminist movement was not directed at advancing the rights of women in the military. In fact, early feminists were pacifists and did not condone the enlistment of women into the military.[2] By the 1980s, however, many feminists advocating for the passage of the Equal Rights Amendment (ERA) were fighting not only for the inclusion of women into combat, but also for a compulsory draft of both men and women.

Many ERA supporters believed that the only position consistent with promoting gender equality was the support of female inclusion in combat MOSs, and the registration of women into the draft.[3] One of the ERA's biggest supporters was President Jimmy Carter. . . .[4]

The Marginalization of Military Women

While arguing for the inclusion of women in combat, feminist activists claim to represent the views of military women. However, feminist activists calling for inclusion actually represent only the policy preferences of a few privileged, predominately white women with similar life experiences, whose beliefs meet the needs of the feminist agenda.[5] Feminist activists accept the current standard and policy for men as the objective standard and seek to apply this policy to women, arguing that women are the same as men and should be treated as such.[6] This brand of activism succeeds in marginalizing the life experiences of military women, who have seen the practical effects of the physiological differences between the sexes, causing the alienation of the very women whom the movement seeks to reach.[7] These feminists argue for the compulsory assignment of both women and men to combat MOSs without a careful analysis of the desires of military women.[8] When asked, many military women tend to feel that implementing compulsory service for either men or women is regressive.[9] When forced to choose between the status quo or the assignment of women to combat MOSs, many military women choose the status quo.[10]

A survey conducted in 1995 asked Army women whether women should be assigned to combat MOSs and whether they felt they were capable of performing in combat.[11] The results varied by rank and race.[12] Enlisted women, and women of color particularly, are more likely to oppose assigning women to combat MOSs.[13] White women and officers are more likely to support assigning women.[14] Consequently, white women and officers were most likely to believe that they could endure the physical challenges.[15] In contrast, only half of black, Hispanic, and other women of color believed they could meet the physical demands of combat.[16] The great majority of

Cloutier, Krystyna M. From *Connecticut Law Review*, July 2008, pp. 1533–1534, 1554, 1557–1561, 1565–1568, 1578–1579. Copyright © 2008 by Connecticut Law Review. Reprinted by permission.

women surveyed would not volunteer for assignment to a combat MOS if they were allowed; only eleven percent of enlisted women, thirteen percent of non-commissioned officers (NCOs), and fourteen percent of officers said they would volunteer.[17] Additionally, a majority of women surveyed believed that the gender-specific physical standards should remain the same.[18]

The strongest argument put forth by opponents of inclusion addresses the physiological differences between men and women.[19] In order to combat this argument, proponents of inclusion have explained that the physiological differences between men and women are merely social constructs that can be overcome.[20] These proponents minimize the physical differences between men and women, dismissing them as irrelevant. Often, proponents argue that "[t]he real issue is training. Some women can indeed carry as much weight, throw as far and run as fast as some men in physical strength and endurance."[21] Proponents reference exceptionally talented Olympic athletes, arguing that "[t]hese women demonstrate that trained individuals can do anything."[22] Thus, the abilities of exceptional women are used to suggest a world in which all girls, if socialized the same as boys, can meet the same physical demands.[23] This world is, of course, fictitious.[24] Moreover, by dismissing arguments based on the physiological differences with references to Olympic athletes, military women are left to explain their physical limitations on their own.[25] Of course, military women could integrate more easily if women could do what men can do; but they cannot, and they are constantly reminded of that fact.[26]

Feminist scholars and activists must accommodate women's arguments that rest partly on the biological differences between the sexes. Recognizing the biological and physical differences between men and women does not render women inferior.[27] Certainly, these differences have been used to oppress and marginalize women. However, understanding their physical differences allows many Army women to adapt to their lives in the military. To reject the relevance of the physical differences between the sexes is to reject the experiences of military women.[28] "To pronounce women either the same or different leaves men as the standard of analysis. Further progress toward gender equality requires an alternative framework that focuses not on difference per se, but on the disadvantages that follow from it."[29] Recognizing these differences validates the experiences of military women and allows the feminist agenda to move in a new direction.[30]

The Author's Personal Experience

I left for Iraq as a female Marine Sergeant E-5 shortly after my twenty-first birthday, assigned to a combat support unit.[31] Our unit's mission was simple: bring supplies, gear, ammunition, food, and mail to the Marines in combat and then bring back their dead, their wounded, and their trash. My job was to track these convoys—I had to know where every soldier, marine, and sailor was located on the battlefield, as well as the location of equipment. I was good at my job; I was smart, organized, and responsible, but I quickly realized that I didn't belong. I was asked to carry ninety pounds or more of gear on my body, enough weight to cause my hips to become numb, my lower back to ache, and blisters to form on my feet, even when there was no skin left, and I began to recognize what real physical strength is. And that I don't have it.

I could not help pick up an injured Marine off the ground, lift him several feet into the air, and place him in the back of a seven-ton. I could not pull my own body weight into the second story window of a building while carrying fifty pounds of gear on my back. The men around me had no trouble performing these physical tasks. I felt weak and inferior, but, most of all, I felt as if I was a detriment to those men. Each time I could not perform a physical task as well as a man, I became aware of how unfair and unintelligent it was to judge me by a male standard, a standard designed to ensure my failure. . . .

Technology and Combat

Proponents of inclusion have argued that technology has changed the face of the modern battlefield. They have argued that infantrymen no longer are required to possess the same physical prowess that once was necessary to ensure success on the battlefield.[32] This argument is often used to minimize the significance of the physiological differences between the sexes. However, despite advances in technology, the physical demands on combat soldiers are high. The "daily life of [a] ground combat soldier in combat circumstances is one of constant physical exertion, often in extreme climatic conditions with the barest of amenities and the inherent risk of injury, capture, and death."[33] Ground combat has not become less hazardous or less physically demanding.[34]

A 1986 study conducted by the Combined Arms Center at Fort Leavenworth, Kansas, concluded that "[t]echnological advances will not, however, eliminate the requirement for a great deal of strenuous human activity in order to perform many of the tasks associated with ground combat forces."[35] Similarly, other experts have come to the same conclusion, noting that strength, power, and endurance remain essential to the soldier engaged in ground combat. "Closing with the enemy and destroying him is a very physical endeavor and modern technology has not changed it at all—nor is it likely to."[36]

Moreover, it is likely that the future battlefield will actually become a more lethal and deadly place, not only because of the advances in technology, but also because of the location of the battlefield. Throughout the past hundred years, battles have become longer, requiring soldiers to fight both day and night and through all kinds of weather.[37] These continuous battles increase the risk of exposure to fatigue, stress, and death.[38] Additionally, because of the nature of combat, the front lines are always more dangerous, and infantrymen today are exposed to more powerful and more versatile weapons systems.[39] Advances in technology and the changing nature of the modern battlefield have also caused an increased reliance on mechanization (i.e., tanks, amphibious assault vehicles, etc.).[40] Infantrymen in particular are more susceptible to accidental death from fratricide, unintended explosions or firings from weapons, and collisions between mechanized vehicles.[41]

Furthermore, the role of the infantry squad, a small group of soldiers, has increasingly been utilized to perform various missions.[42] The decentralization of infantry units is part of established military strategy and is essential to mission success on the modern battlefield because only the smallest groups are likely to remain together.[43] This has been made abundantly clear during Operation Enduring Freedom in both Iraq and Afghanistan. Small squads of infantrymen are constantly called upon to clear buildings, search for bombs, conduct patrols, care for each other and the dead and wounded, help rebuild schools and hospitals, help train the Iraqi Army and police, and perform other peacekeeping missions.[44]

Advances in technology have served not only to increase the physical demands of infantrymen but also the psychological demands.[45] Because of the lethality of weapons, units are more dispersed.[46] Consequently, units increasingly rely on the squad leader, who must make decisions in keeping with the commander's intent, as well as ensure that his soldiers are effectively engaging the enemy.[47] Moreover, the isolation of infantrymen creates a greater reliance on the intangibles; unit cohesion, morale, esprit de corps, and bonding have become more and more essential to the success of the unit.[48] These intangibles are most important to the infantrymen in their ability to cope with battlefield stress, fatigue, and fear. . . .[49]

Conclusion

The current argument calling for the military to adopt gender-neutral physical requirements fails to cement women's position in combat.[50] It is in line with the liberal feminist agenda,[51] and it gives the perception that, if adopted, women in the military would have equal opportunities—but it does not ensure inclusion. Rather, it ensures that women are judged by a male standard, a standard designed to exploit women's physical limitations, causing them to look weak and inferior. It ensures that the everyday life experiences of military women are marginalized and dismissed.[52]

Implementing all-female platoons will guarantee that women are not judged by how similar they are to men but on how well they perform. Qualified women will be assigned to these all-female SOF where they will be trained in unconventional warfare, psychological warfare, and peacekeeping, among other things.[53] The establishment of all-female platoons will serve to promote the efficiency and success of the United States military by giving the military another tool in its arsenal and creating an innovative use of resources.

Notes

1. Both the United States government and military and most proponents of inclusion agree that military effectiveness is the touchstone of the debate concerning whether women should be allowed in combat. Kingsley R. Browne, *Women at War: An Evolutionary Perspective,* 49 BUFF. L. REV. 51,228 (2001); *see* Elaine Donnelly, *Constructing the Co–Ed Military,* 14 DUKE J. GENDER L. & POL'Y 815, 819 (2007) (considering the overarching, classical concerns of the military: military effectiveness, and combat readiness); *see also* Martha McSally, *Women in Combat: Is the Current Policy Obsolete?,* 14 DUKE J. GENDER L. & POL'Y 1011, 1030 (2007) ("Military effectiveness requires that we pick the best qualified person for the job, regardless of gender.").

2. *See* HOLM, *supra* note 11, at 351 (noting that early feminists were pacifist; thus, once President Carter called for both men and women to register for the draft, feminists were forced to choose between their abhorrence of war and their desire that women enjoy the same benefits as men—they chose the latter).

3. *See id.* at 351.

4. *See id.* at 347 (discussing President Carter's advocacy of the ERA).

5. Laura L. Miller, *Feminism and the Exclusion ofArmy Women from Combat, in* WOMEN IN THE MILITARY 103, 104 (Rita James Simon ed., 2001).

6. *Id.* at 103. Many feminists refuse to recognize even the possibility that some differences between the sexes are biologically determined, for fear that this will be used to "Justify the repression, suppression, and oppression of women." TONG, *supra* note 188, at 36. For this reason, many feminists "believe that gender identities are the nearly exclusive product of socialization, changeable at society's will." *Id.* However, many female soldiers "believe that women who enjoy traditional female occupations should not be ashamed of their jobs or forced into traditionally male occupations to meet a quota or prove a feminist point." Miller, *supra* note 201, at 104; *see also* STEPHANIE GUTMANN, THE KINDER, GENTLER MILITARY: CAN AMERICA'S GENDER-NEUTRAL FIGHTING FORCE STILL WIN WARS? 12 (2000).

7. Miller, *supra* note 201, at 103, 126–127. For military women, their life experiences have shown them that the physiological differences between the sexes are real and important, and critically impact their performance, *id.* at 127, with one women stating that "women should be kept out of direct combat units. . . . I served in a combat support unit during the war for 6 months and there were many more problems for the female soldiers out there than there were for the males (physically speaking)." *Id.* at 113–114.

8. *See* Miller, *supra* note 201, at 103–04 (noting that some feminist activists "support making women eligible for the draft and assigning

them to combat arms, even on a non-voluntary basis if necessary").

9. *Id.* at 103.

10. *Id.*

11. *Id.* at 104–05.

12. *Id.*

13. *Id.* at 104, 111.

14. *Id.* at 116.

15. *See id.* at 116–18 (noting that if women were assigned to combat positions, because of the hierarchy of the military, it is more likely that enlisted women would actually fight on the front lines and die in combat than their officers).

16. *Id.* at 117–18 tbl.3.

17. *Id.* at 117.

18. *Id.* at 120 tbl.5.

19. *See* GOLDSTEIN, *supra* note 164, at 101; BRIAN MITCHELL, WOMEN IN THE MILITARY: FLIRTING WITH DISASTER 49 (1998).

20. *See* Miller, *supra* note 201, at 127 (noting that liberal feminists downplay gender differences).

21. *Id.* at 108 (quoting Representative Patricia Schroeder of the House Armed Services Committee).

22. *Id.* Representative Patricia Schroeder specifically mentioned "pitching ace Kathy Arendsen, who throws a softball 96 miles per hour underhand, and Florence Griffith Joyner, who runs the 100 meters faster than O.J. Simpson ever ran." *Id.*

23. *Id.*

24. *Id.*

25. *Id.*

26. *Id.* at 127.

27. *See* LYNDA BIRKE, WOMEN, FEMINISM, AND BIOLOGY: THE FEMINIST CHALLENGE 106 (1986) ("[G]ender differentiation does not have to mean gender division in the hierarchical sense.").

28. Miller, *supra* note 201, at 127–28. See Jesse Leavenworth, *War Over Women in Combat: Despite Medals, Debate Persists About Whether They Should Join Men in Ground Units,* HARTFORD COURANT, Mar. 18, 2008, at A1, *available at* LEXIS, News Library, HTCOUR File.

29. THEORETICAL PERSPECTIVES ON SEXUAL DIFFERENCE 204 (Deborah L. Rhode ed., 1990).

30. *See* DOROTHY E. SMITH, THE CONCEPTUAL PRACTICES OF POWER: A FEMINIST SOCIOLOGY OF KNOWLEDGE 13 (1990).

31. Immediately following graduation from high school, the Author enlisted in the Marine Corps and was stationed at Camp Pendleton, CA. The following are excerpts taken from her journal, which was kept during her deployment to Iraq. She was stationed in Iraq from March to July of 2003.

32. *See* Lucinda Joy Peach, *Gender Ideology in the Ethics of Women in Combat, in* IT'S OUR MILITARY, TOO!: WOMEN AND THE U.S. MILITARY 168 (Judith Hicks Stiehm ed., 1996) (arguing that "[p]hysical strength and size has minimal, if any, consideration when weapons are being fired at the touch of a button . . . . Equipment redesign and technological innovations can eliminate most needs for intense physical strength").

33. REPORT TO THE PRESIDENT, *supra* note 121, at 24.

34. *Id.* at C35. "Technology has made combat more lethal—it has not altered the fundamentally physical nature of combat and the offensive requirement and prolonged fighting spirit required to 'close with' the enemy." *Id.* at C35. Closing with the enemy means fighting "over difficult ground, under debilitating loads, under the harshest climatic and environmental conditions, and under the duress of mortal danger." *Id.* at C-34. "Technology has not altered the harshness of the environment on the battlefield nor mitigated the effects of nature which can be more deadly than the enemy. Technology has increased the difficulties which arise from an increased operational tempo and increased requirements for logistical (material) support. Technology, as embodied in increased target acquisition capabilities and increased weapons' ranges, places more people in the area of operations at mortal risk at any given moment in time. Notwithstanding the increased mortal risk to those personnel in combat support and combat service support roles, the units and branches of the Service which by their design and mission are to close with the enemy in close combat and direct fire will remain at far greater risk than those in support roles." *Id.* at C35.

35. CADA, FINAL REPORT, *supra* note 134, at III–1.

36. Tuten, *supra* note 168, at 248. JOHN KEEGAN, THE FACE OF BATTLE 329 (1976) ("There is no such thing as 'getting used to combat' . . . . Each moment of combat imposes a strain so great that men will break down in direct relation to the intensity and duration of their exposure."); Women in Combat: Frequently Asked Questions, Center for Military Readiness (Nov. 22, 2004), http://www.cmrlink.org/WomenInCombat.asp?DocID=237

37. George J. Woods, Women in the Infantry: The Effect on the Moral Domain (Dec. 19, 1992) (unpublished monograph, School of Advanced Military Studies, United States Army Command, General Staff College, Fort Leavenworth, KS) (on file with Naval War College Library, Newport, R.I.) (citing KEEGAN, *supra* note 241, at 302).

38. *Id.* (manuscript at 7).

39. *Id.*

40. *Id.* For example, England has relied on mechanized infantry and artillery units, and the United States Army has established complete divisions of light infantry. JOHN A. ENGLISH & BRUCE I. GUDMUNSSON, ON INFANTRY 175 (1994).

41. KEEGAN, *supra* note 241, at 311–14 ("Accident has always caused a proportion of the battlefield's deaths."); Tuten, *supra* note 168, at 240 ("Technology has expanded the range and destructiveness of weaponry.").

42. United States Marine Corps, Tactics 72 (1997), *available at* http://www.dtic.mil/doctrine/jel/service_pubs/mcdp1_3.pdf [hereinafter Tactics]. The decentralization of command is an "important concept in the execution of maneuver warfare." *Id.*

43. Tactics, *supra* note 247, at 73. "[E]ach leader can act quickly as the situation changes without passing information up the chain of command and waiting for orders to come back down. Speed is greatly increased by this decentralization process." *Id. See* Keegan, *supra* note 241, at 285–90.

44. *See e.g.*, Master Sergeant Gideon Rogers, *Marine Squad Leaders,* Marine Corps News Service, Dec. 18, 2005 (describing the role of a squad leader and daily patrols); Lance Corporal Paul Robbins Jr., *Marine Corps Squad Leaders,* Marine Corps News Service, Aug. 11, 2005, Gordon Trowbridge, *Building an Iraqi Army,* Armed Forces J., Jan. 2006.

45. *See* Keegan, *supra* note 241, at 299 ("Men can stand only so much of anything . . . so that what needs to be established . . . is not the factor by which mechanization of battle has multiplied the cost of waging war to the states involved but the degree to which it has increased the strain thrown on the human participants.").

46. Woods, *supra* note 242 (manuscript at 8). John Matsumura et al., Lightning over Water: Sharpening America's Light Forces for Rapid Reaction Missions iii, 18 (2001).

47. Tactics, *supra* note 247, at 73. Not only does decentralization increase the overall speed and effectiveness of the military, it also employs subordinate commanders to make their own decisions without consulting the chain of command. *Id.* at 86. Often these decisions are in line with the commander's intent which provides the overall purpose for accomplishing any given task. *Id.*; Matsumura, *supra* note 251, at 17 ("[T]here was considerable merit in making light forces even smaller than they are now."); Woods, *supra* note 242 (manuscript at 8).

48. Woods, *supra* note 242 (manuscript at 8); Anthony Kellett, Combat Motivation: The Behavior of Soldiers in Battle 271–72 (1982).

49. *See infra* notes 258–74 and accompanying text (discussing the importance of group cohesion).

50. Of course, the proposals calling for inclusion are dependent in large part upon the technology of war and the political climate of the nation.

51. *See supra* notes 188–92 and accompanying text (discussing liberal feminism); *see also* notes 174–87 and accompanying text (discussing the feminist movement's call for compulsory service for both women and men).

52. *See supra* notes 201–22 and accompanying text (discussing the feminist movement's marginalization of military women because the movement minimizes, and often refuses to recognize, the existence of biological differences between the sexes).

53. *See supra* note 310–12 and accompanying test (discussing the various duties of SOF).

Krystyna M. Cloutier is the managing editor of the *Connecticut Law Review.*

George Neumayr

 **NO**

Your Mother's Army

The casualty lists from the Middle East contain a sick progress report on feminism in the U.S. military. Mothers sent into the war on terrorism are coming home to their children in body bags. Among the war dead: Lori Ann Piestewa, 23, mother of two preschoolers; Melissa J. Hobart, 22, mother of a 3-year-old; Jessica L. Cawvey, 21, single mother of a 6-year-old; Pamela Osbourne, 38, mother of three children, ages 9–19; Katrina L. Bell-Johnson, 32, mother of a 1-year-old.

George Bush's military isn't reconsidering the feminist experiment devised under Bill Clinton; it is completing it. The Army increasingly relies on women even as it lethargically and ineffectually recruits men. (The Army missed its recruiting goal in February by 27 percent.) Women now constitute 15 percent of the active Army, 23 percent of the Army Reserve, and 13 percent of the Army National Guard. It is commonly estimated that 30 percent of the Army will be female by 2010.

Claudia Kennedy, a general under Bill Clinton who entered the military after filling out an Army enlistment coupon she found in *Cosmopolitan* magazine and is credited with launching the Army's "Consideration of Others" program, once said to West Point cadets, "This is not your father's Army anymore!" Her boast is even truer under Bush's Pentagon, which has been pushing more and more women onto the battlefield, forming the beginnings of a coed front line. As of this spring, roughly 17,000 female soldiers had been in Iraq and Afghanistan, serving in de facto combat roles even though their positions are technically described as "support."

In February, even as the Army insisted that it wasn't abolishing the prohibition on women in ground combat units, its 3rd Infantry Division confirmed that it was placing women side by side with combat troops in "forward support" positions, a policy called "collocation." The Army cited as its reason for the new policy a shortage of qualified men. But Elaine Donnelly of the Center for Military Readiness was told by Pentagon officials that "this is how women grow their careers." (A military source who e-mailed *TAS* also pinpointed feminist careerism as the real reason for the change, writing, "All of this is entirely for the purpose of ensuring that women in the military have the opportunity to become generals, even though the only real purpose of having generals at all is for the leading of military units in actual combat and making and deciding on overall strategic considerations as they pertain to the impending battles.")

When the policy drew fire from critics like Donnelly (who established that it skirted the law and that the Army has been secretly tinkering with gender codes for units in an unclassified document titled "Combat Exclusion Quick Look Options"), the Army offered up the absurd sop of promising to evacuate the female troops should these collocated units run into battle conditions—an outrageously convoluted plan which only underscored the Army's willingness to juggle feminism at the expense of its essential military mission.

One soldier who heard about the new gender-integrated collocation policy described it as a formula for losing battles and getting soldiers killed, since evacuating female troops will mean dissipating crucial resources at the very moment these ground combat units will need them most. Assets, he said, "cannot be spared simply to move females to the rear. . . . Imagine an entire brigade trying to chopper out these female contingents before combat—it would require almost half of a division's worth of aviation assets to move them all at once."

Given the choice between feminism and maximum military effectiveness, the Army is choosing feminism. But as the Army nudges women to the frontlines and unfolds the feminist logic of equal rights requiring equal risks, the shocks of war are becoming more terrifyingly real to women, the majority of whom reveal in surveys that they have no desire to serve on the frontlines. Many female soldiers had an image of life in the military as careerism without combat—an image military recruiters eager to meet female quotas don't discourage. "You're not generally told as a female that you will be in that type of situation where you are in harm's way directly," said National Guard Sergeant Brenda Monroe to the *Sacramento Bee*. "I never dreamed that I would wake up every night and have to run to a bunker and take cover because we were being attacked or under direct fire."

The rescued soldier Jessica Lynch makes a similar observation in her memoirs, noting that she never anticipated even being in a position to be raped and kidnapped by the enemy. After former Notre Dame basketball player Danielle Green had her left hand blown off during an attack in Iraq, her old Irish coach Muffet McGraw said to reporters, "It was just a shock to hear she had been injured because she had said that her job was going to keep her on the sidelines."

The first shock of war for female soldiers is that they are actually in it. But it is not the last one. A story that much of the media have ignored is that a significant number of female soldiers exposed to the traumas of war are returning from the Middle East with serious psychological problems. The *Sacramento Bee* to its credit reported in March that female soldiers are suffering a high incidence of post-traumatic stress disorder: "Returning female vets are bringing back wounded minds, beset by post-traumatic stress disorder, an illness that affects women at twice the rate of men." Military doctors fear an "avalanche of cases among female vets will smother the military health care system," it reported.

The *Bee* added that at the Veteran Affairs' Post-Traumatic Stress Disorder (PTSD) center in White River Junction, Vermont, researchers "are completing a $5 million study of 384 female vets with PTSD." Several studies are underway and doctors are reaching the obvious conclusion, that war is more traumatic for women than men.

Researchers, according to the *Bee*, "have found female brains may be less efficient than male brains at producing the neurosteroids that help human beings cope with stress. Other studies have shown women deplete serotonin, a substance that helps combat depression, more quickly than men and regenerate it more slowly. And menstrual cycles may also play a role in making women more vulnerable in stressful situations."

Meanwhile, the Army itches to send even more women into crippling combat conditions, as ambitious generals glance anxiously over their shoulders at Hillary Clinton on the Armed Services Committee. (Stephanie Gutmann, author of *The Kinder, Gentler Military*, has reported that many in Congress have long demanded an Army composed of 50 percent women, and that the Army's recruiting philosophy of women is, "Get'em on the plane.") While George Bush has said "no women in combat," he acts as if the matter is out of his hands. "There's no change of policy as far as I'm concerned," he passively said to the *Washington Times* in January.

In a "Message from the Army Leadership" earlier this year, its heads proudly related how "women are exposed to combat danger as they perform aviation missions, ground convoy security, united resupply operations, and a host of other critical functions:" Nothing has given the Pentagon pause—not reports of eroding standards in training, not the Abu Ghraib debacle of women wardens and run-amok female jailers, not bodybags carrying the nation's mothers and daughters, not women soldiers tortured and held in captivity, not the growing list of orphans.

The Army's blatantly barbaric policy of separating mothers from their toddlers is even a point of pride, cast as a principled refusal to surrender the feminist idea that men and women must carry the same responsibilities if they wish to enjoy the same benefits. (By contrast, in the Korean War, no woman with a child under 18 was permitted to serve.) Before separating children from their mothers, the Army issues to military moms ludicrous literature on "children and deployment" (one of the accompanying pictures is of a woman cradling an infant) in which books on "Family-Change Situations" are extolled, such as "All Kinds of Families" and "The Good-bye Painting."

"The child may become confused and fearful that Mommy or Daddy will abandon them," the Army counsels, and suggests female troops leave behind a laminated photo of themselves: "the 'I want my daddy/mommy syndrome' can be helped by supplying the child with a laminated photo. . ." The Army also suggests that "children record cassettes to the soldier. This is good for toddlers who are learning how to talk; it keeps the soldier in touch with their progress." (It is not uncommon for mothers still nursing their children to be deployed. Since many of the mothers in the military are single mothers—women in the military are twice as likely as men to be single parents—many luckless children are left with no parents.)

GEORGE NEUMAYR is the executive editor of *The American Spectator*.

EXPLORING THE ISSUE

Should Women Serve in Military Combat Positions?

Critical Thinking and Reflection

1. What barriers to women's full participation in combat roles remain?
2. How should Congress address current law concerning the draft and Selective Service?
3. Are there any areas of combat or military service that *should* remain unavailable to women? Why or why not?
4. How should the military classify pregnancy for female soldiers?

Is There Common Ground?

In January 2013, Defense Secretary Leon Panetta announced that the Pentagon would lift the ban on women in combat and take steps to open previously off-limit frontline positions to women. The change in policy does not mean that all combat positions with all services will be lifted immediately. Each branch has the opportunity to make a case for retaining bans on certain positions as the new policy is phased in between 2013 and 2016. The reaction from government officials reflected changing notions about women's roles in society and the evolution in how women have served the country over the last decade.

> "Not every woman makes a good soldier, but not every man makes a good soldier. So women will compete," said Rep. Loretta Sanchez, D-Calif. "We're not asking that standards be lowered. We're saying that if they can be effective and they can be a good soldier or a good Marine in that particular operation, then give them a shot."

—(Baldor, 2013)

Women military leaders also noted that the policy change was long overdue, especially in light of twenty-first century military reality:

> Retired Air Force Colonel Martha McSally, the first woman to fly in combat, told *American Thinker* that opening up roles "Is lining up with the reality what is really happening. Women have come back wounded and have paid the ultimate sacrifice. In the Iraq and Afghanistan Wars we saw that women were not allowed to be assigned to any direct combat units, but there was not a restriction for them being attached to ground combat units. Medics and dog handlers, for example, have been attached to infantry units. Take, for example, Monica Brown, a woman medic who served

with a cavalry unit in a remote Pakistan province and was awarded the Silver Star in 2007 for risking her life to shield and treat her wounded comrades. She was placed in that position because there was no other medic and went out on combat patrols days at a time. A few days after receiving the award she was pulled out because of the restrictions of women in direct combat roles. This shows how very confusing, inefficient, and not effective the past policy has been".

—(Cooper, 2013)

Women in the military will continue to face challenges as each restriction is lifted and new ground is broken across different service branches. Each newly opened door will pose fresh questions for military officials to address while the American public becomes accustomed to the changing face of the nation's armed forces.

Additional Resources

Baldor, L. (2013, January 23). "Women in Combat: Leon Panetta Removes Military Ban, Opening Front-Line Positions." *The Huffington Post.* Retrieved from: www.huffingtonpost.com/2013/01/23/women-in-combat_n_2535954.html

Cooper, E. (2013, February 21). "Women in Combat: The Soldiers Speak." *American Thinker.* Retrieved from: http://www.americanthinker.com/2013/02/women_in_combat_the_soldiers_speak.html

Baker, K.J.M. (2012). "Female Soldiers Sue for Their Right to Fight in Combat." *Jezebel.* Retrieved from: http://jezebel.com/5913015/female-soldiers-sue-for-their-right-to-fight-in-combat

Create Central

www.mhhe.com/createcentral

Internet References . . .

Alliance For National Defense

http://www.4militarywomen.org/Women_in_Combat.
htm

Selected, Edited, and with Issue Framing Material by:
Rachel Pienta, *Valdosta State University*

ISSUE

Can Sex Work Be Empowering?

YES: Peter A. Newman, from "Reflections on Sonagachi: An Empowerment-Based HIV-Preventive Intervention for Female Sex Workers in West Bengal, India," *Women's Studies Quarterly* (vol. 31, no. 1, Spring/Summer 2003)

NO: Jeffery P. Dennis, from "Women Are Victims, Men Make Choices: The Invisibility of Men and Boys in the Global Sex Trade," *Gender Issues* (March 2008)

Learning Outcomes

As you read the issue, focus on the following points:

- Can an individual find self-preserving tools in a demeaning and harmful work environment such as the sex work industry?
- How can heteronormative stereotypes contribute to exploitation?

ISSUE SUMMARY

YES: Peter Newman examines sex work and the issue of empowerment within a framework of workers' rights. Newman discusses how female sex workers' autonomy and individual agency are impacted by the implementation of a harm reduction strategy aimed at giving women tools to first safeguard their health and ultimately to make personal choices as conscious actors engaging in a self-determinative process.

NO: Jeffery Dennis examines the double standard of current research on the global sex trade. In his article, Dennis notes that language denoting male and female sex workers differs by gender and that men seem to be the invisible laborers in the sex work industry.

In any discussion on sex work, it is important to draw distinctions on how people enter the sex work industry. Issues of agency and empowerment are rendered moot points when individuals are sold or coerced into modern day slavery.

The United Nations Office on Drugs and Crime provides a definition of what it means to buy and sell humans as a commodity, whether for sex work or other forms of servitude:

> *Trafficking in Persons as the recruitment, transportation, transfer, harbouring or receipt of persons, by means of the threat or use of force or other forms of coercion, of abduction, of fraud, of deception, of the abuse of power or of a position of vulnerability or of the giving or receiving of payments or benefits to achieve the consent of a person having control over another person, for the purpose of exploitation. Exploitation shall include, at a minimum, the exploitation of the prostitution of others or other forms of sexual exploitation, forced labour or services, slavery or practices similar to slavery, servitude or the removal of organs.*

—(United Nations Office on Drugs and Crime, 2012)

In the United States and overseas, groups have organized to advocate for the rights of sex workers. Activists, advocates, and researchers adopt harm reduction and human rights models to address human rights and safety issues in the sex industry.

Factors contributing to the inequality and subordinate status of women have implications for how the experience of sex workers differs by gender. Perceived experience by observers and lived experience within the industry are also impacted by cultural constructions of gender and sex stratification.

Research suggests that local policies focused on addressing sex work as a social evil subject to criminal prosecution contribute to the victimization of sex industry workers. For example, if the presence of condoms is viewed as a marker of sex solicitation then sex workers will avoid the use of condoms in an effort to mask the criminality of the transaction.

The underlying social issues that propel any individual into sex work include factors such as social position, restricted access to education, scarcity of other income earning opportunities, and a general lack of life opportunities all present reasons for voluntary entry into the sex trade. Coercion and other forms of bondage that contribute to human trafficking pose other challenges to sex workers' relative social autonomy and empowerment.

In "Reflections on Sonagachi: An Empowerment-Based HIV-Preventive Intervention for Female Sex Workers in West Bengal, India," Peter Newman examines sex work within a workers' rights framework in order to analyze the effectiveness of a "harm reduction" model applied to an HIV-prevention community intervention program.

In "Women Are Victims, Men Make Choices: The Invisibility of Men and Boys in the Global Sex Trade," Jeffery Dennis suggests that men in the sex work industry are perceived as empowered actors with personal agency. His analysis of the relative invisibility of men and boys in discourse on the global sex trade examines the possibility that heteronormative stereotypes contribute to the dearth of attention given to potential male exploitation and victimization.

YES ⬅

Peter A. Newman

Reflections on Sonagachi: An Empowerment-Based HIV-Preventive Intervention for Female Sex Workers in West Bengal, India

India is second only to South Africa in the number of persons diagnosed with HIV/AIDS, with an estimated 4 million HIV infected persons. Nevertheless, overall HIV seroprevalence in India remains relatively low, estimated at about 1%. With annual sexually transmitted disease (STD) incidence at 5%, however, the potential increase in the HIV epidemic is staggering. Accordingly, India has been designated one of five nations worldwide in which HIV/AIDS poses a national security threat.

Early reports of HIV/AIDS in India were largely among female sex workers in the south. HIV spread rapidly among sex workers in major Indian cities; by the late 1990s, it was estimated that 80% to 95% of HIV seropositive persons in most major Indian cities were sex workers. At present, HIV seroprevalence rates are 50% and higher among sex workers in Delhi, Pune, and Chennai. Yet in Calcutta, a gateway to the Golden Triangle, the nexus of many national truck routes, and home to an extensive red light district, the HIV seroprevalence rate among sex workers is estimated at 11.9%. This stark contrast seems to be the result of a model HIV-prevention program started in Calcutta in 1991, the Sonagachi Project.

The Sonagachi Project has achieved worldwide recognition, including through World Health Organization (WHO) acknowledgment and funding and coverage in the New York Times, for its innovative approach to public health. The cornerstone of Sonagachi is workers' rights. Sex work is viewed as a valid profession, akin to any other, and sex workers are viewed as providing a valuable service to society. As workers, they merit protection from violence, harassment, STDs, and other occupational safety and health risks. The establishment of the Sonagachi Project was the undertaking of Dr. Smarajit Jana, whose training as a physician in occupational health helped to frame his vision of the initial program.

How this simple-sounding yet revolutionary-certainly for India, if not for many developed nations as well-proposition of workers' rights is translated into practice in the form of Sonagachi may provide valuable lessons for public health among sex workers in other societies, particularly in the face of the HIV/AIDS pandemic.

Sex Work

Understanding sex work as a profession is a necessary premise for adopting a workers' rights approach to HIV prevention among sex workers. The status of sex work, however, is a complex and contested issue, not least because of traditional religious, legal, and ethical injunctions against it. It should be noted, as well, that several feminist authors have proposed convincing arguments against seeing sex work as simply another profession. As someone trained in clinical social work and health psychology who has worked firsthand with clients traumatized by sexual abuse and violence, I have an ambivalent perspective on equating sex work with other professions. Still, having seen the ravages of HIV/AIDS both in developed and developing countries over the past 2 decades, as well as observing numerous approaches to prevention, I have developed a strong affinity for the approach known as "harm reduction." It is in the context of a harm reduction approach to HIV prevention that I understand the Sonagachi Project and its equating sex work with other professions. Furthermore, my role with Sonagachi over the course of 2 years was to implement and oversee a community trial of the Sonagachi intervention as an HIV-prevention program; the focus of my work was to evaluate the program's effectiveness.

Harm Reduction

Harm reduction evolved throughout the past 20 years as an approach to HIV prevention. The initial focus was minimization of HIV risk and harm for injecting drug users. Rather than requiring injecting drug users (IDUs) to immediately cease their drug use or face the likely risk of HIV infection, particularly in the context of a paucity of drug treatment programs, a harm reduction approach suggested IDUs be educated about how HIV is transmitted and how to avoid it. Injecting drug use, per se, does not lead to HIV infection; sharing unclean needles and other drug paraphernalia, however, are very efficient means of transmitting the virus. By teaching IDUs how to clean their "works," distributing bleach, and making available clean syringes, several cities around the world were able to curtail new HIV infections among IDUs. A harm reduction approach would also advocate having drug treatment programs available and encouraging IDUs to make use of them as a further step in the minimization of harm.

Thus, rather than posing the equations IDU = AIDS and stopping IDU = preventing AIDS, as the only options, a harm reduction approach offers individuals the opportunity to move their behavior to the next-lowest level of possible harm. Drug users may engage in injecting drug use in a safer way, one in which they exponentially lower the risk of HIV (and Hepatitis C) infection. Of course, there are other risks to injecting drug use that are not immediately addressed by the use of clean syringes, but the latter do a great service in minimizing the transmission of HIV, which results in tremendous morbidity and mortality.

Sonagachi is not avowedly a harm reduction program; rather, it is strongly aligned with an empowerment and social justice perspective. The concept of harm reduction, in general, has remained largely tied to illicit drug use. There is no reason, however, why harm reduction cannot be applied to other populations and health risks, such as the sexual transmission of HIV. Importantly, empowerment and harm reduction paradigms are not mutually exclusive; in fact, they may complement one another. Part of the credo, and efficacy, of harm reduction is that of respecting the individual's right to self-determination. This right is also a core concept of empowerment. An individual who is empowered to make her own decisions will be much more able to protect her health and to avoid HIV to enact harm reduction strategies.

Paramount in many HIV prevention models, most of which focus on the individual level of behavior change, is the underlying, but not always acknowledged, assumption that the individual has enough self-respect, feeling of self-worth, and will to live that she is motivated to implement efforts to protect herself from HIV. Sonagachi offers condoms and HIV/STD education, but also as part of its program works to build self-esteem, self-respect, and modes for increasing self-reliance. Along the lines of harm reduction, the Sonagachi Project aims to reduce the immediate harm to sex workers from HIV and STDs by empowering them to protect themselves against HIV. Characterizing sex work as a profession is not incongruent with building options for other means of subsistence for those sex workers who choose to and who are capable of pursuing them. And, contrariwise, it seems disingenuous and incongruous to on the one hand tell these women that they are valued and cared for, and on the other hand that they are engaged in an ignominious and shameful means of making money, or to solely focus on ways to get out of sex work.

On a personal level, my conceptualization of Sonagachi in a harm reduction framework helped me to suspend reservations that I had about unquestioningly equating sex work with other professions. Additionally, as a white male from the United States working largely with Indian women in a well-established and indigenous prevention program, I took as my first stance one of listening and understanding rather than of presumptuously offering advice or judgment.

The Sonagachi Method

Sonagachi seeks to empower sex workers by simultaneously working on individual, group, and structural levels. While individual women are seen as potential agents of change in their own lives and for their own community, the intervention program also effects change on a structural level to facilitate individual- and group-level growth and empowerment. The different modes of empowerment become mutually reinforcing as the sex workers themselves assume increasingly greater roles and responsibility in program administration and decision making.

Individual Empowerment

Peer educators are the cornerstone of Sonagachi. Initially, women who are seen as having leadership abilities, and who are often more literate than their peers, are asked by Sonagachi workers to participate in educational workshops. Workshops are held on HIV, STDs and their prevention, condom use, and basic STD and HIV care in an environment in which sex work is addressed as a profession. A core of peer educators are engaged in training workshops, which also involve exercises that build individual self-esteem and group cohesion-factors that are at least as important as knowledge. Peer educators subsequently conduct street-level outreach in their own communities to offer basic education and skill building to other sex workers. Peer educators report back to team leaders of Sonagachi, who offer feedback, ongoing training and support, and quality control. Gradually, new women who evince similar characteristics to the initial peer leaders are brought into intensive peer educator workshops, and in turn they permeate ever widening pathways into red light districts.

Modeling is a vital process in the peer education method. Many women who never received formal schooling and remain illiterate are offered basic information about health and well-being. Many sex workers, not unlike the rest of Indian society, have misconceptions about HIV and its transmission (e.g., sexual intercourse with a virgin can cure the male of HIV; risks from casual contact). At least as important as their having accurate information, the sex workers see women like themselves taking on leadership positions, learning to read and write, being trusted with responsibility, and taking home a paycheck from a recognized nongovernmental organization (NGO). Engendering hope and allowing others to envision themselves as having potential through the modeling process are potent mechanisms of empowerment. In the process, women are also instilled with the feeling that someone values them; this may be a revelation for someone who has understood her position in society as immovable and largely as a conduit for the needs of others. Indeed, the early focus on sex workers, if not women in general, in U.S. HFV-prevention efforts largely focused on women's roles as vectors for infection (i.e., to men), not as valid and valued consumers of public health in their own right.

Another vital component of the Sonagachi method is conscientization, a process described and promulgated by Paolo Freire. Conscientization involves seeing oneself as part of a whole, as part of a context and a system, rather than as a victim of one's individual fate, as if unrelated to structural context. Furthermore, one is not an unchangeable part of a fixed system; both oneself and the system are malleable. Conscientization involves both adopting this mental framework and taking action (praxis) to change one's position in the system and to change the system itself. Through education, modeling, the inculcation of self-worth, and the building of hope and positive expectancies (e.g., "I can learn how to read"; "my children may be able to attend school"), sex workers are facilitated in moving along a path of empowerment.

Through individual empowerment, women not only come to understand HIV and its transmission, but also develop increasing motivation and capacity to implement condom use, sometimes in the face of active resistance from male clients. Along the lines of Conscientization, a woman becomes more able to perceive her right and ability to implement condom use rather than accept HIV disease as her "natural" or deserved fate as a sex worker.

Group Empowerment

In addition to building self-esteem and self-worth-because one is engaged in a valid form of work, and through becoming a change agent rather than a passive object-the gradual destigmatization of sex work operates powerfully on the group level. Stigma is, in general, anti-thetical to HIV prevention, as it is precisely disempowering. Stigma acts as one deterrent to sex workers' (or any other stigmatized group's) meeting together in public, or advocating for themselves, as in so doing the sex workers call increasing attention to themselves on that dimension in which they are stigmatized, in turn, garnering disapprobation, and sometimes violence, from others.

Group empowerment involves building cohesion and a sense of solidarity with other sex workers. In becoming more able to identify oneself, with evolving pride, as a member of a group, albeit a disenfranchised group, one can experience oneself as engaged in a legitimate struggle for human rights and social justice. Sonagachi has conducted several stadium-size gatherings of sex workers from all over India to promote the struggle for legal rights and social justice. These gatherings are tremendous sources of pride and accomplishment for the sex workers-and

the Sonagachi intervention staff-and serve to powerfully combat stigma.

Group empowerment is also key to HIV prevention among sex workers. Even with adequate knowledge of HIV and its transmission, and a growing sense of self-worth, there is an ever present economic temptation for sex workers to forego condom use. Some clients offer at least double the going rate to engage in sexual intercourse without a condom. Additionally, if a woman refuses to forego condoms, there is a risk to her business, as the male client may simply approach other sex workers with the same offer until he succeeds. The initial worker may lose a client, a vital source of income. In order for HIV education and prevention to work in practice, sex workers must band together in a united front that makes condom use a given. As a result, condom use is not at odds with economic survival but is, rather, coextensive with physical health and economic well-being.

Structural Empowerment

As potent as are the processes of individual and group empowerment, numerous entrenched and powerful interests saw themselves as benefiting from the status quo of sex workers in Calcutta. As in other contexts around the world, most sex workers retain less than half the money generated from their own work, frequently much less. Some female sex workers in India (chukrees) are engaged in a form of bonded labor and earn only basic room and board for years as they pay off their debt to the madam to buy their freedom. Numerous stakeholders in the process-madams who run the brothels, landlords who rent the rooms and the brothel property, male clients, police (who often receive kickbacks), local politicians (who may receive money indirectly), local crime syndicates that often control aspects of the sex trade and receive protection money-benefit from the sex work industry. It would be naive to expect an individual or group disenfranchised because of poverty, social class, sexism, and stigma to subvert the entire power structure through individual or group empowerment processes alone. Thus, in addition to the peer education process and the building of group solidarity, Sonagachi engages in a systematic program of social advocacy and structural change.

Initially, Dr. Jana, a respected physician, engaged the help of his colleagues in the local government and public health infrastructure to gain limited support for his vision of a noncoercive approach to STD/HIV prevention, based on an occupational health model. Dr. Jana opened a clinic to serve sex workers, one in which, for the first time for many, the women were treated with dignity and respect. He encouraged sex workers to undergo HIV testing, avoiding coercive tactics, which had previously been tried in Calcutta and had failed. As word of the clinic spread, sex workers brought their friends and colleagues-and children. Interestingly, many of the women described a desire to provide for and build a better life for their children as their primary motivation for engaging in sex work.

Dr. Jana used his insider status with government and health officials to gain credibility and support for the program. Over time, he lent his status to the disenfranchised group to open doors and build their credibility. It is arguable whether any sex worker would have initially had the connections or credibility to support the establishment of such a program. As I worked intermittently in Calcutta and met with Dr. Jana in 2000 and 2001, I never witnessed his attending a press conference or meeting with officials accompanied by less than three to five sex workers, who had become the fabric and voice of Sonagachi.

An important key to the evolving empowerment process is for more-enfranchised members, and often the initiators of the program, to cede power and responsibility to the initial clients. That Dr. Jana has been in Dhaka, Bangladesh, for several years working on implementing a similar program there is not incidental, as the Sonagachi Project in Calcutta is largely managed and administered by interventionists and volunteers, many of them present or former sex workers.

Another aspect of structural empowerment is meetings held by Sonagachi program staff, some of whom have higher education and who come from higher social classes in Indian society, with local politicians, police, and madams. These interventionists include sex workers among them and are accompanied by present sex workers to the meetings. An important element of the Sonagachi success was that of gaining the support of the madams, all women, who are closest in the hierarchy to the sex workers and are thereby responsible for many important decisions in the sex workers' lives. For HIV prevention, that entails decisions around condom use. Early in the program, and as now replicated in other locales, the interventionist and sex worker team offered HIV/AIDS education to the madams and explained how it was in the madams' economic interest to have healthy, non-HIV-infected workers. A small investment in condoms would reap greater profits for the madams in the end. The madams are a key element in the success of Sonagachi. Many have engaged in sex work themselves, and the program includes an element of solidarity building with and empowerment of madams. The aim, at least initially, is not to usurp the power of the madams, but to respect their authority and good sense.

As the program evolved, teams of interventionists and sex workers also met with local police to gain their support. To win over police, Sonagachi has used a mix of education, acknowledgment of police authority, and threat: no police station wants a band of hundreds or thousands of sex workers protesting outside. I witnessed the success of these strategies during the replication of the Sonagachi program for our research project in several sites in North Bengal. The intervention team approached local authorities with a mix of education and the threat of bringing a contingent of dozens of sex workers from the "big city" to a rural village. In rural North Bengal, local politicians initially showed mixed reactions. One local mayor, after a few educational visits with the intervention

team, was supportive of having a clinic for sex workers set up in his village. Leverage was less an issue in this case, as this local official had an earnest interest in anything that would benefit the health and well-being of his community. For other communities and politicians, the mix of gentle pressure from outside and the enlistment of local madams were more key to establishing a Sonagachi-type intervention.

Another element of structural empowerment evolved at a later stage of the Sonagachi Project in Calcutta. After years of outreach, there is now an identified group of male clients who are the main or "fixed" clients (babus) of some of the sex workers (not all sex workers have such a relationship) and who are actively engaged in promoting condom use, safety, and respect for sex workers. This dimension of Sonagachi, like many others, was not initially envisioned as part of any blueprint for success; rather, through the empowerment process, a small handful of these men became interested in the program and began to organize male clients.

All these elements of structural empowerment provide opportunities as well as rays of hope for the local sex workers. Increased police law enforcement and brutality against sex workers might dampen spirits and scare women away from participating; when the initiation of the program is accompanied, however, by even a slight decrease in these aversive elements, positive change is facilitated. Gradually, as is evident in Sonagachi in Calcutta, the sex workers themselves become the primary agents of advocacy. Thus, from the program's inception and throughout its evolution, individual, group, and structural empowerment have been mutually reinforcing, with different components and methods depending on the developmental stage of the program and the regional sociopolitical context. Early on, more active participation was needed by outside leaders and professionals; as the program evolved, the initial leaders needed to cede power and decision making to the sex workers as the workers assumed ever greater roles in the program's implementation and direction.

Conclusion

Sonagachi has been highly successful as a sustained, 12-year HFV-preventive intervention in Calcutta, apparently resulting in vastly lower rates of HIV infection among sex workers there as compared with most other major Indian cities. It is nonetheless important to acknowledge that in facilitating this grassroots social movement, as was accomplished by Dr. Jana, there was no implementation plan, blueprint, or schedule that existed from the program's inception. The principles of empowerment enacted in a multidimensional spectrum-on individual, group, and structural levels-and the underlying premise of sex work as a valid profession, may well function in other locales, but the specific dimensions of the evolving program depend largely on the local context. Different communities of sex workers in different, and even in the same, countries may have disparate needs in growing a Sonagachi-type project. Trust and relationship building, between sex workers and program professionals, among sex workers, and among staff, and an earnest commitment to letting the initial objects of the intervention, the sex workers, assume greater responsibility and decision making seem to be crucial components of the Sonagachi success.

Now, more than a decade into the evolution of Sonagachi, the program has established a credit union for sex workers. Paradoxically, sex work remains illegal in India; yet a worker's collaborative credit union provides low-cost loans to sex workers so they may begin a small business or for emergencies. Our university-based research program, in fact, used the credit union to make payments to the Indian team to implement our joint project. Again, no one in the program would say that they envisioned such a credit union in 1991 as part of Sonagachi. And in attempting to replicate the program elsewhere in India and Bangladesh, a credit union is not seen as an imperative. In Calcutta, however, the credit union is a powerful mechanism in support of HIV prevention and empowerment. Given that many women's primary motivation is to support their children to provide them with a better life, even the woman most well educated in HIV and its transmission may be tempted to forego condom use when her child is sick, often for the chance to earn more money. Now women can borrow in such emergencies and save for such emergencies in the future. Economic self-reliance is another powerful ingredient in empowerment. Additionally, while Sonagachi conveys a clear message that sex work is valid work, that these women are valued members of society, the sex workers are offered the opportunity to explore and develop other talents, as is consistent with a harm reduction approach. If a sex worker wants to begin a small basket-weaving business, for example, she may negotiate a loan with the credit union at a rate more akin

to that for other Indian citizens than the usurious rates charged by crime syndicates.

Finally, another important but often overlooked aspect of empowerment is celebration, which also acts as a form of positive reinforcement for success. In the past 5 years, a cultural wing of Sonagachi has begun. Komal Gandhar celebrates sex workers in song and dance. Several Sonagachi staff and sex workers recently participated in an international meeting of sex workers in Thailand, at which they gave a performance and participated in workshops promoting a workers' rights agenda for sex workers.

The Sonagachi Project, which offers a way for sex workers to go from being disenfranchised and stigmatized individuals to being empowered agents who see themselves as part of an international human rights movement, is one of several oases of hope in the worldwide struggle in the face of the HIV/AIDS pandemic. One of the foremost lessons of Sonagachi for HIV prevention, particularly in addressing women, sex workers, or other disenfranchised communities, may be that risk behavior (e.g., unprotected sex) is only the tip of the iceberg. As a successful HIV-preventive intervention for female sex workers that has sustained itself for a decade, Sonagachi continues to address multiple needs among sex workers as defined by sex workers. Not contracting HIV becomes a subgoal rather than the overarching agenda of the intervention. The avoidance of HIV is a traditional public health agenda; Sonagachi may push the envelope by envisioning a broader public health outlook that encompasses human rights and psychosocial and economic well-being, in addition to physical health.

PETER A. NEWMAN has published over 60 peer-reviewed articles and has received over a dozen external research grants.

Jeffery P. Dennis

 NO

Women Are Victims, Men Make Choices: The Invisibility of Men and Boys in the Global Sex Trade

Introduction

Male sex workers are easy to spot anywhere in the world. They lounge outside a doughnut shop on Highland Street in Los Angeles and a Lebanese cafe near the Center Pompidou in Paris, in an arcade in Prague, and in a sex club in Cleveland. They pretend to study the train schedules at Pennsylvania Station in Manhattan and the shop windows at the Grand Place in Brussels. They mingle with the crowds at York Minster; they dance at strip clubs in Dayton. On a certain street in Tijuana, any man or boy who makes eye contact with you is for sale. They wait in Internet chatrooms for men whose profile contains the keyword "generous." They post advertisements as escorts, masseurs, or models, or openly as sex workers; one Internet directory lists over 5000 in the USA, searchable by physical attributes, services provided, and price.

Yet they are almost completely ignored by social service agencies, administrative bodies, the mass media, and scholarship. The rigor of academic arguments and the immediacy of fieldwork usually allow scholars to qualify or even reject popular stereotypes, but in this case they do not: scholarly discussions of sex workers nearly always specify "she," "her," or "the woman," as if no man ever sold his sexual services. Scholarly discussions about children exploited through prostitution nearly always specify "she," "her," or "the girl," as if no boy has ever been exploited. This study will investigate the extent of the invisibility of men and boys in scholarly discussions of the global sex trade, and suggest explanations in the combined discourses of Orientalism, sexism, and heteronormativity.

Method

To locate articles concerning the global sex trade as a social and political phenomenon, a search was performed on JSTOR and SocInfo, the two largest social science databases, for articles in peer-reviewed journals, published between January 2002 and March 2007, with any of several keywords or phrases in the abstracts: prostitution, prostitutes, sex workers, sex work, male prostitution, male prostitutes, male sex workers. After reviews, opinion pieces and historical studies were excluded, 166 articles remained. . . .

The Sex Worker as "She"

As Table 1 indicates, 84% of the articles in the sample discussed only female sex workers, 10% only male, and 6% both:

Some of the unequal distribution probably results from the belief that a negligible proportion of sex workers are male; authors reason that most clients are men, straight men outnumber gay men, and surely only gay men patronize male sex workers. Gay men actually comprise 5–10% of the male population, hardly a "negligible proportion" to begin with, but the demand for male sex workers is by no means contained within gay communities. In many countries, sexual practices are conceptualized according to roles played by the partners (active/passive or masculine/feminine) rather than their genders, so the client's sexual identity is irrelevant to the transaction. Even in the West, men who self-identify as heterosexual often patronize male sex workers. They may believe that a transvestite or pre-operative transsexual is female; they may be on the "down low," expressing same-sex desire without a gay identity; or they may believe that same-sex behavior does not count as infidelity to their wives or girlfriends. Thus, there is a significant demand for male sex workers. Men comprise about 20% of the individuals arrested as vendors of sexual services in the USA each year, and about 30% of those in France. Since the police often mistake male sex workers for MSM, men seeking same-sex liaisons without a monetary exchange, the actual male proportion is probably higher. . . .

Table 1

Gender of the Sex Worker Population

	N	%
Female assumed	111	67
Female specified	28	17
Male specified	17	10
Both female and male	10	6

Trafficking in Women

Table 2 depicts the gender assigned to the sex workers in the 141 articles that specified a location of the population studied. A chi-square analysis was unreliable because the variables were both nominal and some cells contained only a few cases (or no cases at all), but a nominal-by-nominal analysis yielded a contingency coefficient of 0.369 ($p = 0.004$), suggesting a high association between the independent and dependent variables.

In world-system theory, the core states, the colonial powers of Western Europe and their auxiliaries (the USA, Canada, Australia, and New Zealand), controlled almost all of the world's population for nearly 500 years, and still exercise a great deal of dominance in politics, economics, technology, and mass media. The periphery (sub-Saharan Africa, East and South Asia, and the Middle East) provided capital for the core, and today they continue to provide human capital, in the form of millions of low-wage immigrants, guest workers, and sex workers. Every year, 500,000–800,000 people are trafficked across international borders; some go to work in factories and farms, but many enter the sex trade. Men, women, and children of both sexes can and do become sex workers, yet none of the 33 articles on trafficking specified a male population, and only one specified both genders. Two others dismissed the male victims in a single phrase ("women, girls, and a smaller number of men and boys"), and for the rest, trafficking in men and boys simply does not occur. Mameli writes about the "illegal trafficking of human beings," but does not mention male human beings at all. Huda discusses" human trafficking" in Lebanon, but likewise equates "human" with "woman only."

One of the most pervasive of the ideologies, protocols, and social practices developed to maintain and justify the core's exploitation of the periphery was Orientalism, the Western depiction of the colonized "native" as soft, passive, savage, and childlike, requiring surveillance and supervision. Several scholars have noted the gender-polarized frame of Orientalism, the male-coded European or American exerting a controlling gaze over a female-coded native. The lack of discussion of the male victims of trafficking may represent a gendering of Orientalism, the presumption that the trafficked human being, usually from a periphery state, is by definition female.

Of the articles concerning female sex workers (either specified or assumed), 54% located the populations in core states, and 28% in periphery states. However, of the articles concerning men, 80% located the populations in core states, and 7% in the periphery (a single article about rent-boys in Thailand), even though male sex workers are commonplace in nearly every periphery country. The location of the male prostitute in the West replicates the heterosexist notion that the heterosexual desire and practice is the natural state of humanity. Thus, the native, untainted by civilized "decadence," is always heterosexual; as Rinaldi writes of local attitudes in Zimbabwe, "Gay? We don't have that here." Since same-sex practice supposedly occurs only in the West, male sex work is perceived as a strictly Western phenomenon, a form of recreation for gay sophisticates in Manhattan, irrelevant to the struggles of the "real" (i.e., female) sex workers in the brothels of Mumbai.

When the clients are from periphery or semi-periphery countries, the vendors they patronize are always assumed female. Parrado et al. use the gender-neutral term "commercial sex workers," but then argue that their popularity among Hispanic immigrant men in North Carolina can be attributed to the "male-dominated immigrant flow," which "hinders the ability of migrants to find partners of the opposite sex." They thus contend that none of the immigrant men are gay or bisexual, or select providers on the basis of masculine/feminine or active/passive roles irrelevant to sexual orientation, in spite of ample documentation that such identities and practices exist in Hispanic communities. Luke studied informal sexual relationships in Kenya, specified as "male non-marital partnerships," temporary and unofficial, sometimes with a sex worker, sometimes not; but he offers no hint that any men ever create non-marital partnerships with other men, in spite of documentation that such partnerships are commonplace in sub-Saharan Africa.

The Ideal Type Is Female

None of the 29 articles in the Legality category (legal, philosophical, and theoretical studies) discussed both genders, and only one specified men. Five specified women, and the other 23, 79% of the total, simply assumed that sex workers are always female. Since there were no field observations or interviews, authors were free to discuss sex work as "an ideal type," a distillation of the many details of social life into what Max Weber calls "the one-sided accentuation of one or more points of view." This

Table 2

Location of the Sex Worker Population

	Female Only	Male Only	Both
Core			
Western Europe (%)	29	7	56
North America (%)	29	67	11
Australia (%)	6	7	22
Semi-periphery			
Eastern Europe (%)	6	0	0
Latin America (%)	3	13	0
Periphery			
Africa (%)	7	0	0
Asia (%)	21	7	11
N	117	15	9

sort of typification is necessarily reductive, often excluding escorts, exotic dancers, performers in adult videos, and other sorts of "indoor" workers, even though they comprise 80–90% of all erotic laborers, as well as individuals who casually offer sex in exchange for food, drugs, or a place to spend the night, even though they surely outnumber the professionals who proffer formal verbal contracts. It also reduces the many possible gendered transactions (male, female, and transgendered vendors, male, female, and transgendered clients) to a simple model of male clients and female vendors.

Only one article in the Legality category, "A Theory of Prostitution" by Edlund and Korn, addressed its exclusion of "homosexual prostitution." The authors assert that prostitution is by definition "low-skill, labor-intensive, female," and thus can be explained as the result of male attempts to maintain their social dominance by regulating and oppressing women. When men purchase the services of male prostitutes, they do not contribute to the regulation and oppression of women; thus they can be safely excluded from further consideration.

Most of the other authors of articles in the Legality category found no need to justify their exclusion of male sex workers, as if they were not aware that they were excluding anyone. Discussions of sex work are usually informed by heteronormativity, the cognitive universalization of heterosexual desire and practice. So powerful is the heteronormative definition of "male" as "one who desires the female" that evidence of male–male liaisons is "considered merely an unusual aberration, sometimes mentioned as an afterthought but more often ignored altogether". Thus, scholars who write about the theoretical, ethical, or legal aspects of sex work literally do not recall that male sex workers exist, or else frame them as a trivial aside, irrelevant to what prostitution or sex work is "really" about. . . .

Female Coercion, Male Choice

Table 3 portrays the use of the term "prostitute," implying coercion and degradation, and "sex worker," implying active choice of a work situation, in the titles of the articles in the sample, excluding those that use both or some other term (contingency coefficient 0.259, $p = 0.022$).

The term "prostitute" or its equivalents was preferred in 66% of the articles concerning women (specified or assumed), but in only 25% of the articles concerning men, while 75% of the articles concerning men preferred the

Table 3

Expressions of Agency

	Female Only	Male Only	Both
Prostitute (%)	66	25	71
Sex worker (%)	34	75	29
N	87	12	7

term "sex worker" or its equivalents. The implication is clear: women are forced to participate in sexual exchanges, but men are not.

Even the articles concerning women that did use the term "sex worker" usually depended on a discourse of coercion: the women were victimized, brutalized, forced, commodified. Pochagina discusses the factors that "force women to become involved in the sex business." McKeganey argues that "it would be inaccurate to use the language of choice to describe the women's routes into prostitution." Conversely, articles concerning male sex workers usually involved the discourse of choice. They were never forced or coerced; they made career decisions. Indeed, sex work was often framed as a pleasurable, positive use of their talents.

While some high-profile, high-salaried male sex workers do describe idyllic suburban childhoods, with academic and sports accomplishments at prestigious universities, and a decision to earn some extra money by capitalizing on their superior physiques, most enter the world of sex work through desperation. They are unlikely to be literally coerced by romantic partners or pimps, but their "decisions" are hardly based on a comparison of options. Many recall abusive childhoods, no opportunity to acquire legitimate marketable skills, days or months of living on the street, and a choice of sex work or starvation.

An allied discourse frames female but not male sex work as degrading, causing deep feelings of shame and remorse. Some commentators argue that women are socialized to view their sexuality as a precious commodity, and men as a form of recreation; thus men are simply less likely to feel shame or remorse over their sexual activities. However, this binary assessment oversimplifies the many possible meanings assigned to sexual acts. Many male sex workers, especially juveniles, are homophobic, despising themselves for the "failed" masculinity that their acts imply. Those who are gay are rarely out and proud, rarely the "New Gay Teenagers" who come out at age 13 to fully supportive, fully aware parents, join Gay-Straight Alliances in their middle schools, and petition their high schools to add Queer Studies to the curriculum. They often grew up among homophobic parents and peers, and in fact often enter sex work after being ejected from their homes for being gay; they may believe that their sexual acts brand them as inferior, sinful, wrong, unwelcome in the "normal" world. Even those who are gay and self-actualized may easily feel that they are being "used" and therefore degraded by the sexual exchange.

Discussions of sex work are inextricably bound up in discussions of patriarchy, of men subjugating, objectifying, purchasing, possessing, and degrading the female body in order to maintain or increase their political, social, and economic dominance; prostitution thus becomes a form of slavery, even when it is putatively consensual, a form of degradation even when it is framed as "labor." Miriam notes that "men create the demand, women are the supply." Letiche and van Mens state that "women are necessary in the exchange economy as status objects and in the operation of male desire," promoting the heteronormative notion that "male desire" is precisely the same thing as "desire for women," unaware that a significant proportion of the male population desires men, prefers men as providers in economic transactions, or finds the gender of the provider irrelevant.

The inclusion of the male body as an object of possession, objectification, and degradation by a man would disrupt the assumption that sex exchanges are by nature heterosexual, that the power differential is part of a heterosexual "sexual contract" that forms the basis of all social relations. Therefore, when male prostitutes are mentioned at all, they must be active, agentive, capitalizing on their talents, running their own business, never coerced, never degraded. Only women "can" be objectified.

Protecting Youth

Considering the vast public concern over the sexual exploitation of children and the overrepresentation of children and adolescents in the sex worker population, it is surprising that juveniles were underrepresented in the articles studied. While many empirical reports describe the extent of child prostitution, scholarship tends to mention juveniles in passing, if at all, and present the sex worker as an adult woman. Only 15 articles specified a juvenile population to the exclusion of adults; ten of these concerned girls only, one boys only, and four both genders. Thus, girls were ten times more likely than boys to be the subjects of scholarly scrutiny and intervention, even though when one uses the scholarly definition of prostitution as any sex for money exchange rather than the contractual street-hustling of the popular imagination, more adolescent boys than adolescent girls participate, at least in Western countries.

The teenage boy sex worker is thus subject to redoubled invisibility, his gender and his age causing him to virtually vanish from scholarly scrutiny. Scott notes that male prostitution was conceptualized in the early years of the 20th century within the parameters of two newfound "social problems," homosexuality and adolescence: the male prostitute was envisioned as a young heterosexual boy being victimized by predatory gay adults. Today, however, the male prostitute is almost always depicted as a gay adult himself. Perhaps some scholars suffer from the heteronormative model of the child as by definition heterosexual, and shy away from acknowledging that gay boys exist, or that straight boys might participate in same-sex activity. Perhaps they presume that adolescent males cannot be coerced into sexual acts; if arousal occurs, then the act must be desired and consensual, and without arousal no sexual act can occur. However, it is more likely that they have again fallen prey to gender stereotypes, perceiving girls as soft, passive, fragile, and in need of intervention and support, but boys as hard and tough, able to take care of themselves.

Significantly, the articles that specified children usually limited their populations to teenagers, although one survey found that 25% of underaged prostitutes were prepubescent. By avoiding the younger children, specifically prepubescent boys, they could continue to maintain the cultural myth of the passive girl and the active boy, the girl who is victimized and brutalized by men and the boy who is ignored by men and therefore a free agent, his masculinity making him an active participant in every social milieu, using his talents to make his own way in the world.

Only Men Are Gay

The sexual orientation variable coded whether researchers in field studies gave any indication that they had asked or were aware of the sexual orientations of their respondents. No table is necessary, since only one of the articles concerning women did so. Sanders discusses how female sex workers adopt a "heterosexualized image" in order to better perform their sexual labor, even though some are in "long-term straight or gay relationships." The others either failed to report on the sexual orientations of the women or failed to inquire in the first place, as if the question was unnecessary, as if no lesbian or bisexual women exist, or none are sex workers. Dalla is quite thorough about demographics, recording the women's race, age, educational level, number of children, and marital status, but not their sexual orientation. Hwang and Bedford examine many factors, including age, education, pathways to prostitution, and various aberrant behaviors, but not sexual orientation, nor even same-sex behavior, as if lesbian activity simply does not exist.

The authors may presume that the sexual orientation of the female sex workers is irrelevant, since they are selling sex primarily to men regardless of whether they are interested in women in their private life, but more likely they are expressing the heteronormative position that everyone on earth is by definition heterosexual. McKay argues that female sex workers disrupt heteronormativity by feigning heterosexual desire for pay, thus calling attention to the artificiality and "constructedness" of heterosexual desire itself. In lieu of facing the possibility that heterosexual desire is not normal, natural, innate, and universal, that it can be performed, researchers fall back on the most heteronormative equations of "female" with "desiring men." Thus there are endless evocations of the female sex workers' "boyfriends," never "boyfriends and girlfriends," and "male partners," never "male or female partners."

However, every field research article concerning male sex workers, without exception, asked about their sexual orientation: what percentage was straight? What percentage gay? What percentage bisexual? What percentage questioning? Was there a connection between sexual orientation and type of service performed, or pathway into sex work, or drug use, or unprotected sex?

Researchers were particularly fascinated by the spectacle of straight men having sex with men for pay. Their comments sometimes suggest relief (at least they are not gay, they are not enjoying it) and sometimes disbelief (how can a man have a sexual encounter *without* enjoying it, without desiring his partner?). Female sex workers were never asked if they enjoyed their heterosexual activity. Perhaps if male sex workers can be presented as "really straight," not experiencing same-sex desire, then the presumption of universal heterosexuality might not be challenged.

Discussion

The invisibility of men and boys in discussions of the global sex trade may derive from nothing more profound than discomfort among heterosexuals scholars (and tenure committees and institutional review boards) over the acts that the men and boys are engaging in. The acts that female sex workers engage in can be understood as merely a coercive, degraded, brutalized form of acts that the heterosexual researchers have engaged in with their own husbands or wives; they depict a desire that heterosexual researchers themselves experience and can comprehend; but the acts of male sex workers are wholly alien, the desire they enact beyond the realm of what heterosexual researchers can envision. Thus the question then becomes not "why do men and boys have sex *for money*?" but "why do men and boys have sex *with men*?" For this reason, male sex workers are often lumped together with MSM, men who have sex with men without a monetary exchange; the part that requires explanation is not the remuneration, but the sex. Female sex workers are never lumped together with "women who have sex with men."

The remedy to the invisibility is not simply more articles, more research studies, more scholarly investment into the lives of the men and boys who saunter down Polk Street in San Francisco or Las Ramblas in Barcelona, who are pimped out of hustler bars in Houston or perform in erotic videos in Berlin. More research studies might still present the male sex worker as active, as in control, as a strong, powerful force more often victimizing than victimized. What is needed is more subtle and more difficult, a re-evaluation of scholarly preconceptions about male and female bodies, about objectification, about the inevitability of heterosexual identity and about the impossibility of same-sex desire.

References

Bell, S. (1994). *Reading, writing, and rewriting the prostitute body.* Bloomington: Indiana University Press.

Calhoun, T. C., & Weaver, G. (1996). Rational decision-making among male street prostitutes. *Deviant Behavior, 17*(2), 209–227.

Coleman, E. (1989). The development of male prostitute activity among gay and bisexual adolescents. *Journal of Homosexuality, 17*(1–2), 131–149.

Connell, R. W. (1995). *Masculinities.* Berkeley: University of California Press.

Dalla, R. (2002). Night moves: A qualitative investigation of street-level sex work. *Psychology of Women Quarterly, 26*(1), 63.

Davies, M., & Rogers, P. (2006). Perceptions of male victims in depicted sexual assaults: A review of the literature. *Aggression and Violent Behavior, 11*(4), 367–377.

Dorais, M. (2005). *Rent-boys: The world of male sex trade workers.* Me Gill-Queens University Press.

Edlund, L., & Korn, E. (2002). A theory of prostitution. *Journal of Political Economy, 110*(1), 181.

Estes, R. J., & Weiner, N. A. (2001). *The commercial sexual exploitation of children in the U.S., Canada, and Mexico.* Philadelphia: University of Pennsylvania.

Farley, M. (2004). Bad for the body, bad for the heart: Prostitution harms women even if legalized or decriminalized. *Violence Against Women, 10*(10), 1087–1125.

Federal Bureau of Investigation. (2006). *Unified Crime Reports.*

Finkelhor, D., & Ormrod, R. (2004). *Prostitution of juveniles: Patterns from NIBRS.* Washington, DC: Office of Justice Programs.

Finlinson, H., Colon, H., Robles, R., & Soto, M. (2006). Sexual identity formation and AIDS prevention: An exploratory study of non-gay-identified Puerto Rican MSM from working class neighborhoods. *AIDS and Behavior, 10*(5), 531–539.

Flowers, R. B. (2001). Runaway kids and teenage prostitution: America's lost, abandoned, and sexually exploited children. Westport, CT: Greenwood Press.

Friedman, M. (2003). *Strapped for cash: A history of American hustler culture.* San Francisco: Alyson Publications.

Huda, S. (2006). Human trafficking in Lebanon. *Forced Migration Review, 25,* 36.

Hwang, S., & Bedford, O. (2003). Precursors and pathways to adolescent prostitution in Taiwan. *Journal of Sex Research, 40*(2), 201.

Itiel, J. (1998). *A consumer's guide to male hustlers.* Binghamton, NY: Haworth Press.

Kesler, K. (2002). Is a feminist stance in support of prostitution possible? An exploration of current trends. *Sexualities, 5*(2), 219.

Lawrence, A. (1999). Suburban hustler: Stories of a high-tech call-boy. New York: Late Nite Press.

Letiche, H., & van Mens, L. (2002). Prostitution as a male object of epistemological pain. *Gender, Work and Organization, 9*(2), 167–185.

Leichtentritt, R. D., & Davidson, B. A. (1996). Young male street workers: Life histories and current experiences. *British Journal of Social Work, 35*(5), 483–509.

Levine, P. (2003). *Prostitution, race and politics: Policing venereal disease in the British empire.* New York: Routledge.

Luke, N. (2006). Exchange and condom use in informal sexual relationships in urban Kenya. *Economic Development & Cultural Change, 54*(2), 319–348.

Mameli, P. (2002). Stopping the illegal trafficking of human beings. *Crime, Law and Social Change, 38*(1), 67–80.

Matthews, F. (2006). *The invisible boy: Revisioning the victimization of male children and teens.* Ottawa: Public Health Clearinghouse of Canada.

McKay, C. (1999). Is sex work queer? *Social Alternatives, 18*(3), 48–53.

McKeganey, N. (2006). Street prostitution in Scotland: The views of working women. *Drugs: Education, Prevention and Policy, 13*(2), 151–166.

Miriam, K. (2005). Stopping the traffic in women: Power, agency and abolition in feminist debates over sex-trafficking. *Journal of Social Philosophy, 36*(1), 1–17.

Mirkin, H. (1999). The pattern of sexual politics: Feminism, homosexuality and pedophilia. *Journal of Homosexuality, 37*(2), 1–24.

Murray, S. (1997). The will not to know: Islamic accommodations of male homosexuality. In S. Murray, & W. Roscoe (Eds.), *Islamic homosexualities* (pp. 14–54). New York: New York University Press.

Nielsen, J., Walden, G., & Kunkel, C. (2000). Gendered heteronormativity: Empirical illustrations in everyday life. *Sociological Quarterly, 41*(2), 283–296.

Parrado, E., Flippen, C., & McQuiston, C. (2004). Use of commercial sex workers among hispanic migrants in North Carolina: Implications for the spread of HIV. *Perspectives on Sexual and Reproductive Health, 36*(4), 150–156.

Pateman, C. (1988). *The sexual contract.* Cambridge: Polity Press.

Pedesen, W., & Hegna, K. (2003). Children and adolescents who sell sex. *Social Science and Medicine, 56*, 135–147.

Pettersson, T., & Tiby, E. (2002). The production and reproduction of prostitution. *Journal of Scandinavian Studies in Criminology and Crime Prevention, 3*(2), 154–172.

Pochagina, O. (2005). The sex business as a social phenomenon in contemporary China. *Far Eastern Affairs, 33*(4), 86–102.

Prestage, G. (1990). *Sex work and sex workers in Australia.* Sydney: University of New South Wales Press.

Quiroga, J. (2000). *Tropics of desire: Interventions from Queer Latin America.* New York: New York University Press.

Ratnapala, N. (1999). Male sex work in Sri Lanka. In P. Aggleton (Ed.) *Men who sell sex* (pp. 213–222). Philadelphia: Temple University Press.

Rinaldi, A. (1998). Gay? We don't have that here. *New Statesman, 127*(4396), 17.

Roscoe, W., & Murray, S. (2004). *Boy-wives and female husbands: Studies of African homosexualities.* London: Palgrave-Macmillan.

Said, E. (1979). *Orientalism. Revised edition, 2003.* New York: Penguin Books.

Sanders, T. (2005). It's just acting: Sex workers' strategies for capitalizing on sexuality. *Gender, Work and Organization, 12*(4), 319–342.

Saphira, M. (2001). *Commercial exploitation of children.* Auckland, New Zealand: ECPAT.

Savin-Williams, R. C. (2006). *The new gay teenager.* Cambridge, MA: Harvard University Press.

Scott, J. (2003). A prostitute's progress: Male prostitution in scientific discourse. *Social Semiotics, 13*(2), 179–191.

Svedin, C., & Priebe, G. (2007). Selling sex in a population-based study of high school seniors in Sweden: Demographic and psychosocial correlates. *Archives of Sexual Behavior, 36*(1), 21–32.

Tan, M. (1999). Walking the tightrope: Sexual risk and male sex work in the Philippines. In P. Aggleton (Ed.), *Men who sell sex* (pp. 241–262). Philadelphia: Temple University Press.

U.S. Department of Justice. (2007). Bureau of justice statistics, http://www.ojp.usdoj.gov/bjs/.

Wallerstein, I. (2004). *World-systems analysis: An introduction.* Durham: Duke University Press.

Weber, M., Gerth, H. H., & Mills, C. W. (1958). *From Max Weber.* Oxford: Oxford University Press.

Weitzer, R. (2000). Why we need more research on sex work. In R. Weitzer (Ed.), *Sex for sale: Prostitution, pornography, and the sex industry* (pp. 1–16). New York: Routledge.

Whitaker, R. (1999). *Assuming the position: A memoir of hustling.* New York: Four Walls Eight Windows Press.

Whitam, F. L. (1992). Baijot and the callboy: Homosexual-heterosexual relations in the Philippines. In S. Murray (Ed.), *Oceanic homosexualities* (pp. 231–248). New York: Garland.

Wiegman, R. (2006). Heteronormativity and the desire for gender. *Feminist Theory, 7*(1), 89–103.

Yegenoglu, M. (2005). *Colonial fantasies: Towards a feminist reading of orientalism.* Cambridge: Cambridge University Press.

JEFFERY P. DENNIS has written extensively on the intersection of crime and gender.

EXPLORING THE ISSUE

Can Sex Work Be Empowering?

Critical Thinking and Reflection

1. How do issues of empowerment, agency, and choice intersect with the gendered nature of sex work?
2. How do cultural and gender biases impact how victims of trafficking are treated by law enforcement agencies?

Is There Common Ground?

The sex industry takes on many forms—from the woman or man with the web camera and the pay per view website to the brothels where sex workers toil to pay debts that grow exponentially with each passing day. Where does the line between sex work as a choice end and human trafficking for use as sex slaves begin? The easy answer to this question might be that a person in the role of sex worker retains individual autonomy and can quit the work as if it were any other job. Human trafficking involves the sale and purchase of people as commodities in the sex trade. Trafficking victims have owners who exercise control over their actions. Free will is lost and efforts to resist may be met with threats, abuse, or death.

Additional Resources

United Nations Office on Drugs and Crime. (2012). "Human Trafficking." United Nations: New York, 2012. Retrieved from: www.unodc.org/unodc/en/human-trafficking/what-is-human-trafficking.html?ref=menuside

Create Central

www.mhhe.com/createcentral

Internet References . . .

Sex Worker Rights

http://sexworkerrights.org

Sex Workers Project

http://sexworkersproject.org

Selected, Edited, and with Issue Framing Material by:
Rachel Pienta, *Valdosta State University*

ISSUE

Have Working Women Destroyed the American Family?

YES: Siwei Liu and Kathryn Hynes, from "Are Difficulties Balancing Work and Family Associated with Subsequent Fertility?" *Family Relations* (February 2012)

NO: Caryn E. Medved and William K. Rawlins, from "At-Home Fathers and Breadwinning Mothers: Variations in Constructing Work and Family Lives," *Women and Language* (Fall 2011)

Learning Outcomes

As you read the issue, focus on the following points:

• How has the need for sufficient income led women into the workplace?
• Does occupational parity influence traditional gender roles within the home?

ISSUE SUMMARY

YES: Siwei Liu and Kathryn Hynes suggest that American women make life choices that favor higher education and competitive careers at the expense of fertility, resulting in smaller families.

NO: Caryn E. Medved and William K. Rawlins suggest that changing social norms about gender roles have increased the acceptance of at-home fathers and breadwinning mothers, allowing men and women to pursue life choices that provide for greater flexible family structure.

The debate regarding the impact of working mothers on the structure of the American family is rooted in notions of the middle class ideal for economic achievement. In the early twentieth century, a marker of male professional achievement was a key element in Henry Ford's business model. The "Ford Five Dollar Day" was a component of social engineering designed to conflate earning power with achievement of a particular life ideal and men who were "living right" became eligible for bonuses (Bloomfield, 1983). Earning sufficient income to allow a man to have a stay-at-home wife was a sign of economic and social achievement.

The early twentieth century saw increasing numbers of women enter the workplace. Historical events such as the Great Depression and World War II paved the way for women to enter the paid labor force in increasing numbers. Social changes in the 1960s brought about changes in labor laws. Women began to earn college degrees in greater numbers and increased access to birth control including the availability of oral contraceptives all became contributing factors in changing how women would plan their adult lives.

By the late 1960s, the amount of time women spent in the workforce had increased dramatically. However, the time women spend on childcare and other household obligations has not decreased (Mitchell, 2012). Life has become a balancing act of time management for working mothers in America. Traditional gender roles still support the idea that a woman's place is in the home and that a man's place is in the workplace; variations on this structure continue to make working women easy targets for social criticism (Eddleston & Powell, 2012).

In the late 1990s, cultural and social messages in the United States would have suggested the mistaken idea that the problems of gender inequality for working mothers had been resolved. The efforts that began with the passage of Title VII in the 1960s and culminated with the passage of the Family Medical Leave Act during the Clinton years may have led many to believe that working mothers had achieved occupational parity. Persistent structural and institutional issues continue to perpetuate gender-based economic disparities that not only pose barriers to occupational parity but also present challenges to achieving egalitarian parenting roles that might ultimately transcend traditional sex role beliefs in family relationships.

In "Are Difficulties Balancing Work and Family Associated with Subsequent Fertility?" Liu and Hynes examine the life choices women make in order to achieve work and fertility goals. Their research suggests women will sacrifice career goals rather than forgo childbearing and that women report greater achieved life satisfaction from family than work.

In "At-Home Fathers and Breadwinning Mothers: Variations in Constructing Work and Family Lives," Medved and Rawlins examine variations in family structure that suggest men and women engage in role compromises to create functional family structure in the face of new economic realities.

YES ↵

Liu and Hynes

Are Difficulties Balancing Work and Family Associated with Subsequent Fertility?

Ever since mothers entered the labor market in large numbers, there has been concern about the challenges they face trying to balance their work and family roles. Work-family conflict has been linked to poor health outcomes as well as low performance and satisfaction in both family and work domains (Allen, Herst, Bruck, & Sutton, 2000; Perry-Jenkins, Repetti, & Crouter, 2000). Most recently, scholars have suggested that women's struggle to reconcile their work and family roles may be one of the causes of the rapid decline in fertility rates in several developed countries (Frejka & Calot, 2001; Lesthaeghe, 2000). Indeed, it is evident that women with higher education levels who are most likely to try and juggle work and family simultaneously are delaying first births and forgoing higher parity births (d'Addil & d'Ercole, 2005; Sleebos, 2003). But it is unclear whether the conflict they experience trying to balance these roles is indeed leading to their fertility behavior or whether other factors may be involved. In addition, U.S. fertility rates have not dropped to the levels seen in other developed countries, leading some to hypothesize that despite less generous social policies, women in the United States must somehow be managing to handle their work and family roles.

Although there are many hypotheses in the literature, few empirical studies directly examine the association between women's perceived difficulty in balancing work and family and their subsequent fertility decisions. In this study, we use longitudinal data on a sample of working mothers in the United States to examine whether mothers who have more difficulty in balancing work and family make different decisions about subsequent fertility than mothers who navigate these two domains with greater ease. Because employment and fertility decisions are often made simultaneously, we further examine whether difficulty in balancing work and family is associated with subsequent fertility and or subsequent labor market exits.

The current study contributes to both the demographic and work-family literatures. Demographic research on subsequent fertility has relied primarily on socioeconomic characteristics as predictors (e.g., Bumpass, Rindfuss, & Janosik, 1978; Morgan & Rindfuss, 1999). Our models extend prior demographic work by examining the role of subjective factors, such as attitudes and feelings, in fertility behavior. We consider attitudes and feelings subjective because they are based on a woman's interpretation of her situation. Research has indicated that women's attitudes and feelings play an important part in predicting childbearing (Barber & Axinn, 2005). Further, work-family researchers have studied many causes and consequences of work-family conflict, but none have studied whether it is associated with subsequent fertility. In this study, we directly test the association between work-family conflict and subsequent fertility. We discuss the implications of our findings in the concluding section.

Background and Conceptual Framework

Work, Family, and Subsequent Fertility

The challenges of balancing work and family have been well documented (Bellavia & Frone, 2005; Duxbury & Higgins, 2001). Both work and family are "greedy institutions" that require substantial time and energy (Coser, 1974). To reconcile the difficulties balancing the two domains, women have often reduced their work hours or exited the labor market during or immediately after a pregnancy (Desai & Waite, 1991; Hynes & Clarkberg, 2005), thereby lightening their work burden to make time for their increasing family responsibilities. Women's roles, however, have changed dramatically over the past few decades. Today many women invest heavily in higher education and careers, and many more are working to offset the decline in the wages men garner for less skilled work (Oppenheimer, 1994). Recently, there has been concern in some developed countries that women may try to manage the competing responsibilities of work and family by reducing their family responsibilities, specifically by having fewer children.

At a cross-national level, women's labor force participation rate was negatively correlated with total fertility rate (TFR) across developed countries in the 1970s (d'Addil & d'Ercole, 2005). During the past two decades, this correlation has switched from negative to positive, with some countries high on both TFR and women's labor force participation (e.g., the United States and Sweden) and some countries low on both dimensions (e.g., Italy and Japan). Demographers speculate that social and institutional changes—such as increasing social

Liu, Siwei and Hynes, Kathryn. From *Family Relations*, February 2012, pp. 16–20, 23–24, 27–30. Copyright © 2012 by National Council on Family Relations. Reprinted by permission of Wiley-Blackwell via Rightslink.

acceptance of working mothers and improvements in child-care availability and maternity leave—have reduced the incompatibility between employment and motherhood in some countries. Where this incompatibility has been reduced, they hypothesize that women can work and fertility rates have remained higher, but where social and institutional supports for working mothers are less apparent, women may be delaying the transition to parenthood and ultimately having fewer children (d'Addil & d'Ercole, 2005; Rindfuss, Guzzo, & Morgan, 2003; Sleebos, 2003).

Although these cross-national comparisons may indicate that women are able to manage both these roles in the United States, *within the United States* there appears to be a negative relationship between women's employment and fertility. Women with more education and stronger attachment to the labor market are more likely to remain employed after a birth than women with fewer labor market investments. They also tend to have children at an older age and to have fewer children (Rindfuss, Morgan, & Offutt, 1996). Neoclassical economic theory hypothesizes that the within-country negative association between work and fertility is because of the opportunity costs incurred when women have and raise children (G. S. Becker, 1993). Therefore, on the basis of prior research, it is unclear whether we will see fewer subsequent births among women in the United States who experience difficulty in balancing work and family.

Processes Linking Difficulty in Balancing Work and Family to Subsequent Fertility

Despite the focus in the literature on the challenges of working and raising children, there is little research linking individual women's subjective experiences balancing work and family to their decisions about subsequent fertility. Yet we can use existing research and theory to consider why we might or might not see such an association.

Research has shown that parents adapt their work, family, and child-care arrangements in order to create a good fit between their desired situation and their actual situation (Barnett, 1998; Hynes & Habasevich-Brooks, 2008; Moen & Wethington, 1992; Singley & Hynes, 2005; Voydanoff, 2002). For example, P. E. Becker and Moen (1999) found that middle-class dual-earner couples often use "scaling back" strategies to buffer the family from work encroachments. These strategies include placing limits on work, having a one-job, one-career marriage, and trading off job and career status in response to career opportunities and life course events. As with other work-family decisions, subsequent fertility decisions need to be contextualized. Whereas women may have images of their ideal number of children, those fertility expectations change as the opportunities and constraints in their environments change (Sleebos, 2003). As a result, women often end up with fewer children than they desired (d'Addil & d'Ercole, 2005; Hagewen & Morgan, 2005).

The notion that women who struggle to balance work and family may make different decisions about subsequent fertility than women at ease balancing these two spheres is supported by role theory. Adding a new baby to the family can be thought of as adding a new role for the mother. From the role theory perspective, this may create role strain as the mother feels inadequate in meeting the demands of her role system (Goode, 1960; Perry-Jenkins et al., 2000). Mothers who are already struggling to manage their work and family roles may delay or forgo subsequent fertility to avoid adding more burdens to their role system. In contrast, mothers who are able to combine work and family are in a state of role ease (Marks & MacDermid, 1996). They may feel they can add another baby to the family (if they so desire) and still manage the competing demands of work and family. Therefore, our first hypothesis is that mothers who have difficulty in balancing their work and family roles will be *less likely* to have a subsequent birth than mothers without such difficulty. We present one set of analyses testing this first hypothesis.

An important consideration when examining women's fertility behavior, however, is that women's employment history is often interdependent with their fertility history (Budig, 2003). On the one hand, we expect that women who experience difficulty in balancing their work and family roles will have fewer subsequent births. On the other hand, many women exit the labor market at least temporarily during early parenthood—around first births but also around subsequent births and even at times that do not correspond to births (Hynes & Clarkberg, 2005). From the role theory perspective, role strain in balancing work and family can be resolved by either reducing the family role *or* by reducing the work role. We may see that instead of forgoing subsequent births, women exit the labor market to reduce their strain. Therefore, our competing hypothesis is that difficulty in balancing work and family will not be associated with fewer subsequent births; instead, it will be associated with job exits. We present a second set of models to test this competing hypothesis.

Measuring Difficulty in Balancing Work and Family

Over the years, scholars have developed a variety of instruments to measure work-family experiences from different angles (Milkie, Denny, Kendig, & Schieman, 2010). We rely on three measures in this study that capture different aspects of women's perceived difficulty in balancing work and family: satisfaction with working, work-to-family spillover, and family-to-work spillover. Satisfaction with working measures the mother's satisfaction with her decision about whether to work or not (see Measures section for detail). Work-to-family spillover and family-to-work spillover measure the degree to which women's work affects family functioning and vice versa. Because these three measures capture different components of women's experiences, we may expect slightly different results. For instance, women who report low satisfaction with working may be more likely to change their work behavior than their fertility behavior because the question places the focus of dissatisfaction on working. Similarly, women who report that their work is interfering with their family may change their work roles, as again, work is identified as the culprit. In contrast, women who report that their family life is interfering with their work life may be particularly likely to forgo subsequent fertility, as additional children would only increase their family demands, thereby exacerbating the problem.

Additional Factors Influencing Work and Family Decisions

Both work and fertility decisions are influenced by myriad factors. We consider three groups of factors in this study. First, women's fertility and work decisions are likely to be influenced by their spouse or partner. The presence of a partner clearly affects the likelihood of a subsequent birth. Partners also provide social capital. For instance, they can share the responsibility of domestic labor and thereby make it easier for women to combine their work and family roles. Therefore, we control for the presence of a spouse or partner. We also control for women's unearned income in our models. Unearned income measures the amount of money available to a woman excluding her own income (typically the income of her spouse or partner or welfare benefits). This captures a woman's ability to leave the labor market if she desires. In addition, women's human capital is likely to influence their underlying fertility and work propensities; therefore, we control for women's education and age. The number of prior children in the family is also controlled for, given its clear influence on subsequent fertility.

Second, we control for the woman's underlying beliefs about the costs and benefits of work for children's well-being, as these beliefs are likely to influence both perceptions of work-family conflict and subsequent work and fertility behavior. For instance, women who believe that work has negative effects on children are probably more likely to report high dissatisfaction with working and are more likely to exit the labor force. Therefore controlling for this underlying belief system is important.

Finally, we control for women's work characteristics, including work hours and work flexibility. Although long hours and low flexibility may lead to work-family conflict (Frone, Russell, & Cooper, 1992), they do not necessarily correspond to each other. For instance, a woman who works long hours may have no difficulty in balancing work and family because she has purchased consistent child care, whereas a woman whose work hours are flexible may still find it difficult to combine her work and family roles if she is trying to outsource as little caregiving as possible. Because these work characteristics reflect women's constraints and resources at work, they are likely to influence women's work and fertility decisions.

Method
Data

We drew data from the National Institute of Child Health and Human Development's (NICHD) longitudinal Study of Early Child Care (SECC). The SECC was designed to examine the effects of child care on children's development, but includes many of the measures necessary for work-family and fertility research. In 1991, families experiencing a birth were recruited from hospitals in 10 study sites for an initial sample of 1,364 children. Participants were contacted approximately every 3 months for information about their family composition, work arrangements, and child-care arrangements. More detailed data collection occurred at 6, 15, 24, 36, and 54 months after the child's birth, including information on subjective experiences balancing work and family. Although the experiences of rural families were underrepresented, the detailed time-varying measures of key constructs made these data uniquely suited to this study.

Because the panel began with the birth of a child (of any parity), "time" in our analysis was in months since that birth. Thus, we were examining transitions that occurred 6 to 54 months (4.5 years) after the observed birth, a period when subsequent fertility was most likely. Because work-family measures are available only for mothers who were working or on leave 6 months after giving birth, we limited our analyses to these 809 women. Therefore, our analyses reflect the experiences of working mothers, not all women. Mothers in our sample in general were older, more educated, more likely to be White, more likely to be living with their spouse or partner, and had fewer children than those who were excluded. They also had higher average unearned income before the birth, although the difference is not significant. This is consistent with prior research indicating that women with more human capital and higher socioeconomic status (SES) are more likely to remain employed after birth (Hynes & Clarkberg, 2005). We discuss the limitation of our sample in the discussion section.

Analysis Plan

To test our initial hypothesis that mothers experiencing difficulty in balancing work and family may be less likely to have subsequent births, we used discrete-time event history models. Because our theory predicts that difficulty in balancing work and family will reduce the likelihood that a woman will choose to have a subsequent birth, our main dependent variable was whether the woman conceived a child or not. To ensure the proper temporal ordering of events, we used difficulty in balancing work and family at a given data collection point (e.g., at 6 months) to predict conception in the following study window (e.g., between 6 and 15 months). We linked balancing work and family to conception, not births, because conception is generally the time when the fertility decision is made. Our measure of conception, however, was calculated by moving backward from an observed birth; therefore, we are not catching unintended pregnancies that were aborted or intended pregnancies that resulted in miscarriages.

As in all event history models, we created a person-spell data set in which each woman contributed one "spell" or observation for each time period in which we had our key independent variables. Satisfaction with working was collected at 6, 15, 24, and 36 months, allowing mothers to contribute up to 4 person-spells to the analysis; measures of work-family conflict were collected at 6, 15, and 36 months, allowing mothers to contribute up to 3 person-spells. The person-spells were not identical in duration; instead, there were two 9-month windows (6–15 months and 15–24 months), followed by a 12-month window (24–36 months) and a 10-month window (36–46 months). Although birth data were available through 54 months, we ended our analysis at 46 months because we had to move back in time from the birth to the conception. Because our focus was on working mothers, women were included in our models only if they were working at the beginning of each spell.

Our final analysis samples varied slightly across models because of small amounts of missing data on the measures of work-family balance and the control variables. Our event-history data set using satisfaction with working as the major predictor included 773 women, contributing a total of 2,251 person-spells. Work-family conflict was only measured at 6, 15, and 36 months, leading to a sample of 766 women contributing 1,696 person-spells.

To test our competing hypothesis that women experiencing difficulty in balancing work and family may exit the labor market rather than reduce their fertility, we also ran a series of multinomial logit models. These models were structured similarly to the models described above, but the dependent variable captured women's decisions about working and about having a subsequent birth. The dependent variable had four categories: 1 = no job exit and no conception, 2 = conception only, 3 = job exit only, and 4 = both conception and related job exit. We describe the creation of this variable below.

All analyses were clustered by id, and robust standard errors were estimated to account for the nonindependence of observations. . . .

Results
Subsequent Fertility

We began by testing discrete-time event history models to examine whether difficulty in balancing work and family was associated with subsequent fertility. These are logit coefficients, not odds ratios, so a positive number indicates a positive association and a number less than 0 indicates a negative association. The standard errors are in parentheses. Each column represents one model; the only difference between the models is the variable used

to measure difficulty in balancing work and family. These measures represent different ways of capturing women's work-family experiences.

According to our first hypothesis, mothers who struggle to balance their work and family roles may postpone or forgo subsequent fertility. If this is the case, we should see a negative relationship between our measures of balancing work and family and the likelihood of having a subsequent birth. Our results, however, provided no support for this hypothesis: None of the models showed a negative relationship between any of our measures of difficulty in balancing work and family and subsequent fertility. Specification tests indicated that using linear work-family balance measures also did not net any significant associations between different measures on work-family balance and subsequent fertility.

Our control variables generally showed expected patterns. Mother's age was negatively related to subsequent fertility, which conforms to the general trend that older mothers are less likely to give birth. Mother's education had a significant positive association with the likelihood of having a subsequent birth in the model with satisfaction as the key predictor, and this relationship is marginally significant in the other two models. This is contrary to the general pattern that women who are more educated tend to have lower fertility rates but is consistent with a few studies based on European countries (Kreyenfeld, 2002) and with demographic literature indicating that the negative relation between women's education and fertility is mainly because of the postponement of first birth (d'Addil & d'Ercole, 2005; Rindfuss, Bumpass, & John, 1980). Our sample consists of women who have already had at least one child. Within this group of women, those who have more education may feel a stronger "time squeeze" in childbearing, as they may have delayed their first births (Kreyenfeld, 2002). Once they made the transition to motherhood, they may be prone to have more children within a relatively short period of time, leading to a positive relation that we see shortly after a birth. Finally, we see that women who already had more children were less likely to have another child.

Looking at the effects of our ideology measures, we see that women who reported more benefits to children from working were less likely than those who saw fewer benefits from working to have a subsequent birth. This association is in line with prior research indicating that women who have more positive attitudes toward maternal employment may be more committed to work, and work oriented women tend to have fewer children (Greenberger & O'Neil, 1990; Rindfuss et al., 1996). Beliefs in the cost of working, however, did not predict subsequent births. This is a sample of working mothers; therefore, those with very strong beliefs and the resources to exit the labor market may have made the transition out of work already. We do not see strong associations between mother's work characteristics and their fertility behavior. There is a negative relationship between work hours and subsequent birth, but this relationship is significant only in one model. Work flexibility does not have a significant effect on subsequent birth in any model. . . .

Discussion

There has been considerable speculation in international literature that difficulty in balancing work and family roles may be part of the reason for low fertility rates in several developed countries. Although low fertility per se is not a problem in the United States, there is evidence from prior research that women's fertility and labor market decisions are interconnected: Women with stronger attachments to the labor market are more likely to delay the onset of fertility and have lower completed fertility rates. As always, aggregate patterns contain considerable variation, with some working mothers stopping at one child and others continuing on to have higher parity births. Decades of work-family research in the United States points to the complex intersection of preferences, opportunities, and constraints in forming both the work and family decisions of parents. Further, research highlights the way that challenges in balancing work and family can lead women to exit the labor market. Yet, little research has focused on the role of subjective experiences balancing work and family in fertility decisions.

This study provides a direct test of the hypothesis that mothers' perceived difficulty in balancing work and family may influence their subsequent fertility behavior. Using longitudinal data on a sample of working mothers in the United States, we found no evidence that mothers experiencing difficulty in balancing work and family were forgoing subsequent births. This was true for a measure that focused broadly on satisfaction with working and for more specific measures of work-to-family spillover and family-to-work spillover. We found more support—although the results are less consistent across models—for the hypothesis that women may choose to reconcile work-family conflict by exiting the labor market.

On the basis of prior literature, both competing hypotheses were plausible. In this study, our results indicate that although women may struggle to balance work and family in the United States, that struggle is not systematically associated with lower rates of subsequent fertility among working mothers. These findings are not surprising for two reasons. First, our study is based on women in the United States. The fertility rate and women's labor force participation rates in the United States remain high compared to many European countries (Brewster & Rindfuss, 2000). It would be interesting to see results from a similarly designed study in a lower-fertility country, as we might expect to see a stronger association between difficulties in balancing work and family and subsequent fertility. In addition, we know that although women's employment rates are relatively high in the United States, there are still many women who exit the labor market at some point during early parenthood. It may be that women's

fertility behavior is more stable and less sensitive to contextual influences than their work behavior. Qualitative research would be interesting in this area, helping us to understand how women make decisions about work and fertility across early parenthood.

A different way to explore these issues would be to ask young women, who have not yet begun having children, about whether they *think* they will experience work-family conflict and how those perceptions influence the timing and likelihood of their transition to parenthood. In this study, we have examined subsequent fertility among working mothers. As an initial study this makes sense, given the research indicating that lower fertility rates are often because of forgoing subsequent births. But sometimes these forgone subsequent births are in part because of delayed first births. This area would benefit greatly from research in the United States and in other countries about whether women's perceptions about how difficult it will be to balance work and family influence the timing of first births.

Our study fills an important gap in the literature, but it has several limitations as well. First, our analysis sample did not include women who moved out of the labor market prior to the observed birth or immediately after the birth. But the inclusion of these women is only likely to strengthen our findings about the link between perceived work-family conflict and labor market exits and should not alter our findings about subsequent fertility. Similarly, although our interest was primarily in understanding subsequent fertility, those interested in women's employment behavior may wish to examine less dramatic changes to work including job changes, schedule changes, and other "scaling back" tactics (P. E. Becker & Moen, 1999; Singley & Hynes, 2005). Understanding the various ways women respond to work-family conflict and the long-term effects of these changes on happiness, labor market success, and parenting would provide valuable information about the costs and benefits of different decisions.

Our focus on working mothers also raises questions about differential patterns for lower and higher socioeconomic status women. Consistent with prior research, we found that women with lower education levels are less likely to work 6 months after giving birth than those with higher education levels. There are many reasons for this pattern, including lower opportunity costs associated with labor market exits, child-care costs consuming a larger proportion of pay, and gender ideology. Unfortunately, we did not have an adequate sample size to examine whether the association between work-family conflict and subsequent work and fertility decisions differs by socioeconomic status. It may be that lower socioeconomic status women experiencing difficulty in balancing work and family are more likely to forgo having subsequent births and stay in the labor market because they have a greater need to work. On the other hand, it may be that lower socioeconomic status women are more likely to have subsequent births and transition out of the labor market, given their lower opportunity costs. A similar set of mixed hypotheses could be generated for higher socioeconomic status women. Given the different opportunities and constraints of these two groups, an examination of their various responses is merited. Similarly, our sample consisted primarily of women who are White. In our models, we controlled for minority status but did not have a large enough sample of minority women to conduct subgroup analyses.

Our analysis was based mostly on information obtained from mothers, because the NICHD-SECC does not provide comparable data about fathers' work characteristics. We did control for the unearned income available to the mother, which is likely the factor most strongly influencing women's work and fertility decisions. But incorporating other variables related to fathers may be an important avenue for future research.

Because there are few data sets that include detailed work history, fertility, and subjective measures of work-family conflict, we relied on data collected in the early 1990s. We do not think, however, that there are compelling reasons to believe these results would be different for a more recent cohort of mothers. There have not been major changes in national policies that influence women's work-family decisions around births except the adoption of the Family and Medical Leave Act in 1993. But research on access to unpaid leaves shows that they are much less likely to impact work decisions than paid leaves (for review, see Hynes, 2003). Women's rates of labor market participation and fertility have not changed much, nor has the work environment changed in ways that would help

women better balance work and family (Bond, Thompson, Galinsky, & Prottas, 2002).

Finally, in this study we used the event of an actual birth to infer mothers' decisions about having additional children. This may have blurred the relationship between work-family conflict and subsequent fertility, because not all subsequent births are planned. Unfortunately, we do not have measures on women's fertility intentions to test the effect of this assumption. We do know, however, that the unintended pregnancy rate is substantially higher for younger, less educated, and lower income women (Finer & Henshaw, 2006), whereas women in our sample were, on average, relatively advantaged. Future research that directly measures women's fertility decisions would be valuable.

The finding that women with young children who struggle to balance work and family may exit the labor market has implications for work-family practitioners and policymakers. Labor market exits are costly for women because breaks in employment can have negative impacts on women's wages and job status and may increase gender inequality in the long run (Felmlee, 1995; Hynes, 2003). Labor market exits can also be costly for employers because they can increase expenses related to hiring and training replacement workers. Our findings about labor market exits are only suggestive, but we are interested to see findings from on-going studies that are examining whether work-life policies aimed at reducing mothers' work-family conflict, such as those allowing women to have greater control in their work hours (Kelly & Moen, 2007; Kossek & Ozeki, 1999), may help mothers remain employed.

References

Allen, T. D., Herst, D. E. L., Bruck, C. S., & Sutton, M. (2000). Consequences associated with work-to-family conflict: A review and agenda for future research. *Journal of Occupational Health Psychology, 5,* 278–308.

Barber, J. S., & Axinn, W. G. (2005). How do attitudes shape childbearing in the United States? In A. Booth & A. C. Crouter (Eds.), *The new population problem: Why families in developed countries are shrinking and what it means* (pp. 59–92). Mahwah, NJ: Erlbaum.

Barnett, R. C. (1998). Toward a review and reconceptualization of the work/family literature. *Genetic, Social and General Psychology Monographs, 124,* 125–182.

Becker, G. S. (1993). *A treatise on the family.* Cambridge, MA: Harvard University Press.

Becker, P. E., & Moen, P. (1999). Scaling back: Dual-earner couples' work-family strategies. *Journal of Marriage and the Family, 61,* 995–1007.

Bellavia, G. M., & Frone, M. R. (2005). Work family conflict. In J. Barling, E. K. Kelloway, & M. R. Frone (Eds.), *Handbook of work stress* (pp. 113–148). Thousand Oaks, CA: Sage.

Bond, J. T., Thompson, C., Galinsky, E., & Prottas, D. (2002). *Highlights of the national study of the changing workforce.* New York: Families and Work Institute.

Brewster, K. L., & Rindfuss, R. R. (2000). Fertility and women's employment in industrialized nations. *Annual Review of Sociology, 26,* 271–296.

Budig, M. J. (2003). Are women's employment and fertility histories interdependent? An examination of causal order using event history analysis. *Social Science Research, 32,* 376–401.

Bumpass, L. L., Rindfuss, R. R., & Janosik, R. B. (1978). Age and marital status at first birth and the pace of subsequent fertility. *Demography, 15,* 75–86.

Coser, L. A. (1974). *Greedy institutions: Patterns of undivided commitment.* New York: The Free Press.

d'Addil, A. C., & d'Ercole, M. M. (2005). Trends and determinants of fertility rates: The role of policies. In *OECD Social Employment and Migration Working Papers* (Vol. 27). Paris: OECD Directorate for Employment, Labour and Social Affairs.

Desai, S., & Waite, L. J. (1991). Women's employment during pregnancy and after the first birth: Occupational characteristics and work commitment. *American Sociological Review, 56,* 551–566.

Duxbury, L., & Higgins, C. (2001). *Work-life balance in the new millennium: Where are we? Where do we need to go?* Ottawa: Canadian Policy Research Networks.

Felmlee, D. H. (1995). Causes and consequences of women's employment discontinuity, 1967–1973. *Work and Occupations, 22,* 167–187.

Finer, L., & Henshaw, S. K. (2006). Disparities in rates of unintended pregnancy in the United States, 1994 and 2001. *Perspectives on Sexual and Reproductive Health, 38,* 90–96.

Frejka, T., & Calot, G. (2001). Cohort reproductive patterns in low-fertility countries. *Population and Development Review, 27,* 103–132.

Frone, M. R., Russell, M., & Cooper, M. L. (1992). Antecedents and outcomes of work-family conflict: Testing a model of the work-family interface. *Journal of Applied Psychology, 77,* 65–78.

Goode, W. J. (1960). A theory of role strain. *American Sociological Review, 25,* 483–496.

Greenberger, E., & O'Neil, R. (1990). Parents' concerns about their child's development: Implications for fathers' and mothers' well-being and attitudes toward work. *Journal of Marriage and the Family, 52,* 621–635.

Hagewen, K. J., & Morgan, S. P. (2005). Intended and ideal family size in the United States, 1970–2002. *Population and Development Review, 31,* 507–527.

Hynes, K. (2003), *What should we consider when assessing the impacts of maternity leave policies?* Bronfenbrenner Life Course Center Working Paper #03-03, Ithaca, NY.

Hynes, K., & Clarkberg, M. (2005). Women's employment patterns during early parenthood: A group-based trajectory analysis. *Journal of Marriage and Family, 67,* 222.

Hynes, K., & Habasevich-Brooks, T. (2008). The ups and downs of child care: Variations in child care quality and exposure across the early years. *Early Childhood Research Quarterly, 23,* 559–574.

Kelly, E. L., & Moen, P. (2007). Rethinking the clockwork of work: Why schedule control may pay off at work and at home. *Advances in Developing Human Resources, 9,* 487–506.

Kossek, E. E., & Ozeki, C. (1999). Bridging the work-family policy and productivity gap: A literature review. *Community, Work & Family, 2,* 7–32.

Kreyenfeld, M. (2002). Time-squeeze, partner effect of self-selection? An investigation into the positive effect of women's education on second birth risks in West Germany. *Demographic Research (Electronic version), 7.*

Lesthaeghe, R. (2000). *Postponement and recuperation: Recent fertility trends and forecasts in six Western European countries.* Brussels: Interface Demography.

Marks, S. R., & MacDermid, S. M. (1996). Multiple roles and the self: A theory of role balance. *Journal of Marriage and the Family, 58,* 417–432.

Marshall, N. L., & Barnett, R. C. (1993). Work-family strains and gains among two-earner couples. *Journal of Community Psychology, 21,* 64–78.

Milkie, M. A., Denny, K. E., Kendig, S., & Schieman, S. (2010). Measurement of the work-family interface. In *Work and Family Encyclopedia.* Retrieved from http://wfnetwork.bc.edu/ encyclopedia_entry.php?id=16822&area=All

Moen, P., & Wethington, E. (1992). The concept of family adaptive strategies. *Annual Review of Sociology, 18,* 233–251.

Morgan, S. P., & Rindfuss, R. R. (1999). Reexamining the link of early childbearing to marriage and to subsequent fertility. *Demography, 36,* 59–75.

NICH D-SECC Phase I Instrument Document. (n.d.) [Electronic Version]. Retrieved from https://secc.rti.org/

Oppenheimer, V. K. (1994). Women's rising employment and the future of the family in industrial societies. *Population and Development Review, 20,* 293–342.

Perry-Jenkins, M., Repetti, R. L., & Crouter, A. C. (2000). Work and family in the 1990s. *Journal of Marriage and the Family, 62,* 981–998.

Rindfuss, R. R., Bumpass, L., & John, C. S. (1980). Education and fertility: Implications for the roles women occupy. *American Sociological Review, 45,* 431–447.

Rindfuss, R. R., Guzzo, K. B., & Morgan, S. P. (2003). The changing institutional context of low fertility. *Population Research and Policy Review, 22,* 411–438.

Rindfuss, R. R., Morgan, S. P., & Offutt, K. (1996). Education and the changing age pattern of American fertility: 1963–1989. *Demography, 33,* 277–290.

Singley, S. G., & Hynes, K. (2005). Transitions to parenthood: Work-family policies, gender, and the couple context. *Gender & Society, 19,* 376–397.

Sleebos, J. (2003). Low fertility rates in OECD countries: Facts and policy responses. *OECD Social, Employment and Migration Working Papers,* 13.

Voydanoff, P. (2002). Linkages between the work-family interface and work, family, and individual outcomes. *Journal of Family Issues, 23,* 138–164.

Siwei Liu is an assistant professor of human development and family studies at the University of California Davis.

Kathryn Hynes is an assistant professor of human development and family studies at Pennsylvania State University.

Medved and Rawlins

 **NO**

At-Home Fathers and Breadwinning Mothers: Variations in Constructing Work and Family Lives

"At times I used to dream about when they are older [and] I will be able to write; when they are older, the house will get cleaned lickety split . . . I do the dishes and I do the laundry and all the mundane household stuff [but] now I don't get to cuddle and watch Sesame Street."

The above excerpt is from an interview with Bob, an at-home father, reminiscing about the memorable times he used to spend with his daughters when they were younger. Bob is married to Julie, a senior manager working at a large firm in the Midwest. He continues, "There was always a realization between us that she was like the, I guess, the corporate person," and he humorously adds, "I have a lot of patience with kids, but with adults, less so." Alternative ways of composing and talking about work and family life as evidenced in Bob and Julie's story are slowly making their way into mainstream U.S. culture. The number of couples reporting to be primarily or solely financially dependent on a wife's income range from 12% of women who earn more than 60% of the family's income to just under 3% who report being entirely dependent on a wife's earnings. The U.S. also saw a 200% increase in the number of reported at-home fathers between 1994 and 2005. Further, men were disproportionately affected early on during the recent recession as the most significant layoffs hit male-dominated industries. The Pew Research Center also reports that women continue to outpace men in education and earnings growth. Undoubtedly, substantial changes in the discourse and related practices of marriage and earning are underway. . . .

Review of Literature
Dual-Earner Couples' Negotiations

Marital structures and communication strategies are often-studied sites for the (re) negotiation of gender. The post-World War II rise of the middle-class, White, dual-earner couple brought gender issues center stage for scholars and feminist activists alike. The category "dual-earner" has always encompassed a wide array of earning arrangements ranging from dual labor force participation regardless

of income level to professional dual *careers* couples and even asymmetrical earnings with "wives as senior partners." Various theoretical perspectives have been evoked to explore these couples' experiences and negotiations, including social exchange, economic bargaining, feminist and gender construction, and integrated theoretical perspectives.

We know that increases in dual-career women's incomes do not inevitably or neatly translate into greater marital power. Gender and other social and discursive forces, not simply earning differentials, need to be taken into account to understand divisions of household labor, and marital decision making and satisfaction. Even when market hours are fairly equal, wives still do more housework than their husbands. What spouses consider a fair division of labor remains gendered and complexly related to marital satisfaction. Generally speaking, as dual-career women's incomes rise, women do less and men perform more housework. Yet men at the extremes of the income range slightly *reduce* their participation in housework. Finally, higher income-earning women, at times, use communication strategies that downplay their financial contributions and refrain from exercising the traditional masculine link between money and power. What is less understood is how couples negotiate gender and identity when husbands effectively opt out or remain out of the workforce after layoffs and wives remain tied to paid labor. How does this context shape how these couples make sense out of work and family? Key to understanding this process of negotiation is exploring how these couples talk about their approaches to caring and earning.

Labor Force Decision Making and Opting Out

Stone found that while only a minority of professional women plan ahead to leave their careers for full-time motherhood, many exit due to frustration with both organizational as well as spousal flexibility and support, along with intensive mothering pressures. Stone argues that these women do not make this choice lightly and voice concerns about likely problems with career re-entry in professional positions. Many fail to plan for potential unintended consequences of financial dependency such as the possibility of divorce or husbands' job loss or disability. Gerson's arguments remain relevant as she contends that women's workforce decisions are products of: (a) "pushing" women out of the workforce (i.e., desires for traditional motherhood, lack of spousal assistance, lack of supportive work environments, falling career aspirations); as well as (b) "pulling" them into paid labor (i.e., career aspirations, ambivalence toward motherhood, financial necessity). She notes that "women [may] . . . resemble men who find themselves in jobs they would prefer to leave, except for one important difference . . . few men enjoy the traditional, although shrinking, female option of trading paid work for domestic work." Meaning construction in the lives of men (and their wives) who *do* trade career for domestic work is the focus of the present study. Further, we believe that to richly understand this inherently communicative process, we must investigate and juxtapose *both* men and women's interrelated accounts of labor force participation and exit. Just as life course theorists argue that work and family is constituted by "linked lives," we argue that marital identities, at times are also linked identities and must be explored as joint-constructions or co-constructions.

Stay-at-Home Fathering

Bridges, Etaugh, and Barnes-Farrell report that stay-at-home fathers are judged more harshly than stay-at-home mothers for ostensibly sacrificing their families' financial security. In other words, thay are sanctioned for engaging in caregiving and *not* breadwinning per conventional gender expectations. For their parts, working mothers are perceived as less communal (i.e., sensitive, warm, nurturing, and dedicated to family) and less effective as parents than fathers. Even so, Wentworth and Chell explain that "male cross-gender behavior is treated more harshly than female cross-gender behavior." They suggest "there is a stronger link between gender roles and perceived sexuality for men than for women." Although we must not forget that the sexuality of powerful career women is also challenged, a man performing household labor of childcare may be perceived minimally as "less of a man," perhaps even threatening to children or homosexual. In an early study of primary caregiving fathers, Radin reported that men did not persist in at-home roles for extended periods of time due to gendered pressures to conform. Radin, however, found four commonalities among men who *did* remain in full-time caregiving roles for more than two years (versus reverting to traditional patterns) including: (a) viewing their own fathers as inattentive, (b) being in their 30s and/or with prior career experience, (c) enjoying the support of extended family members, and (d) having a small family. Rochlen and colleagues' work also found that men exit paid work when (a) their wives have a high value for career, (b) they see full-time parenting as an opportunity, and (c) caregiving aligns with their preference or personality. Both at-home mothering and father-ing couples report similar levels of marital satisfaction, but women in either arrangement report higher levels of stress and exhaustion than men. . . .

In sum, we know that gender and power are intertwined with dual-career couples' negotiation of childcare, domestic labor, and labor force participation. Men's power and privilege in the home persists to a certain extent, despite women's increased contributions to household income. Yet lived moments of "undoing gender" cannot be discounted and warrant investigation. What is less well known is how couples engaging in gender atypical arrangements—particularly primary breadwinning mothers married to at-home fathers—come to understand, enact, and potentially resist or rework conventional gendered tasks and identities through language and social interaction. Given the relatively uncharted and exploratory nature of this study, we frame this investigation around one central research question: *How do stay-at-home fathers and breadwinning mothers articulate their stances toward moneymaking and homemaking?*

Doing, Undoing, and Reworking Gender

Gender operates on multiple, dynamic, and interdependent levels. We take up social constructionist and feminist arguments that the interactive and discursive expressions of gender are complexly intertwined with their structural and institutional manifestations. Studying the discourse of these couples concurrently gives us (a) insight into their ongoing negotiations and coordination of gendered tasks and identities, as well as (b) examples of how available language shapes and is reshaped by what these couples see as possible performances of homemaking and moneymaking. We "do gender" in everyday discourse and related practices in the context of larger cultural and structural forces. Equally important, we can *undo* and rework gender through our language and social interactions. We must not only explore the ways we perpetuate modern gendered assumptions about caregiving and wage-earning, but also the ways we resist and 'break the bowls' of gender. We also need to pay attention to dissembling binaries; that is exploring the various enactments of gender in-between simply doing and undoing, public and private, or masculine and feminine. Multiple masculinities and femininities exist as interdependent discourses, co-constructed identities, and lived experiences. Gender role prescriptions still exist although they are not as static or fixed as in the past. Instead, they persist in ongoing interplay with gendered identities, understandings of selves and as co-constructed processes in marital relationships. Sometimes gendered social change is subtle and can only be seen in small acts and words at the margins of our lived experiences. Further, fathering and housework are feminist issues just as are women's access to and success in the workplace. We embrace these theoretical assumptions about language and gender in the five stories below that (re)present varying gendered co-constructions of homemaking-moneymaking tasks and identities. . . .

Discussion and Implications

In framing our study, we asked, *how do stay-at-home fathers and breadwinning mothers articulate their stances toward moneymaking and homemaking?* Analyzing our participants' discourses, we found these couples orchestrating their private and public lives differently depending on how they jointly framed tasks, identities, and role eligibilities. While some couples temporarily sojourned and retained traditionally gendered associations for their activities and selves, others keenly reconstituted historical alignments between femininity and care as well as masculinity and economic provision. Other couples relegated gender to a relatively minimal role in their articulations of daily life. We have (re) presented their diverse efforts through five stances: reversing, conflicting, collaborating, improvising, and sharing. Following Deutsch, we adopt a perspective on "doing gender" that attempts to tease out not only how gender is perpetuated through language and social interaction but also how it *is adapted and even disassembled* in subtle and not so subtle ways. Further, across these five stances, we vividly illustrate different micro-level approaches to "working out" social change with respect to work and family roles, identities and tasks. In our final section, we examine these stances more deeply with respect to the social construction of masculinities and femininities and its potential to segue into transformative social change, as well as directions for future research. Here we mainly focus on gender while recognizing that our insights are bound by class, race, and sexuality.

The language of 'role reversal' has captured popular imagination with respect to stay-at-home fathers and breadwinning mothers. In some ways, the reversing stance exemplified by Scott and Alicia's early parenting experiences most straightforwardly depicts gender maintenance through both language and behaviors that appear to preserve traditional gendered assumptions of caregiving and paid employment. At the time of the interview, presupposed differences in biology and socialization seemed to trump the economics of their situation (assuming that earning more money is the valued economic outcome). Within a six-month period of time, Scott's identity crisis led to his move back into full-time paid employment. Like other professional women electing to opt out, Alicia's desire to 'mother' and her difficulties managing work responsibilities motivated her shift into the central caregiver role. In the reversing stance, traditional distinctions remain between masculinity and public sphere participation as well as femininity and private sphere constructions.

While observing their reproduction of hegemonic forms of masculinity and femininity, we also must respect their situation's complexity and ongoing identity struggles. For most of their marriage, Alicia had earned more money than Scott; her role as primary wage-earner can be seen as part of women's growing structural access to workplace opportunities as well as Scott's willingness to embrace

marriage as the secondary earner. Thus, during early marriage and the relatively short time of their reversal, they jointly constructed and lived moments of social change that cannot be discounted in their relational biography. And, while Scott and Alicia reverted to conventional societal gendered roles, they ostensibly made this decision by choice. Future research needs to probe constructions of choice and/or agency with respect to marital work and life arrangements along with their political implications. Scott, for example, spoke of the profundity of his experience choosing to be home with his newborn daughter. While his time as an at-home father might have been relatively short, its personal and relational impact could be far-reaching. Perhaps Scott's caregiving experiences shifted his own understandings and/or performances of masculinity, regardless of his choice to return to paid employment. Further, other men in his workplace might have seen Scott take time off to care for his daughter and, as a result, considered this option in their own lives. The importance of role models as signaling or opening up social change must not be undervalued. We see in this first snapshot how existing gendered assumptions about work and family life can be reproduced through SAHFC's communication strategies, even in the context of reversing the performance of caring and earning duties while still holding out the potential for social change.

The conflicting stance illustrates how couples performing gender atypical duties can simultaneously experience the colliding forces of frustration *and* satisfaction, gender maintenance *and* resistance, as well as gender consciousness *and* a lack of gender awareness. These couples often articulated relational tensions or moments when the reality of their choices, duties, and identities clashed with how they wistfully thought their lives would progress, or the inflexibility of employment structures. For instance, like Sue, successful women's greater earning power may be framed as trapping couples (or individual wives or husbands) into enacting work and family lives that contradict or confuse their experiences of an authentic self. Sue's and Mike's narratives express both frustration about being constrained by Sue's ability to earn a greater income at the time of the interview as well as joy and competence in carrying out their respective tasks. She also noted Mike's discomfort over not contributing more significantly to the family income. This conflicting couple wanted the opportunity to change their arrangement but felt constrained by the conditions of their financial situation. Masculinities and femininities are portrayed in this stance as complex, contradictory, and dynamic constructions in relation to caring and earning.

Before we default to marking the conflicting stance as also simply perpetuating hegemonic forms of gender, we must recognize that conflict has always been part of social change—the very feelings of discomfort expressed by conflicting couples illustrate the social constructionist perspective in action. Unconventional gendered arrangements involving conflictual interactions can evidence social change, including real moments of relational renegotiation. Indeed, identity construction under such circumstances itself is a struggle at times; and, through Mike and Sue's (as well as all of our participants') words, we can see the struggle more vividly. Change at all levels isn't simply an either/or proposition, but a *process* of becoming or doing and undoing that we richly see in Mike and Sue's struggles and successes. Both the reversing and conflicting stances portray examples of difficult interactions occurring as these couples wrestle with shifting discourses and practices of work and family. The antagonistic sound of their conflicting narrative can be contrasted with another SAHC story framing change as collaboration.

The collaborating stance illustrates the concurrent *holding onto* and *letting go* of masculinities and femininities in relation to homemaking and moneymaking. Ty's and Lisa's abilities both to acknowledge and parody traditional gendered assumptions about who "ought" to do particular tasks and how they "should" be performed provides an insightful example of the strategic use of irony in everyday talk and action. As demonstrated by Trethewey, irony is a "lived" strategy individuals may use in managing the "both/ and" quality of life. Together, this couple bridged the exigencies of role eligibility and identity, often doing so communicatively in ways that allowed both historical constructions and current enactments of gender to co-exist. They did not seek resolution of this tension or wholesale transformation of gender but appeared to live with it and use it as a source of insight. Ty, for instance, insightfully invoked irony when he explained how he was both constrained by his understandings of appropriately masculine emotion yet also able to laugh when his well-planned dinner went awry in what he called a "sitcom" moment. Although not easy, he recognized the futility of holding tightly to this narrow view of being a man. Irony permitted Ty (and allows us) to see how seemingly incongruous alternatives (maintaining versus transforming gendered assumptions of care and paid labor) can actually co-exist in various ways.

While collaboration seems a sophisticated and gentile way to manage conflicting gendered selves, conventional masculinity and femininity remain part of the interpretive frame. The locus of conflict, or perhaps tension, in the collaborating stance seems to be more internal than relational, in contrast to the first two homemaking and moneymaking stances. Thus, we need to ask whether ironic collaboration can create enough "gender vertigo" to dismantle traditional forms of gender and power. Can irony sufficiently weaken the link between sex category and gendered divisions of labor? Or, to seriously affect social change, must masculinities and femininities be disassembled, fade into the background, or be degendered in interactions?

Case in point: the improvising stance as viewed through Bob and Julie's narrative seems to let go of gender accountability in their work and family lives. Following Deutsch, we agree that "under some conditions, [gender] may be so irrelevant that it is not even accessed." Perhaps more realistically in the present analysis, we could

say that gender assumed a less important role in Julie and Bob's communication about work and family life than it is often afforded. Bob articulated a sense of self and relationship with Julie grounded in the language of friendship, and Julie explained that Bob was born to be their daughter's primary caregiver. Gender's assumed master status appears to be subsumed in their language of non-hierarchical relations, personal preference, and differing sex-typical abilities. Improvising couples didn't appear, actively or explicitly, to resist gender conventions; rather they seemed not to take them into account in their framing of work and family life. In the improvising stance, we see the undoing of gender most clearly through its relative absence. Bob and Julie minimized traditional masculinities and femininities in assigning duties and crafting selves. Even more interesting is their use of biological and/or natural language to justify *sex atypical* work and family roles. Bob is constructed as born to do caregiving and the more natural one to be at home full-time with their two girls. Most often, biological language is argued by gender theorists to only *reinforce* oppression and inequity between men and women. What are the personal or political implications of positioning some men as more natural caregivers than women? And, does the absence of gendered discourse necessarily equate to its transgression? This stance portrays another way of framing and performing alternative forms of work and family life that raises fascinating questions about SAHFC arrangements and social change across identities, roles, institutions, and discourses.

Of course, the improvising stance comes with its own unique challenges. Tensions emerged, for instance, when Julie got frustrated that Bob did not do laundry the way she wanted it done; Bob retorted that it was his job and he would "do laundry like a guy." Although Bob still used gender to mark his performance of household labor, he owned the task as gender appropriate and even uniquely performed by men versus defining it as "woman's work." Here we see the language of equal role eligibilities producing relational tension (i.e., Julie wanted laundry done her way) but a very different type of tension is constructed than evidenced in discourses of unequal role eligibilites (i.e., if Sue perceived that women still need to perform the "second shift" of household labor). It is not the mere existence of tension that is most instructive about these couples' experiences, but the negotiated nature of these tensions as revealed through close examination of their discourse. While clear divisions of labor existed, Bob and Julie's tensions arose from *how* work should be done rather then *who* should do particular kinds of work. The question then arises whether difference always means inequality. Bob and Julie's situation seems to illustrate one example when differences, sex atypical as they are, do not seem to beget inequality. Does Bob's masculine identity rooted in the daily travails of caregiving evidence maternal thinking or changing norms of masculinity? And, did Bob and Julie (as well as other couples participating in this study), at an earlier point in time, struggle differently with constructing their unconventional identities and, if so, how?

Finally, the sharing stance explicitly and consciously resists traditional masculinities and femininities in both word and deed while also contesting separate but equal allocations of labor. Empowerment through overt resistance is articulated in Tom and Sandra's account of sharing work and family tasks and identities, perhaps more so than in the other four stances. Here we see the post-feminist ideal of equal and fully participative divisions of labor as well as external markers of gender change such as taking each other's names. Tensions arise in this stance due to the lack of role models and resistance to existing work and family structures. Here we see public attempts at reworking gender and creating new forms of language and behavior at the relational level. At the same time, Tom and Sandra also perform micro-acts of resistance by minipulating employment structures to accommodate their desires to share work and family. Theirs is not an easy path; it is one fraught with challenges but expressed as empowering for both of them. Active resistance through gender consciousness is only one means of social change. Future research needs to explore effective and ineffective communication strategies and behavioral practices that aid SAHFCs in their attempts to realize potentially transformative changes in social institutions.

Conclusions and Next Steps

What can we learn from this study of variations in couples' homemaking and moneymaking stances? First, by documenting (and providing our interpretations of) the subtle differences in the performance and articulation of gender in the lives of these couples, we illustrate varieties of masculinities and femininities at play in their work and family lives. Scott, Mike, Ty, Bob, and Tom share with us shades and adaptations of masculinities, differentially caught up in interdependent webs of caregiving, wage earning, heterosexuality, and identity. Likewise, Alicia's enactment of being a woman, successful employee, wife and mother is but one rendering of femininity with similarities and differences from Sue, Lisa, Julie, and Sandra.

Second, the stories embodying these five homemaking-moneymaking stances reinforce that no one right way or single model for success in doing or undoing gender exists. A communication approach to exploring gendered work and family social change recognizes the criticality of process over form or, at minimum, their intimate interaction. The key contribution of this study is to illustrate that ostensibly identical work and family arrangements are lived very differently when we dig deeper into the various ways SAHFCs communicatively frame their work and family lives. We agree with Gerson's assertion that we must get "beyond drawing simple—and overly deterministic—associations between forms and outcome [but rather] we need to explore the forces that shape [work] and family" including often overlooked discursive, relational, and interactional forces.

Third, both the co-constructed and contextual natures of these performances come to the forefront. Could Bob take on the identity of natural, full-time caregiver and gatekeeper of laundry without Julie's symmetrical performance as the determined, non-domestic career woman? If Tom wasn't willing to engage fully in caregiving, wage-earning, and identity transformation, could Sandra claim her empowered shared marital identity? And, isn't Mike's identity struggle also part and parcel of Sue's struggles to craft a coherent, if only transient, sense of self? We believe that these narratives richly display how SAHFCs as relational partners co-construct a life and "participate together in the process of making sense of their local circumstances." These performances are also likely to change over time through the couples' ongoing negotiation of individually and mutually experienced contingencies emerging in their home and work lives. Today, more likely than in the past, families move in and out of assorted family forms and earning/caring arrangements, thereby making critical the present focus on processes of negotiation and renegotiation.

Extending this line of scholarship beyond the issues outlined above, future research should investigate the experiences and attitudes of larger and more diverse samples of couples. We wonder what other stances (or modifications of the five offered in this analysis) might be developed through exploring a larger corpus of discourse and related data such as division of labor diaries or extensive participant-observation field notes. What additional tensions or struggles would their stories reflect? Over time, do couples living the conflicted stance ever articulate feeling reconciled or comfortable in their reversal? If not, (why) do they remain as SAHFC? When and why do reversing couples decide they need to make a change? Additional research also should include the voices of couples from an extensive socio-economic range and various racial and ethnic backgrounds. Choosing to stay-at-home may be a function of economics and not an option for many couples. We also know that historical and contemporary gender roles and identities in African American and Hispanic marriages as well as gay and lesbian relationships may differ at times from White and heterosexual Americans.

There are also important practical implications of this study. Couples also may use this information as a resource in their own decision-making. Couples must listen carefully to how spouses talk about the idea of transposing roles prior to making that decision or in the midst of related conflicts. Spouses might listen for ways husbands or wives talk about who they are or could be as earners or caregivers (identity adoption), their views on who should be doing particular types of work (role eligibility), and what types of work they see men and women legitimately doing (task responsibility). Keying into such language is not easy but might give couples one more tool to make good decisions or better diagnose the potential challenges or frustrations they may experience (or are experiencing) in taking on these types of arrangements.

In closing, our analysis of the five homemaking and moneymaking stances detailed in this study provides a unique glimpse into the diverse ways SAHFCs negotiate gendered tasks, identities, and roles related to caring and earning. In the midst of unconventional ways of composing their lives, these couples' narratives illustrate the variety of subtle and critical communicative processes that facilitate and constrain gendered social change. Their sto-

ries show us what it means to redraw the boundaries of our work and family lives.

CARYN E. MEDVED is an associate professor of Communication Studies at Baruch College, City University of New York.

WILLIAM K. RAWLINS is a stocker professor in the School of Communication Studies at Ohio University.

EXPLORING THE ISSUE

Have Working Women Destroyed the American Family?

Critical Thinking and Reflection

1. What factors influence women to postpone or opt entirely out of childbearing?
2. How does the declining fertility rate in the United States impact other aspects of American culture beyond the economic considerations?
3. How might a "postfamiliar" nation adapt to waning fertility rates over time?

Is There Common Ground?

In a 2013 *Newsweek* article, writers Joel Kotkin and Harry Siegel discuss what they term "postfamilial America" where childbearing has become a lifestyle choice made by fewer people each year. Kotkin and Siegel (2013) note the possible causes of the "postfamiliar" era in other nations across the globe:

> The global causes of postfamilialism are diverse, and many, on their own, are socially favorable or at least benign. The rush of people worldwide into cities, for example, has ushered in prosperity for hundreds of millions, allowing families to be both smaller and more prosperous. Improvements in contraception and increased access to it have given women far greater control of their reproductive options, which has coincided with a decline in religion in most advanced countries. With women's rights largely secured in the First World and their seats in the classroom, the statehouse, and the boardroom no longer tokens or novelties, children have ceased being an economic or cultural necessity for many or an eventual outcome of sex.

The implications of such cultural and demographic shifts are largely uncharted territory for economists and social scientist alike.

Additional Resources

Kotkin, J. and Siegel, H. (2013, February 19). "Where have all the babies gone?" *The Daily Beast,* from Newsweek. Retrieved from: www.thedailybeast.com/newsweek/2013/02/18/why-the-choice-to-be-childless-is-bad-for-america.html

Bloomfield, G. (1983). "The Five Dollar Day: Labour Management and Social Control in the Ford Motor Company, 1908–1921." *Labour/Le Travail, 11,* 291–292.

Eddleston, K. and Powell, G. (2012). "Nurturing Entrepreneurs' Work–Family Balance: A Gendered Perspective." *Entrepreneurship: Theory & Practice, 36*(3), 513–541.

Mitchell, K. (2012). "Mission: Almost Impossible Working Mothers Struggle to Balance Career and Home Life." *Businesswest, 27*(22), 49–55.

Create Central

www.mhhe.com/createcentral

Internet References . . .

The Henry J. Kaiser Family Foundation

http://kff.org/uninsured/issue-brief/women-work-and-family-health-a-balancing/

National Partnership for Women & Families

http://www.nationalpartnership.org/

Selected, Edited, and with Issue Framing Material by:
Rachel Pienta, *Valdosta State University*

ISSUE

Are Lower Fertility Rates Responsible for Economic Downturns?

YES: Tom Bethell, from "Population, Economy, and God," *The American Spectator* (May 2009)

NO: Oded Galor and Andrew Mountford, from "Trading Population for Productivity: Theory and Evidence," *Review of Economic Studies* (October 2008)

Learning Outcomes
As you read the issue, focus on the following points: • How might fertility rates impact a population's economy?   • How does a woman's increased workforce participation impact a nation's productivity?

ISSUE SUMMARY

YES: Tom Bethell, senior editor of *The American Spectator*, examines low birth rates in nations with high GDP per capita. In his analysis, he discusses why the nations most able to afford larger families actually have fewer children per family than those who live in less wealthy countries.

NO: Oded Galor and Andrew Mountford argue that lower fertility rates result in the development of a highly specialized and skilled labor force.

For much of the late twentieth century, concerns about the world's so-called population explosion dominated discussions about development and sustainability. Demographers and other social scientists discussed how the nations of the world might adapt to accommodate the planet's burgeoning population. However, in the years since the century's turn it has become apparent that rapid population growth was not universal across the globe as wealthier, post-industrial nations saw fertility rates decline. Wealthier nations have also seen a trend of population replacement by recent immigrants, a shift that will change the demographic composition of these nations over the next several generations.

In wealthy, post-industrial nations the demand for skilled, specialized labor may exceed the talent available to meet industry needs. For example, Germany's economy is healthy and flourishing while fertility rates continue to decline. In 2011, the Association of German Engineers reported a chronic shortage of needed engineers to support the nation's technical industry (Blau & Gobble, 2012). Other European nations face similar challenges in meeting the need for highly skilled scientists. Faced with declining fertility rates, these countries must consider importing talent. Concomitantly, industry needs will drive and influence policy changes as national governments are

pressured to respond to corporate demands for a specialized labor force.

Bethell, in "Population, Economy, and God," explores the disparity in fertility rates between wealthy and less economically thriving nations through the lens of changing social norms. The foundation of Bethell's analysis is premised on the notion that a shift in views about sex and procreation have resulted in an anti-natal culture at the expense of fertility rates and, furthermore, the traditional family.

In "Trading Population for Productivity: Theory and Evidence," Galor and Mountford discuss a phenomenon termed as the "Great Divergence" in income per capita within the larger framework of two centuries of world demographic transitions. An era of sustained economic growth across the globe, supported by advances in communication and the relative ease of modern international commerce, served to widen the gap between the technologically privileged and those nations still toiling in the pre-industrial era.

Bethell's evaluation of guest worker programs in nations with declining fertility rates differs from that of Galor and Mountford. While Galor and Mountford examine the relationship between fertility rates and national productivity as a demographic factor that can inform government policies, Bethell sounds an alarm bell about unintended consequences and the potential pitfalls for nations that import rather than give birth to the future workforce.

YES ↵

Tom Bethell

Population, Economy, and God

World population, once "exploding," is still increasing, and "momentum" ensures that it will do so for decades to come. But fertility rates have tumbled. In Europe every country has fallen below replacement level. Some governments, especially France's, are beginning to use financial incentives to restore fertility rates but the effort, if generous enough to work—by paying women to have a third child—could bankrupt the welfare state.

In rich countries, a total fertility rate of 2.1 babies per woman is needed if population is to remain stable. But in the European Union as a whole the rate is down to 1.5. Germany is at 1.4, and Italy, Spain, and Greece are at 1.3. The fertility rate in France is now 2.0, or close to replacement. But the uneasy question is whether this is due to subsidies or to the growing Muslim population.

All over the world, with a few anomalies, there is a strong inverse correlation between GDP per capita and babies per family. It's a paradox, because wealthier people can obviously afford lots of children. But very predictably they have fewer. Hong Kong (1.02), Singapore, and Taiwan are three of the richest countries in the world, and three of the four lowest in total fertility. The countries with the highest fertility rates are Mali (7.4), Niger, and Uganda. Guess how low they are on the wealth chart.

Here's a news item. Carl Djerassi, one of the inventors of the birth control pill, recently deplored the sharp decline of total fertility in Austria (1.4), the country of his birth. A Catholic news story seized on that and reported that one of the pill's inventors had said the pill had caused a "demographic catastrophe." Austria's leading Catholic, Cardinal Schönborn, said the Vatican had predicted 40 years ago that the pill would promote a dramatic fall in birth rates.

Djerassi, 85, an emeritus professor of chemistry at Stanford, did warn of a catastrophe and he said that Austria should admit more immigrants. But he denied that people have smaller families "because of the availability of birth control." They do so "for personal, economic, cultural, and other reasons," of which "changes in the status of women" was the most important. Japan has an even worse demographic problem, he said, "yet the pill was only legalized there in 1999 and is still not used widely." (Japan's fertility rate is 1.22.) (In fact, if the pill and abortion really were illegal more children surely would be born, if only because unintentional pregnancies would come to term.)

Austrian families who had decided against children wanted "to enjoy their schnitzels while leaving the rest of the world to get on with it," Djerassi also said. That may have rankled because the country had just put his face on a postage stamp.

So what is causing these dramatic declines? It's under way in many countries outside Europe too. In Mexico, fertility has moved down close to replacement level—having been as high as six babies per woman in the 1970s.

Obviously economic growth has been the dominant factor but there are other considerations.

Young couples hardly read Paul Ehrlich before deciding whether to have children, but scaremongering authors have played a key role in creating our anti-natalist mood. Books warning of a (then) newfangled emergency, the "population explosion," began appearing soon after World War II. Consider *Road to Survival* (1948), by William Vogt, or *People! Challenge to Survival*, by the same author. An anti-people fanatic before his time, Vogt was hypnotized by the Malthusian doctrine that population growth would overtake the food supply. That would lead to a war of all against all. Paul Ehrlich projected that the 1980s would see massive die-offs from starvation. (Obesity turned out to be the greater health threat.)

In that earlier period, the population controllers didn't feel they had to mince words. Vogt wrote in 1960 that "tens of thousands of children born every year in the United States should, solely for their own sakes, never have seen the light of day. . . . There are hundreds of thousands of others, technically legitimate since their parents have engaged in some sort of marriage ritual, but whose birth is as much of a crime against them as it is against the bastards."

At a time when the world population still had not reached 3 billion—today it is 6.7 billion—Vogt thought "drastic measures are inescapable." He warned of "mounting population pressures in the Soviet Union," where, by the century's end, "there may be 300 million Russians." It was time for them "to begin control of one of the most powerful causes of war—overpopulation."

Note: the population of Russia by 2000 was 145 million; today it is 141 million. (Fertility rate: 1.4.)

Population alarmists have long enjoyed the freedom to project their fears onto whatever cause is uppermost in the progressive mind. Then it was war. Today it is the environment, which, we are told, human beings are ruining. This will be shown to have been as false as the earlier warnings, but not before our environmental scares have done much harm to a fragile economy (at the rate things are going with Obama). All previous scares were based on faulty premises, and the latest one, based on "science," will be no different.

I believe that two interacting factors shape population growth or decline: economic prosperity and belief in God. As to the first, there is no doubt that rising material prosperity discourages additional children. Fewer infants die; large families are no longer needed to support older parents. The welfare state—which only rich countries can afford—has greatly compounded this effect. When people believe that the government will take care of them, pay their pensions and treat their maladies, children do seem less essential.

A rise in prosperity also encourages people to think that they can dispense with God. Religion diminishes when wealth increases—that's my theory. But with a twist that I shall come to. Wealth generates independence, including independence from God, or (if you will) Providence. God is gradually forgotten, then assumed not to exist. This will tend to drive childbearing down even further. Hedonism will become predominant. Remember, Jesus warned that it's the rich, not the poor, who are at spiritual hazard.

The legalization of abortion reflected the decline of religious faith in America, but it must also have led others to conclude that God was no longer to be feared. That's why I don't quite believe Djerassi when he tries to disassociate the pill from fertility. The ready availability of the pill told society at large that sex without consequences was perfectly acceptable. Then, by degrees, that self-indulgent view became an anti-natalist worldview.

It became so ingrained that many people now think it obvious. Sex became a "free" pastime as long as it was restricted to consenting adults. Furthermore, anyone who questioned that premise risked denunciation as a bigot.

The U.S. has been seen as the great stumbling block to any theory linking prosperity, lack of faith, and low fertility. Prosperity here has been high, and overall fertility is at replacement. But I am wary of this version of American exceptionalism. How much lower would U. S. fertility fall without the influx of Latino immigrants and their many offspring? Nicholas Eberstadt, a demographer at AEI, tells me that Mexican immigrants now actually have a higher fertility rate in the U.S. than they do in Mexico. (Maybe because they come to American hospitals for free medical care?)

I wonder also if religious vitality here is what it's cracked up to be. Surely it has weakened considerably. A recent survey by Trinity College in Hartford, funded by the Lilly Endowment, showed that the percentage of Americans identifying themselves as Christian dropped to 76 percent from 86 percent in 1990; those with "no" religion, 8.2 percent of the population in 1990, are now 15 percent.

As a social force, the U.S. Catholic bishops have withered away to a shocking extent. Hollywood once respected and feared their opinion. Today, the most highly placed of these bishops are unwilling to publicly rebuke pro-abortion politicians who call themselves Catholic, even when they give scandal by receiving Communion in public. How the mitered have fallen. They daren't challenge the rich and powerful.

But there is another factor. Calling yourself a Christian when the pollster phones imposes no cost and self-reported piety may well be inflated. We have to distinguish between mere self-labelers and actual churchgoers. And beyond that there are groups with intense religious belief who retain the morale to ignore the surrounding materialism and keep on having children.

The ultra-Orthodox in Israel are the best example. Other Jewish congregations may go to synagogue, but they have children at perhaps one-third the ultra-Orthodox rate. At about seven or eight children per family, theirs is one of the highest fertility rates in the world. And they don't permit birth control—Carl Djerassi, please note. In the U.S. Orthodox Jews again far outbreed their more secular sisters.

The Mormons are also distinctive. Utah, about two-thirds Mormon, has the highest fertility rate (2.63 in 2006) among the 50 states; Vermont has the lowest (1.69). In the recent Trinity Survey, Northern New England is now "the least religious section of the country." Vermont is the least religious state; 34 percent of residents say they have "no religion." So minimal faith and low fertility are demonstrably linked. Mormon fertility is declining, to be sure, and I recognize that I am flirting with a circular argument: deciding which groups are the most fervent by looking at their birth rates.

Then there's the Muslim concern. It's hard to avoid concluding that the lost Christian zeal has been appropriated by Islam. In the U.S., Muslims have doubled since 1990 (from a low base, to 0.6% of the population). The rise of Islam suggests that the meager European fertility rates would be even lower if Muslims had not contributed disproportionately to European childbearing.

It's hard to pin down the numbers, though. Fertility in France has risen, but Nick Eberstadt tells me that the French government won't reveal how many of these babies are born to Muslim parents. "They treat it as a state secret," he said. In other countries such as Switzerland, where lots of guest workers are employed, the fertility rate would be much lower than it already is (1.44) were it not for the numerous offspring of those guest workers.

When a population is not replacing itself, the welfare state creates its own hazard. Lots of new workers are needed to support the retirees. Germany's low fertility will require an annual immigration of 200,000 just to maintain the current population. Where will they come from? Many arrive from Turkey, where the fertility rate has also declined (to about 2.0). But not as far as it has declined among native Germans. So the concern is that in the welfare states of Europe, believing Muslims are slowly replacing the low-morale, low-fertility, materialistic non-believers who once formed a Christian majority.

I could summarize the argument with this overstatement: The intelligentsia stopped believing in God in the 19th century. In the 20th it tried to build a new society, man without God. It failed. Then came a new twist. Man stopped believing in himself. He saw himself as a mere polluter—a blot on the landscape. Theologians tell us that creatures cannot exist without the support of God. A corollary may be that societies cannot long endure without being sustained by a *belief* in God.

Tom Bethell is a journalist who writes mainly on economic and scientific issues.

Galor and Mountford

Trading Population for Productivity: Theory and Evidence

Introduction

The dramatic transformation in the distribution of income and population across the globe in the past two centuries is one of the most significant mysteries in the growth process. Some regions have excelled in the growth of income *per capita*, while other regions have been dominant in population growth.[1] This striking contrast between the development paths of large subsets of the world economy gives rise to fundamental questions about the growth process and its implications for current and historical development patterns. Notably, how does one account for the sudden take-off from stagnation to growth in some countries in the world and the persistent stagnation in others? Why have the differences in *per capita* incomes across countries increased so markedly in the last two centuries? Has the pace of transition to sustained economic growth in advanced economies adversely affected the process of development in less-developed economies? Have the forces of international trade contributed to the divergence in the timing of the demographic transition and the emergence of sustained economic growth across countries?

The origin of this "Great Divergence" in income *per capita* has been a source of controversy. The relative roles of geographical and institutional factors, human capital formation, ethnic, linguistic and religious fractionalization, colonialism, and globalization have been at the centre of a debate about this remarkable change in the world income distribution in the past two centuries.[2]

This research suggests that international trade has played a significant role in the differential timing of demographic transitions across countries and has been a major determinant of the distribution of world population and the "Great Divergence" in income *per capita* across countries in the last two centuries. The analysis suggests that international trade has an asymmetrical effect on the evolution of industrial and non-industrial economies. While in the industrial nations the gains from trade have been directed primarily towards investment in education and growth in output *per capita*, a greater portion of the gains from trade in non-industrial nations has been chanelled towards population growth.

The expansion of international trade enhanced the specialization of industrial economies in the production of industrial, skilled intensive, goods. The associated rise in the demand for skilled labour has induced a gradual investment in the quality of the population, expediting a demographic transition, stimulating technological progress and further enhancing the comparative advantage of these industrial economies in the production of skilled intensive goods. In non-industrial economies, in contrast, international trade has generated an incentive to specialize in the production of unskilled intensive, non-industrial, goods. The absence of significant demand for human capital has provided limited incentives to invest in the quality of the population and the gains from trade have been utilized primarily for a further increase in the size of the population, rather than the income of the existing population.[3] The demographic transition in these non-industrial economies has been significantly delayed, increasing further their relative abundance of unskilled labour, enhancing their comparative disadvantage in the production of skilled intensive goods and delaying their process of development. The research suggests, therefore, that international trade has persistently affected the distribution of population, skills, and technologies in the world economy, and has been a significant force behind the "Great Divergence" in income *per capita* across countries.

This paper develops a unified growth theory that captures the asymmetric role that international trade may have played in expediting the transition to sustained economic growth in technologically advanced economies and in delaying the transition in technologically inferior economies. The proposed theory is innovative in two dimensions. First, unlike the recent literature on the transition of economies from an epoch of Malthusian stagnation to a state of sustained economic growth that abstracted from the Great Divergence and focused on the evolution of the world economy from stagnation to growth,[4] the proposed theory examines the differential patterns of take-offs across regions in the world and the emergence of the Great Divergence. Second, in contrast to the existing literature on the dynamics of comparative advantage,[5] the focus on the interaction between population growth and comparative advantage and the persistent effect that this interaction may have on the distribution of population and income in the world economy generates an important new insight regarding the distribution of the gains from trade. The theory suggests that even if trade equalizes output growth in the trading countries (due to the terms of trade effect), income *per capita* of developed and less developed economies will diverge, since in developed economies the growth of total output will be generated primarily by an increase in output *per capita*, whereas in less developed economies the contribution of population growth to the growth of total output will be more significant.[6]

The theory is based on several fundamental elements. The interaction between these elements generates a dynamic pattern that is consistent with the observed asymmetrical evolution of the world economy from the epoch of Malthusian stagnation to the current era of sustained growth, characterized by widened differences in income *per capita* and population growth rates, as well as by persistent patterns of comparative advantage. Economies are initially in a Malthusian epoch in which the growth rate of output *per capita* is rather small and population growth is positively related to the level of income *per capita*. Technological progress leads ultimately to the adoption of more advanced agricultural and industrial technologies which paves the way for the take-off from the Malthusian epoch. International trade induces technologically advanced economies to specialize in the production of skilled intensive manufactured goods whereas technologically inferior economies specialize in the production of unskilled intensive agricultural goods. The increase in the demand for human capital in the technologically advanced economies that is brought about by international trade induces investment in human capital[7] and expedites the demographic transition,[8] whereas the reduction in the demand for human capital in less advanced economies delays the demographic transition and investment in human capital.[9]

The analysis demonstrates that the acceleration of the demographic transition in the technologically advanced economies increases their formation of human capital and brings about sustained technological progress that enhances their comparative advantage in the production of skilled intensive industrial goods.[10] In contrast, the delay in the demographic transition in the less advanced economies increases the supply of unskilled workers and enhances the comparative advantage of these economies in the production of unskilled intensive goods. Thus, consistent with the evidence provided in Sections 5 and 6, the pattern of international trade has reinforced the initial patterns of comparative advantage and has generated a persistent effect on the distribution of population in the world economy and a great divergence in income *per capita* across countries and regions.

The fundamental hypothesis is tested empirically using contemporary cross country data. In accordance with the theory, cross country regressions support the hypothesis that international trade generates opposing effects on fertility rates and education in developed and less developed economies. The analysis establishes that a larger share of trade in GDP *per capita* has a positive effect

on fertility and a negative effect on human capital formation in non-OECD economies, whereas in OECD economies, trade triggers a decline in fertility and an increase in human capital accumulation.

An Autarkic Economy

This section analyzes the path of a closed economy from its Malthusian pre-industrial state through a transitional state of increased fertility, investment in human capital and economic growth to a modern state with high investment in human capital, low population growth, and sustained economic growth.

Consider an overlapping-generations economy in which economic activity extends over infinite discrete time. In every period t, two goods, a manufactured good, Y_t^m, and an agricultural good Y_t^a, may be produced using up to three factors of production, skilled labour, H_t, unskilled labour, L_t, and land, X. The supply of skilled and unskilled labour is endogenously determined and evolves over time, whereas the quantity of land is exogenously determined and remains constant over time.

Production

In each of the sectors of the economy production may take place with either an old technology or a new one. In early stages of development the new production technologies are latent and production is conducted using the old technologies. However, in the process of development the productivity of the new technologies grows faster than those of the old technologies and ultimately the new technologies become economically viable. In the agricultural sector, the introduction of the new technology represents the escape from the Malthusian trap, where wages do not fall despite an increase in population. In the industrial sector, the introduction of the new technology reflects an increase in the skill-intensity of the production process in the second phase of the industrial revolution and the associated increase in the demand for human capital. . . .

Concluding Remarks

This research suggests that the transformation in the distribution of income and population across the globe that accompanied the take-off from an epoch of stagnation to sustained economic growth is partly associated with the contrasting effects of international trade on the timing of the demographic transition in industrial and non-industrial countries. In industrial economies international trade has enhanced the specialization in the production of skilled intensive goods and stimulated technological progress. The rise in the demand for skilled labour has induced an investment in the quality of the population, expediting the demographic transition, stimulating technological progress and further enhancing the comparative advantage of these industrial economies in the produc-

tion of skilled intensive goods. In non-industrial economies, in contrast, the specialization in the production of
unskilled intensive goods that has been triggered by international trade has reduced the demand for skilled labour,
providing limited incentives to invest in population
quality. The demographic transition has been therefore
delayed, increasing further the abundance of unskilled
labour in these economies and enhancing their comparative disadvantage in the production of skilled intensive
goods. International trade has therefore widened the
gap between the technological level as well as the skill
abundance of industrial and non-industrial economies,
enhancing the initial patterns of comparative advantage
and generating sustained differences in income *per capita*
across countries.

The asymmetric effect of international trade on the
timing of the demographic transition in developed and
less-developed economies, and its persistent effect, therefore, on the initial patterns of comparative advantage,
may suggest that the rapid transition of the currently
developed economies into a state of sustained economic
growth is associated with the slow transition of less
developed economies into a state of sustained economic
growth.

The analysis abstracts from several factors that are
relevant for the assessment of the effects of international
trade on population growth and the process of development in less developed economies. Cultural and institutional differences between countries in the determination
of population growth, in the provision of public education, and in the process of technological change would
be reflected in the demographic characteristics and in the
patterns of comparative advantage. Moreover, the adverse
effect of international trade on industrialization and thus
on the timing of the demographic transition could have
been mitigated by the positive effect of trade on technological diffusion across countries. Nevertheless, labour productivity greatly differs across countries and even among
industries in which technologies are very similar. Moreover, since the rate of technological diffusion depends
upon the appropriateness of factor endowments in the
receiving country, the adverse effect of trade on the factor endowment of less developed economies would slow
down the rate of technological diffusion.[11]

In contrast to the existing literature on the dynamics of comparative advantage, the focus on the interaction
between population growth and comparative advantage
and the persistent effect that this interaction may have on
the distribution of population and income in the world
economy generates an important new insight regarding
the distribution of the gains from trade. The theory suggests that even if trade between developed and less developed economies equalizes output growth in the trading
countries, income *per capita* of developed and less developed economies will diverge, since in developed economies the growth of total output will be generated primarily
by an increase in output *per capita*, whereas in less devel-

oped economies the contribution of population growth to
the growth of total output will be more significant.

In accordance with the theory, cross country regression analysis supports the hypothesis that international
trade generates opposing effects on fertility rates and
education in developed and less developed economies. It
demonstrates that international trade has a positive effect
on fertility and a negative effect on human capital formation in non-OECD economies, whereas in OECD economies, trade triggers a decline in fertility and an increase
in human capital accumulation. Thus, international trade
accentuates the initial patterns of comparative advantage
and is likely to affect differently the growth trajectories
of population, human capital, and income *per capita* of
developed and less developed economies.

Notes

1. In the time period 1820–1998, the ratio between
income *per capita* in the richest region of the
world and the poorest region of the world has
increased from about 3 to 19. In particular, the
ratio between income *per capita* in Western
Europe and Asia grew nearly threefold, whereas
the ratio between the Asian population and the
Western European population grew nearly twofold (Maddison, 2001).
2. North (1981), Landes (1998), Mokyr (2002),
Hall and Jones (1999), Acemoglu, Johnson and
Robinson (2005), Easterly and Levine (2003),
Rodrik, Subraminian and Trebbi (2004), Howitt
and Mayer-Foulkes (2005) and Ashraf and
Galor (2007) have argued that institutions that
facilitated the protection of property rights
and enhanced technological research, the diffusion of knowledge, and the transmission of
society specific human capital, have been the
prime factors that enabled the earlier European
take-off and the great technological divergence
across the globe. The effect of geographical factors on economic growth and the great divergence have been emphasized by Jones (1981),
Diamond (1997), Gallup, Sachs and Mellinger
(1998) and Pomeranz (2000). Finally, the role of
human capital in the great divergence is under-
lined in unified growth theory (Galor, 2005;
Galor and Weil 2000; Galor and Moav, 2002;
McDermott, 2002; Doepke, 2004; Lagerlof,
2006; Galor, Moav and Vollrath, 2008) and is
documented empirically by Glaeser, La Porta,
Lopez-De-Silanes and Shleifer (2004).
3. Evidence suggests that the returns to human
capital may have been higher in LDCs. One
can therefore mistakenly suppose that incentives to invest in child quality are higher in
LDCs. However, these higher rates of return are
not applicable to most individuals. They reflect
a suboptimal investment in human capital in
an environment characterized by credit market
imperfections and limited access to schooling.
International trade, therefore reduces further

the modest demand for human capital and reduces further the incentive to substitute child quality for quantity.

4. In particular, Galor and Weil (1999, 2000) argue that the inherent positive interaction between population and technology during the Malthusian regime increased the rate of technological progress sufficiently so as to induce investment in human capital which led to further technological progress, a demographic transition, and sustained economic growth.

5. See Findlay and Kierzkowski (1983), Grossman and Helpman (1991), Stokey (1991), Young (1991), Matsuyama (1992), and Atkeson and Kehoe (2000), among others.

6. See, for example, Acemoglu and Ventura (2002) for the terms of trade effect. Deardorff (1994) suggests that diverging (exogenous) population growth rates can lead to widening international inequality. Similarly, Krugman and Venables (1995) and Baldwin, Martin and Ottaviano (2001) argue that the reduction in transportation costs and the associated expansion in trade, generated geographically based industrialization and divergence.

7. Consistent with empirical evidence, the increased demand for human capital has not resulted necessarily in an increase in the equilibrium rate of return to human capital due to a massive supply response generated by (a) the increase in the incentive for investment in education (for a given cost), and (b) institutional changes (*e.g.* the provision of public education) that lowered the cost of investment in human capital.

8. Unlike Becker's hypothesis (Becker, 1981) where a high level of income induces parents to switch to having fewer, higher quality children, the substitution of quality for quantity is in response to technological progress. The fact that demographic transitions occurred around the same period in Western European countries that differed in their income *per capita*, but shared a similar pattern of future technological progress, supports our technological approach.

9. Moreover, the increased specialization of production within an economy would result, ceteris paribus, in increased income and fertility inequality within the economy, in line with the finding of Haines (2000) that fertility rate in rural areas remained higher than for urban areas for significant periods in the 19th century in both the U.S. and U.K., as well as with the findings of de la Croix and Doepke (2003) that income inequality causes differential fertility patterns within and across economies.

10. Similarly to this element in the theory, Grossman and Helpman (1991) demonstrate that a country that begins with a head start in the accumulation of knowledge often leads in productivity over time.

11. The effect of trade on technological diffusion is discussed by Findlay (1996). The imperfec-

tions in this process are illustrated for instance by Clark (1987) who shows that despite the fact that in 1910 textile machinery was uniform around the world, labour productivity was ten times higher in advanced countries than in the less developed ones. This imperfection may be related to the effect of factor endowments on the adoption of technologies (Basu and Weil, 1998; Zeira, 1998; Acemoglu and Zilibotti, 2001).

References

Acemoglu, D., Johnson, S. and Robinson, J. A. (2005), "Institutions as the Fundamental Cause of Long-Run Growth," in P. Aghion and S. Durlauf (eds.) *Handbook of Economic Growth* (Amsterdam: North-Holland) 395–472.

Acemoglu, D. and Ventura, J. (2002), "The World Income Distribution," *Quarterly Journal of Economics,* **117**, 659–694.

Acemoglu, D. and Zilibotti, F. (2001), "Productivity Differences," *Quarterly Journal of Economics,* **116**, 563–606.

Ashraf, Q. and Galor, O. (2007), "Cultural Assimilation, Cultural Diffusion and the Origin of the Wealth of Nations" (CEPR Discussion Papers 6444).

Atkeson, A. and Kehoe, P. (2000), "Paths of Development for Early and Late Bloomers in a Dynamic Heckscher-Ohlin Model" (Bank of Minneapolis Staff Report #256).

Baldwin, R. E., Martin, P. and Ottaviano, G. I. P. (2001), "Global Income Divergence, Trade and Industrialization: The Geography of Growth Take-Offs," *Journal of Economic Growth,* **6**, 5–37.

Basu, S. and Weil, D. N. (1998), "Appropriate Technology and Growth," *Quarterly Journal of Economics,* **113**, 1025–1054.

Becker, G. S. (1981), *A Treatise on the Family* (Cambridge, MA: Harvard University Press).

Clark, G. (1987), "Why Isn't the Whole World Developed? Lessons from the Cotton Mills," *Journal of Economic History,* **47** (1), 141–174.

Deardorff, A. V. (1994), "Growth and International Investment with Diverging Populations," *Oxford Economic Papers,* **46** (3), 477–91.

De La Croix, D. and Doepke, M. (2003), "Inequality and Growth: Why Differential Fertility Matters," *American Economic Review,* **93**, 1091–1113.

Diamond, J. (1997), *Guns, Germs and Steel: The Fates of Human Societies* (New York: Norton).

Doepke, M. (2004), "Accounting for Fertility Decline During the Transition to Growth," *Journal of Economic Growth,* **9**, 347–383.

Easterly, W. and Levine, R. (2003), "Tropics, Germs, and Crops: The Role of Endowments in Economic Development," *Journal of Monetary Economics*, **50**, 3–39.

Findlay, R. and Keirzkowski, H. (1983), "International Trade and Human Capital: A Simple General Equilibrium Model," *Journal of Political Economy*, **91**, 957–978.

Findlay, R. (1996), "Modeling Global Interdependence: Centers, Peripheries, and Frontiers," *American Economic Review*, **86**, 47–51.

Gallup, J. L., Sachs, J. D. and Mellinger, A. D. (1998), "Geography and Economic Development" (NBER Working Paper No. w6849, Cambridge, MA).

Galor, O. (2005), "Unified Growth Theory: From Stagnation to Growth," in P. Aghion and S. Durlauf (eds.) *Handbook of Economic Growth* (Amsterdam: North-Holland), 171–293.

Galor, O. and Moav, O. (2002), "Natural Selection and the Origin of Economic Growth," *Quarterly Journal of Economics*, **117**, 1133–1192.

Galor, O., Moav, O. and Vollrath, D. (2008), "Inequality in Land Ownership, the Emergence of Human Capital Promoting Institutions and the Great Divergence," *Review of Economic Studies*.

Galor, O. and Weil, D. N. (1999), "From Malthusian Stagnation to Modern Growth," *American Economic Review*, **89**, 150–154.

Galor, O. and Weil, D. N. (2000), "Population, Technology and Growth: From the Malthusian Regime to the Demographic Transition," *American Economic Review*, **90**, 806–828.

Glaeser, E. L., La Porta, R., Lopez-De-Silanes, F. and Shleifer, A. (2004), "Do Institutions Cause Growth?," *Journal of Economic Growth*, **9**, 271–303.

Grossman, G. M. and Helpman, E. (1991), *Innovation and Growth* (Cambridge, MA: MIT Press).

Haines, M. R. (2000), "The Population of the United States, 1790–1920," in S. L. Engermann and R. E. Gallman (eds.) *The Cambridge Economic History of the United States, Vol. II, The Long Nineteenth Century* (Cambridge: Cambridge University Press) 143–205.

Harley, C. K. (1999), "Reassessing the Industrial Revolution: A Macro View," in J. Mokyr (ed.) *The British Industrial Revolution: An Economic Perspective* (Boulder: Westview Press) 160–205.

Hall, R. E. and Jones, C. I. (1999), "Why Do Some Countries Produce So Much More Output Per Worker Than Others?," *Quarterly Journal of Economics*, **114**, 83–116.

Howitt, P. and Mayer-Foulkes, D. (2005), "R&D, Implementation and Stagnation: A Schumpeterian Theory of Convergence Clubs," *Journal of Money Credit and Banking*, **37**, 147–177.

Jones, E. L. (1981), *The European Miracle: Environments, Economies and Geopolitics in the History of Europe and Asia* (Cambridge: Cambridge University Press).

Krugman, P. and Venables, A. (1995), "Globalization and the Inequality of Nations," *Quarterly Journal of Economics*, **90**, 857–880.

Lagerlof, N. P. (2006), "The Galor-Weil Model Revisited: A Quantitative Exercise," *Review of Economic Dynamics*, **9**, 116–142.

Landes, D. S. (1998), *The Wealth and Poverty of Nations* (New York: Norton).

Maddison, A. (2001), *The World Economy* (Paris: OECD).

Matsuyama, K. (1992), "Agricultural Productivity, Comparative Advantage, and Economic Growth," *Journal of Economic Theory*, **58**, 317–334.

Mcdermott, J. (2002), "Development Dynamics: Economic Integration and the Demographic Transition," *Journal of Economic Growth*, **7**, 371–410.

Mokyr, J. (2002), *The Gifts of Athena: Historical Origins of the Knowledge Economy* (Princeton: Princeton University Press).

Pomeranz, K. (2000), *The Great Divergence: China, Europe and the Making of the Modern World Economy* (Princeton: Princeton University Press).

Rodrik, D., Subraminian, A. and Trebbi, F. (2004), "Institutions Rule: The Primacy of Institutions Over Geography and Integration in Economic Development," *Journal of Economic Growth*, **9**, 131–165.

Stokey, N. L. (1991), "The Volume and Composition of Trade Between Rich and Poor Countries," *Review of Economic Studies*, **58**, 63–80.

Young, A. (1991), "Learning by Doing and the Dynamic Effects of International Trade," *Quarterly Journal of Economics*, **106**, 369–405.

Zeira, J. (1998), "Workers, Machines, and Economic Growth," *Quarterly Journal of Economics*, **113**, 1091–1118.

ODED GALOR is the Herbert H. Goldberger Professor of Economics at Brown University.

ANDREW MOUNTFORD is a professor of economics in the Department of Economics, Royal Holloway University of London.

EXPLORING THE ISSUE

Are Lower Fertility Rates Responsible for Economic Downturns?

Critical Thinking and Reflection

1. How is Tom Bethell's analysis of the economy influenced by his perspective regarding the interaction between culture and religious faith?
2. How might the data presented by Oded Galor and Andrew Mountford prove useful to governments in the design and implementation of future national policies in the United States and in Europe?
3. How are cultural attitudes about children and families influenced by social norms about gender roles?

Is There Common Ground?

Research on demographic transitions that occur as a result of falling fertility rates suggest that the greater productivity of women who delay childbirth actually results in increased economic growth for nations that experience this population trend (Lawson, 2008). As definitions of family shift and gender norms associated with families evolve, cultural attitudes about fertility and family size will also change. Lawson (2008) asserts that concurrent "declines in mortality and fertility allows the working-age share of the population to grow" at a relatively quick pace, resulting in per capita gains that impact national gross domestic product over several decades (p. 9). In the case of nations with graying populations with upside-down demographics—where the number of non-working citizens exceeds the number of workers—governments need to consider who will perform the labor of the workforce. However, the changing notion of labor needs in devel-

oping nations combined with technological production advances may also mean that in the future fewer workers will do work that required more people power in prior generations.

Additional Resources

Blau, J., and Gobble, M.M. (2012). "Europe's Battle for Technical Talent." *Research Technology Management, 55*(2), 3.

Lawson, S. (2008). "Women Hold Up Half the Sky." Global Economics Paper No. 164. Goldman Sachs Economic Research. Retrieved from: www.goldmansachs.com/

Create Central

www.mhhe.com/createcentral

Internet References . . .

Pew Social and Demographic Trends

http://www.pewsocialtrends.org/2011/10/12/in-a-down-economy-fewer-births/

Carolina Population Center

http://www.cpc.unc.edu/news/features/low-fertility-rate-of-china

National Council for Research on Women

http://www.ncrw.org/news-center/in-the-news/study-fertility-rates-affected-global-economic-crisi

Unit 4

Gender Equity: Still Unequal After All These Years

*H*ow do we determine what constitutes gender equity and who should benefit? How do we decide when parity has been achieved? Is Title IX still necessary? Are "trans" women who become female entitled to benefit from gender equity policies? Is the Equal Rights Amendment still needed?

The battle for gender equity should really be characterized as a long war because the campaign is deeply rooted and has a long history. In the United States, the framers of the Constitution were famously asked to "remember the ladies." Abigail Adams, wife of John Adams, in a 1776 letter written to her husband and other members of the Continental Congress, asked the men to consider the role of women as citizens as the new nation was formed:

"remember the ladies and be more generous and favorable to them than your ancestors. Do not put such unlimited power into the hands of the husbands. Remember, all men would be tyrants if they could. If particular care and attention is not paid to the ladies, we are determined to foment a rebellion, and will not hold ourselves bound by any laws in which we have no voice or representation."

Women across the globe continue to ask world leaders to "remember the ladies" and perhaps nowhere is the request made more frequently nor more loudly than in America. From the convening of the Seneca Falls Convention in 1848 to the passage of the 19th Amendment in 1920 to the present day, American women continue to ask men to "remember the ladies" and promise rebellion if their voices are not heard.

Butterfield, L.H., ed. *Adams Family Correspondence* (vol. 1, pp. 369–371). Belknap Press of Harvard University Press: Cambridge, Massachusetts, 1963–1993.

Selected, Edited, and with Issue Framing Material by:
Rachel Pienta, *Valdosta State University*

ISSUE

Should "Trans" Women Benefit from Gender Equity Policies?

YES: Laurel Anderson, from "Punishing the Innocent: How the Classification of Male-to-Female Transgender Individuals in Immigration Detention Constitutes Illegal Punishment Under the Fifth Amendment," *Berkeley Journal of Gender, Law & Justice*, vol. 25, issue 1 (Spring 2010)

NO: Stephanie Bloyd, from "'Bathroom Bill' Sparks Accessibility Debate," *Club Industry* (Fitness Business Pro section, Penton Media, August 2009)

Learning Outcomes

As you read the issues, focus on the following points:

- Are current gender equity policies sufficient to protect the rights of transgender individuals?
- Is segregation of transgender individuals a viable option?

ISSUE SUMMARY

YES: Laurel Anderson examines the gap in the justice system's current policies relative to the concerns of the transgender community. She suggests that the detention policies currently in place provide insufficient protection to female detainees and place the safety of "trans" women in particular in jeopardy.

NO: Stephanie Bloyd examines bathroom parity and accessibility within the framework of gender equity relative to the experiences of transgender men and women.

Petra L. Doan, a post-operative transsexual woman, is an urban and regional planning professor who writes about issues related to planning for queer populations. Her research suggests that "trans" women experience greater levels of victimization across all spheres of society (Doan, 2009). Issues of accessibility, discrimination, and safety are key factors in policy discussions concerning accommodations for members of the transgender community.

Part of the challenge in determining how to address the needs of the gender variant community is to consider what framework to apply. Anti-discrimination proponents frame the discourse within civil rights language, while issues surrounding privacy rights further complicate legal considerations in the courts.

In "Punishing the Innocent: How the Classification of Male-to-Female Transgender Individuals in Immigration

Detention Constitutes Illegal Punishment Under the Fifth Amendment," Anderson examines how the current policies of such agencies as Immigration and Customs Enforcement (ICE) hold transgender women in conditions that may violate the Due Process Clause. She suggests that policy reform alone will not ensure the safety of transgender female detainees. According to Anderson, specialized diversity training designed to create a culture of respect and understanding will ultimately be effective in reducing violence toward incarcerated transgender women.

In "'Bathroom Bill' Sparks Accessibility Debate," Bloyd addresses the conflict between anti-discrimination and privacy issues inherent in the debate over accessibility for transgender women. The issue of accessibility and the provision of non-discriminatory, private, and safe space continue to be a source of controversy as states struggle to determine questions of gender in public venues.

YES

Laurel Anderson

Punishing the Innocent: How the Classification of Male-to-Female Transgender Individuals in Immigration Detention Constitutes Illegal Punishment Under the Fifih Amendment

Christina Madrazo, a male-to-female pre-operative transgender immigrant, was detained in Krome Detention Center in Miami, Florida awaiting an appeal of her asylum claim. She fled Mexico after she was violently attacked for being transgender. Madrazo was placed in solitary confinement at Krome because officials were unsure whether to house her with men or women. Solitary confinement was isolating and made her extremely vulnerable to attacks by prison guards. One of the guards, in charge of bringing her meals and watching over her safety, raped her on two separate occasions. The first time, the guard attacked Madrazo in her cell and tried to force her to perform oral sex on him. When she refused, he sodomized her until he heard another person approaching. Madrazo reported the rape, but the officer was still allowed to serve her food the next day. Later that night, he raped her a second time. Unfortunately, this tragic story is not uncommon; transgender detainees, particularly male-to-female transgender women, are at a high risk of sexual assault and harassment.

Although immigrant detainees are technically held in civil custody, there is an inherent inconsistency between their legal status and their detention conditions. Most are housed in jails and prisons, while others are held in prison-like conditions in detention centers without having been convicted of a crime. Detainees are often treated like prisoners: shackled, forced to wear jumpsuits, and permitted to visit with relatives only through glass. Despite their identification as women, most transgender detainees are housed with men. Abuse in male facilities is rampant, and male-to-female transgender women are often the targets. They experience harassment and sexual assault at rates much higher than the general population. For example, a recent study by the University of California, Irvine found that 59 percent of transgender prisoners in California reported being victims of sexual assault, compared to 4.4 percent of the general prison population.

In men's detention facilities, a strict hierarchy is enforced that rewards masculinity and aggression with power and punishes femininity and passivity with violence. An informal but highly enforced code of conduct requires men to "'act tough, lift weights, and be willing to fight to settle grudges,' or risk being labeled weak and subjected to beatings and rape." Detainees and staff victimize other detainees who are perceived as weak or feminine. As one inmate explained, "Smaller, weaker, meeker individuals are usually targets. Meeker individuals tend to 'act Gay' is how it's described here and in turn invites [sic] assault. . . ." Transgender women in men's facilities immediately stand out due to their femininity. Consequently, they find themselves at the bottom of the hierarchy and become targets of sexual victimization and harassment from other inmates and guards.

This commentary focuses on the plight of male-to-female transgender immigrants in men's detention facilities. The term "transgender" signifies people who have a gender identity or expression that is different from the one associated with their assigned sex. A male-to-female transgender person, or a transgender woman, is a person who was deemed a man at birth but who currently identifies as a woman. This paper uses the term "transgender detainees" to refer to transgender women, who are the focus of this inquiry. Additionally, the term "detention facilities" is used as a general term meant to encompass all types of facilities—including prisons, jails, and detention centers—that detain immigrants for immigration purposes.

I argue that the detention policies of Immigration and Customs Enforcement (ICE)—when applied to transgender immigrants—create an environment that constitutes punishment in violation of the Due Process Clause. This note seeks to identify the efficacy of using a due process challenge to force ICE to make the reforms necessary to reduce the punitive nature of immigrant detention and protect the heath and safety of transgender detainees. I identify two necessary reforms: reworking the current gender classification system to reflect gender identity and limiting the use of administrative segregation as the primary means of providing detainee safety. I argue that a

Anderson, Laurel. From *Berkeley Journal of Gender, Law & Justice*, vol. 25, issue 1 (Spring 2010), pp. 1–11, 13–16, 30–31. Copyright © 2010 by the Regents of the University of California. Reprinted by permission of Berkeley Law Journal Publications, University of California.

successful due process claim is possible to compel these reforms. Previous constitutional challenges to conditions of confinement brought by other groups serve as a litigation guide. Cases that define the constitutional rights of convicted prisoners can be utilized to define the rights of detainees as well as support a due process claim. Successful constitutional challenges brought in the context of juvenile immigrant detention provide strategies for shaping this claim.

In [the following sections,] I will give a brief background of ways in which transgender immigrants end up in ICE detention [and] identify the problems caused by the current gender classification system and administrative segregation protocols. I propose changes to these current practices that would increase the safety of transgender detainees and create accountability for the detention centers. [I] will explore the possibility of bringing a constitutional challenge against detention centers to force ICE to implement these proposed changes. By examining the ways in which the courts have defined the proper conditions of confinement for a similar group, namely transgender prisoners, and by proposing several challenges to the current prison jurisprudence, I will provide a roadmap for a successful legal claim by transgender detainees. In fleshing out this roadmap, I look to the successes achieved by juvenile immigrant detainees and suggest that a transgender detainee challenge would benefit from highlighting the similarities between these two groups.

Avenues to Detention

There are two common ways in which a transgender immigrant ends up in detention. The first occurs when ICE arrests a transgender immigrant either crossing the border or living in the United States without proper immigration status. Many male-to-female transgender women migrate to the United States in order to escape persecution on the basis of their gender identity. Because they lack the immigration status necessary to enter or remain in the country legally, they are vulnerable to being detained by ICE. Federal statute requires mandatory detention of all immigrants who do not have valid visas or who entered the country without inspection, even if the immigrant has expressed an intention to file for asylum. Between 2003 and 2009, ICE detained over 48,000 asylum seekers. In 2007 and 2008 alone, over 6,000 asylum seekers were caught while crossing the border or shortly after entering the country. If detained, transgender immigrants can file an asylum application as a defense to deportation, but it rarely results in their release. They are automatically held until they can prove a credible fear of returning home. As a result, an asylum seeker can spend anywhere from several months up to a year in detention waiting for a decision.

Transgender immigrants of any status can also be detained by ICE after completing a jail or prison sentence for a deportable crime. Federal statute requires mandatory detention until removal for non-citizens who have

committed crimes of moral turpitude, aggravated felonies, most controlled substance offenses, or firearms offenses. Crimes of moral turpitude include, but are not limited to, prostitution, fraud, and theft.

Transgender people in general, particularly transgender people of color, have been subjected to extremely high levels of incarceration. One possible explanation for this phenomenon is poverty. Transgender immigrants often experience multiple layers of oppression; the discrimination they face as immigrants is compounded with the discrimination they face because of their transgender status. Their transgender status excludes them from the network of jobs and financial support usually available to immigrants. Additionally, because of pervasive discrimination, transgender people often have difficulty accessing safety nets such as homeless shelters, foster care, and other public services that are supposed to provide for impoverished people. Due to crippling poverty and minimal access to social services, many transgender people turn to illegal economies, such as sex work and the drug trade, to survive.

A second cause of the high incarceration rates is police profiling. Discrimination based on gender identity and race makes transgender individuals especially vulnerable to law enforcement profiling, prosecution, and incarceration. Police profiling of transgender women as sex workers, particularly women of color, is common. Police officers harass and arrest female transgender sex workers even when they have not witnessed sex work related behavior, and even when sex workers are not engaging in work at the time. Many transgender sex workers have reported sexual assaults by police officers. Sometimes sex workers are forced to have sexual relations with the officers; they face arrest if they refuse.

Transgender immigrants who have been convicted of a crime also have the right to apply for asylum defensively, but have to wait in detention until their asylum claims have been adjudicated. They are detained in the meantime, not for their former crime but for the civil violation of living in the U.S. without proper status, and often in deplorable conditions.

Problems with the Current System

The government holds transgender detainees against their will, often for long periods of time, but does not have proper standards set in place to protect their safety. This section will identify the reasons why the current gender classification system creates a dangerous environment for transgender detainees. It will then explain how the current solution to these dangers, administrative segregation, does not alleviate the problems but instead creates additional ones.

Inappropriate Gender Classification System

Whether transgender detainees are defined as male or female for housing purposes has a significant impact on their health and safety. A male-to-female transgender woman is far more likely to experience violence if housed with men instead of women. As victims of sexual assault, harassment, and humiliation, transgender women in detention are likely to suffer serious physical injury and mental anguish. On the extreme end, transgender women are raped and fear for their lives. They also suffer smaller indignities daily: they are spit on, sexually objectified, propositioned, and insulted. Guards may perform sexualized pat downs or strip searches in front of other detainees. Transgender women regularly complain of being watched in the shower by other detainees or guards. They are also denied hormone treatments and grooming products necessary to maintain a feminine appearance.

Furthermore, detention with male prisoners can exacerbate the emotional problems of transgender asylum seekers who suffer from post-traumatic stress disorder (PTSD). Since asylum seekers in general are likely to be survivors of persecution in their home countries, they often suffer from PTSD. Recent studies of PTSD show that asylum seekers are highly susceptible to psychological distress in detention. Being placed in hypermasculine, violent conditions can exacerbate the trauma that transgender asylum seekers have experienced in their home county. One transgender asylum seeker who had been detained, tortured, and raped in her home country said that her detention in the United States triggered flashbacks of these memories. In some cases, detention conditions re-traumatized asylum seekers so severely that they chose to return to the violence in their home country rather than remain in detention.

Despite the significance of gender classification to the health and safety of transgender detainees, ICE does not have any written policies that address how to house the detainees. This leaves the determination entirely up to the individual detention centers. Unfortunately, detention facilities are simply not equipped to handle the basic needs of gender variant people. Most facilities employ very rigid gender definitions that classify sex based on the presence of particular genitalia, thus increasing the risk of violence and emotional harm to the detainees.

Harms of Administrative Segregation

Detention administrators commonly respond to the existence of a transgender person or the complaints made by that person with the problematic solution of administrative segregation—the practice of separating the detainee from the general population. In theory, this approach is supposed to be a protective, non-punitive measure, but in practice the conditions are as restrictive as some of the harshest forms of punitive segregation. Many facilities use the same form of segregation to isolate detainees who complain of assault as they do to isolate the most dangerous detainees, or the ones too violent to live with the general population. Administrative segregation often involves completely eliminating contact with other detainees and confining detainees to locked cells for twenty-three hours a day. It also frequently restricts detainees' access to facilities such as religious services, phones, showers, and recreational facilities. Furthermore, facilities often fail to provide educational, rehabilitative, and vocational programs to those segregated.

One transgender detainee who was placed in administrative segregation after she complained of a threat of violence described her experience in this way:

> They moved me to solitary confinement, lockdown for 23 hours a day. 75–80% of the people there are informants and sexual offenders who are at risk in the general population jail. . . . They never let me come out for a break until late when everyone else has gone away. The phones were available from 8 am until 10 pm. They let me out after the phones shut down—midnight, 1 a.m., so I couldn't call anyone, the ombudsman, the warden, a lawyer. They said I was a security risk, and they were short-staffed, so they couldn't let me go to the law library, and so on. Immigration officers don't come to solitary because that's not where immigration cases are.

Like in this example, administrative segregation often takes the form of solitary confinement. Because of the detrimental emotional effects of the confinement, some commentators have suggested that long-term segregation amounts to torture. The effects of solitary confinement are even more extreme on people who have previously experienced mental trauma, namely asylum seekers. Tellingly, many transgender detainees prefer the risks of housing with the general population to the isolation of administrative segregation.

Additionally, administrative segregation does not always provide more protection than placement in the general population. Administrative segregation that takes the form of solitary confinement makes a detainee extremely vulnerable to violence by guards, because there are few others around to witness the guards' misconduct. Because the segregation creates isolation from potential witnesses and cameras, it gives detainees less opportunity to document abuses against them once they occur.

The story of Esmeralda, a transgender asylum seeker from Mexico, illuminates the many flaws in administrative segregation. Esmeralda came to the United States seeking refuge after being abused in a Mexican jail, but was detained while the final result of her asylum application was pending. The facility automatically placed her in administrative segregation due to her transgender status. She was not allowed to leave her cell to get food or drink, and she was required to go to the bathroom in shackles. Three days after her arrival, a guard forced her to perform oral sex on him while she was shackled. Despite her formal complaint, ICE refused to release her. She became suicidal but was not allowed to see a psychologist. Eventually she opted to return to Mexico rather than to stay in detention any longer.

ICE has a policy addressing administrative segregation, but the policy vests detention facilities with the discretion to determine when and how to implement the practice. The ICE manual defines administrative segregation as a "non-punitive status in which restricted conditions of confinement are required" that may be employed when "the detainee's continued presence in the general population poses a threat to self, staff, [or] other detainees," as well as for "the secure and orderly operation of the facility." According to these regulations, a detainee may initiate the segregation, but an administrator may also place a detainee in segregation against her will when the administration has determined that the segregation is warranted. The ICE policy states that administrative segregation should only be implemented when reasonable alternatives are unavailable, but leaves the determination as to whether reasonable alternatives exist up to each facility. Because of this leeway, facilities often use the system they already have in place to protect detainees—placing them under the same conditions as they do dangerous prisoners—instead of fashioning more appropriate conditions.

ICE guidelines also do not specify how administrative segregation should be implemented. While the manual sets forth basic guidelines for the proper treatment of segregated detainees, these guidelines are inadequate because they leave implementation of the standards up to individual facilities. The ICE manual mandates that detainees in administrative segregation receive "the same privileges as are available to detainees in the general population," but the ultimate allotment of privileges is varied based on the resources and safety concerns of each facility. Additionally, ICE suggests that detainees in administrative segregation be housed separately from those in disciplinary segregation. Instead of being mandatory, however, adherence to the guidelines is determined by the resources of the individual facilities. Prison and jails are often excused from following the explicit guidelines if they create their own equivalent protocols. This gives each institution the latitude to modify the protocols, potentially reducing the rights of detainees. By giving detention facilities leeway, ICE guidelines have allowed them to create dangerous and restrictive forms of administrative segregation. . . .

Gender Classifications Based on Gender Identity

The National Lawyers Guild and the San Francisco Human Rights Commission created a list of recommended reforms for California prisons that can be used as a guideline for updating detention protocols. They recommend that an individualized assessment for appropriate housing be made for each detainee based on a policy of classifying by gender identity, and that each assessment be reviewed periodically thereafter. According to the recommended classification policy, housing status would be determined by referring to a transgender detainee's official identification only if it matched her gender identity. Otherwise, the detainee would be housed according to the gender by which she identified.

Some fear that a policy classifying transgender women according to their gender identity will encourage men to pose as transgender women to gain access to women's facilities, or will permit transgender women to assault female detainees. While there is no evidence to support these fears, there is little data to refute them

because this method of gender classification has not often been employed in the detention context. However, many homeless shelters have integrated transgender women into women's shelters for years without significant problems. In these cases, there have been no documented instances of men dressing as women to gain admittance. Furthermore, these shelters found that transgender women were no more likely to assault other women than were the general female population. In fact, they found that the major concern in the shelters were attacks on transgender women.

One of the greatest challenges to the proposed gender classification will be ensuring the safety of transgender women in women's facilities. While transgender women are less likely to experience violence when housed with other women than with men, they are still likely to be subjected to abuse from other detainees.[1] Furthermore, they are still disproportionately targeted for sexual assault by staff.[2] In order to increase chances of a successful integration of transgender detainees in women's facilities and decrease violence against them both by the staff and the female detainees, administrators should also institute an official policy of respect for transgender people.[3] This includes addressing each detainee by her preferred pronoun and name, even when they conflict with official documents. It also includes providing access to women's clothing and medical hormone treatments. Not only will this policy demonstrate respect to the individual detainee, but it will create an environment where transgender women are seen as women, thus reducing violence directed at transgender women based on their transgender status. Facilities should also provide gender identity training to their guards and healthcare professionals.[4] These trainings can help dispel the gender stereotypes that underlie much of the discrimination. Formal training of detainees on gender identity may be necessary as well, particularly if there are biological women who feel unsafe being housed with transgender women.

Restructuring the gender classification system of detention centers is not a simple solution. It will likely be a complicated and difficult logistical transition for many facilities.[5] When faced with the options provided by the current system, some transgender women may choose to remain in male facilities instead of facing unknown conditions in women's facilities.[6] Until the transition is complete and women's facilities are structured to ensure the safety of transgender detainees, placement in them should be optional.[7]

Protective Custody and Administrative Segregation as a Last Resort

Administrative segregation remains a reasonable method for ensuring the safety of transgender detainees, but it should take a less restrictive form and only be used on a case-by-case basis. The National Lawyers Guild and San Francisco Human Rights Commission's recommendations suggest that transgender detainees be housed in administrative segregation *only* when there is reason to believe the detainees present a heightened risk to themselves or to others, and *only* for that limited period of time during which the heightened risk exists. To guard against indefinite confinement, the facility must prepare a written plan for returning the detainee to less restrictive, but safe, housing. Administrative segregation should be available, but not required, for detainees who express fear of victimization in their current housing. Furthermore, a better form of administrative segregation should be implemented: one which gives detainees access to all of the same services—showers, recreational time, and educational programs—as detainees in the general population, and one that does not isolate them in solitary confinement.

Implementing these new protocols and requiring adherence by detention centers is key to protecting the safety of transgender detainees. Unlike the current ICE protocols, the specificity of these proposed standards will provide each center with clear instructions on how to house and protect transgender detainees, making it more likely that they will receive proper care. In cases where detention centers do not follow the guidelines, harmed detainees can use the protocols to demonstrate a clear violation, force compliance, or gain compensation. . . .

Conclusion

Transgender detainees suffer horrific abuses in immigrant detention when they are housed in men's facilities. The common response to actual or threatened abuse of a detainee is to put the victim in administrative segregation. But segregation is an inadequate solution because it does not properly protect transgender immigrants. In many cases, segregation exposes detainees to further attacks. Thus, there is an urgent need for reform. A policy encouraging the use of alternative measures to detention that ensure an immigrant's presence at removal hearings is the ultimate goal. With many alternative measures demonstrating success rates in the ninetieth percentile, it is illogical that ICE is still using detention as a major form of absconsion prevention.

For those in detention, ICE should change its classification protocol to affirm the gender identities of its detainees instead of relying on genital-based classifications. This is not an easy change to make, but it would protect transgender detainees from conditions that amount to punishment. A change in gender classification procedures should reduce violence against transgender detainees while simultaneously affirming their gender identities. Administrative segregation is inadequate and harmful; thus, ICE should also end the use of segregation as the primary method of violence prevention. Policies that control the violence instead of isolating a particular victim would make detention safer for all immigrants.

A successful legal challenge to the current ICE policies would force them to make these changes or find other methods of ensuring the safety of transgender detainees. While a due process challenge is not the only way of convincing ICE to change its protocols, a successful case would have a monumental impact. A positive ruling that defines the constitutional protections for detainees and specifies violations within the current system in regards to

transgender immigrants would ensure that these protections remain in place regardless of the administration or the political climate. Lobbying ICE through the political process to change its regulations would not have the same guarantee because there is no law preventing ICE from reverting to former policies.

A detainee challenge should incorporate similar cases brought by convicted criminals, but only to illustrate the baseline of protection afforded to detainees. Because current precedent does not afford many protections to convicted criminals, highlighting the distinction between the legal status of the two groups is essential. Linking the vulnerabilities of transgender immigrant detainees with those of juvenile immigrant detainees could bolster a constitutional claim and hopefully provide access to the protections afforded to juveniles. Comprehensive change to ICE protocols geared toward the protection of transgender immigrants could ultimately put an end to the type of violence suffered by Christina Madrazo.

Notes

1. For instance, it is likely that transgender women in women's detention facilities would experience the same type and frequency of abuse as transgender women in homeless shelters. For a brief description of such abuse, see MOTTET & OHLE, *supra* note 111, at 14.
2. Sydney Tarzwell, Note, *The Gender Lines Are Marked with Razor Wire: Addressing State Prison Policies and Practices for the Management of Transgender Prisoners*, 38 COLUM. HUM. RTS. L. REV. 167, 178 (2006).
3. This policy is based on a policy proposed by The National Gay and Lesbian Task Force Policy Institute. *See* MOTTET & OHLE, *supra* note 111, at 11.
4. The Transgender Law Center first provided this suggestion in the context of protecting transgender women in men's prisons, but it is equally necessary to ensure the safety of transgender women in women's facilities. *See* Letter from Christopher Daley, Director, Transgender Law Ctr., to Nat'l Prison Rape Elimination Comm'n, (Aug. 15, 2005), *available at* http://transgenderlawcenter.org/pdf/prisom-ape.pdf.
5. Interview with Alexander Li-Hua Lee, Former Director, Transgender, Gender Variant & Intersex Justice Project (Mar. 16, 2010).
6. *Id.*
7. Allowing transgender individuals to choose their housing during the temporary transitional period would also benefit female to male transgender detainees because they would be at a high risk of violence in male detention centers without protective procedures in place.

LAUREL ANDERSON is a J.D. candidate, 2011, at the University of California, Berkeley, School of Law.

Stephanie Bloyd

 **NO**

'Bathroom Bill' Sparks Accessibility Debate

Boston—An anti-discrimination bill under consideration in Massachusetts could have implications for health club locker room accessibility guidelines.

A Massachusetts state judiciary committee heard testimony last month on House Bill 1728 that supports transgender rights. It would amend the state's nondiscrimination and hate crime laws to make them inclusive for transgendered people.

The Massachusetts Family Institute, a conservative Christian organization, testified against the bill and launched a media campaign that labeled it "the bathroom bill." The group ran a series of radio ads that claimed the legislation would put women and children at risk to male sexual predators, whom they say would be allowed access to public restrooms and locker rooms.

Helen Durkin, executive vice president of public policy for the International Health, Racquet and Sportsclub Association (IHRSA), also testified in opposition to the bill, which the organization says would infringe on the privacy rights of health club members. Durkin asked the judiciary committee to consider exempting health club locker rooms from the bill's language.

"If the proposed legislation becomes law, there would be situations at health clubs where not only adults, but also children, would be in close proximity to an individual with the anatomy of the opposite sex as that individual undressed," Durkin testified.

Some 13 states have passed similar anti-discrimination laws without an increase in restroom-related incidents, according to the Gay and Lesbian Advocates and Defenders (GLAD), a legal rights organization dedicated to ending discrimination based on sexual orientation, HIV status and gender identity and expression.

"A full 37 percent of the American population, in 13 states, live in an area covered by a transgender-inclusive anti-discrimination law, and there have been no reported incidents involving a transgender person threatening the safety of anyone else in a restroom facility," testified Jennifer Levi, attorney and director of GLAD's Transgender Rights Project.

In addition, Levi says privacy concerns can be addressed without discriminating.

"There are very easy ways to address these concerns without jeopardizing passage of the bill," Levi says. "One way people generally address privacy issues is to provide private spaces for anyone who wants to use them."

Levi notes that many health clubs now provide shower curtains and bathroom doors for people who are uncomfortable changing in public.

This is the second time the committee heard testimony on the bill, which needs the judiciary committee's approval before it advances to the state legislature.

STEPHANIE BLOYD is a senior associate editor at *Club Industry*.

EXPLORING THE ISSUE

Should "Trans" Women Benefit from Gender Equity Policies?

Critical Thinking and Reflection

1. How do we balance the civil freedoms of transgender men and women with their basic human right to safety?
2. How do issues of sex, gender, and identity intersect with and sometimes disrupt our cultural rules for social behavior?
3. Would gender equality translate into a post-gender society? Why or why not?

Is There Common Ground?

During the 2012 elections, the voting rights of some citizens were impacted by what many across the nation characterized as "voter suppression" laws. In particular, newly instituted and recently amended voter identification laws posed challenges for transgender voters. However, barriers at the ballot box were not a phenomenon limited to the 2012 elections. Claire Swinford, a transgender woman, recounted her experience at the polls in 2010. Swinford explained how she was stopped by a poll worker:

> While she had an appropriate ID and her name was on the rolls, Swinford, who was early on in her transition from male to female, hadn't yet changed the gender marker and name on her driver's license to reflect her appearance, because of the cost, which she said was more than $200. Despite the poll worker challenging Swinford's gender, she persisted. "Everyone in the place can overhear the conversation where the person is questioning my identity and calling me sir," she said. The poll worker finally offered her a provisional ballot, and Swinford asked to see a supervisor who could contact the county elections office. The office said Swinford met the requirements and could vote

after all, but "it would have been very easy to walk away from that," she said.

—(Berg, 2012)

Swinford's experience at the polls illustrates how transgender issues transcend the logistics of bathroom parity and impact the most basic of citizenship rights.

Additional Resources

Berg, A. (2012, November 2). "Voter Identification Laws Create Unique Problems for Transgender Voters." *The Daily Beast*. Retrieved from: www.thedailybeast.com/articles/2012/11/02/voter-identification-laws-create-unique-problems-for-transgender-voters.html

Doan, P. (2009). "Safety and Urban Environments: Transgendered Experiences of the City." *Women & Environments International Magazine*, No. 78/79, 22–25.

Create Central

www.mhhe.com/createcentral

Internet References . . .

Canadian Transgender Community Network

http://transcommunity.ca/

The Center: The Lesbian, Gay, Bisexual & Transgender Community Center

http://www.gaycenter.org/

PFLAG

http://community.pflag.org/transgender

Out & Equal: Workplace Advocates

http://outandequal.org/diversity/transgendercommunity

Selected, Edited, and with Issue Framing Material by:
Rachel Pienta, *Valdosta State University*

ISSUE

Should Title IX Be Repealed?

YES: **Victoria Langton**, from "Stop the Bleeding: Title IX and the Disappearance of Men's Collegiate Athletic Teams," *Vanderbilt Journal of Entertainment and Technology Law* (vol. 12, no. 1, Fall 2009)

NO: **Charles L. Kennedy**, from "A New Frontier for Women's Sports (Beyond Title IX)," *Gender Issues* (June, 2010)

Learning Outcomes
As you read the issue, focus on the following points:
• What perpetuates gender inequalities in collegiate athletics?
• Could Title IX be reformed to improve its effectiveness? Does it need to be?

ISSUE SUMMARY

YES: Victoria Langton examines the impact of Title IX on men's collegiate sports in the context of diminished opportunities for male athletes.

NO: Charles L. Kennedy discusses the effectiveness of Title IX as a civil rights initiative and the challenges female athletes still face due to inconsistent enforcement of the legislation's equity provisions.

The passage of Title IX in 1972, followed by the implementation of the 1979 Policy Interpretation applied to collegiate athletics, has had far reaching effects on men and women's sports over the last 40 years. Opportunities for collegiate women athletes have expanded while sports options for male athletes have narrowed. However, persistent gender inequities have prompted numerous court challenges over the last four decades.

In "Stop the Bleeding: Title IX and the Disappearance of Men's Collegiate Athletic Teams," Langton examines the pitfalls of proportionality and the deleterious effect that implementation of equity provisions in Title IX have had on men's collegiate sports since 1972. Langton notes the virtual disappearance of certain men's sports such as gymnastics and wrestling at the collegiate level.

In "A New Frontier for Women's Sports (Beyond Title IX)," Kennedy examines the impact of Title IX as a civil rights law. This legislation has exponentially increased opportunities for women in higher education—contributing to the increased number of women students

in college classrooms and on the playing fields. The implementation and enforcement of the provisions of Title IX remains in dispute 40 years after the legislation was passed.

Opponents of Title IX argue for alternative interpretations regarding the proportionality test for compliance. Langton suggests that financial sustainability is a legitimate consideration. According to this interpretation, inability to offer one sport does not justify the elimination of another sport—even in the pursuit of gender parity. The interpretation proposed by Langton raises issues of financial viability and potential advantages of relative profitability between programs within institutions.

Court cases over related Title IX issues such as proportionality and general compliance concerns illustrate the ongoing challenges inherent in achieving full gender equity for female student athletes. The twenty-first century battle for equity and fairness for women will be fought in the financial arena as resource allocation continues to be a shortfall for many scholastic programs in an era of fierce competition for program funds.

YES ↵

Victoria Langton

Stop the Bleeding: Title IX and the Disappearance of Men's Collegiate Athletic Teams

June 23, 2008, marked the thirty-sixth anniversary of the passage of Title IX of the Education Amendments of 1972 (Title IX),[1] which prohibits gender discrimination by programs or activities receiving federal education funding.[2] On the same day, the College Sports Council, an organization dedicated largely to Title IX reform,[3] and the Independent Women's Forum, a nonpartisan research and educational institution,[4] began circulating a petition to Congress calling for "common sense reforms to Title IX enforcement."[5] The petition asserts that reform is needed because "[m]en's collegiate athletic teams are being eliminated and rosters are being capped at an alarming rate in order to comply with the 'proportionality' enforcement prong" of the 1979 Policy Interpretation implementing Title IX.[6] Within six months of its circulation, the petition garnered more than six thousand signatures.[7]

Among the signatories to the petition is 1984 Olympic gymnastics gold medalist Peter Vidmar.[8] Prior to his success at the Olympics, Vidmar was a star collegiate gymnast at the University of California, Los Angeles (UCLA), which eliminated its men's gymnastics program in 1994.[9] While the university officially cited budget concerns as the reason for the elimination of the team, athletes and observers suspect that the real culprit was the need to comply with Title IX.[10] Indeed, UCLA added a women's soccer program the same year it decided to drop the men's gymnastics team, lending support to the theory that the decision was not entirely financially motivated.[11]

Since the passage of Title IX in 1972 and the implementation of the 1979 Policy Interpretation,[12] the number of National Collegiate Athletic Associate (NCAA) men's gymnastics teams has declined dramatically, from 107 in the early 1980s[13] to just seventeen in 2008–2009.[14] Bob Colarossi, the president of USA Gymnastics from 1998 to 2005,[15] has referred to the steady elimination of men's collegiate gymnastics teams as "one of the unintended consequences of Title IX."[16] Ron Galimore, the current USA Gymnastics vice president of events, as well as a 1980 Olympian and former collegiate gymnast,[17] has lamented that "[w]hat we're really focusing on is to stop the bleeding, keep the programs we have and see if there will be any review of Title IX."[18] Galimore has also stated, "I don't think the intention of Title IX was to eliminate sports for some and provide sports for others, but there has been a knee-jerk reaction."[19]

The apparent link between Title IX and the elimination of men's collegiate athletic teams is not alleged to be a byproduct of either the text of the statute or the initial implementing regulation promulgated by the Department of Health, Education, and Welfare (HEW), now the Department of Education (DOE).[20] Instead, the provision that is most frequently cited as the driving force behind the decision to eliminate men's programs is the first prong of the 1979 Policy Interpretation issued by HEW.[21] The Policy Interpretation provides three means of assessing compliance with Title IX and its implementing regulation, the first of which is "[w]hether intercollegiate level participation opportunities for male and female students are provided in numbers substantially proportionate to their respective enrollments. . . ."[22] The move toward compliance with this provision of the Policy Interpretation means a university must either add women's programs or drop men's programs until the number of athletic opportunities for each gender is in accord with the general population of the school.[23] Adding women's programs "often require[s] a lot of money,"[24] which may leave eliminating or capping the rosters of men's teams as the only viable means for compliance under this provision. . . .

A Pending Title IX Challenge

In September of 2006, James Madison University (JMU) announced that it was cutting ten sports teams, seven men's and three women's, in order to comply with Title IX though the proportionality prong of the 1979 Policy Interpretation.[25] The press release stated, "[t]he proportionality requirements of Title IX mandate that collegiate athletics programs mirror each school's undergraduate population in terms of gender. As of the fall semester 2006, JMU's proportions place it fundamentally out of compliance with federal law."[26] The lack of compliance resulted from the fact that JMU's student body was 61% female and 39% male while its participation in athletics was roughly 51% female and 49% male.[27] JMU did not elaborate on why it was unable to comply with Title IX through the second

Langton, Victoria. From *Vanderbilt Journal of Entertainment and Technology Law*, Fall 2009, pp. 184–186, 199–207. Copyright © 2009 by Victoria Langton. Reprinted by permission of the author.

or third prongs, but it did state, through the press release, that "[it had] explored every avenue in search of an alternative to this action . . . this plan is our most viable alternative for reaching compliance with Title IX."[28] Unlike the cases discussed above, the school did not claim that budgetary constraints caused the cuts and announced that the money generated by the cuts would be channeled into funding other sports.[29]

Following the decision to eliminate the teams, a group of coaches, athletes, and parents formed Equity in Athletics, Incorporated (EIA), a not-for-profit organization, to fight the proposed cuts.[30] EIA filed suit against JMU in the Fourth Circuit on March 17, 2007, alleging that the three-prong test of the 1979 Policy Interpretation was a violation of Title IX, the Constitution, and the APA.[31] At the time the lawsuit was filed, the Fourth Circuit had yet to confront a lawsuit challenging the permissibility of the elimination of teams in order to comply with Title IX.

The plaintiffs first sought a preliminary injunction to prevent the university from eliminating the teams, which the district court denied.[32] As part of its analysis, the court considered, among other factors, the likelihood of the plaintiffs succeeding on the merits of their claim.[33] The court cited numerous sources of authority for the general proposition that "[e]very court, in construing the Policy Interpretation and the text of Title IX, has held that a university may bring itself into Title IX compliance by increasing athletic opportunities for the underrepresented gender (women in this case) *or* by decreasing athletic opportunities for the overrepresented gender (men in this case)."[34] However, the court may have overstated the precedent: Several of the cases cited by the court arose as challenges by a university to the 1979 Policy Interpretation in response to lawsuits brought by female students alleging noncompliance,[35] and other cases dealt with circumstances in which institutions were "financially strapped."[36] Still, while the court concluded, based on this authority and in balancing the potential harm against the potential for success on the merits, that a preliminary injunction was not justified,[37] the court went out of its way to state that it was

> not unsympathetic to the plight of the members of the athletic programs that were chosen for elimination by JMU's Board of Visitors. These students are innocent victims of Title IX's benevolent attempt to remedy the effects of past discrimination against women, and JMU's efforts to comply with Title IX.[38]

In affirming the denial of the preliminary injunction, the Fourth Circuit similarly concluded that the plaintiffs had failed to demonstrate the requisite "clear showing of a likelihood of success."[39] The court pointed out that "[c]ourts have consistently rejected EIA's underlying claim that equal opportunity under [the regulation implementing Title IX] should be tied to expressed interest rather than actual participation."[40] However, all of the cases cited

by the court were decided prior to the 2005 Clarification, which specifically recognizes interest of the students as a requisite for a finding of noncompliance under the third prong of the 1979 Policy Interpretation.[41] In fact, the President of the College Sports Council, Jim McCarthy, stated in response to JMU's decision to eliminate the teams, "[l]ast year, the [DOE] issued new guidelines—survey the students and find out what sports they want to do. When they enroll in the fall, answer questions about participating and the school would take those results. . . . We are asking the DOE to strengthen that guideline."[42] Thus, it remains to be seen what impact, if any, a decision on the merits of the case would have on courts' interpretation of compliance under the 1979 Policy Interpretation. . . .

Proportionality as a Title IX Violation

The Supreme Court should grant certiorari in a case addressing this issue and conclude that it is impermissible under Title IX for a university to comply under the proportionality prong of the 1979 Policy Interpretation by eliminating or capping teams when budgetary constraints would not require such action in the absence of a need to comply with Title IX. Title IX specifically states that "[n]o person in the United States shall, on the basis of sex, be excluded from participation in, be denied the benefits of, or be subjected to discrimination under any education program or activity receiving Federal financial assistance."[43] The plain language of the statute indicates that eliminating or capping the roster of a men's (or women's) program when there is sufficient funding and interest to sustain the program is impermissible when done solely on the basis of gender balancing.

The Supreme Court could hold that such use of the first prong is actually a Title IX violation. The first suggestion that schools can comply with Title IX by eliminating programs is found in the 1996 Clarification, which states that "[a]n institution can choose to eliminate or cap teams as a way of complying with part one of the three-part test."[44] However, the 1996 Clarification goes on to state that Title IX is intended to provide institutions with flexibility to comply with the statute in a *nondiscriminatory* manner."[45] It also emphasizes that universities are not required to eliminate or cap teams in order to comply with Title IX.[46] Thus, it seems permissible to argue under the 1996 Clarification that eliminating programs to comply with the 1979 Policy Interpretation is, in fact, discriminatory under the Title IX statute when other, nondiscriminatory means of compliance exist.

Alternatively, the Supreme Court could reach the same conclusion by holding the 1996 Clarification to be an invalid interpretation of Title IX and the 1975 Regulations. In *Christensen v. Harris County*, the Supreme Court held that opinion letters, such as the 1996 Clarification, are not entitled to substantial deference.[47] Instead, the Court held that such letters are merely entitled to "respect," but only when the underlying regulation is ambiguous.[48] In *Chalenor*, the Eighth Circuit deferred to the 1979 Policy Interpretation based on a finding that the 1975 Regulations are ambiguous.[49] However, the provision the court quoted to support its finding of ambiguity describes factors to be considered in determining if a university is providing equal opportunity for participation.[50] The regulation clearly states that "[n]o person shall, on the basis of sex, be excluded from participation in, be denied the benefits of, be treated differently from another person or otherwise be discriminated against in any interscholastic, intercollegiate, club or intramural athletics."[51] Contrary to the conclusion of the Eighth Circuit, this seems to be a clear statement that a student may not be excluded from athletic participation on the basis of gender. Thus, the Supreme Court could find, as it did in *Christenson*, that the regulation is unambiguous and, as a result, that deference to a subsequent opinion letter is unwarranted.[52] The Court could then easily conclude that the cutting or capping of men's teams as a means to comply with the 1979 Policy Interpretation and Title IX, when other, nondiscriminatory means of compliance are available, is impermissible.

In providing guidance to schools attempting to comply under prong three, the 2005 Clarification lends support to the theory that choosing to eliminate or cap a men's team is actually a Title IX violation,[53] given that other, nondiscriminatory means of compliance wi[ll] almost always be available. Under the 2005 Clarification, a university is presumed to be in compliance with prong three unless all of the following conditions are met: "(1) unmet interest sufficient to sustain a varsity team in the sport(s), (2) sufficient ability to sustain an intercollegiate team in the sport, and (3) reasonable expectation of intercollegiate competition for a team in the sport(s) within the school's normal competitive region."[54] Thus, a school that was not in compliance with the proportionality requirement of prong one and could not afford to expand athletic opportunities for women under prong two—and was not required by budgetary constraints to eliminate programs—could still easily comply with the 1979 Policy Interpretation under prong three. The school could either (1) disseminate surveys to demonstrate that the interests of women in participating in athletics are met or (2) demonstrate that it does not "have the ability" to sustain a varsity team in a sport for which there is interest.[55] Thus, under the 2005 Clarification, it seems that a school would never be required to eliminate teams to comply with Title IX, absent a circumstance in which budget constraints independently required cuts. Therefore, a decision to do so could be found to be patently discriminatory under Title IX.

Construing Title IX to prohibit elimination of teams of an underrepresented sex, when not otherwise required by budgetary constraints, would not necessarily prohibit the elimination or capping of a team in a manner that maintains proportionality when a university can prove that it is financially required to cut or cap a team even without the need to comply with Title IX. This accords with both *Kelley*

and *Chalenor*, where the universities presented evidence that the elimination of a team was financially required and that a men's team was cut instead of a women's team in order to maintain proportionality.[56] The reason for allowing a budget exception is that such a situation clearly prevents a school from complying under prong two—since it would not be possible to expand programs for the underrepresented gender[57]—and possibly also prong three, depending on the OCR or a court's construction of "sufficient ability to sustain an intercollegiate team" in the 2005 Clarification.[58] In this circumstance, a university may be concerned about opening itself to Title IX liability if it eliminated a women's team, creating a catch-22 of compliance. Thus, the Supreme Court should find that a university can consider proportionality under prong one in choosing which teams to eliminate or cap if—and only if—it can present evidence sufficient to prove that such action is financially necessary independent of Title IX compliance.

Such a decision by the Supreme Court would be consistent with the plain meaning and intent of the statute and implementing regulation. The Court could leave the 1996 Clarification in place by finding that cutting or capping a team when other alternatives for compliance exist is not a permissible "nondiscriminatory manner" of complying with Title IX.[59] Alternatively, the Court could find that the 1996 Clarification is not entitled to deference and that its acceptance of the cutting or capping of teams of the overrepresented gender as a means of compliance with Title IX is impermissible under the statute and implementing regulation.

Any such holding by the Supreme Court would likely generate significant pressure on universities to end the practice of eliminating or capping men's teams in the name of Title IX compliance. It would also make it possible for men's teams to bring successful actions under Title IX in response to a decision to eliminate or cap a team. As a result, it would help eliminate the gender-based discrepancies that Title IX was passed to combat. Thus, the Supreme Court should grant certiorari on this issue and hold that a decision by a university to cut or cap an athletic team for the sole purpose of gender balancing, in the absence of independent budgetary constraints, is impermissible under Title IX.

Conclusion

Proponents of Title IX and the current framework have recognized the negative impact of the current enforcement mechanisms on men's sports. The former president of the NCAA, Myles Brand, recently predicted that cuts to men's teams will continue as a result of Title IX.[60] In deciding how to comply with Title IX, athletic directors have also noted these cuts as an unfortunate consequence.[61] Nonetheless, the NCAA and athletic departments continue to make decisions to eliminate programs. Thus, it is clear that statements by the DOE, such as the 2005 Clarification, which provides further flexibility in Title IX compliance,[62] and the 2003 Clarification, which discourages universities from complying with Title IX through the elimination of teams,[63] have been ineffective. The Supreme Court must intervene to give effect to the stated regulatory intention.

If the Supreme Court declines to address this issue, the DOE itself could solve the problem of the unintended consequences of Title IX for men's athletics by revisiting its clarifications. Indeed, the 1996 Clarification itself was a response to pressure on the DOE to revise the Policy Interpretation, in the form of a letter written by members of Congress encouraging the DOE to revisit the issue.[64] Thus, it is possible that continuing political pressure could ultimately force the DOE to independently decide to change its position on Title IX enforcement. The current petition to revise Title IX[65] could prompt Congress to once again appeal to the DOE to revise its interpretation of Title IX and the implementing regulation.

In fact, the DOE has recently shown sensitivity to the impact of its policy interpretations on men's collegiate athletics, as illustrated by the 2003 and 2005 Clarifications. With this in mind, the climate may be right to appeal once again to the DOE and to urge it to make a stronger statement, perhaps even by repealing the 1996 Clarification. This would have the same impact as adjudication by the Supreme Court in creating substantial pressure on universities to comply with Title IX through means other than the elimination or capping of programs. It would also make successful action by men's athletic teams under Title IX possible. Thus, action by either the Supreme Court or the DOE on this issue could ultimately save certain men's collegiate sports, such as gymnastics, from a gradual, Title IX-induced extinction.

Notes

1. *See* Press Release, Coll. Sports Council, CSC Issues National Appeal for "Common-Sense Reform" of Title IX (June 23, 2008), *available at* http://collegesportscouncil.org/newsroom/display_releases.cfm?id=23.
2. Jackson v. Birmingham Bd. of Educ., 544 U.S. 167, 173 (2005).
3. College Sports Council, About Us, http://collegesportscouncil.org/about/ (last visited Sept. 22, 2009).
4. Independent Women's Forum, Our Mission, http://www.iwf.org/about/ (last visited Sept. 22, 2009).
5. College Sports Council, Electronic Petition: CSC Issues National Appeal for "Common-Sense Reform" to Title IX, http://www.petitiononline.com/csc2008/petition.html (last visited Sept. 22, 2009).
6. *Id.*
7. College Sports Council, Electronic Petition: CSC Issues National Appeal for "Common-Sense Reform" to Title IX, Petition Signatures, http://www.petitiononline.com/mod_perl/signed.cgi?csc2008 (last visited Sept. 22, 2009).
8. Press Release, Coll. Sports Council, Olympic Greats John Naber, Peter Vidmar, Dan Gable and Cael Sanderson Join with Actor Billy Baldwin Calling for 'Common Sense' Reform of Title IX (Aug. 4, 2008), *available at* http://collegesportscouncil.org/newsroom/display_releases.cfm?id=24.
9. Frank Litsky, *Gymnastics; Colleges Reluctantly Drop Men's Programs*, N.Y. TIMES, Aug. 7, 2001, at D2, *available at* http://www.nytimes.com/2001/08/07/sports/gymnastics-colleges-reluctantly-drop-men-s-programs.html.
10. *See, e.g.,* Jen Brown, *Gymnast Missed '96 Olympics After UCLA Dropped Team*, ABC NEWS, June 28, 2005, http://abcnews.go.com/Sports/story?id=885358; Steve Kim, *Effects of Title IX Felt at UCLA, Northridge*, DAILY BRUIN, Sept. 22, 1997, *available at* http://beta.dailybruin.com/articles/1997/9/22/effects-of-title-ix-felt-at-uc/.
11. Kim, *supra* note 10.
12. *See* Title IX of the Education Amendments of 1972; A Policy Interpretation; Title IX and Intercollegiate Athletics, 44 Fed. Reg. 71,413 (Dec. 11, 1979), *available at* http://www.ed.gov/about/offices/list/ocr/docs/t9interp.html [hereinafter A Policy Interpretation].
13. *60 Minutes: The Battle Over Title IX: Male Athletes Suing to Change the Law* (CBS television broadcast June 29, 2003), *available at* http://www.cbsnews.com/stories/2003/06/27/60minutes/main560723.shtml [hereinafter *The Battle Over Title IX*].
14. NCAA, Current Composition, http://www.ncaa.org/wps/ncaa?ContentID=811 (last visited Sept. 22, 2009).
15. Helene Elliott, *USA Gymnastics Chief to Step Down*, L.A. TIMES, Jan. 13, 2005, at D9.
16. Litsky, *supra* note 9.
17. Press Release, USA Gymnastics, 1980 Olympian Galimore Carries Torch During 2008 Olympic Torch Relay (Apr. 9, 2008), *available at* http://www.usa-gymnastics.org/post.php?PostID=2078.
18. Litsky, *supra* note 9.
19. *Id.*
20. *See, e.g.,* Equity in Athletics, Inc. v. U.S. Dep't of Educ., 291 F. App'x 517, 519 & n.2 (4th Cir. 2008).
21. *See, e.g., id.* at 519–20; Fresno State Bulldogs, Background Fact Sheet, http://gobulldogs.cstv.com/genrel/061506aah.html (citing Title IX among the factors that led to the elimination of the men's wrestling team and explaining that wrestling has a large roster and no equivalent sport for women, thus impeding the school's attempt to equate women's athletic participation with the 60/40 female-to-male ratio of the student body).
22. A Policy Interpretation, *supra* note 12.
23. Litsky, *supra* note 9.
24. *The Battle Over Title IX, supra* note 13.
25. Press Release, James Madison Univ., JMU Enacts Proportionality Plan to Comply with Title IX (Sept. 29, 2006), *available at* http://web.jmu.edu/mediarel/PR-thisRelease.asp?AutoID=846.

26. *Id.*
27. *Id.*
28. *Id.*
29. *Id.; see also* Steve Nearman, *Title IX Enforcement Hits James Madison Hard,* WASH. TIMES, Oct. 28, 2006, at C12 (quoting College Sports Council President Jim McCarthy, stating "track teams have been among the most hurt in college sports. Among the most teams cut. . . . And the budget is minuscule. It's not budgetary reasons; it's to comply with the proportionality of the gender quotas"), *available at* http://www.washingtontimes.com/news/2006/oct/28/20061028-115416-7089r/.
30. Equity in Athletics, Inc. v. U.S. Dep't of Educ., 291 F. App'x 517, 520 (4th Cir. 2008).
31. *Id.*
32. Equity in Athletics, Inc. v. U.S. Dep't of Educ., 504 F. Supp. 2d 88 (W.D. Va. 2007).
33. *Id.* at 99.
34. *Id.* at 101 (citing Neal v. Bd. of Trs., 198 F.3d 763, 769–70 (9th Cir. 1999)).
35. *Id.* (citing, for example, Cohen v. Brown Univ. (*Cohen I*), 991 F.2d 888 (1st Cir. 1993)).
36. *Id.* (citing Roberts v. Colo. State Bd. of Agric., 998 F.2d 824, 830 (10th Cir. 1993)) ("We recognize that in times of economic hardship, few schools will be able to satisfy Title IX's effective accommodation requirement by continuing to expand their women's athletics programs. . . . Financially strapped institutions may still comply with Title IX by cutting athletic programs such that men's and women's athletic participation rates become substantially proportionate to their representation in the undergraduate population.").
37. *Id.* at 99.
38. *Id.* at 112.
39. Equity in Athletics, Inc. v. U.S. Dep't of Educ., 291 F. App'x 517, 522 (4th Cir. 2008).
40. *Id.* at 523 (citing Boulahanis v. Bd. of Regents, 198 F.3d 633, 638–39 (7th Cir. 1999); Neal v. Bd. of Trs., 198 F.3d 763, 767 (9th Cir. 1999); Cohen v. Brown Univ. (*Cohen II*), 101 F.3d 155, 174 (1st Cir. 1996)).
41. Letter from James F. Manning, *supra* note 79.
42. Nearman, *supra* note 146.
43. 20 U.S.C. § 1681 (2000).
44. Nat'l Wrestling Coaches Ass'n v. U.S. Dep't of Educ., *(Nat'l Wrestling Coaches I)*, 263 F. Supp. 2d 82, 93 (D.D.C. 2003).

45. Letter from Norma V. Cantú, *supra* note 71 (emphasis added).
46. *Nat'l Wrestling Coaches Ass'n I,* 263 F. Supp. 2d at 93.
47. Christensen v. Harris County, 529 U.S. 576, 586 (2000).
48. *Id.* at 587–88.
49. Chalenor v. Univ. of N.D., 291 F.3d 1042, 1046–47 (8th Cir. 2002).
50. 34 C.F.R. § 106.41(c) (2007).
51. *Id.* § 106.41(a).
52. *Christensen,* 529 U.S. at 588.
53. *See* text accompanying note 170 (stating that the 1975 Regulations prohibit discrimination on the basis of gender).
54. Letter from James F. Manning, *supra* note 79.
55. *See id.*
56. Chalenor v. Univ. of N.D., 291 F.3d 1042, 1044 (8th Cir. 2002); Kelley v. Bd. of Trs. *(Kelley II),* 35 F.3d 265, 269 (7th Cir. 1994).
57. A Policy Interpretation, *supra* note 12.
58. Letter from James F. Manning, *supra* note 79.
59. *See* Letter from Norma V. Cantú, *supra* note 71.
60. Brady, *supra* note 99.
61. For example, Shelley Appelbaum, senior associate athletic director at Michigan State has stated, "I'm not naïve, I know men's Olympic sports have had a tough time recently." Rexrode, *supra* note 25.
62. Letter from James F. Manning, *supra* note 79.
63. Letter from Gerald Reynolds, *supra* note 77.
64. *Id.* at 92.
65. Press Release, Coll. Sports Council, *supra* note 1.

VICTORIA LANGTON, JD, Vanderbilt University Law School, 2010; BA, International Relations, magna cum laude, Ursinus College, 2006. The author wishes to thank her parents, John and Andrea Langton; her sister, Lynn Langton; and her grandmother, Beatrice Sobeinski, for their constant love and support. She also wishes to thank her club gymnastics coach, Kathy Sanford, who taught her much more than gymnastics, including inspiring her to think critically about Title IX. Finally, she would like to thank the editorial board and staff of the *Vanderbilt Journal of Entertainment and Technology Law* for their hard work in editing this Note.

Charles L. Kennedy

NO

A New Frontier for Women's Sports
(Beyond Title IX)

It is now estimated that more than three million girls participate in interscholastic sports in high school and nearly 200,000 college women play sports. In 1972, there were less than 300,000 high school girls and fewer than 32,000 college women playing sports. 1972, of course, is the year in which Title IX was enacted.

This bill ushered in a real change of opportunity for women in all fields of American society. It was described by Ralph Nader as "one of the most important and successful civil rights laws in US history."

For instance, at the 25th anniversary of Title IX in 1997, the number of women enrolled in advanced degree programs had dramatically increased. As an example the number of women in medical schools had increased from 9 to 41%. The increases were similar in dental, law, business, and engineering schools. Today, the average undergraduate enrollment for women in colleges throughout the country is nearly 57%. This enormous increase has also been very evident regarding the number of girls and women on the playing fields. Female athletic participation has increased by 904% in high schools and 456% in colleges, since the enactment of Title IX in 1972.

However, this success on the playing fields has generated considerable criticism, controversy, and outright opposition. The US Department of Education convened a Commission on Opportunity in Athletics in 2002 to consider changes to Title IX policies and regulations.

Although the commission declined to make any changes, more recently in 2005, the Department issued an *Additional Clarification* of its athletic policies, which permit colleges and high schools to use e-mail surveys as a measure of girls' and women's interest in sports. This is considered a major loophole through which schools can evade their responsibility to provide girls and women with opportunities in athletics.

It should be noted that this continuing controversy was omnipresent in the beginning and should not be surprising. Caspar W. Weinberger, the Secretary of HEW, quipped in 1974, after the Department received 9,700 comments regarding the proposed regulations to Title IX, that "he had not been aware that the most pressing issue facing higher education was the preservation of football."[1]

Amidst this controversy, several interesting books have been published on the debate over Title IX.

- *A Place on The Team: The Triumph and Tragedy of Title IX* by Welsh Suggs (Princeton University Press, [11]). This is an inside story of how Title IX revolutionized sports in the US. It chronicles the law's successes, failures, and opportunities for women.
- *Let Me Play: The Story of Title IX—The Law That Changed the Future of Girls in America* by Karen Blumenthal (Atheneum Books for Young Readers, [1]). Although primarily intended for young readers, it is extremely useful for the general public and the many soccer moms and softball dads, who are spending their weekends cheering their daughters in sports. It reviews the history of Title IX through Player Profiles, Instant Replay of individuals, events and stories. Scorecards tracking progress and Editorial Cartoons providing commentary make for interesting reading.
- *Encyclopedia of Title IX and Sports* by Nicole Mitchell and Lisa A. Ennis (Greenwood Press, [6]). This book "is intended to provide an overview of Title IX and its impact on sports to a broad new range of readers, while serving as a starting point for further research and exploration."[2] It provides summaries of the major court cases, organizations, and individuals involved in the struggle to promote women's sports.
- *Women and Sports in the United States—A Documentary Reader* edited by Jean O'Reilly and Susan K. Cohn (Northeastern University Press, [8]). It "presents a selection of essays and documents to help readers explore and understand conflicting interpretations of gender and sport in the past, present, and projected future."[3]
- *Equal Play: Title IX and Social Change* edited by Nancy Hogshead-Maker and Andrew Zimbalist (Temple University Press, [3]). This book explores the governmental processes that form and continue to shape all public policy, including Title IX . . . The importance of the interconnectivity of the three branches of government and of strategic initiatives in each branch to form public policy is thereby revealed.[4]

All five of these books in their own unique way do an exceptional job of capturing the long struggle of Title IX's march to the 21st century. The common thread in all books is the huge amount of governmental activity involved. The constant conflict and continual controversies became manifest in the public hearings (conducted either by congressional committees, the education department, or the presidential commissions), congressional laws, the HEW and DOE regulations, and the court cases.

It is very obvious that Title IX would not have succeeded were it not for the court cases. Some of the most significant cases include *Franklin v. Gwinnett County Public Schools, Cohen v. Brown, Brentwood v. Tennessee Secondary School Athletic Association, Communities for Equity v. Michigan High School Athletic Association, National Wrestling Coaches Association v. US Department of Education, Jackson v. Birmingham Board of Education*, et al.

The lack of enforcement of the laws and regulations, however, has been one of the major problems with the current Title IX regulations. This has long been a major complaint of Donna Lopiano, the former Athletic Director at Texas and formerly the Executive Director of the Women's Sports Foundation. She wrote in 2002, "The Office of Civil Rights hasn't done a good job, but there have been a number of lawsuits and a number of media articles that have put pressure on schools to make progress. But progress has been slow and steady."[5]

Ralph Nader reiterated the same point, "Title IX has never been adequately enforced . . . The Office of Civil Rights has never initiated a single proceeding to remove federal funds from . . . any college that fails to comply."[6]

It was even before the passage of Title IX, however, that advocates for women's sports suffered one of their most egregious setbacks. In 1971, in a New Haven State Court, Judge John Clark Fitzgerald ruled against a sophomore in high school, Susan Hollander, who wanted to run on the school's cross-country and track teams. The Judge wrote, "Athletic competition builds character in our boys. We do not need that kind of character in our girls."[7] The next year the Connecticut Interscholastic Athletics Association changed its rules and allowed her to run.

Much of the continued controversy involves the *1975 Title IX Regulations* and the *1979 Policy Interpretation: Title IX and Intercollegiate Athletics*, both issued by the Department of Health, Education, and Welfare: Office for Civil Rights, and the *1996 Clarification of Intercollegiate Athletic Policy Guidance: The Three-Part Test*, issued by the US Department of Education: Office of Civil Rights. The test involves the following points:

1. Are Participation Opportunities Substantially Proportionate to Enrollment?
2. Is there a History and Continuing Practice of Program Expansion for the Underrepresented Sex?
3. Is the Institution Fully and Effectively Accommodating the Interests and Abilities of the Underrepresented Sex?

The availability of the three-part test has been frequently litigated. "It has been upheld by every one of the eight federal appeals courts that have considered its legality."[8] In its ruling in the case of *NCAA v. Califano*, the federal district court noted that the case "might be the most over-briefed presentation in the court's recent experience."[9]

Additionally, in a Colorado case (*Roberts v. Colorado State University, 1993*) the 10th Circuit US Court of Appeals ruled that the Education Department's regulations deserved *great deference*, but also commented that, "substantial proportionality between athletic participation and an undergraduate enrollment provides a *safe harbor* for recipients under Title IX."[10]

This "safe harbor" language was adopted by the Department of Education in its accompanying letter to the *Clarification of Intercollegiate Athletic Policy Guidance: The Three Part Test (1996)* and in the *Further Clarification of Intercollegiate Athletics Policy Guidance Regarding Title IX Compliance (2003)*.

This clarity, as expected, was very short lived, when the US Supreme Court ruled on the case of *Jackson v. Birmingham Board of Education*. Rodney Jackson, the girls basketball coach at Ensley High School, complained of a variety of inequities in the treatment of the girls' and boys' teams. These inequities involved facilities, equipment, transportation and monetary support. He was subsequently relieved of his coaching duties. He immediately filed suit claiming "that the school board had violated Title IX by retaliating against him for making an accusation of discriminatory practices."[11]

In 2005 the Supreme Court upheld Jackson's claim and ruled that Title IX provided protection for individuals reporting sex discrimination. The Court established four basic principles that would tremendously impact the future of Title IX: "(1) that its language should be broadly construed; (2) that retaliation for reporting discrimination is, itself, considered discrimination; (3) that guarding against retaliation is essential for ensuring Title IX's effectiveness; and (4) that the law protects indirect, as well as direct, victims of discrimination."[12]

This ruling has led to a series of lawsuits by individuals alleging retaliation and suing for monetary damages in Title IX cases. Fresno State University in California, in particular, has been a hot bed of litigation involving complaints by coaches and staff about inequities in facilities, staffing and fairer treatment of male and female athletes.

There were several cases involving Fresno State that attracted national attention. The three cases involved Lindy Vivas, the women's volleyball coach, Stacy Johnson-Klein, the women's basketball coach, and Diane Milutinovich, a former associate athletic director.

Vivas had been fired in 2004, after a winning season, and after filing a complaint against Fresno State in 2003 and a retaliation complaint, with the Department of Education's Office of Civil Rights (OCR). She filed a discrimination lawsuit against Fresno State in 2006 alleging "she was fired because of her advocacy for gender equity and her perceived sexual orientation."[13] In July, 2007, the jury awarded her $5.85 million. It was later reduced by the judge to $4.52 million plus $660,000 in legal fees.

Johnson-Klein had been fired in March, 2005. The university claimed she had "inappropriately obtained pain medication from students and staff, engaged in deceptive and improper fiscal actions, lied and was insubordinate."[14] In October, 2005, she also filed a discrimination lawsuit against the university claiming that she was fired after she complained about her program's lack of resources. In December, 2007, the jury awarded Johnson-Klein $19.1 million. It was later reduced by the judge to $6.6 million plus $2.5 million in legal fees. Fresno State is appealing both of these verdicts.

Also in 2007, the university reached a settlement with Milutinovich. She was granted $3.5 million and given a new title, associate athletics director emeritus. Milutinovich had been involved in either a litigation or complaints with the OCR since 1995 and had been fired twice by Fresno State. In December, 2006, she filed a lawsuit against the school claiming "she was fired both times due to her advocacy for Title IX and gender equity.[15]

Additionally, Maggie Wright, the current softball coach, has also filed a complaint with the OCR accusing the college of retaliation against her for advocating equal treatment of female athletes.

It should be noted that prior to all this Fresno State had drafted a corrective action plan in response to a DOE-OCR investigation that found Fresno State out of compliance with Title IX in the early 1990s. Additionally, as Fresno State contended, ". . . according to a 2007 report by the Women's Sports Foundation, it ranks high in matching the proportionality of female athletes to female students."[16]

However, Diane Milutinovich, the former associate athletic director, made the point that "the University still lags behind others in its treatment of female athletes."[17] My studies actually confirm *both* of these points. As shown in my "The Gender Equity Scorecard V," Fresno State actually ranked 16th in the country on the *proportionality* test, the first point of the Department's three-part test, with a score of +0.54. The school was one of only 18 colleges among the 115 Division 1-A colleges in my study for the 2005–2006 academic/athletic year to finish with a positive score—meaning the percentage of female athletes was proportionately higher than the percentage of female students.

Additionally, Fresno State scored better than the Western Athletic Conference (WAC) average of −4.48, which was the second highest ranked conference. The school also scored significantly better than the national average, which was −7.29. On the proportionality test, Fresno State finished second in the WAC behind only Nevada. It should be noted that Nevada was the national champion on my Gender Equity Scorecards III and IV, covering the 2003–2004 and 2004–2005 academic/athletic

years. Nevada finished second for the 2005–2006 season behind North Texas.

Interestingly, Fresno State has also demonstrated a consistent pattern of improvement over the past 4 years on the proportionality standard. The Bulldogs have improved from −8.86 in 2002–2003 to +0.54 in 2005–2006. See the following chart.

Fresno State's Scores on Proportionality

Year	Score ±0.0
2005–2006	+0.54
2004–2005	+0.23
2003–2004	−3.00
2002–2003	−8.86

It almost begs the question, if Fresno State scores so high on the proportionality score (the safe harbor part of the test)—higher than 99 other Division 1-A colleges—how could the school not be in compliance and lose a Title IX lawsuit?

The answer may be found in the fact that Fresno State ranked only 62nd in the country with a grade of C− and a score of −37.32 on "The Gender Equity Scorecard V." Note: "The Gender Equity Scorecard and my other articles and studies on women's sports and gender equity may be viewed at http://www2.yk.psu.edu/~clk8/articles. It must be recognized that the scorecard goes beyond the current Title IX criteria. It evaluates the colleges' commitments to gender equity by also examining the four financial criteria of *scholarship money, operating expenses, coaches' salaries,* and *recruiting expenses.* It is based on the simple but all important principle, as best enunciated in the movie *Jerry Maguire,* "Show me the money." It simply defies common sense to claim that any college is adequately, effectively and legally supporting women's sports, if the college is not providing sufficient financial support for the women's athletic programs. The best way to determine this support is by including various financial indicators into the Title IX compliance equation.

It should be noted that in my proposal the participation factor has not been eliminated, but it is now one of five criteria to determine compliance with Title IX. The scorecard is based on the criteria utilized by *The Chronicle of Higher Education* in its study on "gender equity" in 2007.[18] All of the statistics in *The Gender Equity Scorecard V* were obtained from the *Chronicle's* study, according to data submitted to the US Department of Education, as required by the Equity in Athletics Disclosure Act (EADA) of 1994.

One of the major problems with the proportionality criteria, which is used as the "safe harbor" of compliance by many schools, is that it does not accurately or fairly measure the full extent of a college's compliance with the spirit of Title IX.

For instance, of the eighteen colleges in my study that had a positive compliance score on proportionality, eight of the eighteen colleges actually had scores of C or lower on *The Gender Equity Scorecard* V. Additionally, four of the colleges received an F grade. These colleges were, in descending order: Cincinnati, Clemson, West Virginia, and Oklahoma State.

Five of the eighteen colleges received an A grade. North Texas and Nevada had an A+. Oregon State, Utah, and Toledo received an A−. San Diego State received a B+ and Purdue, Central Florida, Miami, and Minnesota received Bs on the Scorecard.

This wide range of scores should raise serious concerns in the use of the proportionality standard as a fair and accurate measure of compliance with Title IX.

It also should raise the question: If Fresno State with a high score on the proportionality criteria and a score of −37.32 (a grade of C−), and a national ranking of 62 of 115 colleges on *The Gender Equity Scorecard,* can lose several Title IX lawsuits, then what about the other 56 colleges that scored lower than Fresno State? This question particularly applies to the eight colleges with a grade of F and the 11 colleges with a grade of F−.

It must be emphasized that a college can have a high score on the participation criteria and still drastically short change its women athletes on the economic related items of operating expenses, coaches' salaries, number of coaches, recruiting expenses, travel and hotels, etc.

There are also several examples of gross inequities at the other end of the spectrum in reliance on the proportionality criteria. There were 65 colleges with a score of −5.0 or lower on proportionality; however, 20 of these schools actually had scores of C+ and higher on *The Gender Equity Scorecard V.*

The most flagrant examples involve Eastern Michigan, Kent State, and Ohio University of the Mid-American Conference (MAC). Eastern Michigan actually ranked 108 of 115 colleges on the proportionality scale with a score of −20.76; only seven schools had a worse compliance rate. Nevertheless, the school ranked 6th in the country with a grade of A− and an overall score of −15.02 on *The Gender Equity Scorecard V.*

Similarly, Kent State ranked 106th in the country with a proportionality score of −18.42. Yet when the broader gender equity factors of scholarships, coaches' salaries, operating expenses, and recruiting budget were also considered with proportionality; Kent State received a grade of B+, a rank of 12th in the nation—narrowly missing the Top ten by only −0.80 with a score of −22.0.

Likewise, Ohio University received a B grade on the scorecard and ranked 17th in the country with a score of −23.29. However, on the proportionality score alone, Ohio received a −10.27 score and a rank of 87th in the country.

Of the other 17 schools with a grade of C+ and higher on the scorecard, yet below −5.0 on proportionality, 11 received a B or B− grade and six received a C+.

Fresno State is not the exception to the rule. Since 2005, gender equity lawsuits have been filed against Montana State, Hawaii, and Florida Gulf Coast Universities. California continues to be the hotbed of the controversy,

however, California-Davis, Sonoma State, and California-Berkeley have paid $4.5 million in jury awards or settlements to the plaintiffs.

The California-Berkeley case involved Karen Moe Humphreys, a former Olympic swimmer and the head coach of the California women's swimming team from 1978 to 1992. She was laid off in 2004 and filed a gender discrimination and retaliation lawsuit in 2004. She claimed she lost her job for complaining about the treatment of women by the athletic department. In 2007, the university settled for $3.5 million, reimbursement of legal costs, reinstatement and back pay.

Moe Humphreys still contends that "women's rights are still not taken seriously. I think that gender discrimination is not taken seriously. And I think Title IX compliance is one piece of that . . . My experience has been, when there was a complaint about race discrimination, or if there was a complaint about a discrimination about Americans with Disabilities, the campus took that very seriously."[19]

Additionally, there are 13 other lawsuits, complaints or appeals pending against colleges in California. One of these involves a complaint against Southern California (USC) to the OCR that has been pending for 9 years. The complaint "alleges discrimination against female athletes in terms of sports offered for women, athletic scholarships, coaching and tutoring services, assignment and compensation of coaches and tutors, and recruitment."[20]

This trend is a movement beyond the proportionality requirements of Title IX with its emphasis on *equal opportunities to participate* toward *equal treatment for female athletes.*

This was the essence of the US District Court's ruling in the Slippery Rock case in western Pennsylvania. The judge ruled that, "The defendants have failed to give their female athletes equal treatment in coaching and training, equipment and supplies, publicity, promotion materials and events, playing fields, locker rooms, and other facilities."[21]

It should also be emphasized that in my 2005 study, *Title IX and College Sports in Pennsylvania,* Slippery Rock ranked 3rd in the West Division of the Pennsylvania State Athletic Conference (PSAC). This again begs the obvious question, if Slippery Rock has failed to give their female athletes equal treatment, then what about the schools that finished below Slippery Rock?

One of the schools that finished below Slippery Rock was Lock Haven, which finished 4th in the PSAC West. Ironically, Lock Haven actually ranked 1st in the PSAC West regarding gender equity among coaches salaries.

The Lock Haven University field hockey coach filed a suit in US District Court in central Pennsylvania, claiming her civil rights were violated, because she was paid $15,000 less than her male counterparts. This also begs the question, if Lock Haven is liable, what about the other teams in the PSAC?

This new era in women's sports appears to be an attempt to move beyond the proportionality requirements of the Title IX three-part test. This new era is calling for equity and fairness in the allocation of resources for school sports. In addition to funding, other factors that should be considered include uniforms, scheduling of practices and games, and practice sites.

This is not a revolutionary or novel concept. This principle of equity and fairness in the allocation of resources is clearly affirmed in all of these DOE Rulings: the *1975 Title IX Regulations,* the *1979 Policy Interpretation,* the *1996 Clarification of Intercollegiate Athletics Policy Guidance: The Three Part Test, and* the *1998 Letter from the U.S. Department of Education to Bowling Green State University.*

For instance, the 98 letter states, "Title IX recognizes the uniqueness of intercollegiate athletics by permitting a college or university to have separate athletic programs and teams for men and women . . . The statute requires institutions to provide equitable opportunities to both male and female athletes in all aspects of its two separate athletic programs."[22]

The *1996 Clarification* clearly states, "OCR considers the effective accommodation of interests and abilities (prong three of the Three-Part Test) in conjunction with equivalence in the availability, quality, and kinds of other athletic benefits . . . These other benefits include coaching, equipment, practice and competitive facilities, recruitment, scheduling of games, and publicity, among others."[23]

The OCR concluded "An institution's failure to provide nondiscriminatory participation (the first prong) opportunities usually amounts to a denial of equal athletic opportunity because these opportunities provide access to all other athletic benefits, treatment, and services."[24]

The *1979 Policy Interpretation* and the *1975 Regulations* itemize the factors the Department will examine to determine if the institution does provide equal athletic opportunities for members of both sexes. The factors of equal athletic opportunity are: "provision and maintenance of equipment and supplies, scheduling of games and practice times, travel and per diem expenses, opportunity to receive coaching and academic tutoring, assignment and compensation of coaches and tutors, provision of locker rooms, practice, and competitive facilities, provision of medical and training services and facilities, provision of housing and dining services, and facilities, and publicity."[25]

The state of California may already be moving beyond Title IX and establishing a new era for determining compliance with Title IX. State Senator Dean Florez (D-Fresno), the Chair of the newly created Senate Select Committee on Gender Discrimination and Title IX Implementation, recommends stricter gender equity standards. Under his plan, *California Title IX,* "all public colleges in California should undergo an annual certification process, based upon state-mandated guidelines covering men's and women's athletic participation, budgets, and scholarships . . . any colleges that failed to meet those guidelines would have percentages of their athletic funds revoked."[26]

He advocates that the state would take 20% of any college's athletic funding, that failed to comply with

Title IX, for two consecutive years. The Select Committee on Gender Discrimination is now examining compliance by other California schools, including the state's 109 community colleges, and plans to look at high schools. The Committee has held hearings to question officials at the California State University system and the University of California system regarding their compliance with Title IX.

This new era of Title IX enforcement is essentially back to the future. It is simply to enforce the current regulations and adhere to the true meaning and intent and spirit of Title IX—to provide equal opportunity for boys and girls and men and women athletes.

With even a casual review of the regulations, is it any wonder why juries are unanimously awarding the plaintiffs huge awards in the sex discrimination cases.

In his article on the Johnson-Klein case, Brad Wolverton wrote in *The Chronicle of Higher Education,* "Legal experts say the latest ruling sends a clear warning to colleges across the country to treat women equally and to adhere to federal gender equity law."[27]

If colleges are going to be faced with the specter of increased lawsuits, negative media articles, and the potential of athletic sanctions, then the colleges will soon be clamoring for reform of Title IX. Over the past 3 years the American Association of University Women has noted an increasing number of lawsuits by coaches referred to its legal advocacy fund.

This problem with increased litigation is underscored and compounded by the simple fact that the other two criteria in the DOE-OCR's three-part test (history of expanding opportunities and accommodating interests) are entirely too vague.

Deborah Yow, the Athletic Director at Maryland and a member of the Secretary's Commission on Opportunity in Athletics, made the point that her school's lawyers advise her to use the proportionality test because the other two are too vague.

In discussing the diverse and opposing views of the members of the Secretary's Commission, Joseph White wrote that there would be no problem "reaching a consensus on at least one topic: The Department of Education must do a better job explaining Title IX guidelines to colleges and high schools."[28]

It is very obvious that any law or regulation or rule that is vague and needs explanation or clarification will inevitably lead to litigation and still more litigation.

The obvious light at the end of the tunnel in the search for gender equity is the need for the development of a new test and standards for compliance with Title IX. This is the *new frontier* of gender equity. Even the Secretary's Commission recommended "that the government come up with ways that the schools can comply with the law beyond the three-part test."[29]

It must be recognized that arguably it should not have to be the responsibility of the US Education Department's Office of Civil Rights, or the Congress, or the US District Courts, or the California State Senate to initiate action.

The National Collegiate Athletic Association could and should be in the forefront of leadership on the development of new Title IX standards and criteria. Nancy J. Latimore, the Athletic Director at Elizabethtown College, a Division III college in south-central Pennsylvania, stated, "I've been disappointed that through the years the NCAA hasn't stepped up and put pressure on colleges to be in compliance with Title IX."[30]

The system could work the same as the NCAA's Academic Progress Rate (APR). The APR is a new academic point system, which requires teams to meet minimum requirements or face the potential loss of scholarship money when academically ineligible athletes leave school. The establishment of the APR represents a major and significant move by the NCAA to hold not just individual players, but entire college teams responsible for poor performance in the classroom. This is merely an extension of the hammer of ineligibility policy over entire college athletic programs.

The same policy could and should apply to gender equity. The NCAA needs to provide the leadership and make gender equity in athletics on college campuses a reality.

The fairest and most equitable approach to this new frontier of gender equity is to adopt the criteria of *The Gender Equity Scorecard* of participation, scholarships, operating expenses, coaches' salaries, and recruiting expenses as the new criteria for compliance with the spirit and intent of Title IX. . . .

For teams that have low compliance rates (Ds & Fs), the penalties are many and varied. In addition to cuts in scholarships, there could also be cuts in operating expenses, number of coaches, and recruiting expenses. Conversely, schools with high compliance rates could be awarded increases. Or, if the NCAA really wanted to send a message, the organization could implement bans on TV and postseason appearances.

The alternative to decisive action by the colleges and the NCAA will be to leave the decisions to the District Courts, Congress, the US Department of Education, or the California State Senate. The decision should be an easy one!

Notes

1. Suggs [11], 69–70.
2. Mitchell and Ennis [6], xv.
3. O'Reilly and Cohn [8], xix.
4. Hogshead-Makar and Zimbalist [3], 2.
5. "Title IX," *Houston Chronicle*, June 23, 2002, 1A.
6. Ralph Nader, *Op cit.*
7. Blumenthal [1], 31.
8. Hogshead-Makar, *Op. cit.*, 54.
9. Hogshead-Makar, *Op. cit.*, 53.
10. Suggs, *Op. cit.*, 107.
11. Mitchell, *Op. cit.*, 62.
12. *Ibid.*, 63.
13. "Timeline of Gender Equity Issues at Fresno State," USATODAY.COM/SPORTS/COLLEGE/2008-05-12-FRESNO-TIMELINE, 2.
14. *Ibid.*
15. *Ibid.*
16. Lipka [4], A30.
17. *Ibid.*
18. "Annual Report on Gender Equity," *The Chronicle of Higher Education*, May, 2007, CHRONICLE.COM/STATS/GENDEREQUITY/2007.
19. Jill Liber Steeg, "Title IX Q&A with Karen Moe Humphreys," *USA TODAY*, USA TODAY, USATODAY.COM/SPORTS/COLLEGE/2008-05-12-TITLE-IX-QANDA.
20. Jill Liber Steeg, "Lawsuits, Disputes Reflect Continuing Tension Over Title IX," *USA TODAY*, USATODAY.COM/SPORTS/COLLEGE/2008-05-12-TITLE-IX-COVER.
21. Ward [12], B4.
22. Hogshead-Makar, *Op. cit.*, 164–165.
23. *Ibid.*, 153.
24. *Ibid.*, 153.
25. *Ibid.*, 73.
26. Lipka [5], A29.
27. Wolverton [13].
28. Phillips [10], C1.
29. Fletcher and Sandovel [2], D1.
30. Phillips [9], C1.

References

1. Blumenthal, K. (2005). *Let me play: The story of title IX—the law that changed the future of girls in America* (p. 31). New York: Atheneum Books for Young Readers.
2. Fletcher, M. A., & Sandovel, G. (2003). Title IX panel acts moderately. *Washington Post,* January 31, 2003, D1.
3. Hogshead-Makar, N., & Zimbalist, A. (Eds.). (2007). *Equal play: Title IX and social change* (p. 2). Philadelphia: Temple University Press.
4. Lipka, S. (2007). Jury orders Fresno State to pay ex-coach $5.85 million in discrimination case. *The Chronicle of Higher Education,* July 20, 2007, A30.
5. Lipka, S. (2007). Fresno State grapples with a spate of sex discrimination claims. *The Chronicle of Higher Education,* August 3, 2007, A29.
6. Mitchell, N., & Ennis, L. A. (2007). *Encyclopedia of title IX and sports* (p. xv). Westport: Greenwood Press.
7. Nader, R. (2003). *Join the fight for title IX.* COMMONDREAMS.ORG.
8. O'Reilly, J., & Cohn, S. K. (Eds.). (2007). *Women and sports in the United States: A documentary reader* (p. xix). Boston: Northeastern University Press.
9. Phillips, J. (2002). Law's impact felt locally. *Harrisburg Patriot-News,* June 21, 2002, C1.

10. Phillips, J. (2006). Title IX dissenting views will be in report. *Harrisburg Patriot-News,* February, 2006, C1.

11. Suggs, W. (2005). *A place on the team: The triumph and tragedy of title IX* (pp. 6–70). Princeton: Princeton University Press.

12. Ward, P. R. (2006). Slippery Rock sued for cutting women's sports teams. *Pittsburgh Post Gazette,* May 10, 2006, B4.

13. Wolverton, B. (2007). Jury awards $19.1 million to former Fresno State coach in sexual-discrimination case. *The Chronicle of Higher Education,* December 7, 2007, CHRONICLE.COM/DAILY/2007/12919 N.

CHARLES L. KENNEDY is an instructor of political science at Pennsylvania State University.

EXPLORING THE ISSUE

Should Title IX Be Repealed?

Critical Thinking and Reflection

1. How might our culture be different if there had never been a Title IX?
2. How might Title IX create disadvantages for men in athletics or in the classroom?
3. How might Title IX be amended to create more equitable opportunities for both men and women?

Is There Common Ground?

The American Civil Liberties Union (ACLU) continues to be a key advocate on several tenets of Title IX and asserts that the law benefits both boys and girls. The ACLU (2013) advocates for gender equity and equal treatment under the law for men and women, working to address issues such as "sex-segregation and sex stereotypes in education, pregnant and parenting teens' rights, gender-based violence, and athletics." The National Women's Law Center (NWLC) has taken Title IX advocacy into new territory with advocacy focused on addressing anti-bullying initiatives. In a 2012 Fact Sheet, the NWLC explored how Title IX addresses harassment and bullying based on sex, asserting that "all forms of sex-based harassment are prohibited, including sexual harassment, harassment based on a student's failure to conform to gender stereotypes, and sexual assault" (NWLC, 2012).

In 2012, the Southern Poverty Law Center (SPLC) addressed sex-based discrimination on behalf of Hueytown High School student Hunter Mahaffey in a dispute with the Jefferson County Board of Education in Alabama. Male students were banned from wearing earrings and Alabama high school student Hunter Mahaffey pierced his ears and wanted to wear earrings to school. The SPLC sent a letter to the county school board on Mahaffey's behalf, influencing the board to amend district policy. The SPLC was able to note the rule's discriminatory nature, which violated more than one federal law:

"The policy violated the Equal Protection Clause of the U.S. Constitution because it discriminated on the basis of sex, lacked any exceedingly persuasive justification, and rested on an archaic sex stereotype that earrings are appropriate only for females. The repealed policy also violated Title IX of the Education Amendments of 1972, which protects against sex discrimination at school. The earring ban also violated students' freedom of expression."

—(Southern Poverty Law Center, 2012)

The advocacy of the SPLC helped Hunter Mahaffey take a stand against gender conformity based on sex stereotypes. The board's favorable ruling was also a victory for freedom of speech.

Organizations such as the American Civil Liberties Union, the National Women's Law Center, and the Southern Poverty Law Center, among others, have worked to raise awareness and be advocates on behalf of boys and girls who have experienced bullying or harassment based on sex or gender. This application of Title IX breaks new ground in the area of human rights advocacy. Title IX affords every person equal protection, including

"boys and girls; men and women; students and employees—from sex-based harassment in schools and colleges that receive federal funding. This means that school districts or colleges may violate Title IX when sexual- or gender-based harassment by classmates (or peers) is so serious that it interferes with or limits a student's ability to participate in or benefit from the school or school activities, and such harassment is encouraged, tolerated, not adequately addressed, or ignored by school employees."

—(NWLC, 2012)

Additional Resources

American Civil Liberties Union. (2013). "Title IX—Gender Equity in Education." Retrieved from: www.aclu.org/title-ix-gender-equity-education

National Women's Law Center. (2012). "The Next Generation of Title IX: Harassment and Bullying Based on Sex." Retrieved from: www.nwlc.org/sites/default/files/pdfs/nwlcharassbullying_titleixfactsheet.pdf

National Women's Law Center. (2013). "Education and Title IX." Retrieved from: www.nwlc.org/our-issues/education-%2526-title-ix

Southern Poverty Law Center. (2012, June 18). "Responding to SPLC Demand, Alabama's Jefferson County Board of Education Lifts Ban on Male Earrings." Retrieved from: www.splcenter.org/get-informed/news/responding-to-splc-demand-alabama-s-jefferson-county-board-of-education-lifts-ban-

Create Central

www.mhhe.com/createcentral

Internet References . . .

Title IX information

http://www.titleix.info/

American Civil Liberties Union

http://www.aclu.org/title-ix-gender-equity-education

U.S. Department of Education

http://www.ed.gov/category/keyword/titleix

National Center for Education Statistics

http://nces.ed.gov/fastfacts/display.asp?id=93

Selected, Edited, and with Issue Framing Material by:
Rachel Pienta, *Valdosta State University*

ISSUE

Do We Need the Equal Rights Amendment?

YES: Katha Pollitt, from "ERA: Once More Unto the Breach?" *The Nation* (vol. 296, no. 7, February 2013)

NO: Donald T. Critchlow and Cynthia L. Stachecki, from "The Equal Rights Amendment Reconsidered: Politics, Policy, and Social Mobilization in a Democracy," *Journal of Policy History* (vol. 20, no.1, January 2008)

Learning Outcomes

As you read the issue, focus on the following points:

- How would the ERA change the lives of American women and men?
- Has the original intent that motivated the first ERA activists already been accomplished? If not, what else needs to be achieved?
- If public debate surrounding a constitutional amendment results in a change in public opinion, should ratification of the amendment be pursued?

ISSUE SUMMARY

YES: Katha Pollitt examines how the changing cultural and social landscape of American culture should lead to the ratification of the Equal Rights Amendment. She argues that the objections to the ERA long upheld by the opposition are no longer relevant in modern society.

NO: Donald T. Critchlow and Cynthia L. Stachecki examine the political factors that hampered the Equal Rights Amendment ratification process. They argue that the legacy of the ERA, despite the lingering death of the actual legislation, was the spark that provided for the political mobilization of women.

In 1918, President Woodrow Wilson urged a joint session of Congress to guarantee women the right to vote. In his September 30 speech, Wilson said, "We have made partners of the women in this war. . . . Shall we admit them only to a partnership of suffering and sacrifice and toil and not to a partnership of privilege and right?"

Proponents of the ERA frame their support in this perspective—it is the twenty-first century and women in the United States are still fighting for comparable worth, gender parity, and decision rights over their own bodies. The need for a law like the Lily Ledbetter Act of 2010 exemplifies the continued legal disparity and power shortfalls faced by women in the twenty-first century. The work of organizations like the American Civil Liberties Union on initiatives such as the Reproductive Freedom Project illustrates the ongoing need for a comprehensive human rights amendment that specifically enfranchises women.

Pollitt, in "ERA: Once More Unto the Breach?," argues that the "straw men" laundry list of reasons long given for opposition to ERA ratification have been debunked or made irrelevant in the decades since the amendment was first proposed. The main arguments against ERA were based on notions that women would lose special protections and be "forced" into combat, lose court-awarded alimony, be forced to pay child support, or lose access to sex-segregated bathroom facilities. In the twenty-first century, the last barriers to women serving in combat have all but toppled. Few women are awarded permanent alimony and some women do pay child support to lesser-earning spouses. Modern women fight for equal access to golf clubs and executive dining rooms. Some pop culture scholars would argue that the issue of "potty parity" and possibility of unisex bathrooms was laid to rest with the popular television series "Ally McBeal"—where the "uni" figured prominently in many of the dramatic comedies' plot lines.

Pollitt argues that despite the significant gains and social evolution since 1973, women still face an uphill battle to true equality. She cites examples of Congress's failure to renew the Violence Against Women Act, court cases that allow women to be dismissed from employment for perceived attractiveness, and states that uphold the legal concept of fetal personhood. Pollitt notes that Justice Antonin Scalia cast doubt on the Fourteenth Amendment's applicability to women. Justice Scalia's comment suggests that equal treatment for women before the highest court is not necessarily codified by national law; the need for women's rights to be explicitly recognized in the form of an amendment to the Constitution seems as relevant and timely today as it did in 1973.

Conversely, Critchlow and Stachecki, in "The Equal Rights Amendment Reconsidered: Politics, Policy, and Social Mobilization in a Democracy," argue that efforts to pass the Equal Rights Amendment acted as the catalyst to sufficiently shift the national discourse and ultimately resulted in public policy changes that would help women to achieve equal standing under the law. According to Critchlow and Stachecki, the battle over the Equal Rights Amendment was ultimately empowering to all women and illustrated the effective functioning of a democracy in which women could impact the political process.

YES ↵

Katha Pollitt

ERA: Once More Unto the Breach?

Now that women will be allowed in combat, can we please have the ERA? One of the biggest arguments against the Equal Rights Amendment was that women would be drafted and sent to the front. Of course, we haven't had the draft since 1973, although men still have to register for it at age 18. But in the unlikely event that the draft is reinstated tomorrow, it's not hard to imagine women being included. Since 1982, when the ERA was defeated three states short of ratification, opposition to women in the military has faded. In the wake of the combat announcement, only dinosaurs like George Will still argue that women are too weak and incompetent to kill their fair share of Muslims. Three decades have transformed attitudes: we are way past seeing women as delicate maidens in need of male protection.

Indeed, the fears exploited by ERA opponents to such great effect have mostly come to pass. Stayhome mothers will lose their right to alimony? Check—unless she has a very special lawyer, a wife who stays home with her children will be lucky to get a few years of "rehabilitative maintenance" to retool herself for paid employment. Women will have to pay child support to men? Check again—that also happens these days, when the woman is the breadwinner—just ask Britney Spears. Unisex public toilets? I'm not keen on them myself, but generations of college students have grown up in coed dorms with less privacy than you'd find at the dog run in Central Park. I'm sure we can all work something out.

"The arguments against the ERA are melting away," Feminist Majority head Ellie Smeal told me by phone. "Insurance pricing by gender? The Affordable Care Act takes care of that. Marriage equality? We're getting that too." By the end of the struggle for ratification, courts had used the Fourteenth Amendment and Title VII to dismantle the legal structure of sex discrimination. So would the ERA really change anything? Smeal thinks it would strengthen anti-discrimination law, and also promote the case for equal pay for work of equivalent value. "Right now the burden in these cases is on us. The ERA would change that."

Not so fast, says Phyllis Schlafly, the ERA's archnemesis, who argues that supporters could never show what good the amendment would do—and, moreover, that what it would accomplish would be unpopular. Americans still oppose drafting women, she claims (but there is no draft! Why are we even talking about it?), as well as gay marriage (actually, not so much), taxpayer-funded abortion and other outcomes that chill conservative hearts. "We don't believe that every factory and office should be 50 percent men and women," Schlafly told me in her brisk fashion. "Should Congress have to be half women?" I must say that sounds like a great idea, especially when you consider that at the present rate it will take about 5,000 years for the United States to achieve it.

And that's the thing. Of course the ERA won't mandate equal representation in Congress or anywhere else, but the very fact that it evokes the possibility is what's exciting about it. The ERA would switch the paradigm from how much equality you can wring from a Constitution that does not specifically grant women any rights except the vote to a Constitution that says equality is the basic understanding, for sex as well as for race. Why shouldn't the onus be on those who enjoy and profit from the subordination of women, instead of on women who want to be treated as equals? Why did it take until last year, for example, to ban charging women more for health insurance just because they are women?

A lot of women just roll their eyes when the ERA comes up, I know. It looks like a bit of a relic—"as retro as men wearing bell-bottom trousers," Schlafly quipped, quoting Jeb Bush. Today it's treasured by a small number of older activists, some of whom argue that there's a legal path by which it's potentially alive and only in need of three more states to pass (Google "Madison Amendment"). Stout-hearted Carolyn Maloney reintroduces it every session in Congress, to no effect. It's not only anti-feminists who feel its time has passed. But maybe we need to think again.

The great thing about the ERA is that it isn't a piecemeal, derivative thing. It's a grand statement about the dignity of women—and, yes, gays and transgendered people and men—as bearers of rights and citizenship, about our right to full participation in life. We could use that now, in this era of flourishing backlash in virtually every area—politicians setting up as medieval gynecologists, religious pizza manufacturers seeking to deprive their workers of contraception coverage, churches fighting for the right to fire unmarried pregnant women, public schools that push out pregnant students. We've just seen a Congress that couldn't even renew the Violence Against Women Act, an all-male Iowa Supreme Court that upheld a male dentist's right to fire a female assistant he found too attractive, and an Alabama judge who declared fertilized eggs to be persons. Misogyny is rampant on the Internet, where revenge porn is the latest fad, and women who speak up about anything related to gender are threatened with rape and murder by anonymous creeps. Maybe the Fourteenth Amendment can't do everything. At one point, Justice Scalia suggested that it didn't even apply to women. "It's extremely important to have women's rights explicitly recognized in the Constitution," says Jane Mansbridge, author of the indispensable *Why We Lost the ERA*. "Like the First Amendment, which was originally understood very narrowly, it would have important good effects over time."

Reproductive rights, pay equity, marriage equality, no more discrimination against mothers, basic social respect: maybe it's time to get those old ERA banners out of mothballs and fight for all of our rights, once and for all.

KATHA POLLITT is an American feminist poet, essayist, and critic. She is the author of four essay collections and two book of poetry.

Critchlow and Stachecki

The Equal Rights Amendment Reconsidered: Politics, Policy, and Social Mobilization in a Democracy

In the early 1970s, fifty years after its first appearance in the U.S. Congress, the Equal Rights Amendment came the closest it ever would to ratification. The ERA declared: "Equality of rights under the law shall not be denied or abridged by the United States or by any State on account of sex." After sailing through Congress in 1972 with bipartisan support, the amendment went to the states for ratification. The response was positive and immediate: Hawaii approved the ERA the same day, twenty-one other states approved it before the end of the year, and eight more states the following year. Yet, by 1982 the amendment lay dead, having fallen three states short of the thirty-eight states needed for ratification.

This essay explores the close connection between constitutional change, public opinion, and political activism. The failure of the ERA is explained within a context of social mobilization that shifted public opinion over time. ERA ratification reveals the political dimensions of constitutional change. In this way, the ERA battle was a successful exercise in democratic mobilization, although it created profound acrimony at the time, as is fitting in a mature democracy.[1] A close examination of social science survey literature, often ignored in earlier historical studies, shows that public opinion, particularly in key battleground states, shifted over time against ERA ratification. Opponents of ERA, working on the community and state levels, effectively won over public opinion to their side and, in doing so, prevailed upon their state legislators in battleground states to defeat the ERA. Social science surveys reveal that by 1978 there was a precipitous overall decline in support of the amendment among women in nonratifying states, plummeting below 40 percent. Political leadership working on both the national and local levels proved essential to the success of the anti-ERA movement. Furthermore, this essay posits that politics unique to individual states is critical to understanding the defeat of the ERA. For example, factionalism within the Democratic Party in Illinois—Mayor Richard Daley party regulars versus New Democrat reformers—benefited anti-ERA activists in that state. In the end, however, opponents of ERA ratification won over Democratic legislators in states controlled by the Democrats, including Florida, North Carolina, Oklahoma,

and Missouri. More important, anti-ERA forces were more effective in mobilizing public opinion against ratification.

The interaction of these forces—public opinion, political climate, and social mobilization—are necessary to understand the battle over the Equal Rights Amendment in particular and the amendment process in general.[2] While the history of ERA is often seen as a policy failure, it is important to note that thirty-five states did ratify it, although five of these changed their minds and rescinded. The initial success of ERA ratification and its ultimate failure to win the necessary thirty-eight states indicates the importance of integrating this social science literature into a new historical narrative. Social science literature details how social mobilization by pro- and anti-ERA forces changed public opinion over time and affected voting outcomes in state legislatures.[3]

The proponents of ERA tended to see its defeat as a failure of democracy. Many supporters of ERA blamed the defeat of the amendment on the insurance industry, New Right organizations, and other special interests for providing funding for a well-organized, highly financed opposition that subverted the democratic process and the will of the majority. The defeat of ERA led, inevitably it seemed, to conclusions about the valetudinarian state of American democracy. By contrast, the opponents of the amendment claimed that victory was achieved because the average person, especially women, had been aroused by a maneuver on the part of a political elite—feminist organizations and their political supporters in Washington, D.C., and certain state capitals—to foist an out-of-the-mainstream amendment on the American people. Anti-ERA forces claimed that they represented the average American and that the defeat of ERA represented a victory for democracy.[4]

Scholars have offered many explanations as to why ERA failed. Early literature maintained that it failed ratification for what might be described as internal and external factors. The major internal factor included organization failure on the part of ERA supporters. Scholars argued that by relying on centralized organizations based in Washington, D.C., ERA proponents failed to organize their supporters at the grassroots.[5] Furthermore, factionalism within the pro-ERA movement reflected deep divisions within the principal pro-ERA organization over strategy and tactics. Specifically, ERAmerica, an umbrella organization representing more than a hundred organizations, pursued a strategy of traditional lobbying on the state level to enact ratification, while the leading feminist organization, the National Organization for Women (NOW), used a civil rights protest model to pressure state legislators through mass rallies to ratify the amendment.[6] External factors are found in the origins of the New Right. This explanation maintains that outside political organizations and corporate interests funded Phyllis Schlafly's STOP ERA organization and other antiratification groups. The external argument claimed that Schlafly and her allies persuaded a minority of anxious housewives to pressure their state legislators to vote against ERA.[7] Both the internal and the external explanations assumed that the general will of the people was thwarted in the defeat of the equal rights amendment. In addition, scholars found procedural obstacles in winning ratification by three-quarters of the state legislatures, especially in the state of Illinois, which required a supermajority vote of three-fifths of its members of both houses to ratify a constitutional amendment.

Still, when passed by a two-thirds majority in Congress in 1972, the ERA amendment was seen as winning easy approval in the states. In the House, 354 members voted for the amendment with only 23 opposed, one of whom was the senior female member, Representative Leonor Sullivan (D-Mo.). In the Senate, Sam Ervin, a North Carolina Democrat, tried to block passage by proposing nine separate amendments to the ERA to protect what he saw as the traditional rights of women, including female labor protection laws, exemption from the draft, and family and spousal rights. These amendments were soundly defeated in roll-call votes on March 21 and 22, 1972. The ERA then passed the Senate by 84 to 8, a decisive, sound victory for proponents. ERA ratification swept the states. Within a year of its passage by Congress, thirty states had ratified the ERA. Only eight more states were needed for final ratification when opposition emerged.

Although the focal point for opposition was represented by Phyllis Schlafly and her STOP ERA organization, other anti-ERA groups were active on the state level as well. The important National Council of Catholic Women opposed the ERA, and until 1973 the AFL-CIO did as well. Schlafly and her STOP-ERA movement gained momentum by drawing on the support of many evangelical Christians, Mormons, Orthodox Jews, and Roman Catholic women. After winning quick ratification in 1972, only nine states approved the amendment in 1973, and only four states voted for ratification from 1974 to 1977. The last state to ratify ERA was Indiana in January 1977. Following the extension of the deadline by Congress from March 22, 1979, to June 30, 1982, not a single state endorsed the ERA. The Illinois legislature voted on the ERA every year from 1972 through 1982; the Florida legislature considered it nearly every year; and the North Carolina and Oklahoma legislatures considered it every two years. The ERA failed to win ratification in those other states. . . .

Studies of the ERA battle on the state level reveal that anti-ERA forces were more effective in mobilizing public opinion against the ERA. As a result, legislative organizational structures and procedures were less important in determining state outcomes than was public opinion. As Ernest B. Wohlenberg noted in his survey of fifteen states where ERA failed, "Legislative voting on ERA in non-ratifying states accurately reflects the attitudes and sentiments of constituents."[8] His conclusion is supported by other scholars. For example, in 1987 political scientists Louis Bolce, Gerald De Maio, and Douglas Muzzio found that majority support for the amendment "was neither stable nor sustained." Rather, it "declined a full 27 percent between 1976 and 1980 in those states that rejected ratification of the ERA." In addition, they found that "while nearly three-fifths of the respondents in the rejecting states expressed support for ERA in 1976, their numbers declined to a plurality by 1978." They concluded that by 1980 "opponents and supporters were at a virtual standoff."[9] Moreover, they found that there was a precipitous overall decline among women in supporting the amendment in the nonratifying states. In 1976 the majority of women in these states supported the amendment by more than two-and-a half to one. In these same states, fewer than two in five favored the amendment two years later. In addition, support among white voters "had plummeted below 40 percent" in the rejecting states.[10]

For ERA supporters, the problems presented by this decline were more than quantitative; they were qualitative. Surveys conducted in 1978 and 1980, cited by Bolce et al., revealed that ERA opponents were "clearly" more politically knowledgeable about the ERA in their states and found the issue more salient. Substantial majorities of those surveyed in both ratifying states and rejecting states did not know whether their legislators had acted on ERA. In nonratifying states, only slightly more than one-fifth knew that their states had voted against ratification. Opponents of the ERA were more than twice as likely as supporters to be informed as to their state legislature's vote—and "this tendency for opponents to have been better informed holds when race and sex are isolated."[11] The likely explanation as to why opponents were better informed on this issue is because they felt more strongly about it and this intensity translated into political activism. ERA supporters on the state level were more educated, but they took less interest in politics within their state legislatures. Why this was so remains unclear, although a number of hypotheses come to mind, including an assumption by ERA activists that the politics of protest could substitute for hands-on lobbying.

In 1976, approximately 9 percent of the total population in the rejecting states, both for and against the amendment, was informed about the ERA issue and primary voters. In other words, the battle over ERA in the nonratifying states involved about 9 percent of the total population. Within this small population, supporters represented about 5 percent, opponents 4 percent. Opponents outweighed supporters, however, among those holding an opinion "who were also knowledgeable and politically active." ERA opponents were "better informed and more intense" in their political involvement. Using surveys conducted by the Center for Political Studies (CPS), Bolce et al. discovered that opponents in the rejecting states were more likely to have registered to vote (85 to 77 percent) and voted in the presidential primary (67 to 59 percent) and in the general election (82 to 69 percent). Moreover, opponents were more active politically in general. This pattern of political activity continued in 1980.[12]

Even more revealing was a comparison between those supporters and opponents who felt "intensity" about the ERA. The 1980 CPS survey showed that the number of supporters and opponents were virtually even in states that rejected the ERA. Among those with strongly held opinions, however, the results were significantly different. Bolce et al. found that "among those who engaged in four or more political acts" (such as registering, voting, donating money, participating in a political campaign), "intense opponents surpassed intense supporters by nearly 40 percent." In the end, the evidence suggests that state legislators in nonratifying states were not out of touch with the voters. Bolce et al. concluded, "All we can say with certainty about the public opinion context within which state legislators acted is that in the rejecting states as a whole, it was qualitatively and, in the latter years, quantitatively unfavorable to the ERA."[13]

These findings suggest an important reconsideration of the ERA battle that was not fully addressed in the survey literature: Why were opponents of the ERA successful in mobilizing minority opinion against the amendment, while ERA activists appear to have allowed majority opinion in these states to dissipate? In order to fully answer this question, further detailed studies of the ERA battle at the state level will need to be undertaken. Until then, tentative suggestions as to why the ERA failed can be offered.

Political leadership proved critical in the battle over the ERA. The defeat of the ERA must begin with Phyllis Schlafly herself.[14] If Schlafly had not entered into the fray, the ERA would have been ratified. She provided the leadership in key battleground states by giving guidance to statewide organizations and local chapters of anti-ERA groups, including her STOP ERA organization. As the author of *A Choice Not an Echo*, a campaign book that had played a critical role in winning the Republican nomination for Barry Goldwater in 1964, she carried into the ERA campaign a national reputation. Moreover, she brought to the campaign grassroots organizing skills not found among many of her opponents. She had run for Congress in 1952 and 1970, served as president of the Illinois Federation of Republican Women from 1960 to 1964, and was vice president of the national federation from 1964 to 1967. Following a bitter election fight for the presidency of the National Federation of Republican Women in 1967, she withdrew from the organization and began a monthly national publication, the *Phyllis Schlafly Report*. Many of the women who had supported her in the NFRW election quickly joined the crusade to stop ERA.

Her involvement in the ERA fight came about serendipitously when she was invited to debate the issue before a conservative women's group in 1971. Before this debate she had not taken much of a stand on social issues or feminism. Her involvement in the ERA marked, as many scholars have noted, a turn in the conservative movement to social issues.[15] No longer would grassroots conservatives be solely linked to anticommunism, fiscal restraint, and national defense. Schlafly took the lead in rallying opposition to the ERA when she published "What's Wrong with 'Equal Rights' for Women?" in the *Phyllis Schlafly Report* in February 1972. She followed this article with a more detailed criticism of the ERA in "The Fraud Called the Equal Rights Amendment" in her report in May 1972. In the ensuing ten years, Schlafly published close to a hundred articles on ERA in her monthly report. These articles provided the intellectual ammunition for grassroots activists working in their states, local communities, churches, and social clubs.

Schlafly's attack on the ERA was multiple: it threatened to deprive women workers of protective labor legislation; it threatened the right of wives and mothers to financial support; and it held the potential to draft women into military combat, institute abortion on demand, take away statutory rights of wives and mothers, and federalize laws that were properly in the jurisdiction of the fifty states. She argued that the issue was not whether women should be given better employment opportunities, appointments to higher positions, or more admissions to medical schools. Such goals were desirable, she said, and she supported any necessary legislation to achieve these goals. But feminists were claiming these goals as their own in order to sugarcoat an agenda that was "anti-family, anti-children, and pro-abortion. Feminists believe that the home was a prison and the wife and mother a prisoner."[16] Later in the campaign, she raised the issue that the ERA would allow the legalization of same-sex marriages. Although her critics charged her with simplifying the consequences of the ERA, her challenge to the amendment did not focus on unisex bathrooms, which in itself is a simplification of her attack.[17]

Coalitions were formed in key battleground states. Coalitions within the states varied but often included church groups and women's organizations, such as the National Council of Catholic Women chapters, and ad hoc groups such as Women Who Want to Be Women and the Family Preservation League, as well as right-wing political organizations such as the John Birch Society and Pro America. The *Phyllis Schlafly Report* provided her supporters with a steady stream of arguments against the ERA, while providing information to local activists and handouts to be distributed to state legislators. Because Schlafly became the central spokesperson against the ERA, opponents had to face an experienced and articulate debater.

Her background in politics enabled her to know which legislators to lobby, how to dress, how to speak before the camera, and how to form alliances with legislators, and which legislators to target with campaign contributions through her STOP ERA PAC. Anti-ERA women typically dressed up and brought home-baked breads and pies when lobbying their legislators.[18]

This anti-ERA movement spread like wildfire among traditional women.[19] The mobilization of this antifeminist counterattack took their opponents off guard. Leaders of the National Organization for Women (NOW), ERAmerica, and other supporters of ERA, underestimated the depth of the grassroots opposition. Only later they admitted that they had failed to win over the average homemaker.[20] Simply put, Schlafly outmaneuvered her opponents.[21]

Initially, Schlafly drew support from her network of conservative Republican women across the country, but as the movement gained strength she effectively reached out to bring in average women who previously had not been involved in politics. Schlafly tapped into a new constituency—women from the Church of Christ, Southern Baptists, and fundamentalist Christian groups.[22] Most of these women were mothers, but their church activities had given them skills in public speaking and in converting unbelievers. Equally important, these women brought an evangelical enthusiasm to the cause. Schlafly's movement brought together Roman Catholics, evangelical Protestants, Mormons, and Orthodox Jews. While mostly white, STOP ERA also attracted evangelical African Americans. Especially important in this regard was Reverend Henry Mitchell's congregation from his Black Star Mission Church in Chicago.

This appeal to religion interjected an enthusiasm to the movement. As historian Donald G. Mathews noted, anti-ERA activists brought to their battle a sense of mortal combat. Ratification was translated into a religious issue, "one that addressed the very foundation of their social and personal selves. . . . The sense of mortal combat was expressed in intense predictions of sexual 'chaos' and tremulous condemnation of those who rejected traditional sexual-cultural categories to embrace the innovation of an ambiguous gender order."[23] While not all anti-ERA activists were religious, and Roman Catholic participants differed in their tone and enthusiasm from their evangelical sisters, the mobilization of evangelical Christians added a dynamic to the cause that would not have existed otherwise. Evangelical Christian women proved an especially powerful force in the southern battleground states. Moreover, evangelical Christianity provided an ideological orientation that framed the battle for many of these women. In a widely circulated leaflet, "A Christian View of the Equal Rights Amendment" (1975), Rosemary Thomson declared, "As Christians, we ought to support laws that provide equal opportunity for women, but we must oppose a sweeping constitutional change that would take away their individual choices and alter America's lifestyle. Jesus cautioned us about wolves in

sheep's clothing . . . of Satan coming as an angel of light so even the elect will be deceived."[24]

In mobilizing these women, Schlafly tapped into a wellspring of resentment about cultural changes that were occurring as the secular left challenged long-standing traditions and customs. A mood of opposition to secular culture had been simmering at least since the Supreme Court's ban on school prayer in 1962. The Court's decision in *Roe v. Wade* in 1973 to legalize abortion intensified their opposition. These issues of school prayer and abortion were especially important to evangelical Christians and traditional Roman Catholics who became involved in the anti-ERA campaign. Overall, anti-ERA activists mirrored pro-ERA activists, although with important differences. Both drew from largely white middle-class women. Most were over the age of thirty. Pro-ERA activists were slightly more educated, but the important difference was church membership: 98 percent of anti-ERA supporters claimed church membership, while only 31 percent of pro-ERA supporters did.[25] ERA supporters welcomed the new morality of sexual liberation and reproductive rights. Antifeminist activists saw themselves as upholding the ideal of the two-parent family, which they feared was being replaced in the 1970s by the single-parent family and cohabitating couples, both heterosexual and homosexual.

These antifeminist activists were not driven by a sense of political alienation from the system. Empirical studies of these women showed that they believed, like their counterparts on the other side of the debate, that they controlled their own lives. These studies revealed that anti-ERA activists were not motivated by any sense of alienation from society, urbanization, industrialization, or status anxiety caused by declining social positions. Most of these women placed themselves close to the center of the political spectrum and repudiated groups such as the KKK, the Minutemen, or white separatist groups.[26]

By framing the ERA issue on the social and legal implications of the ERA and the alleged harm it would cause women, Schlafly allowed a broad coalition to be formed that included Republican women, grassroots activists, and average women motivated by religious concerns. In other words, Schlafly framed the cause as a single issue under the slogan, STOP ERA. This general call allowed female activists to emphasize aspects of the movement that appealed to different constituencies within their districts and the sentiments of their legislators. Women with daughters might oppose ERA because it might mean the conscription of females into the military and put women in combat. A traditional-minded woman could oppose the amendment because it might allow same-sex marriages. A conservative who distrusted big government might fear that state power would be further eroded by the enhancement of congressional power. Those people who already distrusted activist courts saw the ambiguity of the ERA as opening the door wider for judicial interpretation.

At the same time, ERA proponents differed among themselves as to the full implications of the amendment. Especially problematic for the pro-ERA side was the linking by some activists of legalized abortion and gay rights. The National Organization for Women reflected the pro-choice position of the feminist movement in the late 1960s.[27] Leaders in NOW and some local American Civil Liberties Union lawyers brought suit under state ERA laws to extend reproductive rights. Specifically, briefs were filed in Hawaii and Massachusetts by pro-choice activists claiming that their state ERAs provided the right for women to use tax funds for abortions based on the doctrine that "equality of rights under the law shall not be denied or abridged by the state on account of sex." A decade later, similar briefs would be filed in suits under state ERA laws claiming the right for same-sex marriage. Not all proponents agreed with these legal claims, and more moderate ERA advocates believed that linking the amendment to abortion, lesbianism, and same-sex marriages was a mistake.[28]

Another factor that must be considered in understanding the defeat of the ERA in the key battleground states is organizational capacity on the grassroots level. The importance of social-movement organization was critical to the final results of the amendment in the states.[29] The organizational capacity of pro- and anti-ERA groups to mobilize their constituencies and public opinion to affect the votes of their state representatives was decisive in the end. The pro-ERA campaign was mostly centralized out of Washington, D.C. Only late in the campaign did the pro-ERA organizations realize the problems created by the lack of grassroots organizations and input. The anti-ERA forces showed greater capacity for social mobilization on the local and state levels, especially in the later stages of the battle. Although STOP-ERA was hierarchical in that Schlafly appointed state leaders and set general strategy, tactics were decided on the local level. Furthermore, because many anti-ERA activists had been involved in local politics or church affairs, they knew their state legislators. When they visited their representatives in state capitols, they wore dresses and makeup and thanked their legislators for voting their way.

The pro-ERA movement was fractious. The two principal organizations involved in the pro-ERA ratification movement, the National Organization for Women (NOW) and ERAmerica, often found themselves at loggerheads over general strategy and tactics. ERAmerica was formed in 1976 after proponents of the amendment realized that they had been caught off guard by Schlafly's STOP ERA movement. ERAmerica was an umbrella organization of 120 groups, but NOW refused to join, so the two groups conducted separate fund-raising and political activities. NOW pursued a strategy modeled on the civil rights movement of the 1960s. This involved mass demonstrations and marches, while working with national political and cultural elites to rally support for the ERA.

In the end, however, the fight over the ERA was to be fought in the state capitols, and many representatives reacted negatively against the intrusion of outsiders into what they considered state affairs. ERAmerica and allies such as the National Federation of Business and Professional Women's Clubs argued against NOW's strategy of confrontation and urged a more subtle lobbying campaign. They held workshops on developing skills in targeting and lobbying state legislators. In pursuing this lobbying strategy, ERAmerica leaders complained that NOW activists actually hurt lobby efforts by their radical demeanor and appearance and their open hostility to the older white male politicos who dominated state legislatures in the 1970s. In the later stages of the struggle, NOW and ERAmerica reconciled their differences and undertook coordinated efforts in lobbying, television advertising, and campaign involvement on behalf of pro-ERA candidates and opposition to anti-ERA candidates, but these efforts came too late in the struggle. By that time, their opponents had outflanked them, public opinion had turned against ERA, and many state legislators had grown tired of the debate and saw no political gain in the issue.[30] . . .

The battle for the ERA amendment met the expectation of those who framed the U.S. Constitution in 1787. In Federalist No. 85, Alexander Hamilton observed that the Constitution being considered by the states was not perfect. "I never expect to see," he wrote, "a perfect work from imperfect man. The result of the deliberations of all collective bodies must necessarily be a compound as well of the errors and prejudices, as of the good sense and wisdom of the individuals of whom they are composed." For this reason, Hamilton understood the need for future generations to amend the Constitution, adding "And the FEELING of inconveniences must correct the mistakes which they *inevitably* fall into, in their first trials and experiments." Those who met in Philadelphia understood that political institutions guarded the Republic from unrestrained human passion that leads to what Hamilton described as "anarchy, civil war, a perpetual alienation of the states from each other, and perhaps the military despotism of a victorious demagogue."[31] Human imperfection required the right of people to amend the Constitution, but human passion necessitated deliberation through the state legislatures to temper the final outcome. The Equal Rights Amendment battle that waged from 1972 through 1982, while acrimonious, manifested a mature democracy at work.

Reflecting a strong, if not majority, sentiment in the nation, Congress in 1972 had passed the Equal Rights Amendment. It went before the states and quickly gained ratification by the majority of states. Yet, as opposition arose—opposition that reflected a significant portion of the population—the ratification slowed in the states and finally would be defeated. Opponents of the ERA mobilized a counter social movement that proved effective in swaying public opinion and state legislators to their side. These anti-ERA activists proved more determined, more politically active and politically knowledgeable, and more effectively organized than were their opponents. This was especially the case in the key battleground states. The result was that ERA was defeated.

This defeat was of profound disappointment to many feminists at the time, but this defeat inspired the call for more effective political organization to gain election to office and achieve desired social legislation on behalf of their cause. For the political right, ERA marked not only political victory but also the revival of the conservative cause that would dominate American politics in the 1980s. In short, the ERA battle sparked social mobilization of feminists and counterfeminists during the struggle over ratification, and its defeat inspired new social mobilization that effected policy, law, and politics in subsequent decades.

Notes

1. In his 1996 prize-winning *Explicit and Authentic Acts: Amending the U.S. Constitution, 1776–1995*, historian David Kyvig challenges the view that the constitutional process failed in the case of the ERA. While Kyvig judges the ratification process a success in that it achieved what the Founding Fathers envisioned in drafting Article V, he believes that the ERA might have won ratification had supporters pursued different strategies. He declares, "The process for achieving constitutional change demanded a consensus beyond what the proponents of reformed gender relationships could fashion" in a contentious political environment. Placing the ERA ratification debate in a larger historical perspective, he defends the importance of constitutional amendment as a means of ensuring "the durability of fundamental reforms in governmental structure and obligation." David Kyvig, *Explicit and Authentic Acts: Amending the U.S. Constitution, 1776–1995* (Lawrence, Kans., 1996), 418, xii.

2. For an interactive approach considering these factors, see Sarah A. Soule and Susan Olzak, "When Do Movements Matter? The Politics of Contingency and the Equal Rights Amendment," *American Sociological Review* 69 (August 2004): 473–97.

3. The importance of social mobilization within a favorable political environment in positively influencing social policy is argued by Edwin Amenta, Kathleen Dunleavy, and Mary Bernstein, in "Stolen Thunder? Huey Long's 'Share Our Wealth,' Political Mediation, and the Second New Deal," *American Sociological Review* 59 (October 1994): 678–702; Edwin Amenta and Michael P. Young, "Making an Impact: Conceptual and Methodological Implications of the Collective Goods Criterion," in Marc Giugni, Doug McAdam, and Charles Tilly, eds., *How Social Movements Matter* (Minneapolis, 1999), 22–41; Hanspeter Kriesi et al., *New Social Movements in Western Europe: A Comparative Analysis*, Vol. 5, *Social Movements, Protest, and Contention* (Minneapolis, 1995); and to some extent in Amenta, *Bold Relief* (Princeton, 2000). For political mobilization and countermobilization, see David S. Meyer and Suzanne Staggenborg, "Movements, Countermovements, and the Structure of Political Opportunity," *American Journal of Sociology* 101 (May 1996): 1628–60. For an interesting slant on the importance of political climate for understanding successful feminist campaigns, see Holly McCammon et al., "How Movements Win: Gendered Opportunity Structures and U.S. Women's Suffrage Movements, 1866–1919," *American Sociological Review* 66 (February 2001): 49–70.

4. For a useful study of ERA that integrates structural problems inherent in the amendment process as well as the failure of ERA activists to win over state legislators, see Jane J. Mansbridge, *Why We Lost the ERA* (Chicago, 1986). The emergence of the New Right and ERA is explored in Mathews and De Hart, *Sex, Gender and the Politics of ERA A State and the Nation* (New York: Oxford University Press, 1990); Val Burris, "Who Opposed the ERA? An Analysis of the Social Bases of Antifeminism," *Social Science Quarterly* 64 (June 1983): 305–17; and Pamela Johnston Conover and Virginia Gray, *Feminism and the New Right: Conflict Over the American Family* (New York, 1983).

5. Mansbridge, *Why We Lost the ERA;* and Mary Frances Berry, *Why ERA Failed: Politics, Women's Rights, and the Amending Process of the Constitution* (Bloomington, 1986).

6. Donald T Critchlow, *Phyllis Schlafly and Grassroots Conservatism: A Woman's Crusade* (Princeton, 2005).

7. Donald G. Mathews and Jane Sherron DeHart, *Sex, Gender, and the Politics of ERA;* Berry, *Why ERA Failed;* and Janet K. Boles, *The Politics of the Equal Rights Amendment: Conflict and the Decision Process* (New York, 1979). See also Conover and Gray, *Feminism and the New Right.*

8. Wolhenberg included in his study Alabama, Arizona, Arkansas, Florida, Georgia, Illinois, Louisiana, Mississippi, Missouri, Nevada, North Carolina, Oklahoma, South Carolina, Utah, and Virginia. Ernest H. Wohlenberg, "Correlates of Equal Rights Amendment Ratification," *Social Science Quarterly* 60 (March 1980): 676–84, quoted on 681.

9. Bolce, De Maio, and Muzzio, "The Equal Rights Amendment, Public Opinion, and American Constitutionalism," 558.

10. Ibid., 559.

11. Ibid., 563.

12. Ibid., 564–65.

13. Ibid., 563–64, 569.

14. Carol Felsenthal, *The Sweetheart of the Silent Majority: The Biography of Phyllis Schlafly* (Garden City, N.Y., 1981); and Critchlow, *Phyllis Schlafly and Grassroots Conservatism.*

15. Critchlow, *Phyllis Schlafly and Grassroots Conservatism.*

16. Detailed arguments against ERA are found in the *Phyllis Schlafly Report* from 1972 to 1982. Also of importance in understanding the legal opposition to ERA is Paul A. Freund, "The Equal Rights Amendment Is Not the Way," *Harvard Civil Rights-Civil Liberties Law Review* 6 (March 1971): 234–42.

17. David Kyvig maintains that Ervin and Schlafly raised the issue of unisex bathrooms as a way of fostering racial fears of blacks and whites having to share bathrooms at a time when Jim Crow was being challenged in the South by the civil rights movement. Kyvig correctly points out that Ervin was no friend of racial desegregation, but Schlafly had supported racial integration in her hometown of St. Louis and supported desegregation in the South. It is worth noting that she campaigned against George Wallace in his presidential bid in 1968. Critchlow, *Phyllis Schlafly and Grassroots Conservatism*, 28–29, 185, 188–94; Kyvig, *Amending the Constitution*, 410–11.

18. Critchlow, *Phyllis Schlafly and Grassroots Conservatism*, 225.

19. A good study of conservative women in this period is found in Lisa McGirr, *Suburban Warriors: The Origins of the New American Right* (Princeton, 2001). See also Rebecca Klatch, *Women of the New Right* (Philadelphia, 1987); Sara Diamond, *Road to Dominion: Right-Wing Movements and Political Power in the United States* (New York, 1995); and Elinor Burkett, *The Right Women: A Journey Through the Heart of Conservative America* (New York, 1998).

    The tradition of women as moral reformers is found in an extensive literature on the subject. For the purpose of this essay, especially useful are Jane Sherron Dehart, "Gender on the Right: Meanings behind the Existential Scream," *Gender and History* 3 (Autumn 1991): 246–67; Zillah R. Eisenstein, "The Sexual Politics of the New Right," *Feminist Theory* 7 (Spring 1982); Kathleen M. Blee, *Women of the Klan: Racism and Gender in the 1920s* (Berkeley and Los Angeles, 1991); and Leonard J. Moore, *Citizen Klansmen: The Ku Klux Klan in Indiana, 1921–1928* (Chapel Hill, 1991). Of particular value for understanding the role of women in public life in the nineteenth century are Mary P. Ryan, *Cradle of the Middle Class: The Family in Oneida County, New York, 1790–1865* (Cambridge, 1981); Mary P. Ryan, "The Power of Women's Networks: A Case Study of Female Moral Reform in Antebellum America," *Feminist Studies* 5 (Spring 1979): 66–85; Barbara Leslie Epstein, *The Politics of Domesticity: Women, Evangelism, and Temperance in Nineteenth-Century America* (Middletown, Conn., 1981); Ruth Bordin, *Women and Temperance: The Quest for Power and Liberty, 1873–1900* (Philadelphia, 1981); Lori D. Ginzberg, "'Moral Suasion is Moral Balderdash': Women, Politics, and Social Activism in the 1850s," *Journal of American History* 73 (December 1986): 601–22; Karen J. Blair, *The Clubwoman as Feminist: True Womanhood Redefined, 1868–1914* (New York, 1980); Kathryn Kish Sklar, "Hull House in the 1890s: A Community of Women Reformers," Signs 10 (Summer 1985): 658–77; Paula Baker, "Domestication of Politics: Women and American Political Society, 1780–1920," *American Historical Review* 89 June 1984): 620–47; Ellen Carol DuBois, *Feminism and Suffrage: The Emergence of an Independent Women's Movement in America, 1848–1869* (Ithaca, 1978); and Susan Lebsock, "Women and American Politics, 1880–1920," in Louise Tilly and Patricia Gurin, eds., *Women, Politics, and Change in Twentieth-Century America* (New York, 1992).

20. The view that women's groups had failed to connect with "homemakers" is found in Bonnie Cowan to Jane Wells (National Coordinator ERAmerica), 19 March 1976, ERAmerica, Box 1, Library of Congress, Washington, D.C.

21. Jane Mansbridge, *Why We Lost the ERA*, 135–38 and 173–78.

22. Brady and Tedin, "*Ladies in Pink*," 564–75.

23. Donald G. Mathews, "'Spiritual Warfare': Cultural Fundamentalism and the Equal Rights Amendment," *Religion and American Culture* 3 (Summer 1993): 129–54, quoted at 133–34. Mathews might have added that pro-ERA feminists in framing the ERA as a "rights" issue also brought an equal passion to their cause.

24. Rosemary Thomson, "A Christian View of the Equal Rights Amendment" (1975). For an understanding of evangelical Christian mobilization in this period, see Clyde Wilcox, *God's Warriors: The Christian Right in Twentieth-Century America* (Baltimore, 1992); Wilcox, *Onward Christian Soldiers? The Religious Right in American Politics* (Boulder, 1996); Steve Bruce, *The Rise and Fall of the New Christian Right: Conservative Protestant Politics in America, 1978–1988* (New York, 1998); and Oran P. Smith, *The Rise of Baptist Republicanism* (New York, 1997). See also Steve Bruce et al., *The Rapture of Politics: The Christian Right as the United States Approaches the Year 2000* (New Brunswick, N.J., 1995); Matthew Moen, *The Christian Right and Congress* (Tuscaloosa, 1989); Robert Liebman and Robert Wuthnow, eds., *The New Christian Right: Mobilization and Legitimation* (Hawthorne, N.Y., 1993); and David Bromley and Anson Shupe, eds., *New Christian Politics* (Macon, Ga., 1984).

25. Although Wohlenberg and others maintained that the level of religious conservatism within a state has a direct correlation to the likelihood of ERA passage, Soule and Olzak "found no effect of religious fundamentalism on ratification." Soule and Olzak, "When Do Movements Matter?" 484.

26. Brady and Tedin, "Ladies in Pink"; Kent L. Tedin et al., "Social Background and Political

Differences Between Pro- and Anti-ERA Activists," *American Politics Quarterly 5* (July 1977): 395–404; Mueler and Dimieri, "The Structure of Belief Systems among Contending ERA Activists"; and Pamela Johnston Conover; "The Mobilization of the New Right: A Test of Various Explanations," *Western Political Quarterly* 36 (December 1983): 632–49. For an argument in favor of status politics, see Wilbur J. Scott, "The Equal Rights Amendment as Status Politics," *Social Forces* 64 (December 1985): 499–506.

27. Especially useful is Ruth Rosen, *The World Split Open: How the Modern Women's Movement Changed America* (New York, 2000), and Daniel Horowitz, *Betty Friedan and the Making of the Feminine Mystique: The American Left, the Cold War, and Modern Feminism* (Amherst, Mass., 1998).

28. This point is developed in Critchlow, *Phyllis Schlafly and Grassroots Conservatism*, 224–25, and in Mansbridge, *Why We Lost the ERA*.

29. Theda Skocpol et al., "Women's Associations and the Enactment of Mothers' Pensions in the United States," *American Political Science Review* 87 (September 1993): 686–701. This argument is developed at length in Skocpol, *Protecting Soldiers and Mothers: The Political Origins of Social Policy in the United States* (Cambridge, Mass., 1995).

30. Differences between ERA and NOW are evident in the archives of ERAmerica located in the Library of Congress. For an outline of these differences, see Critchlow, *Phyllis Schlafly and Grassroots Conservatism*, 227–32.

31. Alexander Hamilton, "The Federalist No. *85,"* *The Federalist,* ed. Jacob E. Cook, 587–95, quotation, 591, 594.

DONALD T. CRITCHLOW is a historian specializing in American political history.

CYNTHIA L. STACHECKI is a doctoral student at Saint Louis University.

EXPLORING THE ISSUE

Do We Need the Equal Rights Amendment?

Critical Thinking and Reflection

1. How might the battle to ratify the Equal Rights Amendment have helped to achieve as much or more than actual ratification might have accomplished?
2. If we still need the Equal Rights Amendment, might the wording of the Amendment need a twenty-first century modernization? Why or why not?

Is There Common Ground?

On Wednesday, March 6, 2013, Senator Robert Menendez (D-NJ) and Representative Carolyn Maloney (D-NY) reintroduced the traditional ERA ratification bills. At the same time, efforts to achieve state-by-state ratification continue. The language of the ERA Amendment is as simple today as it was when it was first proposed by suffragist Alice Paul in 1923:

> The Equal Rights Amendment
>
> Section 1. Equality of rights under the law shall not be denied or abridged by the United States or by any state on account of sex.
>
> Section 2. The Congress shall have the power to enforce, by appropriate legislation, the provisions of this article.
>
> Section 3. This amendment shall take effect two years after the date of ratification.
>
> —(Francis, 2013)

The reasons underlying the recurring failure to ratify the ERA range from political vendettas to entrenched sexism embedded in the fabric of our social institutions. Passage of the ERA, if it happens, will boil down to a vote count—whether in a state legislature or on the floor of Congress. Only history and time will tell how ERA ratification will change American culture and the lives of men and women across the nation.

Additional Resources

Global Economics Paper No. 164. "The Paper Was Underwritten by Goldman Sachs and Authored by Sandra Lawson." Retrieved from: www2 .goldmansachs.com/ideas/demographic-change/ women-hold-up-half-of-the-sky.pdf

Francis, R.W. (2013). "The Equal Rights Amendment." The Alice Paul Institute and the National Council of Women's Organizations. Retrieved from: www.equalrightsamendment.org/

Kristof, N. and WuDunn, S. (2009). *Half the Sky: Turning Oppression into Opportunity for Women Worldwide*. Random House: New York. Retrieved from: www.halftheskymovement.org/

Create Central

www.mhhe.com/createcentral

Internet References . . .

Equal Rights Amendment

http://equalrightsamendment.org/

National Organization for Women

http://www.now.org/issues/economic/cea/history .html

Eagle Forum

http://www.eagleforum.org/era/

Unit 5

UNIT

Feminism in the 21st Century: You've Come a Long Way, Baby

*T*he debates women's roles in society have ignited culture wars that continue to fuel the fires of political discourse in American culture. In 2008, feminism experienced a national identity crisis when the nascent Tea Party arrived on the scene and followers of Alaska Governor and 2008 Vice Presidential nominee Sarah Palin embraced a "New Right" conservative form of feminism. The liberal wing of the feminist movement stood their ground on the belief that conservative perspectives and feminist viewpoints could not peacefully coexist.

Can a woman be a conservative feminist? Are those concepts compatible or mutually exclusive? Can women be misogynistic? Do women always support other women? Why or why not?

Feminism has always been a moving target and the shifting landscape of the women's movement has been magnified by the 24-hour news cycle of the twenty-first century. Competing perspectives on what it means to be a feminist and battles over who can wear the feminism mantle dominate the discourse as women navigate new, largely uncharted waters of personal, political, and professional life in the modern era.

Selected, Edited, and with Issue Framing Material by:
Rachel Pienta, *Valdosta State University*

ISSUE

Can a Woman with Conservative Political Views Be a Feminist?

YES: Christina Hoff Sommers, from "Feminism and Freedom," *The American Spectator* (July/August 2008)

NO: Jessica Valenti, from "Who Stole Feminism?" *The Nation* (October 18, 2010)

Learning Outcomes

As you read the issue, focus on the following points:

• How has feminism evolved over the past decade?

• How is the influence of various subgroups expressed in feminism?

ISSUE SUMMARY

YES: Christina Hoff Sommers, in "Feminism and Freedom," makes an argument for a broader representation and a redefinition of feminism that diverges from what she characterizes as a revisionist and radical feminist agenda.

NO: Jessica Valenti, in "Who Stole Feminism?," makes an argument against what she frames as a co-optation and re-branding of feminism by conservative women.

The fragmentation of the women's movement is not a recent phenomenon. Scholars who study the suffrage efforts of the late nineteenth and early twentieth century would note that a single monolithic movement wholly representative of all women has never existed. The contemporary battle for ownership of the feminist title and, by association, the women's movement has gained particular notoriety in recent years due to an eagerness on the part of both pundits and politicians to claim the sobriquet.

During the 2008 election cycle, vice presidential candidate Sarah Palin claimed the feminist designation and inspired young conservative women throughout the nation to try the label on for size. In "Feminism and Freedom," conservative scholar Christina Hoff Sommers reexamines the women's movement of the eighteenth and nineteenth century. Sommers characterizes egalitarian feminism as radical and conservative feminism as family-centered. She credits egalitarian feminism with earning women important legal rights but makes a case for the conservative feminism school of thought as an option for living a feminist life.

Sommers characterizes the conservative women's movement as one of philanthropy and volunteerism. Historically, the conservative women's movement embraced and celebrated the "Angel in the house" role for women. In fact, the conservative branch of the suffrage movement depicted the fight for the women's vote as a battle for the "home protection ballot." This conservative home-focused

messaging would prove successful with talking points that framed the political enfranchisement of women as "a mother's sacred duty to vote."

In "Who Stole Feminism?," Jessica Valenti examines how conservative women co-opted feminism during the 2008 presidential cycle. The popularity of conservative GOP women who became national political stars in the months leading up to the historic election of President Barack Obama was underscored by the subversion of progressive feminist labels by members of the nascent Tea Party movement. The conservative spin on feminism was hailed by pundits as the "new feminism" and the standard bearer of the movement was Alaska's Governor Sarah Palin, tapped to run as president candidate John McCain's running mate. Valenti makes the argument that feminism is not simply about women ascending to positions of power and influence but encompasses much larger and harder to achieve goals of equity and social justice.

Modern-day conservative women represent a diverse demographic group. Conservative women hold political office and serve as CEOs of Fortune 500 companies. The dividing line between conservative and liberal women often rests on issues of choice. Liberal feminists posit that a key tenet of feminism is a woman's right to choose. Conservative women who embrace the feminist label believe that feminism is not a single issue movement and that being a feminist is about economic opportunity and shattering glass ceilings in the workplace.

YES ←

Christina Hoff Sommers

Feminism and Freedom

On February 10, 2001, 18,000 women filled Madison Square Garden for one of the more notable feminist gatherings of our time. The event—"Take Back the Garden"—centered on a performance of Eve Ensler's raunchy play, *The Vagina Monologues*. The "Vulva Choir" sang; self-described "Vagina Warriors"—including Gloria Steinem, Jane Fonda, and Donna Hanover (Rudolph Giuliani's ex-wife)—recited pet names for vaginas: Mimi, Gladys. Glenn Close led the crowd in spelling out the obscene word for women's intimate anatomy, "Give me a C...!!!" A huge banner declared the Garden to be a "RAPE FREE ZONE." The mood grew solemn when Oprah Winfrey came forward to read a new monologue called "Under the Burqa," which described the plight of Afghan women living under the Taliban. At its climax, an actual Afghan woman named Zoya, who represented RAWA—the Revolutionary Association of the Women of Afghanistan—appeared on stage covered from head to toe in a burqa. Oprah approached her and, with a dramatic sweep of her arm, lifted and removed it. The crowd roared in delight.

Later, an exposé in the progressive *American Prospect* would reveal that RAWA is a Maoist organization whose fanatical members are so feared by Afghan women that one human rights activist has dubbed them the "Talibabes." According to the *Prospect*, when *Ms.* magazine tried to distance itself from RAWA in 2002, a RAWA spokeswoman denounced *Ms.* as the "mouthpiece of hegemonic, U.S.-centric corporate feminism." But on that magical February night at the Garden, few knew or cared about Zoya's political views or affiliations.

The evening was a near-perfect distillation of contemporary feminism. Pick up a women's studies textbook, visit a college women's center, or look at the websites of leading feminist organizations and you will be likely to find the same fixation on intimate anatomy, combined with left-wing politics, and a poisonous antipathy to men. (Campus feminists were among the most vocal and zealous accusers of the young men on the Duke University lacrosse team who were falsely indicted for rape in 2006.) Contemporary feminism routinely depicts American society as a dangerous patriarchy where women are under siege—that is the message of the "RAPE FREE ZONE" banner in the Garden. It therefore presents itself as a movement of "liberation,"

defying the patriarchal oppressor and offering women everywhere the opportunity to make contact with their "real selves."

But modern "women's liberation" has little to do with liberty. It aims not to free women to pursue their own interests and inclinations, but rather to re-educate them to attitudes often profoundly contrary to their natures. In *Professing Feminism: Education and Indoctrination in Women's Studies* (2003), two once-committed women's studies professors, Daphne Patai and Noretta Koertge, describe how the feminist classroom transforms idealistic female students into "relentless grievance collectors." In 1991, the culture critic and dissident feminist Camille Paglia put the matter even more bluntly: she described women's studies as "a jumble of vulgarians, bunglers, whiners, French faddicts, apparatchiks, dough-faced party-liners, pie-in-the-sky utopians and bullying sanctimonious sermonizers. Reasonable, moderate feminists hang back and keep silent in the face of fascism."

The embarrassing spectacle at Madison Square Garden, the erratic state of women's studies, the outbreak of feminist vigilantism at Duke University may tempt some to conclude that the women's movement in the United States is in a state of hopeless, hapless, and permanent disarray. Perhaps American feminism has become hysterical because it has ceased to be useful. After all, women in this country have their freedom; they have achieved parity with men in most of the ways that count. Why not let the feminist movement fade from the scene? The sooner the better. Good riddance.

That is an understandable but unwarranted reaction. Women in the West *did* form a movement and *did* liberate themselves in ways of vital importance to the evolution of liberal society. Feminism, in its classical phase, was a critical chapter in the history of freedom. For most of the world's women, that history has just begun; for them, classical feminism offers a tried and true roadmap to equality and freedom. And even in the West there are unresolved equity issues and the work of feminism is not over. Who needs feminism? We do. The world does. Women everywhere need the liberty to be what they are—not, as contemporary feminism insists, liberation *from* what they are. This we can see if we look back at the history of women's liberation—not as it is taught in women's studies departments, but as it truly was.

The classical feminism of the 18th and 19th centuries embodied two distinct schools of thought and social activism. The first, egalitarian feminism, was progressive (in the view of many contemporaries of both sexes, radical), and it centered on women as independent agents rather than wives and mothers. It held that men and women are, in their essential nature, the same, and it sought to liberate women through abstract appeals to social justice and universal rights. The second school, conservative feminism, was traditionalist and family-centered. It embraced rather than rejected women's established roles as homemakers, caregivers, and providers of domestic tranquility—and it promoted women's rights by redefining, strengthening, and expanding those roles. Conservative feminists argued that a practical, responsible femininity could be a force for good in the world beyond the family, through charitable works and more enlightened politics and government.

Of the two schools, conservative feminism was much the more influential. Unlike its more radical sister, conservative feminism has always had great appeal to large majorities of women. By contrast, egalitarian feminists often appeared strange and frightening with their salons and little journals. It is not, however, my purpose to denigrate egalitarian feminism—quite the contrary. Historically, proponents of the two schools were forthright and sometimes fierce competitors, but their competition sharpened the arguments on both sides, and they often cooperated on practical causes to great effect. The two movements were (and will remain) rivals in principle but complementary in practice. Thanks to egalitarian feminism, women now have the same rights and opportunities as men. But, as conservative feminists have always insisted, free women seldom aspire to be just like men, but rather employ their freedom in distinctive ways and for distinctive purposes.

Egalitarian feminism had its historical beginnings in the writings of the British philosopher Mary Wollstonecraft (1759–1797). Wollstonecraft, a rebel and a free thinker, believed that women were as intelligent as men and as worthy of respect. Her *A Vindication of the Rights of Woman* became an instant sensation. She wrote it in the spirit of the European Enlightenment—whose primary principle was the essential dignity and moral equality of all rational beings. However, Wollstonecraft's insistence that women too are rational and deserving of the same rights as men was then a contentious thesis.

Wollstonecraft's demand was a dramatic break with the past. In 1776, Abigail Adams famously wrote a letter to her husband, John, urging him and his colleagues in the Continental Congress to "remember the ladies. . . and to be more generous and favorable to them than your ancestors." Adams was appealing to a tradition of chivalry and gallantry that enjoined male protectiveness toward women. Sixteen years later, in her *Vindication*, Wollstonecraft was doing something markedly different. She was not urging legislators in France and England to "remember the ladies" or appealing to their generous or protective impulses. Reason, she said, demanded that

women be granted the same rights as men. She wanted nothing less than total political and moral equality. Wollstonecraft was perhaps the first woman in history to insist that biology is not destiny: "I view with indignation the mistaken notions that enslave my sex."

For Wollstonecraft, education was the key to female liberation: "Strengthen the female mind by enlarging it, and there will be an end to blind obedience." She was a proponent of co-education and insisted that women be educated on a par with men—with all fields and disciplines being open to them. In the opening lines of *Vindication*, she expresses her "profound conviction that the neglected education of [women] is the grand source of the misery I deplore."

Wollstonecraft led one of the most daring, dramatic, and consequential lives of the 18th century. She was a lower-middle-class, semi-educated "nobody" (as one British historian has described her) who was to become the first woman to enter the Western canon of political philosophy. Her friends included Thomas Paine, William Wordsworth, and William Blake. She carried on a famous debate with Edmund Burke about the merits of the French Revolution. Soon after she published her *Vindication of the Rights of Woman* she ran off to Paris to write about the revolution.

After her death, her husband William Godwin wrote what he thought was an adulatory biography. He talked honestly about her unorthodox lifestyle that included love affairs, an out-of wedlock child, and two suicide attempts over her faithless American lover. He even praised her—completely inaccurately—for having rejected Christianity. Godwin all but destroyed her reputation for the next hundred years. The public reaction to his disclosures was fascination, horror, and repulsion. Former friends denounced her. Feminists distanced themselves. Political enemies called her a "whore." Today, however, her reputation is secure. In an essay published in 1932, Virginia Woolf wrote, "One form of immortality is hers undoubtedly: she is alive and active, she argues and experiments, we hear her voice and trace her influence even now among the living." Woolf summarizes Wollstonecraft's egalitarian teachings in one sentence: "The staple of her doctrine was that nothing matters save independence." Another way of putting it is to say that what Wollstonecraft wanted for women was the full liberty of citizenship.

At the time Wollstonecraft was writing, Hannah More (1745–1833)—novelist, poet, pamphleteer, political activist, evangelical reformer, and abolitionist—was waging a very different campaign to improve the status of women. More is well-known to scholars who specialize in eighteenth century culture. The late UCLA literary historian Mitzi Myers calls her a "female crusader infinitely more successful than Wollstonecraft or any other competitor," but More is rarely given the credit she deserves. The story of what she initiated and how she did it is integral to the story of women's quest for freedom. But few contemporary feminist historians have wanted that story to be told.

Virginia Woolf once said that if she were in charge of assigning names to critical historical epochs, along with the Crusades, or the War of the Roses, she would give a special name to that world-transforming period at the end of the 18th century in England when, in her words, "The middleclass woman began to write." One disparaging historian called this unprecedented cohort of writing women (borrowing a phrase from the 16th-century religious reformer John Knox) "a monstrous regiment." It was a regiment that was destined to win decisive battles in women's struggle for freedom and opportunity. Its three most important members were Mary Wollstonecraft, Jane Austen, and Hannah More.

If Wollstonecraft was the founder of egalitarian feminism, More was the founder of conservative feminism. Like Wollstonecraft, More was a religiously inspired, self-made woman who became an intellectual peer of several of the most accomplished men of her age. But whereas Wollstonecraft befriended Paine and debated Burke, More was a friend and admirer of Burke, a close friend of Samuel Johnson and of Horace Walpole, and an indispensable ally and confidante to William Wilberforce, a father of British abolitionism. Concerning the French revolution which Wollstonecraft initially championed, More wrote, "From liberty, equality, and the rights of man, good Lord deliver *us.*" And she was surely the most prominent woman of her age. As one biographer notes, "In her time she was better known than Mary Wollstonecraft and her books outsold Jane Austen's many times over." Her various pamphlets sold in the millions and her tract against the French revolution enjoyed a greater circulation than Burke's *Reflections* or Paine's *Rights of Man*. Some historians credit her political writings with saving England from the kind of brutal revolutionary upheaval that traumatized France.

More (who never married) was active in the Bluestocking society. The "Blues" were a group of intellectual women (and men) who would meet to discuss politics, literature, science, and philosophy. It was started in 1750 by intelligent but education-starved upper- and middleclass women who yearned for serious conversation rather than the customary chatter and gossip typical of elite gatherings. "I was educated at random," More would say, and women's education became one of her most passionate causes.

More is hard to classify politically. It is possible to find passages in her novels, pamphlets, and letters that make her look like an arch conservative; others show her as a progressive reformer. Through selective citation she can be made to seem like an insufferable prude—Lord Byron dismissed her as "Morality's prim personification"—but it is doubtful that a "prim personification" would have attracted the devotion and respect of men like Johnson, Walpole, and Wilberforce.

More was a British patriot, a champion of constitutional monarchy, and a friend and admirer of Edmund Burke, but she was no defender of the status quo. She called for revolutionary change—not in politics, but in morals.

In her novels and pamphlets, she sharply reproached members of the upper classes for their amorality, hedonism, indifference to the poor, and tolerance of the crime of slavery. In the many Sunday schools she established she encouraged the poor to be sober, thrifty, hard-working, and religious. More shared Adam Smith's enthusiasm for the free market as a force for good. But for the market to thrive, she believed England's poor and rich would need to develop good moral habits and virtuous characters.

Historians have referred to her as "bourgeois progressivist," a "Christian capitalist," "Burke for beginners," the "first Victorian." She could also be called the first conservative feminist. Unlike Wollstonecraft, More believed the sexes were significantly different in their propensities, aptitudes, and life preferences. She envisioned a society where women's characteristic virtues and graces could be developed, refined, and freely expressed. She was persuaded that these virtues could be realized only when women were given more freedom and a serious education:

> [T]ill women shall be more reasonably educated, and until the native growth of their mind shall cease to be stilted and cramped, we shall have no juster ground for pronouncing that their understanding has already reached its highest attainable perfection, than the Chinese would have for affirming that their women have attained to the greatest possible perfection in walking, while their first care is, during their infancy, to cripple their feet.

She loathed the mindless pastimes that absorbed upper-class women of her day, and encouraged middle- and upper-class women to leave their homes and salons so as to take up serious philanthropic pursuits. According to More, women were more tender-minded than men and were the natural caretakers of the nation. She told women that it was their patriotic duty to apply their natural gifts—nurturing, organizing, and educating—not merely to their own households, but to society at large. "Charity," said one of More's fictional characters, "is the calling of a lady: the care of the poor is her profession." More envisioned armies of intelligent, informed, and well-trained women working in hospitals, orphanages, and schools. She appealed to women to exert themselves "with a patriotism at once firm and feminine for the greater good of all." And women listened.

Her didactic 1880 novel, *Coelebs in Search of a Wife*, which valorized a new kind of wise, effective, active, and responsible femininity, went into 11 editions in nine months, and to 30 by the time of More's death. UCLA literary scholar Anne Mellor comments on the extent of More's influence:

> She urged her women readers to participate actively in the organization of voluntary benevolent societies and in the foundation of hospitals,

orphanages, Sunday Schools. . . .And her call was heard: literally thousands of voluntary societies sprang up in the opening decades of the nineteenth century to serve the needs of every imaginable group of sufferers.

It is hard to overstate the positive impact of widespread volunteerism on the fate of women. As women became engaged in charitable works, other parts of the public sphere became accessible. British historian F.K. Prochaska, in his seminal *Women and Philanthropy in Nineteenth-Century England* (1980), wrote, "The charitable experience of women was a lever which they used to open the doors closed to them in other spheres." According to Prochaska, as women began to become active in the outside world and form philanthropic organizations, they became interested in "government, administration and the law." Their volunteer work in charity schools focused their minds on education reform—for women of their own social class and for the poor women they sought to help. Prochaska, who calls More "probably the most influential woman of her day," concludes, "It should not come as a surprise that in 1866 women trained in charitable society were prominent among those who petitioned the House of Commons praying for the enfranchisement of their sex."

It was taken for granted in More's time that women were less intelligent and less serious than men, and thus less worthy as human beings. More flatly rejected these assumptions. She did so without rejecting the idea of a special women's sphere. She embraced that sphere, giving it greater dignity and power. That was her signature Burkean style of feminism. More initiated a humane revolution in the relations of the sexes that was decorous, civilized, and in no way socially divisive. Above all, it was a feminism that women themselves could comfortably embrace: a feminism that granted women the liberty to be themselves without ceasing to be women. Indeed, if More's name and fame had not been brushed out of women's history, many women today might well be identifying with a modernized version of her femalefriendly feminism.

Fortunately, her ideals and her style of feminism are well represented in the novels of Jane Austen. We don't know for sure whether Austen read More, but scholars claim to see the unmistakable influence in her writings of both More and Wollstonecraft. Her heroines are paragons of rational, merciful, and responsible womanhood. Austen also honors a style of enlightened and chivalrous manhood. Austen's heroes—men like Mr. Darcy, Captain Wentworth, and Mr. Knightley—esteem female strength, rationality, and intelligence.

Egalitarian feminists like Wollstonecraft (and later, John Stuart Mill and Harriet Taylor) are staple figures in the intellectual history of feminism, but they have never attracted a very large following among the rank and file of women of their time. More succeeded brilliantly with all classes of women. She awakened a nation and changed the way it saw itself. What she achieved was unprecedented. But

the feminist scholar Elizabeth Kowaleski Wallace speaks for many when she describes More as a case study of "patriarchal complicity" and an "uninvited guest" who "makes the process of celebrating our HERITAGE as women more difficult."

Hannah More is not the only once-famous women's advocate to have vanished from the official "herstorical" record. Ken Burns, the celebrated documentarian, followed his award-winning *Civil War* with a 1999 film about Elizabeth Cady Stanton (1815–1902) and Susan B. Anthony (1820–1906) and their struggle to win the vote for American women. There is one brief sequence in which the narrator explains that in the last quarter of the 19th century, Anthony forged coalitions with conservative mainstream groups. The mood darkens and a pioneer in the field of women's studies—Professor Sally Roesch Wagner—appears on the screen. Wagner informs viewers that Anthony was so determined to win the vote, she established alliances with pro-suffrage women who were "enemies of freedom in every other way—Frances Willard is a case in point." The camera then shows a photo of a menacing-looking Willard.

One would never imagine from Burns's film that Frances Willard (1839–1898) was one of the most beloved and respected women of the 19th century. When she died, one newspaper wrote, "No woman's name is better known in the English-speaking world than that of Miss Willard, save that of England's great queen." Because of her prodigious good works and kindly nature, Willard was often called the "Saint Frances of American Womanhood."

But Willard, a suffragist and leader of the Women's Christian Temperance Union, is another once esteemed figure in women's history who is today unmentioned and unmentionable. Willard brought mainstream women into the suffrage movement, and some historians credit her with doing far more to win the vote for women than any other suffragist. But her fondness for saying things like "Womanliness first—afterwards what you will" was her ticket to historical obliquy.

Approved feminist founders like Elizabeth Cady Stanton and Susan B. Anthony promoted women's suffrage through Wollstonecraft-like appeals to universal rights. Their inspirations were John Locke, Thomas Jefferson, and Wollstonecraft herself. Stanton wrote affectingly on "the individuality of each human soul," and on a woman's need to be the "arbiter of her own destiny." She and her sister suffragists brought a feminist Enlightenment to women, but to their abiding disappointment, American women greeted the offer with a mixture of indifference and hostility. Stanton's words were effective with a relatively small coterie of educated women, mostly on the East Coast. When a suffrage amendment failed dismally in the state of Colorado in 1877, one newspaper editorial called the suffragists "carpetbaggers" promoting an elitist "eastern issue." The headline read: "Good-bye to the Female Tramps of Boston."

For many decades the average American woman simply ignored the cause of suffrage. In a 1902 history of women's suffrage, Anthony and her co-author wrote, "the indifference and inertia, the apathy of women lies the greatest obstacle to their enfranchisement." Throughout the 1880s and 1890s many women actively organized against it. Stanford historian Carl Degler, in his classic 1980 social history, *At Odds: Women and the Family in America from the Revolution to the Present,* notes that in 1890, more than 20,000 women had joined an *anti*-suffrage group in New York State alone.

To prove once and for all that the majority of women wanted the vote, suffragists organized a referendum in Massachusetts in 1895. Both men and women were allowed to take part. The initiative lost, with 187,000 voting against the franchise and only 110,000 in favor—and of those who voted yes, only 23,000 were women! According to Anthony, "The average man would not vote against granting women the suffrage if all those of his own family brought a strong pressure to bear upon him in its favor." It is the conventional wisdom that men denied women the ballot. But even a cursory look at the historical record suggests that men were not the only problem.

Degler and other historians believe that, because the vote was associated with individualism and personal assertiveness, many women saw it as both selfish and an attack on their unique and valued place in the family. Feminist historians denigrate what they call the "cult of domesticity" that proved so beguiling to nineteenth century women. But they forget that this "cult" freed many rural women from manual labor, improved the material conditions of women's lives and coincided with an increase in female life expectancy. Furthermore, as Degler shows, in nineteenth-century America, both the public and private spheres were prized and valued. The companionate marriages described by Jane Austen were the American domestic ideal. Alexis de Tocqueville commented on the essential equality of the male and female spheres in *Democracy in America* (1840) "Americans," he said, did not think that men and women should perform the same tasks, "but they show an equal regard for both their perspective parts; and though their lot is different, they consider both of them as being of equal value."

Hence as long as women saw the vote as a threat to their sphere, suffrage was a lost cause. Impassioned feminist rhetoric about freedom, dignity, autonomy, and individual rights fell on deaf ears. If the American women's movement was going to move forward, the suffrage movement needed new arguments and new ways of thinking that were more respectful and protective of women's role. Frances Willard showed the way.

Frances Willard served as president of the Woman's Christian Temperance Union from 1879 until her death in 1898. Under her leadership it grew to be the largest and most influential women's organization in the nation. Today we associate temperance with Puritanism. But in the late 19th century, most feminists, including Elizabeth Cady Stanton and Susan B. Anthony, supported it. Temper-

ance advocates believed that a ban on the sale of alcohol would greatly diminish wife abuse, desertion, destitution, and crime. In other words, temperance was a movement in defense of the home—the female sphere.

Willard was proud of women's role as the "Angel in the house." But why, she asked, limit these angels to the home? With the vote, said Willard, women could greatly increase their civilizing and humane influence on society. With the vote, they could protect the homes they so dearly loved. Indeed, Willard referred to the "vote" as "the home protection ballot." Women were moved by this, and men were disarmed.

Anthony admired Willard; Stanton, a skeptic in religious matters, was leery. Both were startled by her ability to attract unprecedented numbers of dedicated women to the suffrage cause. The membership figures for the various women's organizations are striking. In 1890, two leading egalitarian suffragist groups merged because they were worried that the cause was dying. They formed the National American Woman Suffrage Association and elected Elizabeth Cady Stanton president. The total membership of these combined groups, according to University of Michigan historian Ruth Bordin, was 13,000. By comparison, Willard had built an organization with more than ten times that number; by 1890 she had 150,000 adult dues-paying members. Moreover, Willard and her followers began to bring the suffrage movement something new and unfamiliar: victories.

In 1893 the state of Colorado held a second election on women's suffrage. Unlike 1877, when the suffragists lost and the so-called "tramps of Boston" were sent packing, this time the suffragists won the vote by a 55 percent majority. Many historians agree that Willard's new conservative approach explains the success. She had persuaded large numbers of men and women that it was a mother's sacred duty to vote.

Thomas Carlyle has ascribed the insights of genius to "cooperation with the tendency of the world." Like Hannah More before her, Willard cooperated with the world and discerned novel and effective ways to improve it. Feminists do not honor the memory of these women. Indeed, with the exception of a small group of professional historians and literary critics, almost no one knows who they are. Still, it is interesting to note, today the Hannah More/Frances Willard style of conservative feminism is on the verge of a powerful resurgence.

In her 1990 book, *In Search of Islamic Feminism,* the University of Texas Middle Eastern studies professor Elizabeth Warnock Fernea described a new style of feminism coming to life throughout the Muslim world. Traveling through Uzbekistan, Saudi Arabia, Morocco, Turkey, and Iraq, Fernea met great numbers of women's advocates working hard to improve the status of women. There have always been Western-style egalitarian feminists in these countries. But they are small in number and tend to be found among the most educated elites. The "Islamic feminists" Fernea was meeting were different. They were traditional, religious, and family-centered—and they had a following among women from all social classes. They were proud of women's role as mother, wife, and caregiver. Several rejected what they see as divisiveness in today's American women's movement. As one Iraqi women's advocate, Haifa Abdul Rahman, told her, "We see feminism in America as dividing women from men, separating women from the family. This is bad for everyone." Fernea settled on the term "family feminism" to describe this new movement. Experts on the history of Western feminism will here recognize its affinities with Frances Willard's long-lost teachings. Today, almost 20 years after Fernea's book, conservative feminism is surging in the Muslim world.

When Frances Willard died in 1898, her younger feminist colleague Carrie Chapman Catt remarked, "There has never been a woman leader in this country greater than Frances Willard." But today's feminists remain implacably hostile to Willard's notions of "womanly virtue" and have no sympathy with her family-centered feminism. These are unforgivable defects in their eyes, but they are precisely the traits that make Willard's style of feminism highly relevant to the many millions of women all over the world who are struggling for their rights and freedoms in strongly traditional societies, and who do not want to be liberated from their love for family, children, and husband.

Truth be told, there are also great numbers of contemporary American women who would today readily label themselves as feminists were they aware of a conservative alternative, in which liberty rather than "liberation" is the dominant idea. Today, more than 70 percent of American women reject the label "feminist," largely because the label has been appropriated by those who reject the very idea of a feminine sphere.

Clare Boothe Luce, a conservative feminist who in her heyday in the 1940s was a popular playwright and a member of the United States Congress, wrote and spoke about women at a time when feminism's Second Wave was still more than 20 years away. Luce's exemplary remarks on Mother Nature and sex differences are especially relevant today.

> It is time to leave the question of the role of women in society up to Mother Nature—a difficult lady to fool. You have only to give women the same opportunities as men, and you will soon find out what is or is not in their nature. What is in women's nature to do they will do, and you won't be able to stop them. But you will also find, and so will they, that what is not in their nature, even if they are given every opportunity, they will not do, and you won't be able to make them do it.

Camille Paglia once told me she found these words powerful, persuasive, and even awe-inspiring. So do I. Luce takes the best of both egalitarian and conservative feminism. She is careful to say that women's nature can be made known only in conditions of freedom and opportunity. It is in such conditions of respect and fairness that woman can reveal their true preferences. Clearly Luce does not expect that women will turn out to be interchangeable with men.

When Luce wrote her cautionary words, sex role stereotypes still powerfully limited women's choices and opportunities. Today, women enjoy the equality of opportunity that Luce alluded to. The conventional constraints, confinements, and rigid expectations are largely things of the past. It is now possible to observe "the role of women in society" by taking note of the roles women themselves freely choose. Was Wollstonecraft right to insist that under conditions of freedom the sexes would make similar choices? Or was Hannah More closer to the truth when she suggested that women will always prevail in the private sphere and express themselves as the natural caregivers of the species?

We know from common observation that women are markedly more nurturing and empathetic than men. The female tendency to be empathic and caring shows up very early in life. Female infants, for example, show greater distress and concern than male infants over the plight of others; this difference persists into adulthood. Women don't merely say they want to help others; they enter the helping and caring professions in great numbers. Even today, in an era when equal rights feminism is dominant in education, the media, and the women's movement, women continue to be vastly over-represented in fields like nursing, social work, pediatrics, veterinary medicine, and early childhood education. The great 19th-century psychologist William James said that for men "the world is a theater for heroism." That may be an overstatement, but it finds a lot of support in modern social science—and evidence of everyday life. Women are numerically dominant in the helping professions; men prevail in the saving and rescuing vocations such as policemen, firefighters, and soldiers.

Here we come to the central paradox of egalitarian feminism: when women are liberated from the domestic sphere and no longer forced into the role of nurturers, when they are granted their full Lockean/Jeffersonian freedoms to pursue happiness in all the multitudinous ways a free society has to offer, many, perhaps most, still give priority to the domestic sphere.

In a 1975 exchange in the *Saturday Review*, the feminist pioneer Betty Friedan and the French philosopher and women's rights advocate Simone de Beauvoir discussed the "problem" of stay-at-home mothers. Friedan told Beauvoir that she believed women should have the choice to stay home to raise their children if that is what they wished to do. Beauvoir candidly disagreed:

> No, we don't believe that any woman should have this choice. No woman should be authorized to stay at home to raise her children. Society should be totally different. Women should not have that choice, precisely because if there is such a choice, too many women will make that one . . .

In Simone de Beauvoir, we see how starkly the ideology of liberation has come to oppose actual, practical liberty—even "choice." Her intolerance and condescension toward family-centered women is shared by many in today's feminist establishment, and has affected the education of American students. Historian Christine Rosen, in a recent survey of women's studies texts, found that every one disparaged traditional marriage, stay-at-home mothers, and the culture of romance. Perhaps there is a sensible women's studies text out there somewhere, but, for the most part, the sphere of life that has the greatest appeal to most women, and is inseparable from traditional ideas of feminine fulfillment, is rejected in the name of liberation.

Today's feminist establishment in the United States is dominated by the radical wing of the egalitarian tradition. Not only do its members not cooperate with their conservative sisters, but they also often denigrate and vilify them; indeed they have all but eliminated them from the history of American feminism. Revisionist history is never a pretty sight. But feminist revisionists are destructive in special ways. They seek to obliterate not only feminist history but the femininity that made it a success.

Contemporary feminism needs to make peace with Hannah More and Frances Willard and their modern-day heirs or face a complete loss of appeal and effectiveness. Eve Ensler and her most devoted disciple, Jane Fonda, may not be amenable to change. But there is hope for the younger generation. Over the years, I have lectured on more than 100 college campuses where I meet both conservative and radical women activists. The former invite me and the latter come to jeer and wrangle—but as a rule we all part as friends. "Why do you like the Vagina Monologues so much?", I ask them. Most tell me that, by acting in the play or supporting it, they are both having fun (girls, too, like to push the limits) and serving a good cause (funds raised by the performances support local domestic violence shelters). I have yet to meet a single one who shares the play's misandry.

These young women can be reasoned with and many are fully capable of allying themselves with moderate and conservative women to work for common interests. My advice to them: Don't bother "taking back the Garden." Take back feminism. Restore its lost history. Make the movement attractive once again to the silent majority of American women, who really don't want to be liberated from their womanhood. And then take on the cause of the women who have yet to find the liberty that western women have won for themselves and that all women everywhere deserve.

CHRISTINA HOFF SOMMERS is an associate professor of philosophy at Clark University.

Jessica Valenti

Who Stole Feminism?

Sarah Palin opposes abortion and comprehensive sex education. While mayor of Wasilla she made sexual assault victims pay for their own rape kits. She also calls herself a feminist. Delaware GOP Senate nominee Christine O'Donnell has said that allowing women to attend military academies "cripples the readiness of our defense" and that wives should "graciously submit" to their husbands—but her website touts her "commitment to the women's movement." Pundits who once mocked women's rights activists as ugly bra burners are abuzz over the "new conservative feminism," and the Tea Party is lauding itself as a women's movement.

The right once disparaged feminism as man-hating and baby-killing, but now "feminist" is the must-have label for women on the right. Whether or not this rebranding strategy actually succeeds in overcoming the GOP's anti-women reputation is unclear (see Betsy Reed, "Sex and the GOP," page 11). After all, Republicans have long supported overturning *Roe v. Wade*, voted against family and maternity leave, and fought groundbreaking legislation like the Lilly Ledbettter Fair Pay Act. When it comes to wooing women's votes for the GOP, there's a lot of damage control to do.

Feminists are understandably horrified—the movement we've fought so hard for is suddenly being appropriated by the very people who are trying to dismantle it. But this co-opting hasn't happened in a vacuum; the mainstream feminist movement's instability and stalled ideology have made stealing it that much easier. The failure of feminists to prop up the next generation of activists, and the focus on gender as the sole requisite for feminism, has led to a crisis of our own making.

Conservative women have been trying to steal feminism for more than a decade—organizations like the Independent Women's Forum and Feminists for Life have long fought for antiwoman policies while identifying themselves as the "real" feminists. But their "prowoman" messaging didn't garner national attention until actual feminists paved the way for them in the 2008 presidential election. During the Democratic primary, feminist icons and leaders of mainstream women's organizations insisted that the only acceptable vote was for Hillary Clinton; female Barack Obama supporters were derided as traitors or chided for their naïveté. I even heard from women working in feminist organizations who kept mum on their vote for fear of losing their jobs. Perhaps most representative of the internal strife was a *New York Times* op-ed (and the fallout that followed) by Gloria Steinem in which the icon wrote, "Gender is probably the most restricting force in American life."

Soon after, Melissa Harris-Lacewell, an associate professor of politics and African-American studies at Princeton University, responded in a *Democracy Now!* segment, "Part of what, again, has been sort of an anxiety for African-American women feminists like myself is that we're often asked to join up with white women's feminism, but only on their own terms, as long as we sort of remain silent about the ways in which our gender, our class, our sexual identity doesn't intersect, as long as we can be quiet about those things and join onto a single agenda."

The argument was not a new one—women of color and younger feminists have often taken white second-wave feminists to task for focusing on gender inequities over a more intersectional approach that also takes race, class and sexuality into account. But this intrafeminist skirmish over identity politics took on a life of its own in the aftermath of the bitter primary struggle. By pushing a vote for Clinton on the basis of her gender alone, establishment feminists not only rehashed internal grievances—they opened the door for conservatives to demand support for Palin for the very same reason. Unwittingly, the feminist argument for Clinton gave credence to the GOP's hope that the mere presence of a female on the ticket would deliver women's votes.

Is it any wonder, then, that everyone from Palin's supporters to the mainstream media was eager to paint the vice presidential candidate as a feminist? If all it took was being a woman, well, then Palin was it! The *Wall Street Journal* called it "Sarah Palin Feminism." The *New York Post* called her "a feminist dream," while the *Los Angeles Times* ran a piece headlined "Sarah Palin's 'New Feminism' Is Hailed."

In much the same way Obama-supporting feminists were criticized, women who didn't back Palin were swiftly denounced as hypocrites by those on the right. Rick Santorum called Palin the "Clarence Thomas for feminists," blasting women who didn't support her. Janice Shaw Crouse of Concerned Women for America said, "Even feminists—who supposedly promote women's equality and the so-called 'women's rights' agenda—are questioning a female candidate's ability to get the job done." The criticism of women who failed to back Palin even indulged in sexism. Dennis Miller said that women who weren't behind Palin were simply jealous of the candidate's sex life, and *Time* magazine reporter Belinda Luscombe wrote that some women had a "hatred" for Palin simply because she was "too pretty." (My favorite, however, was Kevin Burke's argument in *National Review* that women who didn't support Palin were suffering from "post-abortion symptoms.") Palin even managed to divide some feminists. Elaine Lafferty—a former editor of *Ms.* magazine who had endorsed Clinton but then signed on as a consultant to the McCain campaign—condemned feminist leaders for "sink[ing] this low" and called feminism an "exclusionary club" for not welcoming Palin with open arms.

If there was ever proof that the feminist movement needs to leave gender essentialism at the door—this is it. If powerful feminists continue to insist that gender matters above all else, the movement will become meaningless. If any woman can be a feminist simply because of her gender, then the right will continue to use this faux feminism to advance conservative values and roll back women's rights.

Ensuring feminism's future doesn't stop at embracing intersectionality—we must also shine a spotlight on the real feminists. Part of the reason Palin and her cohort are so successful at positioning themselves as the "new" women's movement is because we fail to push forward and support new feminists of our own. This is not to say that younger women aren't at the forefront of the movement—they certainly are. But their work is often made invisible by an older generation of feminists who prefer to believe young women are apathetic rather than admitting their movement is shifting into something they don't recognize and can't control.

For example, in an April *Newsweek* article about young people's supposed apathy over reproductive rights, NARAL Pro-Choice America President Nancy Keenan suggested that it was only the "postmenopausal militia" on the front lines of reproductive justice. Yet when I asked a NARAL spokesperson about employee demographics, I was told that people younger than 35 make up around 60 percent of the organization. And when they're not ignored, young feminists are painted as vapid and sexualized. Take feminist writer Debra Dickerson, who wrote in a 2009 *Mother Jones* article that today's feminists are all about "pole-dancing, walking around half-naked, posting drunk photos on Facebook and blogging about [their]

sex lives." This insistence that a new wave doesn't exist or isn't worth paying attention to has left open the cultural space for antifeminist women like O'Donnell and Palin to swoop in and lay claim to the movement

If the new wave of feminists—the leaders of small grassroots organizations across the country, the bloggers who are organizing hundreds of thousands of women online, the advocates for reproductive justice, racial equality and queer rights—aren't recognized as the real advocates for women, then the future of the movement will be lost.

Women vote for their interests—not their gender or age—but they still want to see themselves represented. If the only young women Americans see identified as "feminists" are those on the right, we run the risk of losing the larger cultural battle and the many younger women who are seeking an answer to the mixed messages about what feminism really is. And frankly, if we position vibrant young activists front and center, there will be no question as to who is creating the best change for women.

So instead of wringing our hands every time a new female candidate with distinctly antiwoman policies pops up, let's use it as an opportunity to re-establish what feminism is about and to support the up-and-comers in our midst. Let's focus on building power for the new wave of feminists by giving money to the organizations that best represent the future of the movement (like SAFER, NY Abortion Access Fund and Girls for Gender Equity); by providing media training and placing young activists on television and in the op-ed pages (as the great Women's Media Center does); and by pushing young feminists—not just women—to run for office.

Feminism isn't simply about being a woman in a position of power. It's battling systemic inequities; it's a social justice movement that believes sexism, racism and classism exist and interconnect, and that they should be consistently challenged. What's most important to remember as we fight back against conservative appropriation is that the battle over who "owns" the movement is not just about feminists; feminism's future affects all American women. And if we let the lie of conservative feminism stand—if real feminists don't lay claim to the movement and outline their vision for the future—all of us will suffer.

JESSICA VALENTI is an American blogger and feminist writer, known for having founded the feminist blog *Feministing*.

EXPLORING THE ISSUE

Can a Woman with Conservative Political Views Be a Feminist?

Critical Thinking and Reflection

1. How did conservative perspectives come to be perceived as antithetical to the dominant feminist viewpoint?
2. How do the competing voices in the feminist movement contribute to the contested terrain of the feminist narrative?

Is There Common Ground?

Sarah Palin, the former governor of Alaska and 2008 Republican vice presidential candidate, categorized herself as a "conservative feminist." When she accepted the role of vice presidential candidate to form the McCain–Palin ticket, she referenced Hillary Clinton's unsuccessful effort to become the Democratic nominee for president and talked about shattering glass ceilings. In doing so, Palin attempted to carve out a place within the realm of feminism for conservative women. If the Margaret Thatchers and Sarah Palins of the world can be trailblazers and serve as role models for young women, is it possible that there might also be a place for them in a feminist continuum that does not skew to the left of left in liberal ideology? Along the same lines, the role of Condoleeza Rice in breaking new ground to lift the aspirations for young African American women should not be discounted.

Additional Resources

Celis, K. and Childs, S. (2012). "The Substantive Representation of Women: What to Do with Conservative Claims?" *Political Studies, 60*(1), 213–225.

McCarver, V. (2012). "The New Oxymoron: Socially Conservative Feminism." *Women & Language, 35*(1), 57–76.

Create Central

www.mhhe.com/createcentral

Internet References . . .

Feministing

http://feministing.com/

The Heritage Foundation

http://www.heritage.org/events/2013/05/cwn-christina-hoff-sommers-freedom-feminism

Selected, Edited, and with Issue Framing Material by:
Rachel Pienta, *Valdosta State University*

ISSUE

Can Women Be Misogynistic?

YES: Christine Stansell, from "All Fired Up: Women, Feminism, and Misogyny in the Democratic Primaries," *Dissent* (Fall 2008)

NO: Dawn M. Szymanski, Arpana Gupta, Erika R. Carr, and Destin Stewart, from "Internalized Misogyny as a Moderator of the Link between Sexist Events and Women's Psychological Distress," *Sex Roles* (March 28, 2009)

Learning Outcomes
As you read the issue, focus on the following points: • Do women fail to support other women due to misogyny? • What role do the media play in the perception of misogyny?

ISSUE SUMMARY

YES: Christine Stansell, in "All Fired Up: Women, Feminism, and Misogyny in the Democratic Primaries," examines the sexism manifested by media pundits and the reaction of women voters during the Democratic primaries leading up to Barack Obama's selection as that party's presidential nominee.

NO: Dawn M. Szymanski et al., in "Internalized Misogyny as a Moderator of the Link Between Sexist Events and Women's Psychological Distress," examine the socialization and subsequent behaviors of women who experience sexism over the life course.

Since the 1980s, the question of the women's vote and associated female voting behavior has given fuel to a debate over whether women will vote for other women. During the 2008 presidential primary cycle, faced with the possibility of Hillary Clinton as the potential Democratic nominee for president, the American media explored the idea of a woman as a presidential candidate from every possible angle.

In the aftermath of the 2008 election, when the nation experienced conservative political hysteria over the ascension of Sarah Palin to the media stratosphere as the Republican vice presidential nominee, the debate over internalized misogyny as a predictor of women's potential voting behavior continues to generate media ink.

Christine Stansell, in "All Fired Up: Women, Feminism, and Misogyny in the Democratic Primaries," examines the underlying feminist narrative of Hillary Clinton's unsuccessful 2008 bid for the Democratic presidential nomination. Stansell posits that the debate over Clinton's likability was as much about the inherent and entrenched sexism of political institutions as it was about her actual personality.

Stansell deconstructs the dynamics of the media treatment and audience reception of Hillary Clinton in the months leading up to her eventual concession to Barack Obama. While Clinton drew strength from the adversity and improved her poll numbers over the long months as the primary battle raged across the nation, her success served to further inflame the media and misogynist rhetoric dominated both the conservative and liberal discourse.

Szymanski et al., in "Internalized Misogyny as a Moderator of the Link Between Sexist Events and Women's Psychological Distress," examine the issue of misogyny that occurs between women. The study conducted by Szymanski et al. (2009) examined the relationship between what the researchers term "internalized misogyny" and other forms of internalized sexism including self-objectification and women's acceptance of traditional sex stereotyped gender roles. For purposes of the study, the researchers defined "internalized misogyny" as "a devaluation and distrust of women as well as a belief in male superiority" (p. 107).

The impact of external sexism on the internalization of misogyny may be an underlying factor that influences how women participate in politics, whether in the voting booth or as potential candidates. Do women fail to support other women due to misogyny? While Szymanski et al. suggest that internalized misogyny is a direct effect of external sexism, the research shows that it tends to focus inward on the self rather than as an outward manifestation that would impact how a woman would vote.

Christine Stansell

All Fired Up: Women, Feminism, and Misogyny in the Democratic Primaries

Think back to a year and a half ago, to spring 2007, when this all began. Despite Hillary Clinton's advantages in connections and money going into the primaries, those in the know cited a multitude of reasons she would fall flat on her face. Women were one. "Women don't like her," the pundits declared with relish. They didn't like her even more than men didn't like her. She was too ambitious, a flip-flopper, a trimmer, an opportunist. She didn't deserve to be where she was. She should have left Bill years ago.

The media turned out to be wrong about a lot of things. As we know now, women liked Hillary Clinton, very much, and they poured work, money, and excitement into her campaign, their enthusiasm mounting as the months passed. And they have continued to like her, even after she conceded, forming a major stumbling block for Barack Obama. White and Hispanic working women were the core of the coalition she built. Gays were a hidden factor; so far as I can see, lesbians supported Clinton heavily (there's no polling data on the gay vote). Clinton's solid stance on feminist issues—abortion rights (identical to Obama's) and universal health care and gay rights (to the left of Obama's)—did not put off blue-collar whites and Hispanics, male and female, who were supposed to be conservative on social issues.

What was more remarkable, her candidacy, which started out carefully distanced from feminism and gender issues, over time unintentionally brought feminist ideas about fair treatment to the center of the campaign. For the first time in American history, the desire for a fair deal for women—symbolized by this particular woman—migrated out of feminist identity politics into a presidential campaign and won the interest of a huge portion of the electorate. And amazingly, the main body of the feminist intelligentsia—writers and academics—showed no interest in this unprecedented phenomenon. As of this writing, the feminism of the campaign remains unexamined, occluded by charges that it consists of little more than "whining" and special pleading on the part of Clinton's supporters.

The Women's Vote

Nothing like this has ever happened with female voters. Going into the primary campaign, everyone knew about the "women's vote": it's been materializing since the 1980s, when women migrated to or stayed with the Democrats, while men moved to support Ronald Reagan. In 1992, women were the margin that pushed Bill Clinton over the top; in 2000, they went for Al Gore over George W. Bush by an eleven-point margin. But their numbers in this year's primaries were unprecedented, increasing threefold: from under eight million in 2004 to more than twenty-one million in 2008. The surge came in part from the campaign's length and intensity, but nonetheless it brought in female voters as never before. Overall, they cast 57 percent of the votes. Their preference was marked, an eight-point spread: 52 percent for Clinton, to Obama's 44 percent. African American women counted for almost a fourth of the female support Obama did have: among white and Hispanic women, 60 percent went for Clinton, 35 percent for Obama. Hispanic women voted for Hillary by a remarkable 69 percent to 30 percent. These women made up a bloc that no one had counted on. They changed the electoral map.

We don't know much about them because, as is often the case when women do something unexpected, no one bothered to ask them questions. Nor has anyone asked them questions since Obama clinched the nomination. We heard a lot about the twenty-somethings who thrilled to Obama's candidacy. But as to why, against predictions, women were turning out in such large numbers for Hillary, there was little information. Journalists in Indiana, Kentucky, and Ohio seemed to have limited their work to calling out at the rallies, "Anyone here a racist?" and leaving it at that.

Inside the Beltway, Clinton also had major support from women. She was endorsed by the big feminist organizations: the National Organization for Women, the National Women's Political Caucus, and Emily's List. The pro-choice organizations stayed carefully neutral, although in a surprise move orchestrated from the top, NARAL Pro-Choice America came out for Obama in May, touching off consternation among members and state chapters. Even when Clinton conceded, she had retained the endorsements of thirty-five female members of Congress to Obama's twenty-six; and seven of twelve black female U.S. Representatives.

Obama's Support

Missing were ordinary African American women. Their absence was a big loss in terms of morale, political breadth, and sheer numbers. A gender gap among blacks in the early winter virtually disappeared by spring, with black women lining up for Obama in equal numbers to men. Leaving aside the congressional representatives, few prominent black women remained in Clinton's camp: exceptions who went on record were the ever independent-minded writer Michele Wallace, the artist Faith Ringgold, and the poet Maya Angelou, whom Hillary pressed into service.

In the popular vote, this divide cannot be reduced to whites against minorities, since Hispanic support for Clinton confounds that tidy explanation. But it was predictable. Black women have always supported black advancement when it was feasible; and Obama's viability after Iowa made it feasible. Once the race-baiter slurs against both Clintons began to circulate, it was all but impossible for Hillary to hold black women. Would they have supported her against John Edwards? Given the polls from the fall, most likely.

Nor did Clinton by and large attract the postfeminist young, who were drawn to the semiotics of the new in the Obama campaign: Obama's much-hyped outsider status, the generational change he claimed to represent, and the chance to vote for a black presidential candidate. Once the campaign got rolling as a popular-culture phenomenon, they were also attracted to each others' enthusiasm. Raised in an era that oddly combined real progress and right-wing political hegemony, young women had little of their mothers' romance about a woman in the White House, nor did they have their mothers' belief that Clinton's competence and experience could do much to put the country back on course. For women too young to remember anything about Bill Clinton's administration except the Monica Lewinsky scandal, it was Washington politics, not the Republican Party, that was the problem. Good government seemed an oxymoron. Obama's swashbuckling approach was more cinematically persuasive, promising that with his special combination of savoir-faire and virtue, he could summon up postpartisan superpowers to make the right wing go away.

She's Not Likable

By now the "sexism" charge is an old chestnut in the annals of this campaign. What is the substance, and what exactly happened?

Sexism trailed Clinton's campaign from the start in the form of objections voiced, observations made, jokes cracked, and gossip circulated—the sorts of things that have never been said about a man running for president. From her cleavage to her feminine handwriting (silly) to nepotism and dynastic privilege (never seriously raised during the younger Bush's campaign), Clinton was fair game. She was detail-oriented, not masterful; narrow, not commanding; experienced, maybe, but not charismatic. To feminist-minded women, the chatter was irritatingly familiar. But it was subtle and in its idiocy, vaguely comic.

With Obama's victory in the Iowa caucuses and polling data pointing to a repeat in New Hampshire, the press

and the pundits were gleefully preparing for Clinton's comeuppance. Instead, New Hampshire voters turned out in record numbers to give her a three-point lead in the final tally. It was women who made the difference, voting for her by two to one. On the MSNBC coverage I watched that night, the panel of experts flailed and bumbled as the returns came in. Struggling to explain Clinton's steady lead and what the exit polls were showing about her support from women, they hit upon "racism," gravely debating whether the "Bradley effect" was at work and essentially concluding, without a shred of evidence, that it was. Only Jeff Toobin had the presence of mind to point out that Democratic white women were the most reliable liberal bloc in the entire party, bar none, including on race issues.

It wasn't second thoughts on election day but the events of the preceding week that led to the upset and turned a heated battle into a *Network* moment for millions of women—"We're mad as hell and we're not going to take it anymore." The public humiliation of Clinton went over the top, first at the debate when the likability question popped up—did Clinton's personality turn off voters? When Clinton uncharacteristically crumpled— "that hurts my feelings"—Obama jumped in to offer the smug judgment that she was "likeable enough." Several days later, with defeat hanging in the air, Clinton was asked about the strains of the campaign and she teared up. The media piled on, contemptuous of the cold calculation behind "Clinton's tears" or (alternatively) the pathetic weakness.

It was the moment when sexism went public. The sequence was one with which millions of women identified, including, I daresay, any number in New Hampshire. A talented, experienced woman with a no-nonsense grasp of the importance of hard work and "details" was being invidiously compared to a younger man whose career she had helped to promote. It rang a bell. Ratchet the whole situation down a number of notches, turn it into an issue of who was getting promoted, and Clinton might be consulting a lawyer about suing for sex discrimination. The campaign took on an uncanny resemblance to any number of companies and institutions where a woman is told that her own personality deficits are the reason she didn't get the position.

It was the beginning of an electoral chemistry that no one, including the candidate herself, had anticipated. Recognizing Clinton's qualifications for office and resenting the denigration of those qualifications, female voters marched into the voting booths. It was the likability effect, not the Bradley effect, which operated in New Hampshire, and it unleashed a new dynamic in the campaign.

The Professors and the Writers

What happened in the run-up to the New Hampshire primary was prejudicial treatment, pure and simple, but feminist writers and intellectuals mostly kept quiet. Most of those women—in the universities, journals of opinion, and on the editorial pages—*did* turn out to dislike

Clinton. They not only disliked her—not just opposed—they loathed her. The reasons seemed to mirror in reverse the reasons the right disliked and loathed her. In regard to her personal characteristics, they were identical: trimmer, opportunist, calculating, self-seeking, maker of despicable marital decisions. The right viewed her as a feminist (feminazi) peacenik, who would emasculate the nation's defenses; feminist opponents saw her in reverse as an unrepentant hawk—an ultranationalist, as I heard from one colleague—who would continue Bush's disastrous foreign policy.

The animus came from two directions. Left feminists have never been especially sympathetic to professional politicians. They have little patience for, and even less respect for, the arts of *realpolitik,* maneuver, and compromise. In their anti-politics they are aligned with a strain of elite liberalism (going back to George McGovern's campaign and, before that, Adlai Stevenson's) which despises the sweaty pols and looks for the knight in shining armor who will clean things up. Feminists see good politics as a grassroots affair, preferably with politicians absent. The Republican ascendancy diluted this long-standing animus, especially in regard to the urgency of electing pro-choice candidates. But the hostility goes deeper; it's coded in the DNA of 1960s women's liberation: the contempt for an equivocating, weakwilled, racist Democratic Party and a mistrust of liberalism as a shill for the ruling class. Like the rest of the left, feminists see political officeholders (except for the renegades and gadflies) as unprincipled, self-interested, and incapable of creating meaningful change.

Bill Clinton was tolerated, just barely, because of his pro-choice stand and the hatefulness of his right-wing enemies. But Obama was a pro-choice candidate, the Chicago pol who presented himself as the white knight, above and beyond politics as usual. Women who detested Bill Clinton's behavior in the Lewinsky scandal and, more important, despised his welfare policy (this last was the most common objection I heard) abandoned his spouse's ship. If the only ethical stance was to "speak truth to power" and to "push from the left," then Hillary Rodham Clinton, who had spent the last decade inside the Democratic Party, close to power and seeking more power, was inherently suspect. A colleague on a recent historian's panel summed up the indictment: Hillary was no different than a man, by which she meant, one of *those* men, the kind who chair congressional committees and ensure there's a budget line that benefits their constituents.

The antipathy between longtime feminist allies, co-conspirators, and friends hardened into Us and Them, exacerbated by female opinion-makers in the press. After the New Hampshire primary, a New York Feminists for Obama petition signed by hundreds, including a number of' high-profile academics and writers, showed that among the intelligentsia, the Obama trend was something like a stampede. Still, shortly thereafter, when fellow historian Ellen Dubois and I circulated a Feminists for Clinton statement to gather what support there existed for Hillary

in our circles, we discovered an important constituency yearning to be visible. Hundreds wrote back with relief at the chance to sign on and break out of the isolation they felt. "I thought no one was going to say anything," was a common response, so ubiquitous in the public eye were the feminists supporting Obama.

On newspaper opinion pages, in journals of opinion across the liberal spectrum from the *New Republic* to the *Nation,* and on popular Web sites like the Huffington Post, one was hard put after January to find a word of' support for Clinton or, barring that, any interest in the fact that women did seem interested in supporting her, after all. The exception was the *New York Times*'s endorsement of Clinton on January 25, rare in its even-handed discussion of both candidates. But the editorial page was at odds with the Op-ed page, where, with the exception of Paul Krugman, the columnists lined up against Clinton. Gloria Steinem's tough piece, "Women Are Never Front Runners," in early January was the last notable pro-Clinton commentary to appear. For Clinton voters, reading the morning papers and watching the news turned into a grim trudge across hostile ground with artillery trained on you.

Over the next six weeks, Obama and Clinton fought each other to a draw. At the end of' January, Obama's landslide in South Carolina, fueled by ginned-up but devastating racebaiter charges completed the defection of blacks from Clinton. Yet two weeks later, on Super Tuesday, Hillary won the big states—Massachusetts, California, and New York. She still lagged behind in the delegate count. The press and the pundits clamored for her to withdraw, but the ranks of female supporters grew as Clinton again flummoxed expectations and secured a lock on Hispanic and blue-collar voters in Ohio and Pennsylvania.

As the hostility to Hillary intensified, she changed. Under attack, she got bigger, not smaller. The stiff, controlled, pant-suited woman loosened up at the podium: her funny, feisty side came out. Never an eloquent speaker—she always looked like she'd rather be at her desk—Clinton's victory speech in Ohio movingly evoked the experience of Americans teetering on the edge: unemployed college graduates, single mothers, laid-off blue-collar men. "For everybody who works hard and never gives up, but is knocked down and counted out," she vowed, this victory was for you. Plenty of women fit that description.

Despite the carping about likability, Clinton is nothing if not personable as a campaigner, warm and skillful at making People feel that she responds to them individually. In the battleground states and beyond, she learned to play to the crowds and the crowds gave back. After March 1, her female support soared to a ten point spread—54 percent to 44 percent. Men, too, responded to her grit and tenacity. For once, fair treatment for women was something men were willing to sign on to.

Not coincidentally, the Ohio win set off a misogynist frenzy. The dreadful election detritus already in circulation proliferated: the Hillary nutcrackers popped up in airport gift shops, bumper stickers sported slogans such as,

Hillary Clinton—just like your ex-wife but bitchier. A fast-food marquee advertised Hillary special 2 fat thighs with small breasts left wing. But it wasn't only the right-wing hoi polloi. A chorus of naysayers screeched and brayed from major newspapers, networks, liberal journals, and cable shows calling for her to drop out of the race. Yet neither Obama, his aides, his supporters, nor the Democratic National Committee condemned the misogyny. Among Obama's feminist supporters, it was common to deny or ignore it by invoking the supposed racism directed at Obama. In Chicago, I heard a young woman refer to "Hillary Clinton's racist rants"—the audience of Democrats nodded sagely.

In April and May, derisive talk that had flourished on the right-wing talk shows migrated to respectable venues and settled in. On CNN, National Public Radio editor Ken Rudin compared the senator to Glenn Close's murderous character in *Fatal Attraction;* the joke went the rounds, with Andrew Sullivan and Representative Steve Cohen (D-TN) joining the fun (Cohen retracted his quip). McCain supporter Alex Castellanos on MSNBC defended a column that called Clinton a "white bitch," insisting that "some women are named that and it's accurate." "Cunt" was also treated as witty badinage, although the newspapers at least drew the line there.

Toxicity levels soared. To venture into the blogosphere—and not too far into it, to the likes of the Daily Kos, Talking Points Memo, and even the *New Republic* Web site—was to step into an alternate universe, where a Mistress of Evil and her attendant warlocks and Southern strategy wizards faced off against a Superhero. All the old Clinton conspiracy stories resurfaced, this time from the left. Indeed, the opprobrium from the left was not always distinguishable from that of the blogs. In the face of the Jeremiah Wright revelations, Barbara Ehrenreich went into print endorsing an exposé of Clinton's Senate prayer group as the hidden hand of a right-wing conspiracy, "the sinister heart of the international right," with Clinton functioning as the Angela Lansbury of Capitol Hill in an updated *Manchurian Candidate.*

The terms of condemnation were so intense that even the estimable Katha Pollitt, usually alert to the terms on which ordinary women engage politics, was silent. In January, before the tide turned, Pollitt was the one feminist in the Obama campaign to denounce the sexism of media coverage. But even as she grudgingly allowed that Clinton's campaign had legitimacy, she spoke of holding one's nose at the woman, "a centrist Democrat, a believing Methodist, a people-pleaser, a trimmer"—in short, a political hack. Gail Collins, too, long a cunning defender of women and parrier of sexism, treated the wave of misogyny as if it were a sideshow. Maureen Dowd became so hysterical in her obsession with Clinton's perfidies that she wrote herself out of democratic discourse into a liberal equivalent of hate speech— "over the line," the public editor of the *New York Times* would judge her columns several months later, slapping her wrist as the dust settled.

All these opinion writers are entitled to their positions. It isn't their support for Obama that I rue; it is that so many leading feminists and prominent women had so little to say about the most appalling public outbreak of misogyny in recent memory.

Mostly, the candidate remained the scapegoat. But with the depth and extent of women's support undeniable, complaints started to bubble up about her supporters, too. They were "privileged white women" (forget the Hispanics). Jonathan Chait in the *New Republic* disparaged the paradigmatic Clinton supporter as "the suburban empty-nester who can't find stylish clothes for herself at the mall"—compared to "the plight of a black man living under Jim Crow" (in Chait's mind, the paradigmatic Obama voter resided in a time warp). But from another angle, Clinton's women were frumpy overweight losers, salving their psychic wounds with religion.

Aftermath

Obama may not have been able to cut into Clinton's core support, but he could have prevented the lines from hardening if he had spoken out against the sexist onslaught. Does he understand how serious these attacks were or how injurious the legacy is for everyone? It seems not. Nor does he seem to understand the legitimate concerns of Clinton supporters, who are asking for a party that is strongly committed, not incidentally committed, to women's rights as a basic democratic struggle. Right now the campaign seems to assume that, Chicago-style, the votes are his for the taking, and that he need take no particular care to reach out to Clinton's women, or, for that matter, to Clinton's men. "They just don't get it," a Washington insider told me. "They think they can win without them." David Axelrod is said to be calculating with a different math, gambling on augmenting Obama's "new" Democratic coalition of' blacks, young people, and well-to-do white liberals, not on securing the "old" Democrats who supported Clinton.

It's this that makes me wonder whether fear of McCain will be enough to push women to the polls or whether many Clinton supporters will just sit it out. The speculation that substantial numbers will defect to McCain has so far proved to be wrong. These are loyal Democrats who stayed with the party in the leanest years. The real concern is that some of them won't vote at all. Blue-collar women are "drop-off" voters. They vote Democratic, but they are pressed for time and they have child care problems, and so they don't always vote. Hillary moved them; Obama may not.

As for educated professional women—like those who signed on to Feminists for Hillary—responses vary. A few die-hards are calling for a boycott of the election. Many more, like me, are good Democrats, and try to muster hope for the party, especially as Clinton herself has pitched in. If she can set aside the last months, we remind each other, surely we can. But the worry is that women will once again be shunted aside as less deserving in their aspirations, less politically interesting or salient, less important; that the women's movement will be reduced to a shell of itself; and that postfeminism—which is to say inertia—will reign. A recent speech by Obama on equal pay for women was welcome, but it has to be balanced against his remarks on late-term abortion (the new battleground for *Roe*), which are troubling, to say the least, as is the political strategy of wooing evangelicals that underlies them.

Overall, as of this writing on the final day of the Democratic Convention, Clinton women are fired up. The campaign's decision to give Hillary Clinton a major slot and, most of all, her show-stopping speech calling for

unity have for the first time since June given her supporters a place to go. Will there be more outreach from Obama, a turn to a different math on the part of his strategists, and a clearer articulation of a commitment to women? With two months to go, I deeply hope so.

CHRISTINE STANSELL is a leading historian of American women, with interests in gender history, American cultural history, and how societies reconstruct themselves after catastrophes.

Dawn M. Szymanski et al.  **NO**

Internalized Misogyny as a Moderator of the Link between Sexist Events and Women's Psychological Distress

Introduction

According to Feminist Therapy Theory, the personal is political, that is, women's personal problems both in the United States and abroad are influenced by the sociocultural and political conditions in which they live and can be conceptualized as reactions to oppression (Brown 1994; Enns 2004). Because women both in the United States and abroad often live in patriarchal cultures, many women are exposed to various forms of sexism that come from a variety of places including the media, religious institutions, political and legal systems, places of work, and familial and interpersonal relationships (American Psychological Association 2007). The personal is political posits that sexism is likely to contribute to women's mental health problems directly through experiences of sexist events and through the internalization of negative and limiting messages about being a woman. In addition, Feminist Therapy Theory postulates that internalized sexism may exacerbate or moderate the effects of sexist events on psychological distress (Brown 1994; Enns 2004; Worell and Remer 2003). Research on potential moderators of the link between sexist events and psychosocial health might identify subgroups of women for whom this link may be more pronounced, which could ultimately inform interventions targeted to these women.

Sexist Events and Psychological Distress

Sexist events have been conceptualized as gender specific, negative life events that are unique to women, socially based (e.g., they stem from relatively stable underlying patriarchal social structures, institutions, and processes beyond the individual), chronic, and cause excess stress (Klonoff and Landrine 1995; Swim et al. 1998). Two measures with good psychometric support have been developed to assess sexist events. The first, the Schedule of Sexist Events (Klonoff and Landrine 1995), assesses sexism in the forms of sexist degradation and its consequences and sexist discrimination in both close and distant relationships and in the workplace. The second, the Daily Sexist Events Scale (Swim et al. 1998; Swim et al. 2001), assesses sexism in the forms of traditional gender role stereotyping and prejudice, demeaning and derogatory comments and behaviors, and unwanted sexually objectifying comments and behaviors.

Recent research, using either the Schedule of Sexist Events (Klonoff and Landrine 1995) or the Daily Sexist Events Scale (Swim et al. 1998; Swim et al. 2001), has built support for a consistent connection between experiences of external sexism and psychological symptoms among women in general and various subgroups of women. For example, previous research has found that more experiences of sexist events are related to greater psychological distress among college women (Fischer and Holz 2007; Moradi and Subich 2002, 2004; Klonoff et al. 2000; Sabik and Tylka 2006; Swim et al. 2001; Zucker and Landry 2007), both a college and community female sample (Landrine et al. 1995), lesbian and bisexual women (Szymanski 2005; Szymanski and Owens 2009), African American females (Moradi and Subich 2003), and women who sought counseling (Moradi and Funderburk 2006). In addition, Landrine et al. found that sexist events are related to psychological distress above and beyond major and minor generic stressful life events, and Klonoff et al. (2000) found that sexist events may account for gender differences in anxious, depressive, and somatic symptoms. Moreover, this relationship between sexist events and poorer mental health holds when sexism is operationalized in other ways including experiences of childhood sexual abuse (Polusny and Follette 1995), sexual assault, rape, and domestic violence (Koss et al. 2003; Wolfe and Kimerling 1997), and workplace harassment and discrimination (Fitzgerald et al. 1997; Pavalko et al. 2003). Thus, these findings are consistent with the feminist therapy tenet of attending to sexist and oppressive power dynamics in the current contexts of women's lives (Brown 1994; Worell and Remer 2003).

Internalized Sexism and Psychological Distress

Similar to research on external sexism, a burgeoning body of research has begun to demonstrate the negative relationship between various manifestations of internalized sexism and women's psychosocial health. One of the most popular manifestations of internalized sexism that has been researched is the construct of self-objectification (McKinley and Hyde 1996; Noll and Fredrickson 1998).

Self-objectification refers to the internalization of sexually objectifying experiences that occurs when women treat themselves as an object to be looked at and evaluated on the basis of appearance (Fredrickson and Roberts 1997). Researchers have consistently found positive correlations between self-objectification and both depression (Miner-Rubino et al. 2002; Szymanski and Henning 2007; Tiggemann and Kuring 2004) and disordered eating (McKinley and Hyde 1996; Moradi et al. 2005; Muehlenkamp and Saris-Baglama 2002; Noll and Fredrickson 1998; Tiggemann and Kuring 2004; Tiggemann and Slater 2001). In addition, Moradi et al. (2005) found that self-objectification mediated the relationships between sexually objectifying experiences and disordered eating. This finding provides evidence for the importance of looking at the influence of third variables in the link between external sexism and psychosocial distress.

Another conceptualization of internalized sexism that has garnered empirical support is passive acceptance of traditional gender roles and unawareness or denial of cultural, institutional, and individual sexism (Bargad and Hyde 1991; Downing and Roush 1985; Fischer et al. 2000; Worell and Remer 2003). Passive acceptance has been found to be positively correlated with foreclosed identity (Fischer et al. 2000) and psychological distress (Moradi and Subich 2002) among presumably heterosexual women. However, contrary to these findings, no support was found for a relationship between passive acceptance and psychological distress among lesbians and bisexual women (Szymanski 2005). In addition, mixed findings have been found concerning symptoms of disordered eating with one study finding a positive relationship between passive acceptance and symptoms of disordered eating (Snyder and Hasbrouck 1996) and another finding no relationship between the two variables (Sabik and Tylka 2006).

Consistent with Feminist Therapy Theory, Moradi and Subich (2002) found that passive acceptance moderated the relationship between sexist events and psychological distress. That is, this form of internalized sexism exacerbated the relationship between experiences of sexist events within the past year and women's psychological distress. Contrary to this finding, Sabik and Tylka (2006) found no support for the moderating role of passive acceptance in the link between sexist events and symptoms of disordered eating. These findings suggest that manifestations of internalized sexism might moderate the sexism-psychological distress link but not the sexism-disordered eating link. Taken together, these studies provide evidence for examining the internalized sexism-distress link among subgroups of women and for the importance of examining moderators in the link between sexism and mental health.

Although self-objectification and passive acceptance appear to be important manifestations of the ways in which sexism can be internalized, they fail to attend to a core construct of sexism which is misogyny or a hatred and devaluation of women (Szymanski and Kashubeck-West 2008). Misogyny is a cultural practice that serves to maintain power of the dominant male group through the subordination of women (Piggot 2004). Women, and their role in society, are thus devalued to increase and maintain the power of men, which results in a fear of femininity and a hatred and devaluing of women and female related characteristics (Burch 1987; O'Neil 1981; Worell and Remer 2003). The negative impact of the devaluation of something as central as gender is perpetuated not only by men but also by women who reinforce the central male culture of devaluing women through acts of horizontal oppression and omission resulting from internalized misogyny (Piggot 2004; Saakvitne and Pearlman 1993).

The only known measure assessing internalized misogyny is the Internalised Misogyny Scale (IMS; Piggot 2004). The IMS consists of 17 items which reflect three dimensions: devaluing of women, distrust of women, and gender bias in favor of men. Validity was supported by feedback from a focus group, exploratory factor analysis, cross-cultural comparisons, and correlating the IMS with measures of modern sexism, internalized heterosexism, body image, depression, self-esteem, psychosexual adjustment, and social desirability in a cross cultural sample of 803 women from Australia, the United States, Canada, Finland, and the United Kingdom. In addition, internalized misogyny assessed via the IMS has been found to related to lower self esteem, less social support, and more psychological distress among sexual minority women living in the United States (Szymanski and Kashubeck-West 2008), and to negative body image, depression, low self-esteem, and less psychosexual adjustment among lesbian and bisexual women living in five different countries; i.e., Australia, Canada, England, Finland, and the United States (Piggot 2004). However, no study has examined if the relationship between internalized misogyny and poorer psychosocial health holds true for heterosexual women.

Taken together, the results of these studies suggest that internalized sexism can manifest in very different ways. However, it is unclear how internalized misogyny is related to these other forms of internalized sexism (i.e., are they essentially measuring the same thing, are they related but conceptually distinct from one another, or are they unrelated to each other). Feminist Theory would suggest that internalized sexism can manifest in many different ways and that internalized misogyny would be related to, but conceptually distinct from self-objectification and passive acceptance. In addition, research largely supports feminist contentions that there is a direct relationship between internalized oppression and women's mental health. However, given the more recent development and measurement of the internalized misogyny construct more research is needed to examine the relationship between internalized misogyny and the psychosocial health of heterosexual women and women from other minority groups. Furthermore, scant research has examined the potential moderating role of various manifestations of internalized sexism in the link between sexist events and women's psychological distress.

Internalized Misogyny as a Potential Moderator of the Sexist Events-Distress Link

Moderators address the question of under what circumstances does a variable most strongly predict an outcome variable (Frazier et al. 2004). Thus, moderators are variables which could potentially intensify or buffer the relationship between sexism and mental health. Feminist Theory postulates an augmenting or synergistic effect of various aspects of internalized sexism in the relationship between sexist events and mental health (Brown 1994; Enns 2004; Worell and Remer 2003). That is, as the level of internalized misogyny (i.e., the moderator) increases, the relationship between sexist events and psychological distress becomes stronger. Internalized sexism represents a form of self-blame and thus may intensify the relationship of sexist events and mental health. That is, an experience of sexist discrimination is more painful when the victim agrees with the sexist attitudes conveyed by the victimization event. Furthermore, oppressive experiences many be more harmful to women who have negative evaluations of women in general and of oneself as a woman than those who hold positive evaluations (Moradi and Subich 2002, 2004).

Summary of the Current Study

In sum, the purpose of this study is to examine: (a) the relationship between internalized misogyny and self-objectification and passive acceptance to determine if these constructs are related but conceptually distinct forms of internalized sexism, (b) the independent and concurrent relationships of sexist events and internalized misogyny to psychological distress, and (c) the potential moderating role of internalized misogyny in the external sexism-distress link in a sample of undergraduate heterosexual women living in the United States. More specifically, the following hypotheses will be examined:

Hypothesis 1: Internalized misogyny will be significantly correlated with self-objectification and passive acceptance.

Hypothesis 2: Sexist events and internalized misogyny will be significantly correlated with psychological distress.

Hypothesis 3: When examined concurrently, both sexist events and internalized misogyny will be significantly related to psychological distress.

Hypothesis 4: Internalized misogyny will moderate the relationship between sexist events and psychological distress.

Hierarchical multiple regression will be used to examine whether internalized misogyny moderates the relationship between sexist events and psychological dis-

tress because it is recognized as the best method to detect the presence or absence of moderating effects (Aiken and West 1991; Frazier et al. 2004). In this analysis, the predictor (i.e., sexist events) and proposed moderator variable (i.e. internalized misogyny) are entered at Step 1. Next, at Step 2, the interaction term (i.e., sexist events X internalized misogyny) is entered. Evidence for a moderator effect is noted at Step 2 by a statistically significant increment in R^2 and beta weight.

Method

Participants

Participants consisted of 274 self-identified heterosexual women who were recruited via undergraduate psychology courses at a large southern university in the United States. Two participants who identified as lesbian and one participant who identified as not sure about her sexual orientation were dropped from the sample and not included in any of the analyses. Participants ranged in age from 18 to 31 years, with a mean age of 18.88 years ($SD = 1.44$). The sample was 68% ($n = 187$) 1st year undergraduates, 21% ($n = 58$) Sophomore, 7% ($n = 20$) Junior, and 3% ($n = 9$) Senior. The sample was 11% ($n = 29$) African American/ Black, 1% ($n = 4$) Asian American/Pacific Islander, 84% ($n = 230$) European American/White, 2% ($n = 5$) Hispanic/ Latina, 1% ($n = 2$) Native American, 1% ($n = 2$) multiracial, and 1% ($n = 2$) other. Twenty four percent ($n = 65$) were single and not dating, 46% ($n = 126$) were single and dating, and 30% ($n = 83$) were married, partnered, or in a committed relationship. Due to rounding percentages may not add up to 100%.

Measure

Sexist events were assessed via the Daily Sexist Events Scale (Swim et al. 1998; Swim et al. 2001), which consists of 26 items assessing sexism in the forms of traditional gender role stereotyping and prejudice and unwanted sexually objectifying comments and behaviors. We chose to use the Daily Sexist Events Scale in our study because it was developed using a series of daily diary studies to examine the incidence and nature of sexist events specifically experienced by college students. Participants are asked to indicate how often during the previous semester they experienced a variety of sexist events. Example items include "Had people shout sexist comments, whistle, or make catcalls at me" and "Heard someone express disapproval of me because I exhibited behavior inconsistent with stereotypes about my gender." Each item is rated using a 5-point Likert scale with the following response options: 1 (*never*), 2 (*about once during the last semester*), 3 (*about once a month during the last semester*), 4 (*about once a week during the last semester*), and 5 (*about two or more times a week during the last semester*). Mean scores were used with higher scores indicating the experience of more sexist events. Content and construct validity was supported via a series of daily diary studies of sexist experiences, exploratory factor analyses, findings indicating that women reported more sexist events than men, correlations demonstrating that more experiences of sexist events was related to more anger, greater depression, decreased comfort, and less self-esteem among women, and that sexist events was not related to neuroticism (Swim et al. 1998; Swim et al. 2001). Alpha for scores in the current sample was .95.

Internalized misogyny was assessed using the Internalised Misogyny Scale (IMS; Piggot 2004), which consists of 17 items reflecting three factors: distrust of women, devaluing of women, and valuing men over women. We chose the IMS measure to assess internalized misogyny because it is the only known measure assessing this form of internalized sexism, has good psychometric support, and was developed using an international sample so it may have more utility in use with both United States and non-United States samples. Example items include "Sometimes other women bother me by just being around," "It is generally safer not to trust women too much," and "Generally, I prefer to work with men." Each item is rated on a 7-point Likert scale from 1 (strongly disagree) to 7 (strongly agree). Mean scores were used with higher scores indicating more internalized misogyny. Reported alpha for scores on the IMS were .88 full scale, .82 Distrust of Women Subscale, .83 Devaluing Women subscale, and .74 Valuing Men subscale. Validity was supported by feedback from a focus group, exploratory factor analysis, cross-cultural comparisons, and correlating the IMS with measures of modern sexism, internalized heterosexism, body image, depression, self-esteem, psychosexual adjustment, and social desirability in a cross cultural sample of 803 sexual minority women (Piggot 2004). Alpha for full scale scores in the current sample was .90.

Self-objectification was assessed using the Self-Objectification Questionnaire (Noll and Fredrickson 1998), which consists of ten items pertaining to physical attributes that reflect the physical self-concept of the respondent. Five items concern attributes that are appearance-based (i.e., physical attractiveness, sex appeal, weight, firm/sculpted muscles, and measurements), and five items concern attributes that are competence-based (i.e., health, energy level, physical coordination, physical fitness level, and strength). Each item is rank ordered by the respondent from most important (rank 1) to least important (rank 10). Scores were computed by summing the ranks for the appearance and competence attributes separately, then computing a difference score. Higher scores reflect a greater emphasis on appearance, thus greater self-objectification. Validity was supported by correlating the Self-Objectification Questionnaire with measures of body dissatisfaction, body shame, appearance anxiety, neuroticism, and negative affect (Noll & Fredrickson; Miner-Rubino et al. 2002).

Passive acceptance was assessed using the passive acceptance subscale of Bargad and Hyde's (1991) Feminist Identity Development Scale (FIDS), which consists of ten items assessing passive acceptance of traditional gender roles and unawareness or denial of cultural, institutional, and individual sexism. Example of items include "I think that rape is sometimes the woman's fault" and "I think that men and women had it better in the 1950s when married women were housewives and their husbands supported them." Each statement is rated on a 5-point Likert scale from 1 (strongly disagree) to 5 (strongly agree). Mean scores were used with higher scores indicating more passive acceptance of traditional gender roles. Reported alpha for scores on the passive acceptance subscale was .85 (Bargad and Hyde 1991). Validity was supported via theoretically predicted significant score changes in pre-post comparisons of students enrolled in women's studies courses (Bargad and Hyde 1991), and significant correlations between extent of exposure to women's issues in graduate psychology programs and less passive acceptance (Worell et al. 1999). Alpha for scores in the current sample was .80.

Psychological distress was assessed using the Hopkins Symptom Checklist (HSCL; Derogatis et al. 1974), which consists of 58 items reflecting psychological distress across five symptom dimensions: depression, somatization, interpersonal sensitivity, anxiety, and obsessive compulsive. We chose to use the HSCL in our study because several studies examining the relationships between external and internalized sexism and psychological distress have used the HSCL (e.g., Klonoff et al. 2000; Landrine et al. 1995; Szymanski 2005; Szymanski and Kashubeck-West 2008) or derivations of it (e.g., Moradi and Funderburk 2006; Moradi and Subich 2002, 2003, 2004) in their studies. Examples of items include "Feeling easily annoyed or irritated" and "Feeling blue." Participants indicate how often they have felt each symptom during the past several days using a 4-point Likert scale from 1 (not at all) to 4 (extremely). Mean scores were used with higher scores indicating more psychological distress. Reported alpha for scores on the HSCL ranged from .84 to .87. Test-retest reliability ranged from .75 to .84. Validity of the HSCL was supported by studies reflecting the factorial invariance of HSCL symptom dimensions, between group differences, and the HSCL's sensitivity to the use of psychotherapeutic drugs.

Reviews of the literature suggest that all versions of the widely used Symptom Checklist, including the HSCL used in the current study as well as the commercially published Symptom Checklist-90-R (SCL-90-R) appear to measure a general distress factor (Cyr et al. 1985). Inter-correlations between HSCL subscales in the current study (r's ranged from .67 to .83) support this assertion. In addition, a global distress measure was used in several studies (e.g., Corning 2002; Klonoff et al. 2000; Landrine et al. 1995; Moradi and Funderburk 2006; Moradi and Subich 2002, 2003, 2004; Szymanski 2005; Szymanski and Kashubeck-West 2008) examining the relationship between external and/or internalized sexism and mental health, so we chose to use the HSCL full scale scores so we could make better and cleaner comparisons to previous studies. Alpha for scores in the current sample was .97.

Procedures

Participants were recruited via undergraduate psychology courses through a psychology department's research website at a large southern university. Potential participants used a hypertext link to access the survey website. After reading an informed consent, participants were instructed to complete the online survey, which included the aforementioned measures. As an incentive to participate, all participants were given course credit for their undergraduate psychology class and were eligible to enter a participant raffle awarding $100 each to five randomly selected participants.

Procedures for this website survey were based on published suggestions (Buchanan and Smith 1999; Michalak and Szabo 1998; Schmidt 1997). Methods for protecting confidentiality included having participants access the research survey via a hypertext link rather than e-mail to ensure participant anonymity and the use of a separate course credit database so there was no way to connect a person's on-line raffle submission with her submitted survey. Methods used for ensuring data integrity included using "cookies" to identify problems associated with multiple submissions of data from the same computer, and use of a secure server protected with a firewall to prevent tampering with data and programs by "hackers" and inadvertent access to confidential information by research participants. Gosling et al. (2004) reported that results from Internet studies are consistent with findings obtained from traditional pen-and-paper methods.

Results

. . . To test hypothesis 1, correlations between internalized misogyny and self-objectification and passive acceptance were conducted to determine if internalized misogyny was a related but conceptually distinct form of internalized sexism. Low to moderate correlations between internalized misogyny and self-objectification ($r = .12$; $p < .05$) and passive acceptance ($r = .53$; $p < .05$) supported this assertion.

To test hypothesis 2, correlations between sexist events and internalized misogyny and psychological distress were conducted. As expected sexist events ($r = .44$, $p < .05$; medium effect size) and internalized misogyny ($r = .12$, $p < .05$; small effect size) were significantly positively correlated with psychological distress. To test hypothesis 3, a simultaneous multiple regression was conducted to test the unique contributions of sexist events and internalized misogyny in predicting psychological distress. The results of this analysis were significant, $R^2 = .197$, $F(2, 263) = 31.915$, $p < .001$, and revealed that sexist events ($\beta = .43$; $t = 7.696$; $p < .001$) was a significant and unique predictor of psychological distress but internalized misogyny was not ($\beta = .065$; $t = 1.161$; $p > .05$).

To test hypothesis 4, a hierarchical multiple regression was conducted to test the moderator effects of internalized misogyny in sexism-distress link. Scores for sexist events and internalized misogyny were centered to reduce multicollinearity between the interaction terms and other predictor variables (Aiken and West 1991; Tabachnick and Fidell 2001). Multicollinearity is a problem that occurs when variables are redundant and too highly correlated which results in an inflation of the size of error terms and weakens an analysis (Tabachnick and Fidell 2001). Absolute value correlations below .90, condition indexes below 30, and variance inflation factors below ten indicate that multicollinearity is not a problem (Myers 1990; Tabachnick and Fidell 2001). Correlations between the predictor variables ($r = .13$), condition index values (range = 1.00 to 1.19), and variance inflation factors (range = 1.01 to 1.03) revealed that multicollinearity was not a problem for the current analysis. Main effects were entered at Step 1 and interaction effects at Step 2. A significant change in R^2 for the interaction term indicated a significant moderator effect. That is, the interaction between sexist events and internalized misogyny ($\beta = .13$) was a significant predictor of psychological distress scores and accounted for 1.6% beyond the variance accounted for by sexist events and internalized misogyny (R^2 Change = .016; F Change = 5.380; Significant F Change = .021).

To interpret the statistically significant interaction, regression lines were plotted using an equation which included terms for the two main effects (sexist events and internalized misogyny), and the interaction term (sexist events X internalized misogyny, along with the corresponding unstandardized regression coefficients and regression constant (Aiken and West 1991; Cohen and Cohen 1983). As recommended by Aiken and West (1991), psychological distress scores for sexist events scores of one standard deviation below and above the mean and low internalized misogyny (one standard deviations below the mean) versus high internalized misogyny (one standard deviations above the mean) were plotted on a graph. Aiken and West's (1991) simple slope analysis showed that sexist events predicted psychological distress for women with low internalized misogyny, $\beta = .327$, $t(260) = 4.606$, $p < .001$, and for women with high internalized misogyny, $\beta = .531$, $t(260) = 7.544$, $p < .001$, indicating that sexist events predicts psychological distress for women with both low and high levels of internalized misogyny but this relationship is stronger for those with high internalized misogyny scores. The difference between the two internalized misogyny groups occurs at the higher levels of sexism when women who have more internalized misogyny have more psychological distress.

Discussion

Consistent with Feminist Therapy Theory and previous research, the findings of this study suggest that sexist events are positively related to psychological distress in an undergraduate sample of heterosexual women. In addition, the medium effect size ($r = .44$) found in this study is consistent with previous research examining the sexism-distress link (c.f., Fischer and Holz 2007; Moradi and Subich 2002, 2003, 2004; Szymanski 2005; Szymanski and Owens 2009). Thus, feminist psychologists are encouraged to assist their female clients in recognizing the potentially negative impact of sexism on their lives, help them see their problems in a contextual light in order to reduce shame and victim blame, and teach them skills for dealing with and confronting oppression. In addition, it provides empirical support to validate feminist psychologists' social justice efforts aimed at eradicating sexism.

The results of our study also support the need to focus on internalized misogyny or a devaluation and distrust of women as well as a belief in male superiority, as a manifestation of internalized sexism that is related to, but conceptually distinct from self-objectification and passive acceptance of traditional gender roles and an unawareness of sexism. The results of the current study indicated a small effect size ($r = .12$) for the relationship between internalized misogyny and psychological distress among a heterosexual female sample. Although consistent with Feminist Therapy Theory and the relations found among sexual minority women, the effect size found in the current study is smaller than that reported for sexual minority women (i.e., $r = .24$ for depression; Piggot 2004; and $r = .26$ for psychological distress; Szymanski & Kashubeck-West 2008). Furthermore, when sexist events and internalized misogyny were examined concurrently, only sexist events emerged as a unique predictor of psychological distress. In addition, the moderator analysis indicated that the interaction of sexism and internalized misogyny was also a unique predictor of psychological distress. This suggests that both main effects and the moderated effects of internalized misogyny in the link between external sexism and psychological distress may be important when working with heterosexual female clients.

The moderated effect of internalized misogyny in the sexism-distress links is consistent with studies demonstrating the moderating role of passive acceptance of traditional gender roles and an unawareness of sexism (Moradi and Subich 2002) and self-esteem in the relationship between external sexism and psychological distress (Corning 2002; Moradi and Subich 2004). The findings of our moderated model suggest that internalized misogyny exacerbates the relationship between sexist events and psychological distress among heterosexual women. Thus, practitioners working with clients with high experiences of sexist events might use therapeutic strategies aimed to decrease their client's internalized misogyny as a way to possibly mute the potentially unfavorable influence of sexist events on their mental health.

This study is limited by sampling method (undergraduate students enrolled in a course at a Southern University in the United States), self-report measures, a correlational design, and a predominately young adult White sample. Respondents recruited from enrollment in undergraduate psychology courses may be biased in some way (e.g.,

being more homogeneous than the larger target population and having lower levels of internalized misogyny than the larger target population). As is true with all self-report data, participants may not have responded honestly to survey items and results could be due to method variance or a general tendency to respond negatively. In addition, individual differences are likely to exist in judgments about what constitutes a sexist event. Inferences about causality cannot be made due to the cross-sectional and correlational nature of this study. For example, sexist events might result in greater psychological distress, psychological distress might result in more frequent perceptions of sexist events, or a circular relationship might exist between sexist events and psychological distress.

Generalizability of this study is limited by the lack of age and racial/ethnic diversity in the sample. It is possible that the relationships between external and internalized sexism and psychological distress become weaker as women age and develop more cognitive, emotional, and/or social resources to buffer themselves from sexism (Szymanski and Henning 2007). It is also important to consider that the experience of both external and internalized sexism may be different for women of color because it is often fused with their experiences of external and internalized racism. Thus, future research examining the sexism-distress links, and potential moderators of these links, with older women, racial/ethnic minority women, and women outside the United States is warranted. Research on other potential moderators, such as resilience, hardiness, cognitive ability, social support, coping styles and strategies, and involvement in feminist activism, that might weaken or intensify the link between sexist events and psychosocial health is also needed. Longitudinal research is necessary to provide stronger evidence that sexist events have deleterious consequences for women. Finally, future research might identify the types of therapeutic experiences that reduce the strength of the relationship between sexist events and poor mental health.

In conclusion, the current study adds to the accumulating body of research demonstrating the potential negative impact that sexism can have on women's lives. This study extends prior research by examining internalized misogyny as a third variable that might explain the relationship between sexism and women's psychological distress. Results indicated that internalized misogyny is an important manifestation of internalized sexism that intensifies the relationship between external sexism and psychological distress.

References

Aiken, L. S., & West, S. G. (1991). *Multiple regression: Testing and interpreting interactions.* Newbury Park, CA: Sage.

American Psychological Association. (2007). Guidelines for Psychological Practice with Girls and Women. *American Psychologist, 62,* 949–979.

Bargad, A., & Hyde, J. S. (1991). Women's studies: A study of feminist identity development in women. *Psychology of Women Quarterly, 15*, 181–201.

Brown, L. S. (1994). *Subversive dialogues.* New York: Basic Books.

Buchanan, T., & Smith, J. L. (1999). Using the Internet for psychological research: Personality testing on the World Wide Web. *British Journal of Psychology, 90*, 125–144.

Burch, B. (1987). Barriers to intimacy: Conflicts over power, dependency, and nurturing in lesbian relationships. In Boston Lesbian Psychologies Collective (Ed.), *Lesbian psychologies: Explorations and challenges*, pp. 126–141. Chicago: University of Illinois Press.

Cohen, J., & Cohen, P. (1983). *Applied multiple regression/correlation analysis for the behavioral sciences* (2nd ed.). Hillsdale, NJ: Lawrence Erlbaum.

Corning, A. F. (2002). Self-esteem as a moderator between perceived discrimination and psychological distress among women. *Journal of Counseling Psychology, 49*, 117–126.

Cyr, J. J., McKenna-Foley, J. M., & Peacock, E. (1985). Facture structure of the SCL-90-R: Is there one? *Journal of Personality Assessment, 49*, 571–578.

Derogatis, L. R., Lipman, R. S., Rickets, K., Uhlenhuth, E. H., & Covi, L. (1974). The Hopkins Symptom Checklist (HSCL): A self-report symptom inventory. *Behavioral Science, 19*, 1–14.

Downing, N., & Roush, K. (1985). From passive acceptance to active commitment: A model of feminist identity development for women. *The Counseling Psychologist, 13*, 695–709.

Enns, C. Z. (2004). *Feminist theories and feminist psychotherapies: Origins, themes, and Diversity* (2nd ed.). New York: Haworth.

Fischer, A. R., & Holz, K. B. (2007). Perceived discrimination and women's psychological distress: The roles of collective and personal self-esteem. *Journal of Counseling Psychology, 54*, 154–164.

Fischer, A. R., Tokar, D. M., Mergl, M. M., Good, G. E., Hill, M. S., & Blum, S. A. (2000). Assessing women's feminist identity development: Studies of convergent, discriminant, and structural validity. *Psychology of Women Quarterly, 24*, 15–29.

Fitzgerald, L. F., Drasgow, F., Hulin, C. L., Gefand, M. J., & Magley, V. J. (1997). Antecedents and consequences of sexual harassment in organizations: A test of an integrated model. *Journal of Applied Psychology, 82*, 578–589.

Frazier, P. A., Tix, A. P., & Barron, K. E. (2004). Testing moderator and mediator effects in counseling psychology research. *Journal of Counseling Psychology, 51*, 115–134.

Fredrickson, B. L., & Roberts, T. (1997). Objectification theory: Toward understanding women's lived experiences and mental health risks. *Psychology of Women Quarterly, 21*, 173–206.

Gosling, S. D., Vazire, S., Srivastava, S., & John, O. P. (2004). Should we trust web-based studies: A comparative analysis of six preconceptions about Internet questionnaires. *American Psychologist, 59*, 93–104.

Klonoff, E. A., & Landrine, H. (1995). The Schedule of Sexist Events: A measure of lifetime and recent sexist discrimination in women's lives. *Psychology of Women Quarterly, 19*, 439–472.

Klonoff, E. A., Landrine, H., & Campbell, R. (2000). Sexist discrimination may account for well-known gender differences in psychiatric symptoms. *Psychology of Women Quarterly, 24*, 93–99.

Koss, M. P., Bailey, J. A., Yan, N. P., Herrera, V. M., & Lichter, E. L. (2003). Depression and PTSD in survivors of male violence: Research and training initiatives to facilitate recovery. *Psychology of Women Quarterly, 27*, 130–142.

Landrine, H., Klonoff, E. A., Gibbs, J., Masnning, V., & Lund, M. (1995). Physical and psychiatric correlates of gender discrimination: An application of the Schedule of Sexist Events. *Psychology of Women Quarterly, 19*, 473–492.

McKinley, N. M., & Hyde, J. S. (1996). The Objectified Body Consciousness Scale: Development and validation. *Psychology of Women Quarterly, 20*, 181–215.

Michalak, E. E., & Szabo, A. (1998). Guidelines for internet research: An update. *European Psychologist, 3*(1), 70–75.

Miner-Rubino, K., Twenge, J. M., & Fredrickson, B. L. (2002). Trait self-objectification in women: Affective and personality correlates. *Journal of Research in Personality, 36*, 147–172.

Moradi, B., & Funderburk, J. R. (2006). Roles of perceived sexist events and perceived social support in the mental health of women seeking counseling. *Journal of Counseling Psychology, 53*, 464–473.

Moradi, B., & Subich, L. M. (2002). Perceived sexist events and feminist identity development attitudes: Links to women's psychological distress. *The Counseling Psychologist, 30*, 44–65.

Moradi, B., & Subich, L. M. (2003). A concomitant examination of the relations of perceived racist and sexist events to psychological distress for African American women. *The Counseling Psychologist, 31*(4), 451–469.

Moradi, B., & Subich, L. M. (2004). Examining the moderating role of self-esteem in the link between experiences of perceived sexist events and psychological distress. *Journal of Counseling Psychology, 51*, 50–56.

Moradi, B., Dirks, D., & Matteson, A. V. (2005). Roles of sexual objectification experiences and internalization of standards of beauty in eating disorder symptomatology: A test and extension of Objectification Theory. *Journal of Counseling Psychology, 52,* 420–428.

Muehlenkamp, J. J., & Saris-Baglama, R. N. (2002). Self-objectification and its psychological outcomes for college women. *Psychology of Women Quarterly, 26,* 371–379.

Myers, R. (1990). *Classical and modern regression with application* (2nd ed.). Boston: Duxbury.

Noll, S. M., & Fredrickson, B. L. (1998). A mediational model linking self-objectification, body shame, and disordered eating. *Psychology of Women Quarterly, 22,* 623–636.

O'Neil, J. (1981). Patterns of gender role conflict and strain: Sexism and fear of femininity in men's lives. *The Personnel and Guidance Journal, 60,* 203–210.

Pavalko, E. K., Mossakowski, K. N., & Hamilton, V. J. (2003). Does perceived discrimination affect health? Longitudinal relationships between workplace discrimination and women's physical and emotional health. *Journal of Health and Social Behavior, 43,* 18–33.

Piggot, M. (2004). *Double jeopardy: Lesbians and the legacy of multiple stigmatized identities.* Psychology Strand at Swinburne University of Technology, Australia: Unpublished thesis.

Polusny, M. A., & Follette, V. M. (1995). Long-term correlates of child sexual abuse: Theory and review of the empirical literature. *Applied and Preventive Psychology, 4,* 143–166.

Saakvitne, K. W., & Pearlman, L. A. (1993). The impact of internalized misogyny and violence against women on feminine identity. In E. P. Cook (Ed.), *Women, relationships, and power: Implications for counseling. Alexandria.* VA: American Counseling Association.

Sabik, N. J., & Tylka, T. L. (2006). Do feminist identity styles moderate the relation between perceived sexist events and disordered eating? *Psychology of Women Quarterly, 30,* 77–84.

Schmidt, W. C. (1997). World-Wide Web survey research: Benefits, potential problems, and solutions. *Behavior Research Methods, Instruments & Computers, 2,* 274–279.

Snyder, R., & Hasbrouck, L. (1996). Feminist identity, gender traits, and symptoms of disturbed eating among college women. *Psychology of Women Quarterly, 20,* 593–598.

Swim, J. K., Cohen, L. L., & Hyers, L. L. (1998). Experiencing everyday prejudice and discrimination. In J. K. Swim & C. Stangor (Eds.), *Prejudice: The target's perspective* (pp. 37–60) San Diego. CA: Academic Press.

Swim, J. K., Hyers, L. L., Cohen, L. L., & Ferguson, M. J. (2001). Everyday sexism: Evidence for its incidence, nature, and psychological impact from three daily diary studies. *Journal of Social Issues, 57,* 31–53.

Szymanski, D. M. (2005). Heterosexism and sexism as correlates of psychological distress in lesbians. *Journal of Counseling & Development, 83,* 355–360.

Szymanski, D. M., & Henning, S. L. (2007). The role of self-objectification in women's depression: A test of Objectification Theory. *Sex Roles, 56,* 45–53.

Szymanski, D. M., & Kashubeck-West, S. (2008). Mediators of the relationship between internalized oppressions and lesbian and bisexual women's psychological distress. *The Counseling Psychologist, 36,* 575–594.

Szymanski, D. M., & Owens, G. P. (2009). Group level coping as a moderator between heterosexism and sexism and psychological distress in sexual minority women. *Psychology of Women Quarterly, 33,* 197–205.

Tabachnick, B. G., & Fidell, L. S. (2001). *Using multivariate statistics* (4th ed.). Needham Heights, MA: Allyn & Bacon.

Tiggemann, M., & Kuring, J. K. (2004). The role of body objectification in disordered eating and depressed mood. *British Journal of Clinical Psychology, 43,* 299–311.

Tiggemann, M., & Slater, A. (2001). A test of objectification theory in former dancers and non-dancers. *Psychology of Women Quarterly, 25,* 57–64.

Wolfe, J., & Kimerling, R. (1997). Gender issues in the assessment of posttraumatic stress disorder. In J. P. Wilson & T. M. Keane (Eds.), *Assessing psychological trauma and PTSD,* pp. 192–238. New York: Guilford.

Worell, J., & Remer, P. (2003). *Feminist perspectives in therapy: Empowering diverse women* (2nd ed.). Hoboken, NJ: Wiley.

Worell, J., Stilwell, D., Oakley, D., & Robinson, D. (1999). Educating about women and gender: Cognitive, personal, and professional outcomes. *Psychology of Women Quarterly, 23,* 797–811.

Zucker, A. N., & Landry, L. J. (2007). Embodied discrimination: The relation of sexism and distress to women's drinking and smoking behaviors. *Sex Roles, 56,* 193–203.

DAWN M. SZYMANSKI is an associate professor in the Department of Psychology at the University of Tennessee.

EXPLORING THE ISSUE

Can Women Be Misogynistic?

Critical Thinking and Reflection

1. How do differing notions of what constitutes misogyny influence how women react to perceptions of sexism?
2. How might misogyny become internalized to the point of acceptance?

Is There Common Ground?

Are there instances in which enacted misogyny is so obvious, so egregious, that all women become united in recognition of the perpetrated wrong? In 2013, the satirical paper known as *The Onion* ignited a firestorm during the Oscars broadcast when a tweet originated from the paper's social media account that referred to nine-year-old best actress nominee Quvenzhane Wallis as a "cunt." The outcry that ensued elicited outrage among women across the social spectrum. The tweet was removed within an hour and an apology soon followed, posted online via *The Onion*'s Facebook page:

> Dear Readers,
>
> On behalf of The Onion, I offer my personal apology to Quvenzhané Wallis and the Academy of Motion Picture Arts and Sciences for the tweet that was circulated last night during the Oscars. It was crude and offensive—not to mention inconsistent with The Onion's commitment to parody and satire, however biting.
>
> No person should be subjected to such a senseless, humorless comment masquerading as satire.
>
> The tweet was taken down within an hour of publication. We have instituted new and tighter Twitter procedures to ensure that this kind of mistake does not occur again. In addition, we are taking immediate steps to discipline those individuals responsible. Miss Wallis, you are young and talented and deserve better. All of us at The Onion are deeply sorry.
>
> Sincerely,
> Steve Hannah
> CEO
> The Onion.
>
> —(Voorhees, 2013)

Inappropriate invective aimed at children aside, the issue of misogyny finds common ground mainly in disagreement about what it is and when it happens.

Additional Resources

Cunningham, G., Miner, K., and Benavides-Espinoza, C. (2012). "Emotional Reactions to Observing Misogyny: Examining the Roles of Gender, Forecasting, Political Orientation, and Religiosity." *Sex Roles, 67*(1/2), 58–68.

Dailey, D. (2013, February 25). "The Onion's Vile Quvenzhané Wallis Tweet." *Salon Media Group.* Retrieved from: www.salon.com/2013/02/25/the_onions_vile_quvenzhane_wallis_tweet/

Rebollo-Gil, G. and Moras, A. (2012). "Black Women and Black Men in Hip Hop Music: Misogyny, Violence and the Negotiation of (White-Owned) Space." *Journal of Popular Culture, 45*(1), 118–132.

Voorhees, J. (2013, February 25). "UPDATE: Not Even the *Onion* Thought Its Quvenzhane Wallis Tweet Was Funny." The Slate Group, LLC. Retrieved from: www.slate.com/blogs/the_slatest/2013/02/25/onion_oscars_tweet_horible_joke_about_quvenzhane_wallis_prompts_twitter.html

Create Central

www.mhhe.com/createcentral

Internet References . . .

Huffington Post

http://www.huffingtonpost.com/melissa-silverstein/
women-misogyny---the-ugly_b_242760.html

Dignity USA

http://www.dignityusa.org/content/misogyny-and-
homophobia

Women's Views on News

http://www.womensviewsonnews.org/2013/02/hip-
hop-rap-and-misogyny/

Selected, Edited, and with Issue Framing Material by:
Rachel Pienta, *Valdosta State University*

ISSUE

Do Women Support the Advancement of Other Women?

YES: Julianne Malveaux, from "Nurturer or Queen Bee?," *Black Issues in Higher Education* (vol. 22, no. 4, April 7, 2005)

NO: Jacqui Poltera, from "Women and the Ethos of Philosophy: Shedding Light on Mentoring and Competition," *Hypatia* (vol. 26, no. 2, Spring 2011)

Learning Outcomes

As you read the issue, focus on the following points:

- How might the lack of a professional support system impede the advancement of one's career?
- How can women serve as role models and mentors while competing for scarce resources?

ISSUE SUMMARY

YES: Julianne Malveaux, in "Nurturer or Queen Bee?," examines the issue of what she terms "sister-hating" between black women in the workplace.

NO: Jacqui Poltera, in "Women and the Ethos of Philosophy: Shedding Light on Mentoring and Competition," examines the issue of how and when women discriminate against other women.

Do women support the advancement of other women? The YES and NO selections examining the issue focus on women's advancement in academia. Curt Rice, vice president of research at the University of Tromso in Norway, discussed the problem in the context of the chemistry field. According to Rice (2012), more women than men turn away from academic studies during their doctoral studies for three reasons: "(i) the characteristics of academic careers are unappealing, (ii) the impediments they will encounter are disproportionate, and (iii) the sacrifices they will have to make are great." The research that supports Rice's conclusion suggests that women perceive professional academia as a potentially hostile environment. What happens once women land the tenure track position and begin their careers?

In "Nurturer or Queen Bee?," Julianne Malveaux examines leadership styles and support systems among women in academia. Malveaux perceives the issue of women's differing leadership styles as a factor that determines whether or not a structure that provides support for women's professional advancement exists. According to Malveaux, the issue becomes more complicated among women of color who often find themselves disproportionately underrepresented in academia. Malveaux

acknowledges the existence of what she terms the "haters" but paints their plight as a lonely peak of accomplishment fraught with the perils of working without a support system. In contrast, Malveaux notes the role that other women have played in her success as nurturing helpers who reached out to her over the course of her career.

In "Women and the Ethos of Philosophy: Shedding Light on Mentoring and Competition," Jacqui Poltera examines the issue of how women relate to other women in the predominantly male philosophy discipline. Poltera suggests that numerous systematic barriers pose challenges to women's ability and willingness to mentor and support other women in academia. According to Poltera, gendered expectations often translate into inordinately heavy service responsibilities for female academicians that leave little time to meet the requisite demands of research and teaching.

Poltera also addresses the issue of competition in academia and how women compete among women as well as with men. The gendered nature of competition between women centers on issues such as appearance, behavior, and sex-stereotyped roles that women may or may not choose to accept. Poltera suggests that women are not the only ones that are not supporting women in academia and challenges the notion that mentoring women is solely women's work.

YES ↵   **Julianne Malveaux**

Nurturer or Queen Bee?

There were about 30 of us seated in a semi-circle on a weekday afternoon, students, faculty, staff, administrators, mostly African-American women, with a couple of White and Latina sisters thrown in. The occasion—an informal chat with women after a talk I gave. But the warmth turned wary when one woman asked why African-American women were so mean to each other.

We talked about it just a bit, discomfited by the question. I retreated into a conversation about two models of women's leadership—Queen Bee or Nurturer. The Queen Bee, of course, is the woman who gets some psychic pleasure by being the first and the only. She doesn't give other women a break because no one ever gave her one. She did it the hard way, by golly, and everyone else had better do the same. She forgets that some queens, like Marie Antoinette, end up with no one to protect them and their heads on a plate.

In contrast, the Nurturer shares, and takes pleasure in sharing. She doesn't want to be the only woman in the room—she wants lots of other women to move along with her, to witness her job and help her through troubles, just as she does for them. She doesn't mind giving a younger sister the lay of the land or a set of strategic tips, because it doesn't reduce her power, it enhances it.

The dichotomy between Queen Bee and Nurturer isn't a Black woman's thing—it's a woman's thing, maybe even a human thing. Thousands of pages in leadership books and management journals have been devoted to the ways that women work, and the fact that some enjoy helping others, while some enjoy standing out as the first and the only. I've seen it in corporate America, in academia, in politics, in journalism. Some people can be extraordinarily generous with contacts, tips and ideas, while others hoard their connections.

Still, the conversation in our semicircle was troubling. African-American women represent fewer than 2 percent of all faculty members at institutions of higher education, and are over-represented only among support staff. With our numbers so small, we need allies wherever we can find them. Why can't we find them among each other?

Fast-forward two days: Another conference, another conversation. This time, the conference focus is women of color in higher education, and the sisterly energy is palpable among African-American, Latina, Asian American and American Indian women. The sisters are warm, generous, and pleasant. But the question comes up again, in gentler terms. Why can't we all get along? When the basis of the question is broader—women of color, not just African-American women, the answers may be complex since some of us, people of color, have a history of not trusting each other, of letting those in the majority pit us against each other. Still, heads nodded when I spoke of the two models of women's leadership, Queen Bee or Nurturer. People recognized those women, had been those women and wanted to understand those women.

Essence senior writer Audrey Edwards tackled the issue of sister-hating at work in the magazine's March issue, noting that bitter and ugly experiences have caused some African-American women to give up, completely, on the myth of sisterhood. Quoting management experts, executive sisters and others, she describes the challenges some corporate sisters face in seeking mentors, road maps and guidance. Much like the academic sisters I've been running into, the corporate sisters affirmed two models of women's leadership, but also noted practical reasons why sisterhood is fractured at work.

Audre Lorde wrote of "sister rage," the fact that we get madder at us than we do at anyone else, that we treat each other worse that we would others, that even slight offenses, when perpetrated by another sister, seem grounds for greater outrage than similar slights from others. A psychologist or sociologist would have a field day with our behavior and the reasons for it, but from a practical perspective one has to wonder what role this destructive behavior has on our progress as a people.

I have been blessed to be nurtured by wonderful African-American women, both through my sorority, Delta Sigma Theta Inc., and in my professional life. Oh, there have been the haters, but I choose not to dwell on them, but instead on the helpers, the folks who have not only opened doors but also escorted me into special places. I've also been grateful for the honest folks who have simply said they can't help—because of a conflict, some ambivalence about me or my work, or for another unstated reason. I prefer that honesty to the Invisible Man tactic of useless tips and futile referrals. And I've learned from the haters, been strengthened by them and learned to put them in perspective. Still, I wonder if the haters wonder what impact they have, especially in higher education. There is an African proverb, "she who teaches must learn." And when the haters are faculty women, I wonder what they've learned and what they see as the future of women of color in higher education.

Jacqui Poltera

 **NO**

Women and the Ethos of Philosophy: Shedding Light on Mentoring and Competition

The ethos of philosophy is notoriously hostile to women. Highly skilled female thinkers leak out at all stages of the pipeline, and philosophy remains one of the most male-dominated disciplines in the humanities (Norlock 2009, 8). I have two main aims here. First, I explain why we should not take for granted that senior women will be supportive mentors to junior women and thereby plug leaks in the pipeline. More importantly, we should not inadvertently place the onus on them to do so. Second, I argue that we need to consider the possibility that some women contribute to the hostile ethos. Women are as susceptible as men to employing gender schemas (Valian 2005). It is a mistake to presuppose that women philosophers are somehow immune from discriminating against other women, competing with them, and deterring them from entering the field. These facets of the problem form a relatively small but significant contribution to the hostile ethos that we need to acknowledge in our efforts to attract and retain women. Accepting this claim does not detract from the seriousness of longstanding gender discrimination against women, or from a widespread lack of recognition by men of women's needs and accomplishments in philosophy (Haslanger 2008).

Mentoring

There is a tendency to assume that if philosophy is to recruit and retain women, senior female philosophers should take up the role of supportive mentors and role models to more junior women.[1] For example, Sharon Crasnow has argued that the scarcity of women in philosophy means that female students may lack access to female role models and fail to receive adequate mentoring, which can contribute to leaks in the pipeline (Crasnow 2009, 14–15). Similarly, Kathryn J. Norlock argues that "we are best off cultivating efforts to mentoring [sic] women who love philosophy, acting as advocates, and materially assisting their genuine desire to stay" (Norlock 2009, 8–9). Although neither Crasnow nor Norlock explicitly states that women philosophers need to act as mentors and role models, the nature of gender schemas is that, on average, we tend to assume that women will be more supportive and available mentors than men.[2]

Briefly, gender schemas denote those implicit, unconscious beliefs we have about gender-based differences. These influence "our expectations of men and women, our evaluations of their work, and their performance as professionals" (Valian 1998, 2). Gender schemas shape our assumptions and judgments about people even when they are unarticulated, unacknowledged, or expressly disavowed. They often result in overrating men and underrating women in professional settings, where this can accumulate "to provide men with more advantages than women" (Valian 2005, 198). Within philosophy, gender schemas can be doubly disadvantageous for women since woman philosopher represents a schema conflict. The schema for philosophy is aggressive, hyperrational, objective, and masculine whereas the schema for women is emotional, non-objective, political, and feminine (Haslanger 2008, 216). In order for philosophy to "reduce the salience of gender schemas, decrease evaluation bias, and slow the accumulation of disadvantage" (Stewart 2009, 17), women need to comprise a sizeable minority. The tipping point for positive change to occur is when women comprise approximately 24–25% of the profession, although in order to fare significantly better, they need to achieve a critical mass of approximately 30% (Valian 1998, 142). Women currently constitute approximately 21% of the philosophy profession in the United States (Norlock 2009, 6) and around 23% of the profession in Australasia (Goddard et al. 2008, 5).

Attempts to achieve a critical mass can be combined with gendered expectations like assuming that women will be more nurturing, supportive, available, and "responsible for maintaining good social dynamics" in socially dysfunctional philosophy departments (Haslanger 2008, 217). When this happens it can lead to the assumption that senior women are best equipped to encourage junior women to stay in the profession through mentoring them. Insofar as gender-normative expectations affect "what kinds of work women do compared to similarly placed men" (Wylie et al. 2007, 6), mentoring junior women can be perceived as "women's work" by men and women alike.[3] I have two main reservations about such assumptions.

First, placing the onus on senior women staff can inadvertently deter junior women from pursuing philosophy. Although mentoring is central to addressing the under-representation of women in the field, it can also be exceptionally time-consuming, demanding, and exhausting, adding to the already disproportionate amounts of service many female academics do (Norlock 2009). As is familiar, women may leave philosophy because they take issue with the male dominated nature of the discipline and/or with the adversarial method. Similarly, female postgraduates and early career researchers who see their female mentors run ragged by service demands and by fulfilling gendered expectations may be turned off philosophy as a result.[4] Key to encouraging a woman to stay in philosophy is for her to be able to imaginatively project herself into a career as a female philosopher where doing so is an appealing prospect, broadly speaking. If she has had contact predominantly with senior women forced to struggle for recognition and exhausted by service and mentoring demands in ways unmatched by their male colleagues (Kourany 2009), it can make it difficult to imagine herself in a philosophy career without also imagining similar demands and difficulties. This can make the prospect of a career in philosophy unattractive, irrespective of how passionate a junior woman is about the discipline. Moreover, the admiration a junior woman feels for her senior female mentors can be tempered by concern for them and for her future self should she decide to persevere with philosophy.

Part of the problem here is that our expectations that senior women will be supportive and available can conflict with the fact that they can be so stretched among fulfilling the demands of teaching, administrative tasks, research, and attending to their own domestic responsibilities that their energy for being supportive and available is diminished. Unwittingly presupposing that senior women will be active mentors plays into assumptions that nurturing and mentoring are women's work. This being so, if we do not address our assumptions about mentoring, we inadvertently run the risk of increasing problematic gendered expectations for women in philosophy. Doing this may exacerbate the problem, prompting junior and senior women to leave the profession.

Second, we should not assume that an individual will be a competent mentor and role model just in virtue of being a senior woman in philosophy. Although this is a straightforward point, given the temptation to treat mentoring as women's work, it needs to be made. On the one hand, mentors and role models come in a range of forms. For example, I have been inspired to stay in philosophy by a combination of role models, not least of whom include a mature-age mother of two who previously had a career in finance, and a forty-something male psychiatric nurse who juggled his career as a nurse with postgraduate studies in philosophy. I have also been fortunate enough to have a range of male and female supervisors, colleagues, and heads of school encourage me when my will to stay in philosophy flagged. On the other hand, some senior women faculty can deter junior women from entering and remaining in the field because they lack the makings of a good mentor. Senior women (and men) who assume

the role of mentor can, for example, systematically fail to operate with sufficient professionalism and to respect appropriate boundaries. Senior women who have had to persistently struggle for recognition to achieve a position of seniority may resent having to mentor junior women or may have appropriated the very adversarial, combative method of doing philosophy that can deter some women from entering the field (Kourany 2009, 9–10). In some cases, senior women may also infantilize junior women, which can be quite counterproductive if it exacerbates any existing insecurities they have or frustrates their attempts at being taken seriously in the field. In short, good mentoring has more to do with an individual mentor's personality, psychology, and professionalism than it does with their gender. With the focus on achieving a critical mass and retaining women we can lose sight of this.

Although there are already well-established practices of male-male mentoring captured in the familiar caricature of a male professor surrounded by a series of eager male minions who doggedly read, write about, and discuss his work, similar practices of mentoring are less common among women. As such, mentoring is something the philosophical community at large needs to address. Mentoring junior men and women should be shared by competent senior men and women alike and should be something in which people at all stages of the pipeline take a keener and more considered interest. Theorists like Crasnow, Haslanger, Kourany, and Norlock would not reject these claims. Nevertheless, the potentially problematic effects of expecting female mentors to improve the ethos of philosophy for more junior women has received insufficient attention to date. Focusing on this issue does not undermine the benefits of having a positive, constructive, mutually respectful relationship with a mentor. In my own case, good mentoring from one female professor in particular has been invaluable to assuaging my recurring ambivalence about pursuing philosophy as a career.

Two Other Features of the Problem

Belief in our sincere concern as women in philosophy for other women in the field can make it exceptionally challenging to see that women in philosophy employ gender schemas and discriminate against other women in more or less subtle ways. And yet "males and females have similar cognitions about gender and make similar judgments and evaluations of men's and women's behaviours" (Valian 2005, 200). Gender schemas can lead "even well-meaning, equity-minded (female as well as male) philosophers to overlook and dismiss the credentials of women philosophers" (Kourany 2009, 10). This being so, although theorists working on the problem of women in philosophy have to date focused on the ways in which women are forced to manage competition with men, and men discriminate against women, competition and discrimination among women in philosophy needs to be considered.

Competition

Philosophy is cutthroat and can be ruthless. As is all too familiar for postgraduates and early career researchers, jobs are scarce and in high demand (Solomon and Clarke 2009).[5] Of those who complete their PhDs only a handful will get full-time, ongoing jobs in philosophy. Of those who get full-time jobs as philosophers, only a minority will ever publish in the top-ranked journals since they are so competitive (Haslanger 2008; Solomon and Clarke 2009, 3–4). Women philosophers fare worse when it comes to securing full-time continuing employment and publishing in the top journals (Valian 2005; Haslanger 2008).[6] Competition for jobs and for recognition in the field is fierce. Further, as a discipline, philosophy is distinctively combative, competitive, and aggressive. Philosophers tend to treat the adversarial method as paradigmatic of good philosophy. Doing philosophy well typically involves subjecting your hypotheses to vicious opposition (Moulton 1993, 149). Competition in philosophy is thus a reality for women and men alike. Yet, in our efforts to document and address women's struggles for recognition within our hypermasculine discipline, we can neglect the extent to which women compete against one another in vying for recognition and respect.

The collected papers in *Competition: A Feminist Taboo* seek to address competition among women, starting from the claim that in criticizing male power struggles women ignore and conceal their own conflicts over "control, position and recognition" (Miner and Longino 1987, 1). It has been argued that women experience different, deeper, and more complicated forms of competition with other women than with their male peers (Keller and Moglen, in Miner and Longino 1987, 22). Miner and Longino urge female academics and feminists in particular to be brutally honest about the role competition with other women plays in their lives. The underlying idea here is that if we discuss competition among women, we are less likely to confuse feelings of anger, resentment, and envy with the competitive process and may avoid misdirecting insecurities or feelings of failure toward ourselves at another's successes (Miner and Longino 1987, 186). These are important insights that we tend to overlook in addressing the hostile ethos of philosophy. Although we readily discuss the ways in which philosophy is competitive and combative in virtue of its hypermasculinity, we far less readily consider the ways in which women compete with one another. This may be in part because men in philosophy are, on average, more aggressively and overtly competitive than women are. As such, competition between men and other men, or between men and women, is easier to detect. As members of the minority, some women may also feel more threatened by other women than they do by men, as well as less inclined to discuss such feelings lest doing so reinforces gendered expectations that they are more emotional and political. Even women who are

exceptionally well respected in the field may be prone to destructive forms of competition with other women, particularly if they enjoy the status afforded them by being a member of the minority. In short, it is a mistake to attribute the competition to men rather than women. Competition is not gender-specific even though the way it manifests might be.

With the increased focus on employing token women in departments where there are few or none at all, demonstrating "women-friendliness," or meeting equal opportunities criteria, women are forced to compete not only against men but against other women for jobs, publications, and recognition in the field. Insofar as competition exists in cases where there is a possibility of recognition, reward, or influence (Miner and Longino 1987), it is unavoidable for women in philosophy. Although in many cases competition among peers can be productive and spur those competing to strive for excellence, it can also be destructive and counter-productive. The marked gender imbalance in philosophy means that many women are already acutely aware of their status as members of the minority. This "solo status" can promote anxiety and underperformance, and make skilled female philosophers feel more inept than they ought to feel (Haslanger 2008, 218). The effects of solo status, combined with "conflict between our commitment to, indeed our longing for, solidarity with other women and our need to compete in the marketplace for work" (Miner and Longino 1987, 1) can make the ethos of philosophy seem even more hostile and unappealing. Given the male-dominated nature of the discipline, competition among women may be more acute in philosophy than in other disciplines in the humanities and social sciences. Yet, the nature and effects of competition among women in philosophy has to date been largely ignored in attempts to explain the hostile ethos or to plug leaks in the pipeline.

When Women Discriminate Against Other Women

The issue of discrimination came up all too briefly at the Women in Philosophy Symposium when one senior female academic admitted that, despite herself, she at times caught herself operating with gender schemas. This comment resonated with me. I have repeatedly found myself initially impressed with what I took to be a male philosopher's philosophical prowess, only to find that my initial impression had less to do with his abilities than it did with my assumptions that in virtue of being a confident male he was more skilled than he actually was. Conversely, I have caught myself underestimating a woman philosopher on first seeing or speaking to her, only to find that she is a formidable thinker and I was wholly wrong in my initial assumptions about her. The comment at the symposium was geared to generate a discussion about discrimination against women and the effects of gender schemas. Interestingly, it was ultimately treated as humorous and not taken up in conversation. This anecdote is indicative of a broader problem, namely, that if women philosophers presuppose that they are immune to employing gender schemas because they are members of the minority and typically discriminated against, women—women discrimination can go unchecked.

My own experience is that some women in philosophy can be more subtly undermining, unsupportive, and hostile than men. For example, on securing my first full-time academic job soon after completing my PhD, women were responsible for some of the most demoralizing responses. Representative here are "You're a lucky girl, no hard slog for you!" "It's not surprising you got a job there." "I'd heard they were trying to increase their women-friendly rating." "It's not a real philosophy job though is it?" "Now you'll have plenty of time to have babies!" Of interest here is not only how widespread such responses were, but how persistent my own gender schemas were. I had to repeatedly remind myself not to assume that women would be more supportive or less discriminatory than men. Although some of these responses are blatantly discriminatory, they make sense when understood in relation to the struggles the women in question have endured. A career in philosophy is meant to be a struggle, particularly for women.

However, this is not an isolated incidence of women discriminating against other women. There is a familiar quip in philosophy that attending conferences is central to furthering your career and catching up on all the gossip. We need only reflect on the content of philosophy gossip to find examples of women being discriminated against by women for a range of reasons including their attire, philosophical ineptitude, poor responses to questions, tendency to present like a man, or even the amount of cleavage they have on display during a presentation. Such comments count as discrimination rather than critique when they have more to do with the fact that an individual is a woman than they do with the objective merits of her work. An unsuspecting graduate student subject to this kind of gossip and discrimination may feel even more anxious about her abilities and dissuaded from a career in philosophy. There is also an asymmetry here, namely, that if a man were to suggest that a woman's cleavage stole the show from her argument, or that her presentation style was too masculine and confident, it would be a straightforward instance of discrimination. From women such comments are often put down to pettiness or bitchiness when in fact they can be similarly discriminatory and fuel the hostile ethos. There are also women who are complicit in discriminating against other women for their decision to have children. For example, a colleague of mine recently said "Did you hear x is pregnant? There goes her career!" When such comments are made in all seriousness and without irony, they are discriminatory. Again here, we tend to expect such comments from men and typically focus on men's propensity to stereotype mothers as unproductive or uncommitted academics. The fact remains,

however, that just as some men operate with destructive stereotypes and discriminate against women, so too do some women.

It is worth pointing out that the degree to which aggression, competition, and discrimination exist among men or women can be context-specific. It can be far worse in certain countries, philosophical communities, or departments than it is in others. As such, it is important to note that my claims here are general ones. I maintain, however, that we need to consider the subtle but significant ways in which women are complicit in and contribute to the hostile ethos of the discipline. Some women compete with, discriminate against, and undermine other women in their efforts to secure or feel secure in their own positions where this can be off-putting for other women. Although we can explain this with reference to the hostile, combative, hyper-masculine, and competitive ethos of the discipline, we cannot ignore it, and perhaps should not excuse it.

My aim here has been twofold: first, to prompt us to take seriously the possibility that in small but notable ways, some women contribute to and are complicit in the ethos of philosophy; second, to draw attention to the fact that although good mentoring by women can be crucial to nurturing female academics and encouraging them to stay in the profession, there should not be a general expectation of this happening. Mentoring can be onerous, and some senior women are not well-suited to it. My claims about women-women mentoring, competition, and discrimination are geared to elucidate a relatively minor, but largely overlooked, facet of the problem. I suspect that we might be able to find some correlation between the kinds of problems I outline here and the hostile ethos of the discipline. There is no question that men in philosophy are predominantly responsible for this ethos, and for the competitive, combative, discriminatory nature of the discipline. My comments here are not geared to detract from men's role in the problem, or from the fact that in many departments, philosophical communities, and on some editorial boards, men still overtly discriminate against women (Haslanger 2008). Rather, I aim to raise some new aspects of the problem for consideration in the hope that doing so will improve our efforts to encourage highly skilled women to stay in the profession.

Recommendations

1. Become more attuned to the ways in which women's gender schemas about other women in the field can influence the ethos of philosophy.
2. Raise and discuss assumptions about mentoring and competition among women.
3. Examine and acknowledge the nature and effects of competition and discrimination among women in philosophy.
4. Make every effort not to treat the mentoring of junior women or fixing leaks in the pipeline as "women's work."

5. Combine quantitative research like that in Haslanger's paper and in *Improving the Participation of Women in the Philosophy Profession* (Goddard et al. 2008) with the results of conducting qualitative, open-ended surveys. For example, philosophy could follow history in inviting participants in such surveys to comment on whether and how gender has affected their career; what factors facilitated or hindered their career; and, whether mentoring or the lack thereof played a salient role in career development (Lunbeck 2005, 3).

Notes

1. This approach to preventing leaks in the pipeline was discussed at the 2009 Women in Philosophy Symposium held at the Australian National University in Canberra. I discuss an aspect of the symposium below.
2. Further, even when gender schemas are not in play, senior women who have been forced to struggle for recognition in the profession may take it upon themselves to encourage more junior women going through the same process.
3. Qualitative surveys on the status of women in history and anthropology respectively found similar assumptions were widespread. See Lunbeck 2005 and Wasson et al. 2008. This is relevant since these disciplines have had trends similar to philosophy, although both have now reached the tipping point toward achieving a critical mass.
4. One reason this may be so is if junior women choose not to seek advice or to demand time from senior women precisely because they seem overburdened, which may leave junior women feeling more isolated and unsupported than they might otherwise feel. Acknowledging this, however, points to a problem with the current culture of mentoring qua women's work, rather than a problem with those senior women mentors who are too exhausted and overburdened to be consistently attentive and available.
5. See also http://www.philosophicalgourmet.com/perspective.asp and www.aap. org.au (both accessed September 22, 2010).
6. Statistically speaking, the average number of articles published by women in the top ranked journals is 12.36%, with feminist content comprising only 2.36% (Solomon and Clarke 2009, 4).

References

Crasnow, Sharon. 2009. What do the numbers mean? *APA Newsletters on Feminism and Philosophy 8* (2): 13–6. http://www.apaonline.org/documents/publications/v08n2_Feminism.pdf (accessed September 22, 2010).

Goddard, Eliza, et al. 2008. *Improving the participation of women in the philosophy profession.* Prepared by the Committee of Senior Academics Addressing the Status of Women in the Philosophy Profession. http://www.aap.org.au/women/reports/IPWPP_ReportA_Staff.pdf (accessed September 22, 2010).

Haslanger, Sally. 2008. Changing the ideology and culture of philosophy: Not by reason (alone). *Hypatia 23* (2): 210–23.

Kourany, Janet A. 2009. Why are women only 21% of philosophy?: Introduction to the panel presentations. *APA Newsletters on Feminism and Philosophy 8* (2): 9–10. http://www.apaonline.org/documents/publications/v08n2-Feminism.pdf (accessed September 22, 2010).

Lunbeck, Elizabeth. 2005. The status of women in the historical profession. Prepared for the American Historical Association Committee on Women Historians. http://www. historians.org/GOVERNANCE/cwh/CWV-Report_5.20.05.pdf (accessed September 22, 2010).

Miner, Valerie, and Helen E. Longino, eds. 1987. *Competition: A Feminist Taboo.* New York: The Feminist Press at CUNY.

Moulton, Janice. 1993. A paradigm of philosophy: The adversarial method. In *Discovering reality: Feminist perspectives on epistemology, metaphysics, methodology and the philosophy of science,* ed. Sandra Harding and Merrill B.P. Hintikka. Dordrecht: Kluwer Publishing.

Norlock, Kathryn J. 2009. Love to count: Arguments for inaccurately measuring the proportion of philosophers who are women. *APA Newsletters on Feminism and Philosophy 8* (2): 6–9. http://www.apaonline.org/documents/publications/v08n2_Feminism.pdf (accessed September 22, 2010).

Solomon, Miriam, and John Clarke. 2009. CSW Jobs for philosophers employment study. *APA Newsletters on Feminism and Philosophy 8* (2): 3–6. http://www.apaonline.org/documents/publications/v08n2-Feminism.pdf (accessed September 22, 2010).

Stewart, Abigail J. 2009. What might be learned from recent efforts in the natural sciences? *APA Newsletters on Feminism and Philosophy 8* (2): 16–9. http://www.apaonline.org/documents/publications/v08n2_Feminism.pdf (accessed September 22, 2010).

Valian, Virginia. 1998. Why so slow? *The advancement of women.* Cambridge, Mass.: MIT Press.

———. 2005. Beyond gender schemas: Improving the advancement of women in academia. *Hypatia 20* (3): 198–213.

Wasson, Christina, et al. 2008. *We've come a long way, maybe: Academic climate report of the Committee on the Status of Women in Anthropology.* Prepared for the American Anthropological Association. http://lwww.aaanet.org/resourcesldepartments/uploadl COSWA-Academic-Climate-Report-2008.pdf (accessed September 22, 2010).

Wylie, Alison, Janet Jakobsen, and Gisela Fosado. 2007. *Women, work, and the academy: Strategies for responding to "post-civil rights era" gender discrimination.* Published by the Barnard Center for Research on Women. http://www.barnard.edu/bcrw/new feministsolutions/reports/NFS2-Women_Work_and_ the_Academy.pdf (accessed September 22, 2010).

EXPLORING THE ISSUE

Do Women Support the Advancement of Other Women?

Critical Thinking and Reflection

1. How can opposite sex mentors fill the gap for women in the workplace?
2. How might the "old boys' network" transform into a post-gender professional network?

Is There Common Ground?

The intersection of race, sex, class, and gender collide in the workplace in ways experienced in few other areas of life. The workplace limits our affinity choices and occupational expediency and, at times, necessity guides our association choices. However, the role that mentoring plays in the lives of the mentor and the mentored is hard to quantify. The transformative possibilities of the mentoring relationship may not make sense to either side of the equation until some time has passed.

Freelance writer Elizabeth Titus described her experience of mentoring women writers as part of the Afghan Women's Writing Project as a feeling of being needed. Power becomes more significant in the context of relative disadvantage and disparities in social relationships within the mentoring dyad. In the case of university students within a women's prison, the mentoring relationships are even more complex. Mentoring is always a transactional relationship, even when the transaction is emotional labor and the exchange is intangible.

Additional Resources

Lempert, L., LaRose, C., Freeman, L., and Liss, L. (2012). "What Is It That These People Want? Are We Part of Some Kind of Experiment?: Mentoring in a Women's Prison." *Humanity & Society, 36*(1), 30–49.

Rice, C. (2012). "Why Women Leave Academia and Why Universities Should Be Worried." *Higher Education Network.* Guardian News and Media Limited. Retrieved from: www.guardian.co.uk/higher-education-network/blog/2012/may/24/why-women-leave-academia

Titus, E. (2013). "The Lives of Others." *Humanist, 73*(2), 39–40.

Create Central

www.mhhe.com/createcentral

Internet References . . .

Women's Leadership & Mentoring Alliance

http://www.wlmaconnect.org/

American Psychological Association

http://www.apa.org/monitor/nov00/mentoring.aspx

Women's Mentoring Network, Inc.

http://wmninc.org/

Business and Professional Women's Foundation

http://www.bpwfoundation.org/index.php/misc/mentoring_applications_for_mentors_and_mentees/

Unit 6

UNIT

Double Standards: The Intersection of Sex, Gender, and Culture

*F*rom Slutwalks to Sandra Fluke, the idea of a double standard for men and women in society can polarize public opinion. What is the double standard? How does it impact the lives of men and women in the twenty-first century? Is there actually still a double standard of sexuality for women and girls?

Questions of female sexuality and reproductive rights continue to drive policy discourse on issues that range from public safety to health care legislation. In 2012, a law student named Sandra Fluke ignited a national media firestorm after her testimony to a congressional committee about birth control access and insurance coverage became fodder for commentary on a syndicated radio show. Conservative radio personality Rush Limbaugh equated oral contraceptive use with promiscuity when he characterized Sandra Fluke as a "slut" and "a prostitute" after she advocated for oral contraceptive insurance coverage.

The word "slut" also generated international headlines after a Canadian police officer admonished women to avoid looking like sluts as a rape prevention measure. An international movement was born and activists took to the streets around the world for mass demonstrations that celebrated a woman's right to self-presentation without fear of sexual attack. The marches were known as "Slutwalks" and drew women and men of all ages to make public statements about sexuality and clothing choices.

Women's roles and the influence of sex and gender on cultural expectations impact how women are perceived across different social spheres. In particular, the expectations people have about women in leadership roles have powerful implications. Issues regarding how women gain, hold, and wield power remain a challenge for women in business and government contexts.

Selected, Edited, and with Issue Framing Material by:
Rachel Pienta, *Valdosta State University*

ISSUE

Is There Still a Double Standard of Sexuality for Women and Girls?

YES: **Michael J. Marks and R. Chris Fraley**, from "The Sexual Double Standard: Fact or Fiction?," *Sex Roles* (vol. 52, no. 3/4, February 2005)

NO: **Gail Collins**, from "The Decline of the Double Standard," in *When Everything Changed: The Amazing Journey of American Women from 1960 to the Present.* (Little, Brown, and Company, 2009)

Learning Outcomes

As you read the issue, focus on the following points:

- What role does pop culture play in setting public norms for sexual behavior?
- How has the widespread availability of affordable birth control changed sexual norms for both men and women?

ISSUE SUMMARY

YES: Michael J. Marks and R. Chris Fraley, in "The Sexual Double Standard: Fact or Fiction?," address contemporary cultural beliefs about the sexual double standard.

NO: Gail Collins, in the chapter titled "The Decline of the Double Standard" from her 2009 book *When Everything Changed: The Amazing Journey of American Women from 1960 to the Present*, discusses how cultural beliefs regarding expectations for women's sexual behaviors have evolved since the 1960s.

The phrase "sexual double standard" refers to the idea that there are different rules for how men and women should conduct their sexual lives. Throughout history, the onus for chastity has largely rested with the party that could experience the postcoital consequence of pregnancy. The advent of the birth control pill and its widespread availability in the latter half of the twentieth century heralded many changes for American women. For many women, reproductive control translated into delayed marriage and the opportunity to earn advanced degrees as well as the chance to pursue careers outside the home.

How do people perceive the sexual behavior of men and women? Is there really a double standard that approves one type of behavior for one sex but not for the other? In "The Sexual Double Standard: Fact or Fiction?" Michael J. Marks and R. Chris Fraley address beliefs about sexual double standards and examine current research on the subject. To test the limits of existing research on the double standard, Marks and Fraley (2005) conducted an experiment to determine "whether people evaluate men and women differently based on the number of sexual

partners they have had" (p. 177). Their objective was to test the hypothesis that a double standard would exist if "as the number of sexual partners reported increases, male targets would be evaluated more positively and female targets more negatively" (Marks & Fraley, 2005, p. 177).

Marks and Fraley's research showed that the sexual double standard exists but is not a simple construct. The fact that people believe a double standard exists becomes, in effect, a self-fulfilling prophecy that is further supported by the phenomenon of confirmation bias. The tendency to notice instances that align with and confirm previously held beliefs while selectively ignoring examples that might disprove the misconception may contribute to the pervasive notion that a sexual double standard exists in contemporary American culture.

In "The Decline of the Double Standard," Gail Collins chronicles the social changes that altered cultural expectations about women's sexual behavior after the 1960s. From widespread acceptance of cohabitation to the relative affordability and widespread availability of the birth control pill, the rules for sexual behavior have changed for both men and women. According to Collins, the sexual revolution that began in the late 1960s and continued into the early 1970s signaled the beginning of the end for the sexual double standard.

The influence of popular culture in setting public norms for sexual behavior cannot be underestimated.

Helen Gurley Brown's 1962 novel *Sex and the Single Girl* extolled the virtues of single life and extramarital sex. The book was a bestseller and set the stage for the sexual revolution that would subsequently sweep across cities and college campuses throughout America.

Michael J. Marks and R. Chris Fraley

The Sexual Double Standard: Fact or Fiction?

In contemporary society it is widely believed that women and men are held to different standards of sexual behavior. As [many have] noted, "a man who is successful with many women is likely to be seen as just that—successful . . . [whereas] a woman known to have 'success' with many men is . . . likely to be known as a 'slut.'" The view that men are socially rewarded and women socially derogated for sexual activity has been labeled the *sexual double standard*.

The sexual double standard has received a lot of attention from contemporary critics of Western culture. Tanenbaum (2000), for example, has documented the harassment and distress experienced by adolescent girls who have been branded as "sluts" by their peers. Other writers have critiqued the way the media help to create and reinforce negative stereotypes of sexually active women and how these stereotypes may contribute to violence against women. Given the attention the sexual double standard has received in contemporary discourse, one might assume that behavioral scientists have documented the double standard extensively and elucidated many of the mechanisms that generate and sustain it. Despite much systematic research, however, there is virtually no consistent evidence for the existence of this allegedly pervasive phenomenon.

We have three objectives in this [paper]. Our first is to review briefly the empirical literature on the sexual double standard. As we discuss, research findings concerning the double standard do not strongly support its existence. Next, we discuss several methodological reasons why previous researchers may not have been able to document a double standard even if one exists. Finally, we report a study that was designed to determine whether the sexual double standard exists by rectifying the methodological limitations of previous studies.

Empirical Research on the Sexual Double Standard

The sexual double standard seems to be a ubiquitous phenomenon in contemporary society; one recent survey revealed that 85% of people believe that a double standard exists in our culture. The double standard is frequently publicized by the media. For example, MTV, a popular cable television channel that specializes in contemporary culture,

recently aired a program called "Fight for Your Rights: Busting the Double Standard" that was designed to convey the idea that a sexual double standard exists and that people should try to transcend it by exhibiting more egalitarian thinking.

Although the sexual double standard seems pervasive, empirical research does not necessarily show that people evaluate sexually active men and women differently. In fact, much of the literature reveals little or no evidence of a double standard. O'Sullivan (1995), for example, conducted a person perception study in which individual participants read vignettes of a male or female target who reported a high or low number of past sexual partners. Participants then evaluated the targets in domains such as likeability, morality, and desirability as a spouse. Although men and women who engaged in casual intercourse were evaluated more negatively than those whose sexual experiences occurred in committed relationships, a double standard was not found. Gentry (1998) also employed a person perception task and found that raters judged both male and female targets who had relatively few past sexual partners and who were in monogamous relationships more positively than targets who had a high number of partners and had frequent casual sex. Again, no evidence of a double standard was found. Sprecher et al. (1988) examined how appropriate certain sexual acts were for men and women of various ages. Although older targets received more permissive responses (i.e., they were allowed more sexual freedom), there were few differences in the standards used for men versus women for any age group.

Researchers have also documented many characteristics of respondents that influence attitudes toward sexuality, but few, if any, of these findings are consistent with a double standard. For instance, Garcia (1982) found that respondents' degree of androgyny was related to the sexual stereotypes they held. Androgynous participants (i.e., people who possess high levels of both masculine and feminine psychological traits) displayed a single standard, whereas gender-typed respondents (i.e., masculine men and feminine women) displayed a slight preference for female targets in the low-sexual experience condition. However, a preference for high-experience male targets over low-experience male targets was not found.

The number of sexual partners respondents have had also appears to influence their judgments of targets. Milhausen and Herold (1999), for example, found that

Marks, Michael J. and Fraley, R. Chris. From *Sex Roles,* February 2005, pp. 175–186 (excerpts). Copyright © 2005 by Springer Science and Business Media. Reprinted by permission via Rightslink.

women with many sexual partners were more tolerant of highly sexually active men than were women with few sexual partners. However, the interaction between target gender, target experience, and participant experience was not tested. The gender of the respondent has also been shown to influence views on sexuality. Women tend to hold sexual standards that are stricter than those of men, but do not necessarily apply those standards differently as a function of the gender of the person being evaluated.

In summary, although it appears that people *do* evaluate others with respect to the number of sexual partners those people have had, research does not consistently show that those evaluations differ for male and female targets. Even in situations in which men and women are evaluated differently, the associations usually vary only in magnitude, not in sign. In other words, there are some situations in which both women and men may be evaluated more negatively as the number of sexual partners they report increases, but this association is only slightly stronger for women than it is for men. As we will explain below, this pattern can be characterized as a "weak" rather than "strong" double standard. If the sexual double standard is as pervasive and powerful as many people believe, empirical research should reveal cross-over interactions such that the association between sexual experience and evaluations is negative for women but positive for men.

Sexual Double Standard Research Methodology

Although the empirical literature would seem to suggest that the sexual double standard is not in operation, it may be the case that behavioral scientists have failed to tap it properly. Commonly used paradigms for studying the sexual double standard may have methodological limitations that prevent the double standard from emerging. If this is the case, changes are needed in the methodology used in sexual double standard research.

One limitation of past research is the likely existence of demand characteristics. For example, if a study explicitly requires participants to rate the appropriateness of certain sexual behaviors for men, immediately followed by identical questions regarding women, participants may try to answer either in an egalitarian manner or in a manner that is consistent with what they believe to be the norm. Given that many people have preconceived notions about the sexual double standard, it is important to minimize demand characteristics when researching attitudes toward sexuality.

A second limitation of past research involves the presentation of sexual activity in a valenced fashion. For example, some researchers have used materials that imply that premarital sexual intercourse "is just wrong" or have described a target as having a number of past sexual partners that is "a lot above average." This kind of language implies that there is something abnormal or inappropriate about the target's activity. Describing sexual activity with value-laden terms or implying that a person is involved in *any* behavior

to an excess may lead to biased evaluations of that person, regardless of whether that person is male or female. If a sexual double standard exists, the use of these kinds of descriptors may occlude researchers' ability to document it clearly.

Finally, much of the past double standard research has not differentiated between attitudes and evaluations. *Attitudes* toward sexual behavior may include general beliefs about the norms of the culture, personal decisions about when sex is permissible, and the perceived appropriateness of certain sexual behaviors. *Evaluations* concern real judgments made about specific people who engage in sexual activity. Attitudes may be independent of the way people actually evaluate one another. Because of this, results concerning attitudinal differences (e.g., women hold less permissive sexual standards than men do) as evidence of the double standard's existence may conflict with results concerning evaluations of others' behavior. We believe that at the core of popular interest in the sexual double standard is the notion that men and women are evaluated differently depending on their sexual experience. Although the general attitudes that people hold about sexuality are of interest to psychologists, these attitudes may not be reflected in the actual evaluations that people make about one another. Therefore, it is imperative to focus on the evaluations that people make about specific individuals.

Overview of the Present Study

The objective of the present experiment was to determine whether people evaluate men and women differently based on the number of sexual partners they have had. To do this, we asked participants to rate a target on a number of evaluative dimensions. We manipulated both (a) the sex of the target and (b) the number of sexual partners reported by the target. This experiment was explicitly designed to rectify some of the limitations of previous research on the sexual double standard. For example, we focused on the evaluations people made about specific targets rather than general perceptions of social norms. We did not include valenced or biased descriptions of sexual activity (e.g., "promiscuous," "above average number of partners"). Moreover, we employed a between-subjects design to reduce potential demand characteristics. These features enabled us to draw attention away from the sexual focus of the study and allowed us to tap the way people evaluate others who vary in gender and sexual experience. . . .

Competing Hypotheses

If a traditional or "strong" sexual double standard exists, then as the number of sexual partners reported increases, male targets would be evaluated more positively and female targets more negatively. . . .

It is also possible that a "weak" double standard exists, such that both men and women are derogated for high levels of sexual experience, but to different degrees. . . . Finally, if there is no sexual double standard, then we would observe equivalent slopes for male and female targets. . . .

Method

Participants

. . . The . . . sample consisted of 144 undergraduates from a large midwestern university (44 men, 100 women) who participated in fulfillment of partial course credit. The mean participant age in this sample was 19.66 ($SD = 3.14$, range 18–30 years). . . .

Design

We employed a 2 (target sex) × 6 (number of partners: 0, 1, 3, 7, 12, or 19) between-subjects design. . . .

Procedure

A page (constructed by the experimenters) that contained five questions and the answers to those questions was given to the participants to read. Participants were told that the page was a section from a general public survey that had been completed by an anonymous individual. The page contained answers to questions such as "What are your hobbies?" and "How do you see yourself?" Information about the target's sexual experience was conveyed in response to the question "What is something not many people know about you?" The key phrase in the response was "I've had sex with [number] [guys/girls]. I don't really have much to say about it. It's just sort of the way I've lived my life."

After reading the page that contained the target's answers, participants were asked to rate 30 evaluative statements about the target. Participants rated each item on a *Disagree* [to] *Agree* [scale]. These items . . . power, intelligence, likeability, morality, quality as a date, quality as a spouse, physical appeal, and friendship [comprised] four evaluative factors: *values* . . . , *peer popularity* . . . , *power/success* . . . , *and intelligence*. . . .

Results

. . . [A statistical technique, called multiple regression was used to analyse the results.]

In the values domain, there was a main effect of number of sexual partners. . . . Targets with more partners were evaluated more negatively. . . . There was no main effect of target sex and no . . . interaction [of number of sexual partners and target sex.]

In the domain of peer popularity, there was a main effect of number of sexual partners. . . . Targets with more partners were evaluated more negatively. . . . There was no main effect of target sex and no . . . interaction [of number of sexual partners and target sex].

In the domain of power/success, there were no main effects of target sex or number of sexual partners, although there was a tendency for participants to evaluate targets with many partners more negatively. . . . There was no . . . interaction [of number of sexual partners and target sex].

In the domain of intelligence, again there was a main effect of number of sexual partners. . . . Targets with

more partners were evaluated more negatively. . . . There was no . . . interaction [of number of sexual partners and target sex].

Discussion

To date, there has been little evidence that women are evaluated more negatively than men for having many sexual partners. However, if the double standard exists, methodological limitations of previous research may have prevented it from emerging clearly. In the present research, we sought to provide a rigorous test of whether or not the sexual double standard exists by rectifying methodological limitations of previous studies. Our data reveal virtually no evidence of a traditional, or "strong," sexual double standard. . . .

These results . . . suggest that although the double standard may not operate in overall evaluations of persons, it may play a role in shaping perceptions of sexually active people in specific domains. Concerning the domain of intelligence, for example, engaging in frequent casual sex may not be a "smart" thing to do in light of the dangers of sexually transmitted diseases (especially AIDS). . . .

These results suggest that even after addressing some of the methodological limitations of previous research, traditional accounts of the sexual double standard do not appear to characterize the manner in which sexually active men and women are evaluated. This raises the question of whether the sexual double standard is more a cultural illusion than an actual phenomenon. If the double standard does not accurately characterize the manner in which people evaluate sexually active others, why does belief in it persist?

One possibility is that people are sensitive to our culture's "sexual lexicon." Many writers have observed that there are more slang terms in our language that degrade sexually active women than sexually active men. On the basis of such observations, people may conclude that a sexual double standard exists. However, one must be cautious when citing sexual slang as evidence of a double standard. It may be more valuable to consider the relative frequency of the use of slang terms than to consider solely the number of slang terms that exist. When Milhausen and Herold (2001) analyzed the frequency of sexual slang used to describe men and women in actual discourse, they found that the majority of men and women used negative terms to describe both sexually experienced men *and* women. They reported that a minority of men (25%) and women (8%) actually used words such as "stud" to describe sexually active men. Moreover, sexually active men were frequently described with words that fall into the category of *sexual predator* (e.g., "womanizer") or *promiscuous* (e.g., "slut," "dirty"). So although a difference exists in the *number* of sexual slang terms to describe men and women, it is not nearly analogous to the difference in the frequency of their *use* for men and women.

The confirmation bias may also help to explain why people believe that the sexual double standard exists. Confirmation bias refers to a type of selective thinking in which one tends to notice evidence that confirms one's beliefs and to ignore or undervalue evidence that contradicts one's beliefs. Confirmation biases may lead people to notice cases that are consistent with the double standard (e.g., a woman being referred to as a "slut") and fail to notice cases inconsistent with the double standard (e.g., a man being referred to as a "whore"). Because the vast majority of people believe that a sexual double standard exists, it is likely that people will process social information that seemingly corroborates the sexual double standard and will ignore information that refutes it. In short, although men and women may have an equal probability of being derogated (or rewarded) for having had many sexual partners, people may tend to notice only the instances in which women are derogated and men are rewarded. Attending to cases that are consistent with the double standard while ignoring cases inconsistent with it may create the illusion that the sexual double standard is more pervasive than it really is.

Limitations of the Present Study

Although we sought to correct some limitations of past research, other limitations remain. First, the statistical power of the student sample was low because of the relatively small sample size. . . .

Second, the results reported here may not generalize to populations outside of Western culture. Culture can be a powerful sculptor of sexual attitudes and behavior; the double standard may exist in one culture, but be absent from another. For instance, a review of the anthropological literature on sex and sexuality in Africa reveals much evidence of a double standard in African culture.

Third, this study, like much previous research, employs an experimental person perception paradigm. Studying the double standard in more naturalistic settings may reveal dynamics not otherwise tapped by more artificial methodologies. For example, observing "hot spots" where social interactions are possibly centered on sex (e.g., bars, locker rooms) may offer insight to the kinds of attitudes expressed concerning the sexual activity of men and women.

Finally, the present research is relatively atheoretical, partly because we believe that it is necessary to document the phenomenon of the double standard systematically (if it exists) before bringing theoretical perspectives to bear on it. Nonetheless, there may be theoretical perspectives that would help guide us in a more effective search for this phenomenon. For example, social psychological theory suggests that people tend to conform to social norms in the presence of others. Because there are strong gender norms concerning the appropriate sexual behavior of men and women, people may behave in accordance with these norms in social situations. Our study, like other studies on the double standard, only focused on individuals in nongroup situations. Social psychological theory suggests that social interaction in group contexts may be a necessary precondition for the emergence of the double standard.

Conclusions

In an effort to denounce the sexual double standard, contemporary authors, critics, and the media may actually be *perpetuating* it by unintentionally providing confirming evidence for the double standard while ignoring disconfirming evidence. Most accounts from these sources cite numerous cases of women being derogated for sexual activity, perhaps in an effort to elicit empathy from the audience. Empathy is a commendable (and desirable) goal, but these writings may also serve to embed the double standard in our collective conscious. Suggesting that a societal double standard is the basis of the derogation of women shifts focus away from those who are truly at fault—those who are engaging in or permitting sexual harassment and other forms of derogation.

In closing, we believe that it may be beneficial to shift the emphasis of sexual double standard research from the question of *whether* the double standard exists to *why* the double standard appears to be such a pervasive phenomenon when it really is not. By addressing this question, future researchers should be able to elucidate the disparity between popular intuitions and the research literature and open doors to novel avenues for our understanding of attitudes toward sexuality.

References

Garcia, L. T. (1982). Sex-role orientation and stereotypes about male-female sexuality. *Sex Roles, 8,* 863–876.

Gentry, M. (1998). The sexual double standard. The influence of number of relationships and level of sexual activity on judgments of women and men. *Psychology of Women Quarterly, 22,* 505–511.

Milhausen, R. R., & Herold, E. S. (1999). Does the sexual double standard still exist? Perceptions of university women. *Journal of Sex Research, 36,* 361–368.

Milhausen, R. R., & Herold, E. S. (2001). Reconceptualizing the sexual double standard. *Journal of Psychology and Human Sexuality, 13,* 63–83.

O'Sullivan, L. F. (1995). Less is more: The effects of sexual experience on judgments of men's and women's personality characteristics and relationship desirability. *Sex Roles, 33,* 159–181.

Sprecher, S., McKinney, K., Walsh, R., & Anderson, C. (1988). A revision of the Reiss Premarital Sexual Permissiveness Scale. *Journal of Marriage and the Family, 50,* 821–828.

Tanenbaum, L. (2000). *Slut!* New York: Harper Collins.

Michael J. Marks is an associate professor in the Department of Psychology at New Mexico State University.

R. Chris Fraley is an associate professor of psychology at the University of Illinois at Urbana-Champaign.

Gail Collins

 **NO**

The Decline of the Double Standard

"They Think I'm a Good Girl."

In 1968 the *New York Times* took note of a startling new trend: "cohabiting." A feature story introduced readers to several couples, mainly New York City college students, who were living together without the benefit of a marriage license. Everyone's identity was disguised in deference to the controversial nature of the subject. "Joan," whose parents believed she was rooming with a girlfriend, said even the mailman was conspiring with her to hide the truth from her family. "It's funny . . . my parents have a lot of confidence in me. They think I'm a good girl," said Joan, who clearly believed that if her parents got a load of her real roommate, "Charles," they might change their minds.

The lead anecdote, however, belonged to "Peter" and "Susan," who were part of a youthful counterculture that the *Times* was still slowly introducing to its readers. The couple was sharing a four-room apartment with "no bed in the bedroom—just six mattresses for their use and that of fellow students who need a place to sleep." And the paper reported that although Peter and Susan had been together for two years, they "had no plans for a wedding because they regard marriage as 'too serious a step.'" Susan was a student at Barnard College, which generally prohibited off-campus living arrangements. But she had gotten around the rule by having a friend tell the college employment bureau she wanted to hire Susan as a live-in nanny.

That was a little too much detail, as it turned out. It didn't take the Barnard administration long to figure out that "Susan" was actually Linda LeClair, a 20-year-old sophomore. When confronted, LeClair admitted she had deceived the housing administrator and broken school regulations. Rather than apologizing, she and her boyfriend, Peter Behr, a junior at Columbia, began leafleting the campus, asking students to demand changes in the rules. Endless debate and newspaper headlines ensued. A student-faculty committee was called to consider the case. After five hours of deliberation, the committee announced that as punishment for deceiving the administration about where she lived, LeClair would be "denied the privilege of using the following college facilities: the snack bar, the cafeteria, and the James Room," a student lounge.

A snack-bar ban was clearly not the kind of penalty likely to deter future cohabitation, and the alumnae wrote to complain. Barnard's president, Martha Peterson, seemed torn between respecting the committee's decision and showing the college's donors that she was not going to let the matter drop. So she sent an open letter to LeClair, asking her opinion on "the importance of integrity among individuals in the college" and "the importance of respect for regularized procedures." She also wanted a letter from LeClair's parents stating whether they approved of their daughter's behavior. The result of all this was another *Times* story, titled "Father Despairs of Barnard Daughter," and an editorial noting that Barnard could have saved itself a lot of grief "by letting sleeping coeds lie."

By May, Peterson was hinting very strongly that Linda LeClair ought to go away (". . . no useful purpose can be served by your continued enrollment in Barnard College"). Yet she insisted that the final judgment would be based neither on sex nor on failure to follow procedures, but on the final grades of a student who, it appeared, had been spending more time passing out leaflets than attending classes. The *Times*, which had been covering the story as if it involved the threat of nuclear war, tracked down LeClair among "a student group flying paper airplanes on the Columbia campus" and found her rather indifferent to her future as an undergraduate. The next time she made an appearance in the paper would be as one of hundreds of students arrested during sit-ins and protests over Columbia's plan to build a gym in Harlem. Ultimately, LeClair dropped out at the end of the semester, went off with Peter Behr to live in a commune in Vermont, hitchhiked to the West Coast, and returned to New York so her boyfriend could refuse induction into the army. On her arrival, LeClair told a *Times* reporter that she had a certain sympathy for President Peterson. "She is aware . . . that recognizing sexual intercourse would cause embarrassment to the ladies that give money to the college."

". . . While I Wasn't Allowed Out After Nine Thirty."

Of all the social uprisings of the late 1960s and early 1970s, none was more popular than the sexual revolution. And while men took an enthusiastic part, it was basically a story about women. Most of the world had always operated under a double standard in which girls were supposed to remain chaste until marriage while boys were allowed—sometimes encouraged—to press for whatever sex they could get. But Linda LeClair's generation had learned from the civil rights movement that just because something had always been the rule did not mean it was right—particularly if that rule gave some people more privileges than others. Even the authority figures had lost some of their confidence in the old morality. The Barnard administration, while trying to get a handle on the LeClair situation, skirted any suggestion that it was wrong for a young woman to shack up with a man she did not intend to marry. Instead, President Peterson focused on the fact that LeClair had lied about where she was living. Even in 1968, everyone on campus tended to agree that lying was bad.

Colleges had always given their unspoken endorsement to the double standard by setting far stricter regulations in girls' dormitories. In her precohabitation days, LeClair would get back to her room in time for curfew, then look out the window to watch her boyfriend walking away. "I can still see the image," she said recently, "of him going across Broadway to do whatever the heck he wanted to do while I wasn't allowed out after nine thirty at night." It was a tradition as old as women's higher education. But by the late 1960s, Barnard was hardly the only college on the defensive. Within a few years, many schools were in full-scale retreat. When Nora Ephron returned to Wellesley for the tenth reunion of the Class of 1962, she heard that one of her old classmates had gone into a dormitory bathroom and seen "a boy and a girl taking a shower together." No one, Ephron said, could believe it. "Ten years ago we were allowed to have men in the rooms on Sunday afternoons only, on the condition the door be left fourteen inches ajar." And Anne Wallach, visiting her daughter at Antioch, prided herself on not reacting when she passed a naked man on her way to Alison's room.

". . . The Technical Virgins Association."

The female warriors of the sexual revolution had been born into a world where the importance of remaining a virgin until marriage was seldom questioned. Nothing was worse than being suspected of casual sleeping around. Ellen Miller, who grew up in Kentucky, remembers that adults were extremely tolerant of their children smoking and that parents routinely chaperoned parties in which underage boys and girls drank alcohol. But permissiveness went only so far. Nobody wanted to hang out with a girl who had "a reputation," Miller said. "I guess the social mores accepted smoking, accepted drinking, but did not accept early sex."

There were, of course, many women who had clear-cut religious reasons for avoiding sex outside wedlock. But for a great many others, virginity had become a social convention without any real ethical roots. Rather, they saw it as a commodity that made women more valuable in the marriage market, and they tried to divert their boyfriends into sexual activity that would leave them satisfied without risking penetration. "We called it the TVA—the Technical Virgins Association," said one coed of the mid-'60s. The task was made all the more challenging because many women of the era found oral sex disgusting. "Now don't turn up your nose and make that ugly face," warned the author of *The Sensuous Woman* in 1969 before embarking on a discussion of oral sex.

The country had been wedded to the old Victorian belief that women had a much lower sex drive than men and that women were the ones responsible for drawing the line. For a boy, manliness meant pressing his dates to go farther, ever farther. It was the girl's duty to call a halt. "A man will go as far as a woman will let him. The girl has to set the standard," a college student told George Gallup. It was the girl who had to decide whether French-kissing on the second date was too fast, how much touching could take place and where. Advice columnists doled out leaflets with titles such as "Necking and Petting and How Far to Go," and boys reported to their friends whether they had gotten to second base or third.

If a home run had been hit, a gentleman never told—unless, of course, the girl in question had a reputation and was therefore fair game. Girls with reputations got asked out on dates for only "one thing," and most people believed they forfeited their chance of a good marriage. In the movies, unmarried women who were sexually active were punished with a life of lonely solitude or sudden death. (Elizabeth Taylor won the 1960 best actress award for *BUtterfield 8*, in which she played a "party girl" whose decision to reform wasn't enough to save her from a fatal car crash.) The most popular actress of the early 1960s was Doris Day, who specialized in playing a working woman protecting her virtue against handsome men who schemed to deflower her. Since Day was well into her 30s at the time, the films drove home the point that a woman was never too old to resist extramarital sex.

The virginity rule was a reason for early marriage—any delay would increase the chances of straying from the path of virtue. And it was an excellent argument against training women for serious careers. If unmarried women—even those as old as Doris Day—were expected to avoid sex, and if married women were not supposed to work, pursuing a career became something very close to taking the veil.

". . . A Lot More Fun by the Dozen."

In 1961 *Ladies' Home Journal* offered its readers an essay that asked, "Is the Double Standard Out of Date?" In it, writer Betsy Marvin McKinney answered her own question with a definite no. Sex for the sake of sex, without the chance of procreation, could be satisfying for a man, she conceded. His only job, after all, was to release some sperm. But a woman was built to have babies, and for her, sex for pleasure alone was far more frustrating than simply remaining chaste. Doris Day knew what she was doing, and once women started behaving like men in the bedroom, life tilted out of balance. "The end of the world would come as surely as atomic warfare could bring it," McKinney warned grimly.

One reader who came away less than convinced was Helen Gurley Brown, an ad-agency executive in her late 30s who had worked her way up from typist to secretary to a high-salaried copywriter in Los Angeles, all the while sleeping with whatever men took her fancy. She paid her own way in the world, supporting her widowed mother and disabled sister back in Little Rock and plunking down cash for an expensive, if used, Mercedes-Benz. That car impressed David Brown, a film producer who had been burned in the past by extravagant women who expected him to pay the bills. They married, and Brown urged his new wife to write an advice book for young women on how to live a modern single life. McKinney's article got Gurley Brown focused, and her response, *Sex and the Single Girl,* was published in 1962. It became a bestseller "that torpedoed the myth that a girl must be married to enjoy a satisfying life," as the cover bragged in bright yellow letters.

It also became one of those books that define an era. Whether Gurley Brown converted large numbers of people to a new way of thinking or simply announced a change that was already well under way, she captured the mood of the moment. Many American women were beginning to realize that they might be fated to be single for a long time, whether they liked it or not. Those who left school without a mate found the demographics stacked against them. Tradition dictated that they marry a man somewhat older than they were, which meant searching among the scanty population born during the war or competing with younger girls for the first wave of male baby boomers. Georgia Panter, who began a career as a stewardess at 23, said that even a job that put her in constant contact with planes full of businessmen didn't produce many prospects: "It was rare that I met single men." Gurley Brown suggested that her readers should just enjoy affairs with other people's husbands: "The statistics merely state that there are not enough *marriageable* men to go around. Nobody said a word about a shortage of *men.*"

Sex and the Single Girl announced that the single woman, "far from being a creature to be pitied and patronized, is emerging as the newest glamour girl of our times." Unlike her married sisters, Gurley Brown declared breezily, the single woman got to spend her life in the interesting public world of men. She could have almost all the fruits of marriage—financial security, a nice home in which to entertain, an active social life. Children could be put off till later or borrowed for the occasional day from a harried friend or relative. "Her world is a far more colorful world than the one of PTA, Dr. Spock, and a jammed clothes dryer," Gurley Brown declared. It was the polar opposite of the conviction that George Gallup brought back from his surveys—that married women were much happier than their single sisters.

The section of the book that really caused a stir was the one in which Brown gave her single girl the right to extramarital sex—lots of extramarital sex. ("You do need a man of course every step of the way, and they are often cheaper emotionally and a lot more fun by the dozen.") For the new breed of single girl, sex was simply another part of her full, exciting life, just like dinner parties and a well-decorated apartment. It was pretty much the same game plan that *Playboy* had been urging on its male readers with so much success and profitability—except that *Sex and the Single Girl,* with a keen eye to its audience, also promised that at the end of all this glamorous independence, there would still probably be a husband. A *better* husband, in fact. Gurley Brown warned the young women of the 1960s that the men who were real catches were not looking for innocence and submission anymore; they wanted a wife who was both interesting and capable of pulling in a good paycheck. She caught her "brainy, charming, and sexy" movie producer because she had spent seventeen years becoming the kind of woman a rich, fascinating man would want to live with. "And when he finally walked into my life I was just worldly enough, relaxed enough, financially secure enough . . . and adorned with enough glitter to attract him."

"We Weren't of the Mind-Set of Saving It for the Husbands Anymore."

The sexual revolution hit hardest and fastest in big cities and in campus communities. But no one who read a newspaper or went to the movies could miss that something new was going on. A series of court decisions had made it far more difficult to ban pornography of any stripe, and the nation's ever-vigilant marketing community responded by churning out sexually explicit movies, books, magazines, and plays. On Broadway, audiences poured in to see the musical *Hair,* which featured onstage nudity and a cast that cheerfully sang, "Masturbation can be fun." A well-known designer introduced a topless women's swimsuit, and although only a few thousand customers actually bought one, the publicity and jokes made it seem as if everybody was going to the beach clad in just a bikini bottom. A fad for topless dancers in bars started in San Francisco, and everyone knew that at the fashionable Playboy Clubs, drinks were served by those glamorous "Bunnies" in their scanty costumes. (Before her incarnation as a feminist leader, Gloria Steinem was famous for her article "I Was a Playboy Bunny," in which she went under cover to discover that the costumes were extremely uncomfortable, the pay low, and the turnover rapid.)

There was certainly a lot more talk about sex, but it's hard to tell how much of it translated into real-world activity. Women had never shared all that much information about their sexual behavior, even with friends. Marie Monsky, who was living on her own in Manhattan and working her way through night school in the early 1960s, hung out with a fairly sophisticated crowd. But she still doesn't remember having a frank discussion about sexual experience. "There was a line you never crossed," she said. "It was a privacy issue." So it's possible that what looked like a great deal of sexual freedom was actually just a great deal more sexual frankness.

Alfred Kinsey had stunned the nation in 1953 with his famous study that found half of American women had had sex before they were married. (The study was limited to white women—Kinsey, like most of the nation, seemed indifferent to what African-Americans, Hispanics, Asians, or other minorities were doing with their private lives.) His findings were denounced as absurd, unbelievable, and morally suspect—the American Medical Association accused him of setting off a "wave of sex hysteria," and given the fact that Kinsey interviewed only people who had volunteered to talk about the most private aspects of their lives, there was reason to question whether the results were representative of the population as a whole. But his conclusions about women and premarital sex were probably close to the mark. Most of the sexually active single women he found had slept with the men they believed would be their future husbands, something that had always been common, if not readily admitted. (As far back as 1695, a minister visiting New York wrote home that young people there seldom married until "a great belly puts it so forward that they must either submit to that, or to shame and disgrace.")

But as the '60s rolled along, it seemed clear that quite a few respectable middle-class young women had ditched the double standard completely. And the respectable middle-class young men responded enthusiastically. "There was a tremendous amount of sex," said Barbara Arnold, who was a nursing student at the University of Bridgeport. "There was a tremendous amount of, literally, free love. There were just orgies all over the place. . . . It was a very crazy time, it really was." Pam Andrews—whose mother, Lillian, was one of the post-war housewives who enjoyed the new suburbs so much—arrived at Wellesley in 1968 and quickly went to a Planned Parenthood clinic and got a diaphragm. "I think I was one of the early ones," she said. But her classmates soon caught up with her, and when she transferred to the University of Wisconsin in 1970, Andrews found that the spirit of free love was completely in bloom. "You could sleep with everybody. Everybody was very open. It was such an unreal world." Sex in those days, she remembered, "was nothing special—just another way to get to know somebody."

In 1972 a survey of eight colleges found that less than a quarter of the women were still virgins in their junior year—the same proportion as men. "We weren't of the mind-set of saving it for the husbands anymore," said Tawana Hinton, who started college in 1970. "You know, it's like, if it feels good, do it. That was the rule. I don't have to be madly in love. It's not all about love; it's really just . . . no big deal. Pretty much everybody was on the Pill . . . and STDs and HIV wasn't of concern. Your only concern back then was, don't get pregnant."

"I Probably Wouldn't Have Done This if It Weren't for the Pill."

The young Americans who took part in the sexual revolution were living at a very particular moment in time, a brief window in which having sex with multiple partners posed very little physical peril. For most of human history, syphilis had been a scourge, and a good deal of the Victorian hysteria about sex—and prostitution in particular—had to do with women's fear that their husbands would stray and infect them with an incurable disease that could put them in peril of sterility, insanity, and death. Parents who feared their children would not be impressed by the moral arguments against premarital sex had an excellent follow-up: the Victorian version of sex education involved lantern shows of pictures of the grisly effects of syphilis. Then penicillin, which became widely available during World War II, provided a cure. By the 1960s sexually transmitted diseases were being treated like a joke by middle-class people who, as the decade went on, began experimenting with group sex, wife-swapping, and other kinds of behavior that would have been regarded as near suicidal by earlier generations.

And then there was the birth control pill, or—as the media called it in deference to its awesome powers—the Pill. The *Times*, in its survey of college cohabitation, noted that all the female roommates described in the story were taking it. "I probably wouldn't have done this if it weren't for the Pill," said Joan, the student who wistfully noted that her parents still thought she was a good girl. The older generation tended to agree with Joan—they blamed the birth control pill for what they saw as a frightening upsurge in premarital sex. "I think that's when morals started to deteriorate, because women weren't afraid they were going to get pregnant anymore, so why not?" said Louise Meyer in Wyoming. Her youngest daughter, who was born in 1968, wound up living with her future husband before they were married, she noted. It was something she felt her older girls, who had been born in the early '50s, "would never have done."

The fact that the birth control pill had been invented did not necessarily mean a woman could get it. In 1960, the year the Pill went on sale, thirty states had laws restricting the sale or advertising of virtually anything related to birth control. The most draconian was in Connecticut, where anyone convicted of using, buying, or helping someone to acquire a birth control device could be fined or sentenced to up to a year in prison. The law was not one of those moldy pieces of antique legislation that the lawmakers had simply forgotten to repeal. Margaret Sanger, the birth control pioneer, had launched an attempt to eliminate it in 1923, and a bill to modify or repeal it had come up continually ever since. "It is a ridiculous and unenforceable law," complained a state senator from Greenwich in 1953, one of the few years in which advocates for change ever managed to get as far as a full debate. (The repeal bill was defeated on a voice vote by what the *Times* reported as an "overwhelming" majority.)

The law did not have much effect on middle-class married women, who could quietly get a prescription from the family doctor. But anyone who needed to go to a clinic—poor women or unmarried women seeking anonymity—was out of luck. Connecticut's Planned Parenthood League ran a van service transporting women in need of birth control pills across the state line to clinics in Rhode Island or New York. (Driving to Massachusetts would have been no help for unmarried women, since the law there barred anyone—even doctors—from helping them obtain contraceptives.) In 1958 the head of Connecticut Planned Parenthood, Estelle Griswold, designed a plan of attack. Griswold, a gray-haired, middle-aged woman of eminent respectability and an equal amount of feistiness, invited Dr. Charles Lee Buxton, the chairman of Yale Medical School's Department of Obstetrics, and Fowler Harper, a Yale law professor, to her home for cocktails. "Her martinis were always notorious," said Catherine Roraback, a New Haven attorney. Soon after, Harper called Roraback and asked her to join the team that was going to challenge the law.

"Are you calling me as an attorney or a single woman?" asked Roraback.

Harper laughed and acknowledged that having a counsel who represented the people who suffered most under the Connecticut law would be a fine thing.

"Well, I'm not taking it," rejoined Roraback, who did not want to be a token. But she added quickly, "I'll do it as an attorney."

Harper was both a Yale professor and a famous free-speech advocate who had been an outspoken critic of the anti-Communist witch hunts of Senator Joseph McCarthy and his followers. Roraback had defended some of the victims of McCarthyism for little or no fee, and it was for that reason that Harper wanted to invite her into what everyone believed might be a history-making, career-building case.

"I think you deserve something like this," he said.

They brought their first case on behalf of a group of clients that included Dr. Buxton, who argued that he was being denied his right to practice medicine; a woman who had been warned that she would die from another pregnancy; and a couple who had had three disabled children. The case went up to the Supreme Court, which rejected it on the grounds that the laws were not actually being enforced.

That was true only if you were a middle-class woman with a private physician. "All of us knew—and Lee Buxton especially knew—that poor women couldn't get contraceptive advice," said Roraback. The last family-planning clinic had closed long ago, and hospitals did not deal in birth control because they knew they would be prosecuted. But because there were no clinics to prosecute, there were no plaintiffs who had standing to bring a case. A Catch-22.

So Griswold and Buxton opened a clinic. The Connecticut Planned Parenthood Center of New Haven immediately attracted customers, even though the women were warned that the police might arrive at any moment. "If they do that, we'll just sit down here until we get the information we came for," replied one patient. But Roraback was worried that the women's privacy might be compromised during a raid. She went to see the local prosecutor and arranged for three volunteer clinic patients to testify that they had indeed received contraceptives. Griswold and Buxton were given the choice of appearing at the police station on their own or being dramatically arrested, handcuffed, and hauled off before the TV cameras. Representatives of an older, more discreet generation, they opted for the police station. They were fined $100—and given the legal grounding they needed to go to court to challenge the law.

In 1965 the Supreme Court ruled 7 to 2 that Connecticut's law violated married couples' constitutional rights, and in 1972 the Court closed the circle by tossing out the Massachusetts law as well, making it clear that the right to use birth control belonged to everyone, not just to married couples. (In 1973, in the ultimate American benediction, the Internal Revenue Service declared that the Pill was a tax-deductible medicine.) All around the nation, women lined up to get prescriptions. "We had an option, so you took it," said June LaValleur, who had always felt using a diaphragm "kind of broke up the spontaneity of things."

Unmarried women who did not have a personal physician—or whose family doctor might disapprove—continued to have a harder time, especially if they were not living in big cities with liberal attitudes toward sex. In the 1960s, in most states, the age of adulthood was 21, and it was illegal for a doctor to prescribe birth control to an unmarried woman under that age without a parent's consent. It was not until the 1970s that Congress, embarrassed by the fact that young men of 18 were being sent off to the war in Vietnam while they were still legally children, passed the Twenty-sixth Amendment, which reduced the age of majority to 18. Until then, even unmarried 20-year-olds generally had to claim they were engaged and on the verge of marriage to cadge a birth control prescription from a physician.

College health services slowly began prescribing birth control pills for students who wanted them, and some parents made sure their children arrived on campus with a supply already in hand. When Tawana Hinton started college in 1970, her mother marched her off to the gynecologist. "It was like, 'You will go to college on the Pill,'" Hinton recalled. "And I did."

Planned Parenthood clinics were another crucial source—Alison Foster remembered that her boarding school ferried interested students to the nearest clinic. "And when I was in college, it was like candy," she said. "You just went to the health center and they gave them to you." But only 4 percent of the women who were taking the Pill in 1969 got it through Planned Parenthood, and even those who had the name of a sympathetic doctor were sometimes too embarrassed to follow through.

Wendy Woythaler got the Pill while she was at Mount Holyoke in the late '60s, and when she looks back, she remembers searching for an office down a dark alley: "It was probably a fine, upstanding gynecologist somewhere in town. But when you're thinking, 'I'm not supposed to be doing this', it feels like you're going down a dark alley."

"There was a stigma attached to it if you weren't married," said Maria K. "I didn't want to go to the drugstore and buy birth control pills because everybody would know I was having sex. Oh, heavens!"

"Whores Don't Get Pregnant."

For every Linda LeClair, who seemed to have her finger right on the '60s zeitgeist, there were many more young women like Maria K. Maria—whose mother had wound up cooking in a home for elderly women when her father died—walked into the new morality without the sophistication to protect herself from its consequences. She got the news she was pregnant while she was working as a secretary at a local college in a small town in upstate New York. "At that time, if you got pregnant, you either got married or you went away and came back unpregnant," she said.

In 1967, when Maria had her child, the idea that an unmarried woman would simply raise a baby herself was almost unheard-of, particularly in small towns. Most girls just married the father. Others got abortions or went off to homes for unwed mothers, where they gave the baby up for adoption and returned from what was generally described as a long stay with an out-of-town relative. Judy Riff remembered that one of her friends at their all-girls Catholic college got pregnant her sophomore year, "and one minute she was there and the next minute she was gone. It was like she was never there. . . . I don't know what happened to her." The very idea of having a baby out of wedlock "was just so awful. . .," Riff said, "that probably would have to be the worst thing that could have happened to any of us."

Most women had no idea how to obtain an abortion, which was illegal everywhere until the late 1960s. Maria, who was Catholic, never considered the option. Consulting her parish priest, she went to a home for unwed mothers in a nearby city. She was interviewed on arrival by a "kind, compassionate, and practical" woman who told her that the baby's chances of being adopted would be low. The man who fathered Maria's baby was blind, and at a time when adoptive parents had a large supply of illegitimate babies to choose from, any hint of a possible imperfection could be disqualifying. "She said even though it couldn't be genetically passed on to my son, that he would be very difficult to adopt if it was known that one of his parents was not sighted. And she told me that I seemed like a nice girl and she believed . . . that I would make a good mother."

When Maria decided to keep her son, her mother told her that a baby is always a wonderful thing and behaved "like an angel," her daughter recalled. But otherwise, "I became an outcast." She had trouble finding a landlord who would rent to an unmarried mother, and she lost her job. "I think they probably thought I was a bad example in the college atmosphere and so forth." And far worse trouble was around the corner. "About a year and a half later, I was pregnant again. And I was really up a creek."

When she got the news, Maria broke down in the doctor's office. "Everybody's going to think that I'm a whore," she cried.

"Whores don't get pregnant," the doctor said. "They're smarter than that."

"Remember, All of Us Had Taken the Pill."

The Pill had been developed by Dr. Gregory Pincus, a biologist recruited by Margaret Sanger, who was more successful in revolutionizing medical contraception than she was in lobbying the Connecticut state legislature. It posed unique questions when it came to safety. Unlike most medication, it was intended to be taken over long periods of time by healthy women. Risks that might seem acceptable if you were, say, controlling diabetes loomed a lot larger if there was no disease to cure. Cases of blood clotting were reported, and women began to worry that they were being put at risk of heart attacks or strokes. The Food and Drug Administration began research, and in 1970 a Senate committee headed by Gaylord Nelson of Wisconsin held hearings on the Pill's safety. Some women immediately noticed that all the senators doing the investigating were male—no small surprise, since 99 percent of the Senate was of one gender and Margaret Chase Smith couldn't be everywhere. But all the people invited to speak were men as well. Barbara Seaman, the author of the powerful book *The Doctors' Case Against the Pill*, had not been invited. There were no women scientists or consumers who had experienced bad effects. "Remember, all of us had taken the Pill, so we were there as activists, but also as concerned women," said Alice Wolfson, who led a protest that disrupted the proceedings.

The FDA eventually ordered that birth control pills come with an insert describing possible health risks, and a Gallup survey found that 18 percent of those who had been taking the Pill stopped. Many turned to intrauterine devices (IUDs)—until the most popular model, known as the Dalkon Shield, had to be pulled from the market due to questions about its own safety. Meanwhile, researchers were discovering that the Pill was far stronger than necessary. Gradually, the amount of estrogen dropped to less than a third of what was in the earliest versions, and progesterone to less than a tenth. The controversy over the Pill died away, but it turned out to be only the first shot in what would become a long-running feud between American women and the traditional medical community.

For generations, women had been American doctors' best clients and abused guinea pigs. When physicians learned how to use a hypodermic syringe in the mid-nineteenth century, one of the first things they did was to inject opium or morphine into their patients, sometimes on a daily basis, creating legions of addicted housewives. Surgeons removed reproductive organs in women who showed signs of promiscuity or masturbation, and castrated more than 100,000 around the turn of the century. And although those abuses were long over by the 1960s, there was still a widespread presumption that a woman's uterus became useless once she passed childbearing age and should be removed—often along with her ovaries—for minor problems or as a precaution against disease developing in the future. When a doctor discovered a lump in a patient's breast, it was standard procedure to have the woman sign a form consenting to have the entire breast removed even before the biopsy was performed. (Susan Ford, whose mother, Betty, saved many American women's lives by being open about her mastectomy when she was first lady, noted that in those days, the patient woke up to discover she "either had a Band-Aid or no breast.")

Doctors, who were overwhelmingly male, had an authoritarian attitude toward all patients in the postwar era, but they saw more women, and they were particularly inclined to treat female patients as children who panicked easily and were better off knowing as little as possible. When 23-year-old Barbara Winslow of Seattle found a lump in her breast, she and her husband went to a doctor. He told them that he would do a biopsy and that if it proved malignant, he would immediately perform a complete mastectomy. He then handed a consent form to her husband to sign. When Winslow asked why she was not the one asked to give permission, the doctor said, "Because women are too emotionally and irrationally tied to their breasts." Nora Ephron wrote that it seemed every week brought "a new gynecological atrocity tale. A friend who specifically asks not to be sedated during childbirth is sedated. Another friend who has a simple infection is treated instead for gonorrhea, and develops a serious infection as a side effect of penicillin. Another woman tells of going to see her doctor one month after he has delivered her first child, a deformed baby, born dead. His first question: 'Why haven't you been to see me in two years?'"

In 1969 a small group of women in Boston decided to get together and share their "feelings of frustration and anger toward . . . doctors who were condescending, paternalistic, judgmental, and noninformative." As time went on, the group felt it was on to something worth sharing. The members created a course on women and their bodies that in turn became the basis for *Our Bodies, Ourselves,* a book that talked simply and explicitly about sex, birth control, venereal disease, lesbianism, childbirth, and menopause. Lessons on anatomy and basic biology were interspersed with personal testimony, offering the reader the comforting sense that whatever she was feeling or was worried about had happened to somebody else before. "I will tell you that a book we all had was *Our*

Bodies, Ourselves," said Kathy Hinder-hofer, who went to college in the early '70s. "You had to have that." Other women started medical self-help projects, some focusing on informal classes that trained students in basics such as breast examinations, and others evolving into full-blown medical clinics. (A few went over the deep end and began urging women to extract their monthly menstrual flow and perform do-it-yourself abortions with a syringe.) By 1975 nearly two thousand projects were scattered across the United States.

"It Is as Easy as Being the Log Itself."

The sexual revolution was about more than whether women should be able to feel as free as men to have sex before marriage. It was also about whether women—single or married—had as much right to *enjoy* sex. Most postwar manuals on how couples could improve their physical relationship centered on the man. The woman's role pretty much involved lying there. The experts did not generally go as far as the authors of *Modern Woman: The Lost Sex,* an influential postwar diatribe against the nontraditional female that decreed that for a woman, having sex was "not as easy as rolling off a log. . . . It is easier. It is as easy as being the log itself." But they almost all seemed to disapprove of too much aggressive activity on her part. And there was a virtual consensus that women should attain satisfaction from conventional penetration.

Many women had little information about what went on in other people's bedrooms. The popular magazines were vague, and what specifics they did impart were about how to make husbands happy, not how to give wives sexual satisfaction. In a 1957 article called "How to Love Your Husband" in *Coronet,* for instance, author Hannah Lees approvingly described an interview with an "unselfish" wife who admitted, in the language of the era, to faking orgasms:

> "I have never had that feeling," she said, "that wild emotion that many other women have. But my husband, he expects it. I love him. So I try to make him happy." She spread her hands and shrugged, and her face was soft and tender. . . . Maybe her husband was missing something by not having a wife who could match his strong physical need with hers. But I had an idea it made no difference.

Even Helen Gurley Brown, so eager to encourage her readers to have affairs, was silent about what a single girl should do if she didn't enjoy the sex—except to suggest seeing a psychiatrist. And less than half of married women and 38 percent of single women said they talked frankly about sex with their friends or female relatives, according to that famous Gallup survey. Even if they did share confidences, what they learned could often be misleading. Jane Alpert, a high school student in the early '60s, was part of a cool bohemian crowd in Queens. Her role model, Beatrice, "the first girl I knew who claimed not to be a virgin," bragged to Alpert that she had had vaginal orgasms, "which were the best kind."

While their mothers had not necessarily been reared to expect real physical pleasure from lovemaking, the postwar generation wanted intimacy and partnership in every aspect of marriage. Many women who failed to get much pleasure themselves found solace in creating the illusion of success by writhing, moaning, and simulating orgasm. (Robin Morgan said that when she confessed to her husband that she often faked orgasm with him, she was convinced "I was the only woman in the world sick enough to have done this.") It was no wonder that experts suspected more than half of American women were "frigid."

Many women got reeducated by *Human Sexual Response*. The book, which was published in 1966 by William Masters and Virginia Johnson, was the product of eleven years of direct laboratory observation of nearly seven hundred people who had volunteered to have sex while the authors ran cameras and measured their heart and brain activity. Masters and Johnson found, among many, many other things, that women were capable of more intense and enduring sexual response than men, and that, contrary to what Jane Alpert's best friend told her, vaginal orgasms were not the best kind. While the book itself was written in hard-to-read scientific terminology, it was interpreted, summarized, explained, and debated all over the mainstream media for the rest of the decade.

Women began to argue—out loud—that the right to satisfying sexual experience was important, perhaps right up there with equal pay. In 1970 "Myth of the Vaginal Orgasm," an essay by Anne Koedt, explained that the reason "the so-called frigidity rate among women is phenomenally high" was because men were looking for their mates' orgasms in the wrong place. In a call to action that was copied, reprinted, and shared all around the country, Koedt urged, "We must begin to demand that if certain sexual positions now defined as 'standard' are not mutually conducive to orgasm, they no longer be defined as standard."

American society had always given women only one big responsibility when it came to sex—stopping boyfriends from going too far. Now they seemed to be in charge of everything, from providing the birth control to making sure they had orgasms. A great deal of research was obviously required. Workshops sprouted up on college campuses, offering women tips on all sorts of hitherto-undiscussed matters. Arriving at Antioch as a freshman, Alison Foster showed up for a meeting of the campus women's group. About half an hour into the proceedings, she recalled, "everybody was supposed to look at their cervix. We all got little mirrors." Nora Ephron, reporting on similar gatherings in New York, commented, "It is hard not to long for the days when an evening with the girls meant bridge."

". . . This Velvet Bathrobe."

The sexual revolution was only one part of an extraordinary era, when a large number of relatively privileged young people felt free to plan the reinvention of the world, confident that the world would pay attention. They had an unprecedented amount of time to devote to the task because the still-booming economy made it easy to drop in and out of the job market at will. The cost of living was very low, particularly for those who were willing to share space in a rural farmhouse or urban tenement. Travel was cheap, and airlines gave students special passes that allowed them to fly standby for cut-rate prices. When you got to wherever you were going, there was almost always a bed where you could crash for the night in the apartments of fellow members of the youth culture.

Political activists shut down their universities over the war in Vietnam, free speech, or the administration's failure to accept their advice on matters ranging from how to invest the endowment to where to locate the new gym. And even the most apolitical took part in the cultural revolution—a '60s watchword for everything from hippie communes to the Beatles. Standards for fashion and physical appearance underwent a drastic makeover. Clothes became comfortable, colorful, and dramatic. Girls tie-dyed everything, dipping knotted fabric into bright colors to produce psychedelic patterns. ("I ruined many a sink in the dorm," recalled Barbara Arnold.) They bought long, loose-fitting peasant dresses and blouses and vintage clothes. "I was really part of that hippie, thrift-store, make-your-own-blouses-out-of-your-mother's-linen-tablecloth scene," said Alison Foster. She still has a very clear memory of the moment she stopped liking anything the department stores sold and gave her patronage to the secondhand shops downtown. "I'd go to the East Village and buy funky furs and velvet coats. . . . I loved that stuff." When it was time to dress up for Sunday dinner at her boarding school, Foster donned "this velvet bathrobe—which I thought was the height of sophistication. It wasn't even mine. It was my roommate's, but I wore it as many times as I could get away with it." The whole point, she concluded, was being creative "and not looking like our parents. That was very important to me. I look at kids now and I'm wearing very similar clothes to what a lot of the girls wear. But those days I didn't want to look like my parents."

It was nothing personal. Alison Foster got along very well with her mother, Anne Wallach. She had not minded being the only girl in her circle whose mother worked, "and I liked it that she didn't hover." Still, whether a young woman adored her mother or loathed her, if she grew up in the '60s, she probably vowed that her life would be far different—more exciting, less concerned about what the neighbors would think, more in touch with her feelings, more *real*. (Or, as Wellesley College's 1969 student commencement speaker, Hillary Rodham, put it: "A more immediate, ecstatic, and penetrating mode of living.") And no matter what else she did to align herself with the revolutions at hand, clothing marked her as part of the brave new world of change and adventure.

Everything was supposed to be natural. Some women stopped shaving their legs, which quickly turned into a political issue. There was, recalled Anselma Dell'Olio, "a tendency to gauge one's feminist credentials by look, address, and degree of hairiness." (A letter writer to the *Times* denounced "arm-pit Feminists, women whose involvement with the ethic of body hair has overpowered other considerations.") It was easy to wear shorter skirts because panty hose had arrived on the scene. Basically the same leotards that dancers had always worn, panty hose quickly displaced stockings as the undergarment of choice. (Wendy Woythaler's mother was shocked at the idea of throwing out two legs' worth of panty hose when only one had a run in it, so she cut off the offending legs and told her daughter to wear a pair with a good right leg over a pair with a good left. "Oh God, it was awful." Woythaler sighed.) And it was easy not to bother with skirts at all, because by the end of the decade women had given themselves permission to spend their entire lives in jeans if they felt like it. "I used to have to go to an army/navy store to buy blue jeans," recalled Alison Foster. "There was a point where nobody sold blue jeans. And then everybody sold blue jeans."

Black women let their hair blossom out into Afros, and white college students let theirs fall straight down their backs, banishing the nighttime roller routine. Neither style, unfortunately, was always as easy to achieve in reality as in theory. Most white women did not actually have perfectly straight hair, and many resorted to ironing it. Some black women discovered that their hair, when left to its own volition, just hung there. "I decided I was going to show some of my blackness and have this Afro," said Tawana Hinton. "My hair was long, and I did it by trying to roll it and wet it. . . . It didn't work. It didn't last but a minute, you know." Josie Bass, who had given up trying to get her hair to cooperate, was invited to a dance at the University of Maryland by a student she fancied, who himself sported an impressive Afro, so she went downtown and invested in an Afro wig. She was so intent on her errand she didn't really notice that one of the many urban riots of the era was beginning to break out. "The dance was canceled and I never wore that wig." She laughed.

"I Thought I Was the Only Person Like that in the World."

It looked for a while as though the sexual revolution applied to only heterosexuals. "The whole idea of homosexuality made me profoundly uneasy," said Betty Friedan. The leader of the National Organization for Women had a tactical concern about the fact that opponents had tried to undermine the movement by depicting it as a lesbian cabal. But beyond that, it was pretty clear Friedan, like many Americans, was just uncomfortable with "the whole idea."

For most of history, lesbianism was so little understood that it was actually pretty easy for gay women to live out their lives in peace and quiet. (When Martha Peterson, the Barnard president who fought the Linda LeClair wars, died in 2006 at the age of 90, the *Times* obituary surprised many alumnae when it reported that she was "survived by her companion, Dr. Maxine Bennett.") Women had always slept together—the draftiness of most homes made cuddling up in bed extremely popular. And they had traditionally expressed their friendship for one another in intense terms that involved kissing and hugging and declarations of love. The shortage of men after major wars created a large population of unmarried women who often lived together. No one ever thought they were sharing their lives for any reason beyond companionship and convenience.

A woman who was attracted to members of her own sex thus had an easy time hiding it, if she chose to do so. But she probably had a hard time putting her feelings in any positive context. "I thought I was the only person like that in the world," said Carol Rumsey, who was 18 in 1960 when she felt stirrings for her girlfriend, the Jackie Kennedy look-alike. They were spending a last day together before the friend's impending marriage, "and we went to the movies and it was cold in Connecticut—and we got in the backseat and we snuggled up and we were just talking and all of a sudden we kissed and that was, you know, the first time that ever happened to me." And like many other women in her circumstances, Rumsey responded to her discovery by pretending nothing had changed and getting unhappily married.

At the time, while conservatives saw homosexuality as a sin, liberals saw it as an illness. (When *Ms.* began publication in 1971, an early issue assured readers that letting their sons play with dolls would not lead them into homosexuality, since "boys become homosexual because of disturbed family relationships, not because their parents allow them to do so-called feminine things.") No one had much of anything positive to say about it. *Time*, which had put the author Kate Millett on the cover when it wrote a glowing article about the women's liberation movement in 1970, rethought the whole issue when Millett acknowledged she was gay. The revelation about Millett's sexuality, *Time* said, was "bound to discredit her as a spokesman for her cause, cast further doubt on her theories, and reinforce the views of those skeptics who routinely dismiss all liberationists as lesbians."

Homosexuality was almost never referred to in the mainstream media, and when it was, the references were generally oblique—jokes that could go over the heads of more innocent readers and viewers. In the movies, gay characters were the cause of problems, if not disaster. In 1961 *The Children's Hour,* starring Audrey Hepburn and Shirley MacLaine, tackled the subject of lesbianism with sensitivity and an ending depressing enough to make the *BUtterfield 8* finale look like a situation comedy. Hepburn's and MacLaine's characters, the owners of a boarding school for young girls, are falsely accused of having an "unnatural" affair by an extraordinarily unpleasant student. They sue unsuccessfully for libel, and the school is destroyed. Curiosity-seekers come to gawk outside the house, and MacLaine—who turns out to have been nursing a secret passion for her friend all along—hangs herself in the bedroom.

The first attempt by lesbians to organize publicly may have been the Daughters of Bilitis, founded in 1953 in San Francisco. (By 1970 the editors of their magazine, *The Ladder*, felt they had made enormous progress when they proudly estimated that each issue was read or at least seen by "approximately 1,200 people.") Gene Damon, a writer for the magazine, said that to be a lesbian was to be regarded as "automatically out of the human race" and that she was constantly being asked questions such as "But what do you Lesbians do in the daytime?" Damon contributed an essay to the feminist book *Sisterhood Is Powerful* in 1970 that captured the feelings of persecution: "Run, reader, run right past this article, because most of you reading this will be women . . . and you are going to be frightened when you hear what this is all about. I am social anathema, even to you brave ones, for I am a Lesbian."

"Society Has Begun to Make It as Rough for Virgins . . ."

The prophets of the sexual revolution had more in mind than simply eliminating the double standard. The big thought of the 1960s was that sex should become a perfectly natural part of everyday life, not much more dramatic and profound than a handshake. If people would just give up the idea of sex as a sacred act between a man and a woman eternally bonded together, the argument went, they could throw off their repressions and inhibitions. Sharing and good feeling would triumph over jealousy and negativism. The world could make love, not war. The other famous slogan of the '60s—"If it feels good, do it"— might mean more than just an excuse for self-indulgence. It might mean a happier society or even world peace. The hippie movement in particular gave great credence to the idea that if people were busy taking off their clothes and coupling, they were not likely to be in the mood for more negative activity.

Alison Foster experienced that side of the sexual revolution very suddenly, after spending her first two years of high school at a private all-girls school in Manhattan with a very strong sense of decorum. "We had dances where they literally had a ruler—if you were dancing too close, the ladies would come and separate you." She transferred in 1970 to a progressive boarding school, where she discovered a very different world. "Everybody was sleeping with everybody. Professors were sleeping with students. I had a poetry teacher sleeping with a tenth grader. "We had professors modeling in the nude in our art classes. We had a lake that we would all skinny-dip in. So I went

from what I thought was this very sophisticated New York girl to—oh my God, I am so over my head." She loved the school. ("Everybody was talking about feelings. It was just the kind of thing I liked.") But she saw the damage that the new theories about free love could do. "I had friends— they acted like it didn't bother them, but they felt very bad the next morning when he didn't call. I figured out pretty early on that I wasn't going to do that. That I could figure out."

The pressure to give in to the code of free love was a lot more difficult to resist when it was ideological as well as personal. A 1966 novel called *The Harrad Experiment* was an enormous hit on college campuses (to the tune of 2.5 million copies sold in a year and a half), and it was one of those bestsellers that attracts readers with its ideas, not riveting prose or well-drawn characters. *Harrad* was the tale of a group of wholesome college students brought together to learn how to experience sex in a completely honest, open atmosphere. By graduation, the heroes and heroines have, as promised, taken "the long step away from primitive emotions of hate and jealousy" and formed a six-person group marriage. "Every Sunday when my new husband for the week joins me in my room, I feel like a new bride all over again," reported one of the women. "Sometimes I wake up in the night and for a sleepy moment I may forget whether I am with Stanley, Jack, or Harry, and then I feel warm and bubbly." As the curtain fell, they were on their way to settle in an underpopulated state out west, where they planned to take over the legislature and create a utopia where every young citizen would have the right to a free college education, along with cohabitation, nude beaches, and humanistic group sex.

The ideology of the sexual revolution meshed into another '60s phenomenon, the political upheaval known as the New Left. Although young leftists came in all sorts of packages, many saw monogamy as just another form of private property, and free love as a kind of socialism of the flesh. "Certainly it was a time of fairly extensive sleeping around, a time when couples who remained monogamous were not proclaiming the fact from the rooftops," said Priscilla Long, a writer and political activist. Jane Alpert, who had traveled a long road from her high school in Queens to a Lower East Side household of two men and two women in intertwining relationships, became suspicious of a new couple her lover wanted to bring into the circle. "I considered their intention to marry reason enough to exclude them," she said.

Of course, if sex was all about *sharing*, anyone who refused to share was seen, in some quarters, as selfish or repressed or both. "I think there was subtle pressure," said Pam Andrews. "You were a truly liberated person that was going to build a new world, a new idealistic world." Women were still in charge of drawing the lines but were left with fewer arguments against going all the way. Rejected men told them they were sexually repressed or accused them of failing to sympathize with the fact that the men might be drafted for the war in Vietnam. At the time, one woman compared the men she knew to "rabbits," adding, "It was so boring you could die." While most women would not have wanted to go back to a time when they were expected to save themselves for the man they would marry, some did feel that things had gone overboard. "The invention of the Pill made millions for the drug companies, made guinea pigs of us, and made us all the more 'available' as sex objects," raged Robin Morgan. "If a woman didn't want to go to bed with a man *now* she must be hung up."

Gloria Steinem wrote that "in the fine old American tradition of conformity, society has begun to make it as rough for virgins . . . as it once did for those who had affairs before marrying."

GAIL COLLINS is an American journalist, op-ed columnist, and author who is most recognized for her work with *The New York Times*.

EXPLORING THE ISSUE

Is There Still a Double Standard of Sexuality for Women and Girls?

Critical Thinking and Reflection

1. How do legislative measures to limit access to birth control represent the perpetuation of traditional sexual double standards?
2. How do media discourses on women, women's appearance, and expressions of women's sexuality support public notions of a sexual standard?

Is There Common Ground?

Do men gain social status from engaging in casual sex from multiple partners? Is there a social stigma attached to women who engage in this behavior? These questions underlie the debate about the existence of a sexual double standard. Further complicating the notion of the sexual double standard are the gendered perceptions about men, women, and statutory rape. Women, such as teachers, who engage in sexual behavior with younger males or underage boys, perhaps students, may be perceived more negatively than men who commit similar non-forcible transgressions.

Issues of power and control relative to women's sexual agency and traditional subjectivity as a sexual object raise cultural hackles over what constitutes acceptable social behavior. The gendered application of rules premised on culture-based constructs of femininity and masculinity continue to create figurative boxes for social interaction. Such rules continue to have very real and restrictive implications for how people enact and experience the social scripts that guide the individual expression of sexuality.

Additional Resources

Koon-Magnin, S. and Ruback, R. (2012). "Young Adults' Perceptions of Non-Forcible Sexual Activity: The Effects of Participant Gender, Respondent Gender, and Sexual Act." *Sex Roles*, *67*(11/12), 646–658.

Lai, Y. and Hynie, M. (2011). "A Tale of Two Standards: An Examination of Young Adults' Endorsement of Gendered and Ageist Sexual Double Standards." *Sex Roles*, *64*(5/6), 360–371.

Rudman, L., Fetteroif, J., and Sanchez, D. (2013). "What Motivates the Sexual Double Standard? More Support for Male Versus Female Control Theory." *Personality & Social Psychology Bulletin*, *39*(2), 250–263.

Create Central

www.mhhe.com/createcentral

Internet References . . .

AlterNet: Alternative news

http://www.alternet.org/story/86736/he%27s_a_ stud%2C_she%27s_a_slut%3A_the_sexual_double_ standard

The Good Men Project

http://goodmenproject.com/sex-relationships/ the-sexual-double-standard-and-you/

Selected, Edited, and with Issue Framing Material by:
Rachel Pienta, *Valdosta State University*

ISSUE

Should the Word Slut Be Redefined?

YES: Laurie Penny, from "Let's Get Those Sluts Walking," *New Statesman* (June 10, 2011)

NO: Feona Attwood, from "Sluts and Riot Grrrls: Female Identity and Sexual Agency," *Journal of Gender Studies* (vol. 16, no. 3, November 2007)

Learning Outcomes

As you read the issue, focus on the following points:

- How might redefining the term slut be counterproductive to feminist objectives?
- How does popular culture influence our perception of what it means to be a slut?

ISSUE SUMMARY

YES: Laurie Penny, in "Let's Get Those Sluts Walking," examines the underlying issues behind the SlutWalk movement and the implications for women and their sexuality.

NO: Feona Attwood, in "Sluts and Riot Grrrls: Female Identity and Sexual Agency," advocates for a reclamation rather than a redefinition of the word slut.

The word "slut" became the focal point of much debate after January 2011 when Toronto police constable Michael Sanguinetti, during a rape prevention talk, offered a tip to women students, advising them to "Avoid dressing like sluts." The public discourse that followed ignited activism across several continents. The first SlutWalk, organized by Heather Jarvis and Sonya Bennett, was held in Toronto on April 3, 2011. More SlutWalks would follow as women on college campuses and in major cities across the globe organized marches and rallies in protest.

In "Let's Get Those Sluts Walking," Laurie Penny examines the word "slut" within the framework of contemporary culture. Penny compares historical meanings of the word with modern notions of what it means to be a slut and asserts that, in contemporary society, "a slut is any woman with the audacity to express herself sexually." According to Penny, this use of the word slut as a derogative term to denigrate women exemplifies the hypocrisy that dominates the popular discourse on female sexuality. Penny advocates that women reject terms such as slut that are used to evaluate women's purity. Furthermore, Penny recommends that women take a stand against any

efforts to classify them according to how they express their sexuality.

In "Sluts and Riot Grrrls: Female Identity and Sexual Agency," Feona Attwood deconstructs the term slut and examines how the definition and usage of the word has evolved. Attwood chronicles how the word slut has been used to denote and connote various negative associations about women and their sexual behavior. Her literature review illustrates how the word has historically been used, alternately, to control or shame women.

Attwood asserts that a redefinition of the word slut is unnecessary and potentially counterproductive to feminist objectives. She suggests that embracing the word slut and appropriating it to denote a way to transgress prescribed social mores offer one avenue for expression. However, Attwood reminds readers that women have traveled this road before with the word bitch. While the act of "linguistic appropriation" can, in and of itself, be an inherently powerful act, there is a fine and often easily blurred line between embodiment and empowerment. Attwood concludes by saying that the discussion of a possible redefinition of the word slut is more powerful and potentially more productive than an actual redefinition.

YES

Laurie Penny

Let's Get Those Sluts Walking

What is a slut? In the past, the word was used simply to mean any woman who didn't behave: a woman who was "dirty, untidy or slovenly," a slack servant girl, a woman who failed to keep her house in order and her legs closed before marriage, a woman who invited violence and contempt. Today, in a world sodden with images of shorn and willing female bodies, a slut is any woman with the audacity to express herself sexually. That should tell you everything you need to know about modern erotic hypocrisy.

On 11 June, London hosts a SlutWalk. The phenomenon began in Toronto after a local policeman instructed a group of female university students to stop "dressing like sluts" if they didn't want to be raped, a point of view not unique among men in positions of power. The protest that followed has infected the imagination of women in cities around the world, from Dallas to Delhi, who are sick of being bullied and intimidated into sexual conformity.

We like to think that we live in a liberal, permissive society—that, if anything, the problem is that there is too much sex about. This is a cruel delusion. We live in a culture that is deeply confused about its erotic impulses; it bombards us with images of airbrushed models and celebrities writhing in a sterile haze of anhedonia while abstinence is preached at the heart of government.

In Britain, the release of an official report declaring that girls are being too "sexualised" has coincided with parliamentary lobbies for young women to be "taught to say no." Join the dots with police officers telling women that "no" is insufficient if they happen not to be dressed like a nun and an ugly picture begins to form. What we're looking at is a concerted cultural backlash against female sexual liberation.

Give Us Protection

Sex is not the problem. Sexism is. Arbitrary moral divisions are being renewed between "innocent" women and "sluts." Young women, in particular, are expected to look hot and available at all times, but if we dare to express desires of our own, we are mocked, shamed and threatened with sexual violence, which, apparently, has nothing to do with the men who inflict it and everything to do with the length of skirt we have on. Some of us have had enough.

Faced with savage public opprobrium, told that our sexuality is dirty and dangerous, today's young women would do well to take inspiration from the gay rights movement.

For decades, LGBT protesters have marched to demand the right to express their sexuality without fear of victimisation and to show that, whatever society thinks of them, being queer is not a source of shame, a threat to innocence or an invitation to violence. Like them, sexually active women deserve protection just as much as those whom polite society considers "pure."

Some may wish to reclaim the word "slut" to celebrate its implications of bad behaviour. What's more important is that we refuse to let the word sting, or draw distinctions between "good" and "bad" women, based on outdated notions of sexual purity. Now, more than ever, it's time for "sluts" to walk—and walk tall.

LAURIE PENNY is a British columnist, blogger, and author who often writes for the New Statesman.

Feona Attwood

 **NO**

Sluts and Riot Grrrls: Female Identity and Sexual Agency

. . .

Girls. Feminists. Sluts

Attempts to reclaim the term 'slut', like all such reclamations, involve contradiction and difficulty. This difficulty manifests in a variety of different sites where women try to appropriate and disturb existing meanings of gender. In the TV series *Sex and the City*, a text that has become emblematic of the mainstream celebration of female sexuality, Carrie Bradshaw uses the term as a way of trying to articulate what is new and possibly uncomfortable about contemporary women's sexual behaviour: 'Are we simply romantically challenged or are we sluts?' (Season 3, Episode 6, 2000). While 'slut' signifies a move away from a traditional—feminine, romantic—sexuality quite clearly, it is less successful in providing a positive model for what this move is *towards*, unless it is what has previously been understood as a masculine sensibility conceptualized as predatory, episodic, recreational, public and risky. Indeed, the first episode of *Sex and the City* begins with the question, 'Can women have sex like men?' (Season 1, Episode 1,1998). Given the longstanding association of active female sexuality with pollution, it is not surprising that attempts to envisage women as sexual actors quite self-consciously use male sexuality as a model. Lady J's 'How to be as horny as a guy' (1999), a submission to the third-wave Grrrl zine *Bust*, for example, exhorts women to cultivate an active and pleasurable sexuality by swapping 'expendable girlie activities' for male ones: masturbating, objectifying the opposite sex, talking about sex, using porn and making orgasm central to everyday life. The difficulty of positively equating women with sexuality is not only visible in cultural texts, but in the experiences of girls and women. In their discussion of the way the related term 'slag' is used amongst adolescents (1981), Cowie and Lees note its complexity and slipperiness, the lack of clear criteria in the way it is applied, its ambiguous use which slides between 'friendly joking', 'bitchy abuse', 'threat' and 'label' (p. 12), the blurriness of distinction that makes it so easy for girls to pass from 'drag' to 'slag' (p. 15) and which demonstrates what a 'very narrow tightrope' girls have to walk in order to achieve the impossible state of being sexually attractive 'without the taint of sexuality' (p. 14).

As the history of the term shows, 'slut' carries a particular class significance. It is the lowly, dirty, sleazy quality of the slut that marks her out, a quality that suggests that overt sexuality in women is precisely not 'classy'. The class connotations of this low and dirty form of sexuality have, of course, been important in developing the aesthetic of sexually explicit media such as pornography—and indeed, in bolstering its condemnation. Pornography, like other forms of carnivalesque low culture, joyfully enacts the overturning of accepted cultural values, revelling in natural urges, physical pleasure and in the body as 'insistently material, defiantly vulgar, corporeal' (Kipnis, 1996, p. 132). Indeed, Constance Penley has argued that pornography, like various other forms of bawdy culture, displays a 'white trash sensibility', expressed through bawdy humour, obscene language, attacks on the middle classes and the valorization of 'trickster women with a hearty appetite for sex' (Penley, 1997, pp. 89–112).

Although we should be wary of seeing all pornography as challenging in this way, and of overemphasizing its transgressiveness, the work of writers like Kipnis and Penley is useful in highlighting how representations of sexuality which focus on the 'low' rely on particular categories of gender, class and race. As Matt Wray and Annalee Newitz have argued, the term 'white trash' is both a 'classist slur' and a 'racial epithet' that marks out some whites as 'a dysgenic race' who are 'incestuous and sexually promiscuous, violent, alcoholic, lazy, and stupid' (1997, p. 2). Emily White's research also indicates that 'the slut is usually a white girl' (2002, p. 166). Future work on the use of the term 'slut' might contribute to the development of our understanding of the way representations of class, gender, race and sexuality are interrelated and what the implications of this are for a feminist theory and practice which is concerned with the way female sexuality is constructed. Kipnis' example is of the film maker and performance artist Jennifer Reeder, who adopted a 'White Trash Girl' persona, and who argues that attacking race, class and gender norms can function quite radically: 'there's this power in being trashy' (in Kipnis & Reeder, 1997, p. 119). For Reeder there is also a strong link between her White Trash Girl persona, Riot Grrrl and a 'new school of feminism' which swaps what she sees as second-wave victim status and 'whining' for 'female anger and craziness', 'taking responsibility for yourself' and playing with femininity—'you can be a bombshell and wear black panties and still be really smart' (in Kipnis & Reeder,

1997, p. 130). In this way, sexuality becomes a position of power and a point of resistance: 'Fuck *me*? No, fuck *you*' (in Kipnis & Reeder, 1997, p. 115).

As Reeder's comments suggest, this kind of strategy avoids the straightforward opposition of earlier feminist reactions to the way women's sexuality is constructed, replacing it with a more complicated response which puts the ambiguity and difficulty of representing female sexuality at the service of women. Linda Williams' (1993) discussion of Annie Sprinkle's work describes the potential of this kind of strategy. Sprinkle has become an object of feminist fascination because of the playful way she has developed her work in the sex industry as a prostitute and porn star who is also a sex educator, performance artist and academic. Williams takes up an argument made by Tania Modleski about the way patriarchy defines women, for example, by using the term 'whore' to 'saturate' them with sexuality. She suggests that embracing patriarchal terms, as Sprinkle does, may offer women a position of sexual agency, if it involves what Judith Butler has described as 'subversive repetition'. In the realm of sexual performance, this repetition may produce 'an articulation of something that is not named in "whore": her own desire' (Williams, 1993, p. 180), and a re-signification of female sexual identity. Williams argues that Annie Sprinkle employs such a wide variety of sex acts, objects and personae in her work that she disturbs patriarchal definitions of sexual normality, transforming them by going 'beyond' rather than 'against' them. This is, in Judith Butler's term, 'a reversal of effects' (1997, p. 14) in which the repetition of injurious speech becomes the 'constitutive possibility of being otherwise' (1997, p. 102). Here, 'the word that wounds becomes an instrument of resistance . . . a repetition in language that forces change' (1997, p. 163). Reappropriations of the term 'slut' may work in a similar way to Annie Sprinkle's performances, by upsetting categories, boundaries and hierarchies. This is true not only in relation to the display of appropriate sex and gender characteristics, but in the way other markers of status are evaluated. The DIY ethos of Riot Grrrl challenged conventions about the musical skills necessary for public performance and about relations between performers and audiences, while Sprinkle's work, mixing up the personae of whore, porn star, sex educator, artist and academic, disturbs the traditional ordering of such occupations in terms of their value.

The challenge to established order mobilized in many deployments of the term 'slut' is, as I have noted, also apparent in the recent reclamation of 'girl'. The struggle over 'girl' is interesting as a site in which femininities and feminisms are fought over by women and provides the broader context for understanding the changing significance of the term 'slut' and of women's sexual objectification. Nowhere is this more apparent than in the contrast between the approach to signifiers of femininity taken by Riot Grrrl in the 1990s and the women's movement in the 1970s. For example, the practice of writing 'slut' on the body is a gesture that parallels the celebrated myth of bra-burning associated with second-wave feminism, and provides an interesting demonstration of the different strategies used by women to challenge dominant notions of femininity.

Although feminist bra-burning is mythical, a second-wave feminist protest against the Miss America Pageant in 1968 did involve throwing 'woman-garbage' such as girdles, false eyelashes and curlers into a 'Freedom Trash Can' (CWLU Herstory Website Archive). While this form of protest enacted the removal of cultural signifiers which conceal and distort the real, body writing manipulates and questions the real through the redeployment of cultural signifiers. The difference between these two gestures says a great deal about the changes between the cultural moments in which they occur, and about the different political strategies that make sense within those moments. The first depends on the notion of a 'natural' femininity and of 'real' meaning, or at least on a belief that it might be possible to remove all existing definitions and start again. It also reveals a deep suspicion of cultural signifiers in general, and the artefacts of femininity in particular. Clothing is seen as especially suspect in this respect, and feminine clothing and accessories are understood as forms of artificial imposition and imprisonment. But in the second example there is an attempt to refashion femininity from existing items, a form of bricolage that insists there is no essential meaning 'underneath' and that meaning depends precisely on intent, placement, combination and performance. As Mary Celeste Kearney writes, Riot Grrrl performance style shunned the celebration of 'femaleness' and attempted to 'show how genders are socially constructed' (1997, p. 221). This style demonstrated a self-awareness which has been part of the increased reflexivity of contemporary cultural movements and the way they express resistance (Leonard, 1997, p. 246).

This difference in approach can also be seen in the association of second-wave feminism with distinctly 'unfeminine' clothes such as dungarees, compared to the more playful relationship with clothing adopted by many Riot Grrrls who chose to wear 'bunched hair and hairslides with patterned dresses' (Leonard, 1997, p. 235). As Ted Polhemus has noted, Riot Grrrl style juxtaposes 'little-girl dresses with Fredericks of Hollywood tacky glamour, rugged boots, small-town-American second-hand garments, and, especially in the USA, prominent tattoos or piercings' (1994, p. 123). This practice of bricolage which messed up child and adult, girlie girl and man, practicality and glamour, mainstream and alternative style, worked to reinvent and recirculate all kinds of meanings. Courtney Love, the most visible performer to be identified with Riot Grrrl,[1] adopted a rather less playful 'kinderwhore' look, combining very girly, sometimes torn, 'babydoll' dresses with heavy and often smudged make-up[2]; 'a slutty, D.I.Y. subversion of the traditional Prom queen look' ('Kinderwhore', *Wikipedia*).

Kim Nicolini (1995) argues that the slut persona as performed by Love involved a rejection of both 'Good Girl' and 'Good Feminist' roles in order to 'take all the mess of female sex and throw it into the public eye'. Combining pretty and ugly qualities; the babydoll and the witch, 'the glistening sex doll and the screeching life buried under the pink plastic', Love created an 'attraction/repulsion dynamic' capable of making audiences question their attitudes towards female sexuality. As Reynolds and Press say, 'it's as though one of Charcot's female patients has taken charge of her own theatre of hysteria and transformed the humiliation of being an exhibit into an empowering exhibitionism' (1995, p. 262). This kind of performance, embodied by Love, but evident elsewhere in girl subcultures, is a complicated kind of alchemy, on the one hand transforming a position of shame and powerlessness into one of confrontation, yet on the other maintaining a sense of ambivalence and hybridity. The awkwardness of this is particularly evident in performances of the slut persona which often literally signify difficulty by appearing cheap, loud, ugly, noisy, broken, repellent, used and out of control, Other and abject, monstrous and possessed. The 'mess' of female and femininity—essence and artifice—appropriates male space and behaviour in loud, angry public appearances. It disturbs the limits of acceptable feminine behaviour and the boundaries of heterosexual style and performance. Gillis and Munford argue that this can be understood as an attempt to capture 'the contradictions shaping female identity for young women whose world has been informed by the struggles and gains of second wave feminism' (2004, p. 169). For example, Love's performance involved a 'dramatic subversion of the polarity between "power" and "victim" feminisms' which characterized key feminist positions in the US during this period. It also combined the characteristics of individualism, combatism, and celebrity with feminist critiques of beauty and male dominance (Gillis & Munford, 2004, p. 172).

What is notable here is the shift from an earlier 'second-wave focus on the politics of representation to an emphasis on the politics of self-representation' and an interrogation of agency (Gillis & Munford, 2004, p. 173). This shift can also be traced in mainstream culture in the growing fascination with Madonna's status as 'postmodern icon and material girl *par excellence*' in the 1980s and early 1990s. In both instances, celebrity, the body, sex, style and language become central in developing and debating contemporary forms of feminist and feminine practice. Although many critics have deplored the sexualized femininity apparent in these manifestations of 'girl power', it is important to recognize that in some cases, an engagement with the pleasures of femininity may function to destabilize existing categories of gender, while providing a space for younger women who 'selfidentify as feminist, but do not necessarily relate to existing (second wave) feminist institutions' (Munford, 2004, p. 148).

How liberating it may be to engage with sexualization has continued to be a matter of debate in the years since the rise of Riot Grrrl. Certainly, to perform the slut

continues to be a risky business. Since the death of her husband, singer, Kurt Cobain, in 1994, Courtney Love has become a regular object of ridicule and abuse in the mainstream press, a position that is attributable to her apparently druggy, bad mother, disrespectful widow and still 'slutty' behaviour.[3] During this same period, the Riot Grrrl practice of writing on the body has been mainstreamed in high street fashion. T-shirts emblazoned with all manner of terms for the sexual woman—'Bitch, Whore, Vixen, Tart . . . Slut . . . Saucy, PUNK, Hard Bitch, Nice Girl, Sex Kitten, Hustler, Sexy, Fluffy, Chick, Porn Star'[4]—have become commonplace. As Rosalind Gill argues in her commentary on the best-selling 'fit chick unbelievable knockers' T-shirt popular in 2002, this process has worked to hypersexualize women's bodies, and is emblematic of the way in which a figure of 'the autonomous, active, desiring subject has become . . . the dominant figure for representing young women' (Gill, 2003, p. 105).

However, the extent to which this hypersexualization represents a positive development for female sexual subjectivity remains a source of dispute. Christine Griffin argues that the space and performance of youthful femininity continues to be difficult precisely because of the continuation of a double standard (2005, p. 3), and is newly so because of contemporary neo-liberal ideals of individual freedom which *oblige* girls to 'be free' and 'have fun'. Griffin's recent research with girls suggests that they must now struggle to perform as the ideal 'sassy girl' who is 'in a state of perpetual youth, assertiveness and optimism', neither too 'girly', nor a 'tomboy' (2005, p. 5). This figure offers the potential to experiment with sexualized practices such as the adoption of revealing clothing, but these are still ambiguous in their significance and potentially risky in signifying sluttiness rather than sassiness (2005, p. 9).

In a similar vein, Buckley and Fawcett explore the changing relationship between young women, sexuality and identity as it is expressed through fashion and leisure in the 'party city' of Newcastle-upon-Tyne (2002, p. 122). They note that in this context young women engage with sexualization, adopting tight, revealing clothing and socializing in 'raucous' girl groups, putting themselves 'on show' in public space (2002, p. 135). They argue that women appear confident, assertive, uninhibited and fun-loving in this context, and that the spectacle they present may even be read as 'heterosexual camp, a hyperfemininity that carries a disorientating visual power and positions women centre-stage in the contemporary urban landscape' (2002, p. 138). However, such a reading would downplay 'local anxieties about the status of masculinity in a city in which traditional industry has been decimated' (2002, p. 138), and in a region characterized by poverty, low educational expectations and the worst record in Britain for teenage pregnancies and sexually transmitted diseases (2002, p. 142).

Gleeson and Frith describe a research project with young women which suggests that tight, revealing 'sexy' clothing and high heels function as important markers for young women in moving away from their younger 'immature, asexual femininity' (2004, p. 105). Yet they note that girls are evasive about the sexual significance of the clothing they adopt, resisting the researchers' attempts to read them in terms of their production of sexualized identities. They argue that not only does this suggest that sexualized clothing practices are an ambiguous source of anxiety and pleasure, but that ambiguity itself may be 'an important resource for young women in a context where being explicit about sexual intentions is inherently fraught' (2004, p. 107). Ambiguity is embraced as a 'crucial means for women to negotiate their way through contradictory identities as women who are attractive without actively seeking admiring glances, who are sexual but not too sexual, and who are clothed without deliberately creating a look'. In this sense, ambiguity becomes a 'powerful resource which allows women to negotiate meaning and position' (2004, p. 112).

Similar negotiations are found in girls' relationships with other facets of popular culture. As Bettina Fritzsche's work with Spice Girl fans shows, young women may use even the most mainstream of performances as a 'toolbox' in which the imitation of celebrity, fashion and dance styles becomes an important way of trying out forms of feminine self-presentation and experimenting with the performance of sexiness. Fritzsche argues that it is important that we 'learn to understand the very common, playful and body-centred ways that girls cope with society's scripts of identity', not least in order to help girls 'pursue aspects of their own identity which do not conform' (2004, p. 161).

What links these pieces of research is a concern with making sense of what looks like younger women's engagement with elements of a consumerized, sexualized culture which an earlier women's movement saw as a key source of women's oppression. In this sense, struggles over sluttiness have become more politically charged in the twentieth and twenty-first century, and in the last ten years they have also become part of a struggle over feminism itself. Making sense of this struggle is not easy. As Gillis and Munford note, there is considerable confusion about the application of key terms such as post-feminism and third-wave feminism which second-wave feminist academics have tended to use interchangeably. In addition, there have been two very different usages of the term post-feminism, one associated with the demise of feminism and often linked to 'mainstream media representations of feminism' (Gillis & Munford, 2004, p. 166), and another which describes a form of post-structuralist feminism which stresses plurality, difference and deconstruction (2004, p. 168). That difference and deconstruction are also characteristics of third-wave feminist practices *and* of some mainstream post-feminist representations, that second-wave feminists have until very recently largely ignored the existence of third-wave feminism, and that most third-wave feminists have distanced themselves

from any form of academic feminism has only served to complicate this situation.

A sense of confusion and struggle marks debates in contemporary feminism, especially where these cross generational boundaries. This is clearly shown in the significance attributed to the term 'girlie' by third-wave feminist writers, Jennifer Baumgardner and Amy Richards. They describe it as a joyous 'state of being' signifying a 'fierce, fun independence' (2004, p. 61), 'a strong and distinct feminist identity' which illustrates the difference between second- and third-wave feminism (2004, p. 63). For them, this is a moment in which young women appear to rebel against their mothers and against second-wave feminism which seems to them to be all about what young women 'can't do' (2004, p. 66). As such, the term is an object of anger and pain for older feminists. In this form of generational politics, young feminists—Riot Grrrls and girlies— are positioned as 'rebellious daughters who refuse to conform to the rule book of their second wave mothers'. But it may be argued that, whoever initiates this positioning, all that is reinforced is a conflict which threatens the progress of feminist politics. Gillis and Munford argue that a different understanding of feminist history, not as a 'succession of waves' in which 'generations are set up in competition with one another' (2004, p. 176), is necessary if women are not doomed to keep 'reinventing the wheel' (2004, p. 177).

As Susanna Paasonen points out, the relation between the adoption of figures of unruly women, young women, third-wave feminism and related movements may be overstated. Documenting the prominence of the term 'bitch' in the late 1990s in Riot Grrrl and other girl sites, pop music, feminist art projects, and in self-help and 'popular power feminist writings' (2005, p. 210), she nevertheless argues that bitches 'have been articulated as figures for emancipated women in the 1970s, 1980s, 1990s and 2000s alike— despite the obvious differences in historical context, with notably similar turns of phrases' (2005, p. 222). Moreover, 'linguistic appropriation as a means of creating spaces for female networking and self-representation' (2005, p. 212) is 'a long-standing feminist practice' (2005, p. 223). Thus, while it may be useful to examine the common ground between contemporary modes of women's expression and their emphasis on difference, sexuality, individuality and individualism, there is a danger of overstating the extent to which these 'new' forms of feminism are clearly distinguishable from—and preferable to—'old' forms (2005, p. 223). In the process, the many different positions that have been taken by feminists on sexuality, technology and popular culture since the 1970s are made invisible (2005, p. 226).

An understanding of the differing contexts in which women struggle over sex, technology, culture and terminology is clearly important if we are to appreciate what is at stake in that struggle. In the contemporary moment, 'slut' functions for some as an impossible space, the space of contradictions that cannot be resolved in language, theory or practice; the source of conflict between generations and feminisms; a trap and a dead end. And certainly, 'slut' has its limits, threatening to obscure as much as it illuminates and always running the risk of merely reproducing a form of 'hate speak' against women. For others, it is precisely its impossibility that marks it as a potentially productive site, a space of resistance, change and new possibility. Whatever position we take, the reclamation of 'slut' provides an interesting development in this term's history, and it is important as a starting point for illuminating how women continue to engage with the representation of female sexuality. Whether our focus is the way 'slut' is used to police women's behaviour, the significance of sluttiness in popular culture, or its appropriation in mainstream and subcultural practices, an understanding of the ways it might unite or divide us as women and as feminists is crucial.

Notes

1. Courtney Love is often mistakenly identified with Riot Grrrl. However, she does share many stylistic characteristics with Riot Grrrl performers. Reynolds and Press identify her as one of the '90s angry women' of popular music (1995, p. 261).
2. It is thought that the kinder-whore look originated with Kat Bjelland of Babes in Toyland.
3. Love's vilification still continues. In 2005, the British men's weekly magazine ran a story on her affair with British comedian Steve Coogan, under the headline 'You put your cock in that?', reporting that Love had 'nasty, lumpy breasts' and 'had an awful lot of sex' with her 'previous owners' (in Turner, 2005, p. 28).
4. Listed at the *Fluffy Mules* website under 'Fashion Rants'. These are good examples of a 'porn-chic' trend in which previously restricted imagery or terminology is recirculated in the mainstream, but in a relatively tame way. *Fluffy Mules* makes fun of this trend by listing 'Bad Ass Hard Gal' T-shirts that 'should exist but won't' for the purposes of comparison: 'I've got crabs, I'm a DVDA sort of gal, I smell of pee, I did the whole team, I shagged your dad, I just masturbated, This is a stuffed wonderbra'. See *tinyninjas* for an example of 'Slut' shirts and other products at http://tinyninjas.com/store/cpshop.cgi/4152686719.

References

Baumgardner, J. & Richards, A. (2004) Feminism and femininity: or how we learned to stop worrying and love the thong, in: A. Harris (Ed.) *All About the Girl: Culture, Power and Identity* (New York and London: Routledge).

Besson, R. G. (1997a) How to make a sacred slut today. *New Age Quest: Dominant–Submissive Lifestyle*, Available at: http://newagequest.com/DS/makeslut .html, accessed 20 July 2004.

Besson, R. G. (1997b) The slut and spiritual sexuality. *New Age Quest: Dominant–Submissive Lifestyle*, Available at: http://newagequest.com/DS/sacredslut .html, accessed 20 July 2004.

Buckley, C. & Fawcett, H. (2002) Doon the toon: young women, fashion & sexuality, *Fashioning the Feminine: Representation and Women's Fashion from the Fin de Siecle to the Present* (London and New York: I.B. Tauris).

BUST (n.d.) Slut! Whore! What does it all mean?? discussion in the BUST lounge, Available at: http://lounge.bust.com/discus/messages/13/36392 .html?1117859104, accessed 4 July 2005.

Butler, J. (1997) *Excitable Speech: A Politics of the Performative* (New York and London: Routledge).

Cowie, C. & Lees, S. (1981) Slags or drags, *Feminist Review*, 9, pp. 11–21.

CWLU Herstory Website Archive (n.d.) No more Miss America! (1968), Available at: http://www.cwluhistory .com/CWLUARchive/miss.html, accessed 16 July 2005.

Fluffy Mules (n.d.) Fashion rants: 'Bad-Ass Slogan T-shirts', Available at: http://www.btinternet .com/~virtuous/fluffymules/fashion_rants/slogan-tshirts .htm, accessed 12 July 2004.

Fritzsche, B. (2004) Spicy strategies: pop feminist and other empowerments in girl culture, in: A. Harris (Ed.) *All About the Girl: Culture, Power and Identity* (New York and London: Routledge).

Gill, R. (2003) From sexual objectification to sexual subjectification: the resexualisation of women's bodies in the media, *Feminist Media Studies*, 3(1), pp. 100–106.

Gillis, S. & Munford, R. (2004) Genealogies and generations: the politics and praxis of third wave feminism, *Women's History Review*, 13(2), pp. 165–182.

Gleeson, K. & Frith, H. (2004) Pretty in pink: young women presenting mature sexual identities, in: A. Harris (Ed.) *All About the Girl: Culture, Power and Identity* (New York and London: Routledge).

Griffin, C. (2005) Impossible spaces? Femininity as an empty category, paper presented at *ESRC Research Seminar Series: New Femininities*, University of East London, December.

Kearney, M. C. (1997) The missing links: riot grrrl–feminism–lesbian culture, in: S. Whiteley (Ed.) *Sexing the Groove: Popular Music and Gender* (London and New York: Routledge).

Kinderwhore (n.d.) *Wikipedia*, Available at: http://en.wikipedia.org/wiki/Kinderwhore, accessed 17 July 2005.

Kipnis, L. (1996) *Bound and Gagged: Pornography and the Politics of Fantasy in America* (New York: Grove Press).

Kipnis, L. & Reeder, J. (1997) White trash girl: the interview, in: M. Wray & A. Newitz (Eds) *White Trash: Race and Class in America* (London and New York: Routledge).

Lady J. (1999) How to be as horny as a guy, in: M. Karp & D. Stoller (Eds) *The BUST Guide to the New Girl Order* (New York: Penguin).

Language Log, Available at: http://itre.cis.upenn.edu/~myl/languagelog/archives/000538.html, accessed 4 July 2005.

Leonard, M. (1997) Rebel girl, you are the queen of my world: feminism, 'subculture' and grrrl power, in: S. Whiteley (Ed.) *Sexing the Groove: Popular Music and Gender* (London and New York: Routledge).

Lindentree, L. & Mortale, B. (n.d.) The original whore with the heart of gold: how the sacred prostitute fell from grace and how she may return, Available at: http://newagequest.com/DS/sacredessay.html, accessed 20 July 2004.

Mills, J. (1991) *Womanwords: A Vocabulary of Culture and Patriarchal Society* (London: Virago).

Morris, G. (n.d.) Interview with Annie Sprinkle, *Bright Lights Film Journal*, Available at: http://www.brightlightsfilm.com/16/annie.html, accessed 27 April 2004.

Munford, R. (2004) Wake up and smell the lipgloss: gender, generation and the (a)politics of girl power, in: S. Gillis, G. Howie & R. Munford (Eds) *Third Wave Feminism: A Critical Exploration* (Basingstoke: Palgrave Macmillan).

Nicolini, K. (1995) Staging the slut: hyper-sexuality in performance, *Bad Subjects: Political Education for Everyday Life*, 20, Available at: http://eserver.org/bs/20/Nicolini.html, accessed 26 April 2004.

Paasonen, S. (2005) *Figures of Fantasy: Internet, Women and Cyberdiscourse* (New York: Peter Lang).

Penley, C. (1997) Crackers and whackers: the white trashing of porn, in: M. Wray & A. Newitz (Eds) *White Trash: Race and Class in America* (London and New York: Routledge).

Polhemus, T. (1994) *Street Style: From Sidewalk to Catwalk* (London: Thames & Hudson).

Reynolds, S. & Press, J. (1995) *The Sex Revolts: Gender, Rebellion and Rock n Roll* (London: Serpent's Tail Press).

Roget, P. M. (1995) *Roget's II: The New Thesaurus* (3rd edition), edited by the Editors of the American Heritage® Dictionaries (Boston: Houghton Mifflin), available at: http://www.batleby.com/62/.

Sex and the City, Sex and the city, Season 1, Episode 1, 1998, HBO/Time Warner.

Sex and the City, Are we sluts?, Season 3, Episode 6, 2000, HBO/Time Warner.

Slut (n.d.) *Wikipedia*, Available at: http://en.wikipedia.org/wiki/Slut, accessed 4 July 2005.

tinyninjas.com, Available at: http://tinyninjas.com/store/cpshop.cgi/4152686719, accessed 4 July 2005.

Turner, J. (2005) Dirty young men. *The Guardian Weekend*, 22 October pp. 28–37.

Williams, L. (1993) A provoking agent: the pornography and performance art of Annie Sprinkle, in: P. Church Gibson & R. Gibson (Eds) *Dirty Looks: Women, Pornography, Power* (London: BFI).

Wray, M. & Newitz, A. (1997) *White Trash: Race and Class in America* (London and New York: Routledge).

FEONA ATTWOOD is a professor in the Media Department at Middlesex University, UK. Her research is in the area of sex in contemporary culture.

EXPLORING THE ISSUE

Should the Word Slut Be Redefined?

Critical Thinking and Reflection

1. How do gendered notions of acceptable behavior for women influence what it means to be a slut?
2. How does heteronormativity impact gender identity and sexual expression, and what impact does it have on preconceived notions of what it means to be a slut?
3. How do social attitudes about what it means to be a slut perpetuate a rape culture?

Is There Common Ground?

In the United States, the concept of a slut is construed to connote a woman who does not follow certain social rules. Idealized notions of femininity guide our social rules for which women are categorized as sluts. The idea that what a woman wears may mark her as a slut or that attire may mark a woman's sexual availability have been at the core of rape cases in court and have served as incendiary fodder for public discourse.

In February 2012, radio personality Rush Limbaugh referred to 30-year-old law student Sandra Fluke as a slut on his show in the wake of her congressional testimony and health care policy and birth control. His characterization of a young woman advocating for equal access to preventive health care covered by health insurance as a slut asking for government subsidy of her sex life ignited a national firestorm. The ensuing media eruption dominated the airwaves for weeks after the incident and Sandra Fluke became a national figure and, subsequently, a surrogate for President Obama's reelection campaign.

At the root of the controversy was a debate over women's autonomy as sexual beings. The idea that a woman's efforts to regulate her fertility in order to attend school, to serve her nation in the armed forces, or for any other reason are tantamount to licentious or wanton behavior is discriminatory and inhibits women's full participation in society as equal citizens. Men who seek treatment for erectile dysfunction are not categorized as sexual deviants. Similarly, men who opt to undergo a vasectomy are not labeled as sluts either. Under such rules, men enjoy greater privileges and enhanced benefits from social institutions.

Additional Resource

Gibson, M. (2012, March 8). "After Limbaugh, Maybe It's Finally Time to Ignore the 'Slut' Slur." *Time.* Time Inc. Retrieved from: http://newsfeed.time.com/2012/03/08/in-rush-limbaughs-wake-women-are-reclaiming-the-word-slut/#ixzz2NLO1m97k

Create Central

www.mhhe.com/createcentral

Internet References . . .

Time Magazine

http://www.time.com/time/nation/article/0,8599,2088234,00.html

College Magazine

http://www.collegemagazine.com/editorial/3639/Slut-The-Dirtiest-Word-In-The-Dictionary

Huffington Post

http://www.huffingtonpost.com/ashley-knierim/pink-embraces-the-word-slut_b_3193814.html

New York Times

http://www.nytimes.com/2006/07/13/fashion/thursdaystyles/13women.html?_r=0

Selected, Edited, and with Issue Framing Material by:
Rachel Pienta, *Valdosta State University*

ISSUE

Are Women "Hard-Wired" to Be Society's Nurturers?

YES: Andrea L. Meltzer and James K. McNulty, from "Contrast Effects of Stereotypes: 'Nurturing' Male Professors Are Evaluated More Positively Than 'Nurturing' Female Professors," *Journal of Men's Studies* (vol. 19, no. 1, pp. 57–64, Winter 2011)

NO: Jennifer Senior, from "Nurturer-in-Chief: Advice for Hillary Clinton from the Former Prime Minister of Pakistan," *New York* (vol. 40, no. 34, October 1, 2007)

Learning Outcomes

As you read the issue, focus on the following points:

• What are some of the stereotypes women encounter while in leadership roles?
• How might these stereotypes influence behavior both within the leadership role and outside of it?

ISSUE SUMMARY

YES: Andrea L. Meltzer and James K. McNulty, in "Contrast Effects of Stereotypes: 'Nurturing' Male Professors Are Evaluated More Positively Than 'Nurturing' Female Professors," examine the gender stereotypes that contribute to how people form perceptions and influence expectations.

NO: Jennifer Senior, in "Nurturer-in-Chief: Advice for Hillary Clinton from the Former Prime Minister of Pakistan," examines how deeply rooted cultural expectations for gender behavior have real implications for how men and women act in everyday life.

The classic question of nature versus nurture has long dominated discussions about gender behavior. Is biology destiny? What role does socialization play in who we become? How do cultural expectations and social influences impact our notions of what it means to be feminine or masculine? These questions and the potential answers provide rich material for discussion and endless fodder for research.

In "Contrast Effects of Stereotypes: 'Nurturing' Male Professors Are Evaluated More Positively Than 'Nurturing' Female Professors," Andrea Meltzer and James McNulty examine how expectations influence perceptions. Meltzer and McNulty note that prevailing stereotypes contribute to expectations that women are natural nurturers and women who deviate from the perceived norm are negatively perceived. Conversely, they posit, because men are not expected to be nurturers, those men that do exhibit nurturing characteristics are evaluated favorably for portraying an unexpected behavior.

In "Nurturer-in-Chief: Advice for Hillary Clinton from the Former Prime Minister of Pakistan," Jennifer

Senior examines the pitfalls of governing while being a female. In 1988, Benazir Bhutto became the first female to be elected prime minister of a Muslim country. In 2007, Bhutto would end eight years of exile from Pakistan. Jennifer Senior interviewed Bhutto in the months preceding her bid to win back the prime minister's seat. Bhutto was assassinated in December 2007 during her election campaign.

Senior asked Bhutto what words of advice she might offer to would-be presidential candidate Hillary Clinton about the challenges of being a woman leader. Bhutto expressed regret about not being able to comfortably adopt what she characterized as a more nurturing and, for her, more natural woman leader persona during her time in office. According to Bhutto, warmth in a woman leader can be perceived as a weakness. In her case, it seemed that assuming a more nurturing persona was not an option open to Bhutto during her tenure as prime minister. In response to Senior's questions, Bhutto expressed the desire to serve a third time as a warmer, more nurturing leader than she had been previously.

YES

Meltzer and McNulty

Contrast Effects of Stereotypes: "Nurturing" Male Professors Are Evaluated More Positively Than "Nurturing" Female Professors

There is a pervasive belief that men are less nurturing and caring than women. People expect men to be less empathic than women (Graham & Ickes, 1997), for example, less warm than women (Broverman, Vogel, Broverman, Clarkson, & Rosenkrantz, 1972), less nurturing than women (Bem, 1974; Diekman & Eagly, 2000; Sprague & Massoni, 2005), and more aggressive than women (Broverman et al.).

Such stereotypes can lead people to evaluate men less favorably than they evaluate equivalent women in domains that require nurturance and care. One function of stereotypes is that they lead to stereotype-consistent perceptions through processes of perceptual confirmation—the tendency to interpret the details of an event in a manner that is consistent with expectancies (Miller & Turnbull, 1986; see Abel & Meltzer, 2007). Such processes can lead people to perceive men as less nurturing than they perceive equivalent women and, accordingly, to evaluate those men more negatively than they evaluate those women in domains that require nurturance. Several studies provide support for this possibility. For example, fathers are sometimes seen as poorer caretakers than mothers (Bryan, Coleman, Ganong, & Bryan, 1986). Male mental heath professionals are sometimes preferred less than female mental health professionals (Kerssens, Bensing, & Andela, 1997). And male teachers are sometimes evaluated more poorly than equivalent female teachers (Bennett, 1982; Williams, 1992).

But, there are theoretical reasons to believe stereotypes, such as those regarding men's lack of nurturance, may sometimes lead people to evaluate stereotyped targets more *positively* than they evaluate equivalent non-stereotyped targets (Biernat, 2003; Burgoon, 1986; Jussim, Coleman, & Lerch, 1987; Kahneman & Miller, 1986). Although *ambiguous* information tends to be perceived in ways that confirm existing stereotypes, *unambiguous* information can violate existing stereotypes (Herr, Sherman, & Fazio, 1993; see also Biernat, 2003). According to expectancy-violation theory (Burgoon, 1986; Jussim et al., 1987), if unambiguous information about a target violates a stereotype, that information can lead to expectancy-inconsistent perceptions of that target that appear more extreme in contrast to the stereotype (see also Kahneman

& Miller, 1986). Accordingly, unambiguous information that indicates a man is in fact nurturing may serve to make him look particularly nurturing and therefore lead people to evaluate him more positively than they evaluate an equivalent woman in situations that require nurturance. Because women are already expected to be nurturing, however, such contrast effects should not influence evaluations of equivalent women who are equally nurturing.

Indeed, contrary to studies demonstrating that people evaluate men more negatively than they evaluate equivalent women in domains that require nurturance, several other studies indicate that people sometimes evaluate men more favorably than they evaluate equivalent women in such domains (Ambert, 1982; Boulware & Holmes, 1970; Williams, 1992). For example, fathers are not always evaluated less positively than mothers—sometimes fathers are evaluated as better caretakers than mothers (Ambert, 1982). And male mental health professionals are not always evaluated less positively than female mental health professionals—sometimes male health professionals are favored (Boulware & Holmes, 1970). It may be that participants in those studies evaluated men more positively than women because unambiguous information indicated those men were nurturing—which violated the stereotype that men are less nurturing and thus made them look particularly nurturing by comparison. Indeed, the fathers who were evaluated more positively than mothers in Ambert's (1982) study were custodial fathers and thus may have been perceived to be especially nurturing.

Of course, to actually demonstrate that unambiguous information that indicates men are nurturing leads people to evaluate those men more positively than they evaluate equivalent women, research would need to randomly assign participants to receive or not receive such information. Although we are aware of no studies that have used such methods to demonstrate that information that violates stereotypes of men leads to stereotype-inconsistent evaluations of those men, at least two studies have demonstrated that information that violates stereotypes of women leads to stereotype–inconsistent evaluations of those women (Luthar, 1996; Taynor & Deaux, 1973). Taynor and Deaux, for example, asked participants to read a scenario in which an equivalent male or female target provided help in a masculine-oriented emergency situation (i.e., the perpetrator possessed a gun). Likely due to the violation of the stereotype that women are less helpful than men in dangerous situations (Eagly & Crowley, 1986), participants evaluated the helping female more favorably than they evaluated the identical helping male. Nevertheless, given recent evidence that stereotypes shape perceptions of female targets more than they shape perceptions of male targets (Sekaquaptewa & Espinoza, 2004), such stereotype-inconsistent evaluations may only emerge in evaluations of women.

Overview of the Current Research

The current study examined whether information that violates a stereotype about men leads to more positive evaluations of a male target compared to an equivalent female target. Specifically, participants evaluated an ostensible male or female candidate for a job as a university professor who either violated or did not violate the stereotype that men are not particularly nurturing. The university classroom is an ideal context in which to examine this issue because university professors are expected to be at least somewhat nurturing and prior research demonstrates that students expect male professors to be less nurturing than female professors (Sprague & Massoni, 2005). Based on expectancy-violation theory, we predicted that participants would evaluate a "particularly nurturing" male professor more favorably than an identical "particularly nurturing" female professor. . . .

Materials

Professor evaluation. After reading the description of the professor, participants responded to the following 7 items on 4- or 5-point Likert scales: "Do you think Dr. Smith will be well organized and prepared for class sessions?," "Do you think Dr. Smith will speak clearly and distinctly?," "Which do you think would best describe Dr Smith's attitude toward the subject matter?" (ranging from "doesn't like the subject" to "great enthusiasm for the subject"), "Do you think Dr. Smith would return assignments and examinations in a reasonable period of time?," "Do you think Dr. Smith's responses to students' questions in class would be helpful?," "If you needed assistance from Dr. Smith outside of class, do you think you would be able to make satisfactory arrangements for a timely meeting?," and "How do you think you would rate Dr. Smith's overall performance in this course?" All scores were standardized, appropriate items were recoded, and all items were averaged to form a mean evaluation score for which more positive scores indicated more positive evaluations. Internal consistency was slightly lower than desired ($\alpha = .61$) which may call into question any null results.

Results

We tested the primary hypothesis that participants would evaluate a male professor who violated the stereotype that men are not particularly nurturing more positively than

an equivalent female professor through a 2 (Sex of Professor) X 2 (Nurturing) ANCOVA that controlled for participant sex and whether the professor was described as organized or disorganized. . . .

Discussion

Prior work demonstrates that gender stereotypes can lead to evaluative differences of the sexes (see Kunda & Thagard, 1996). Nevertheless, the majority of that work has demonstrated the role of those stereotypes in producing stereotype-consistent evaluations of the sexes, particularly when information about the target is ambiguous. The current work, in contrast, tested the prediction that unambiguous information about a male target that violates an existing stereotype that males are not particularly nurturing can produce stereotype-inconsistent evaluations of him relative to an identical female target in situations that require nurturance. Data were consistent with predictions. Specifically, a male professor described as "particularly nurturing" was evaluated more positively than an identically described female professor, likely due to the violation of the stereotype that men are not particularly nurturing compared to women (Bem, 1974; Diekman & Eagly, 2000; Sprague & Massoni, 2005).

This finding has both theoretical and practical implications. Theoretically, this finding extends previous research on the role of gender stereotypes in evaluations of the sexes. Although several theories (e.g., Biernat, 2003; Jussim et al., 1987; Kahneman & Miller, 1986) suggest that unambiguous information that violates existing stereotypes of men may lead to more favorable evaluations of those men, previous research has only provided strong evidence of such effects in evaluations of women (e.g., Luther, 1996; Taynor & Deaux, 1973). Although stereotypes appear to affect the way people process information about women more strongly than they affect the way people process information about men (Sekaquaptewa & Espinoza, 2004), the current study indicates that stereotypes can have such contrast effects in evaluations of men as well.

Practically, the current findings suggest ways in which people may not only escape the negative implications of various negative stereotypes, but benefit from them. Specifically, in contrast to previous research demonstrating that negative stereotypes can lead people to perceive *ambiguous* behaviors, even those that may actually contradict that stereotype, in a stereotype-consistent manner (see Miller & Turnbull, 1986), the current research indicates that *unambiguous* information can violate negative stereotypes and make targets look more positive by comparison. Accordingly, people from any group that faces a negative stereotype (e.g., men, women, African Americans, Muslims, Caucasians) may actually be able to capitalize on that stereotype by engaging in unambiguous stereotype-inconsistent behaviors that violate the stereotype.

Limitations

Several qualities of this research limit conclusions until these findings can be replicated and extended. First, the fact that the current study examined evaluations of a hypothetical professor limits the generalizability of the findings. Future research may benefit by systematically examining whether similar effects emerge in more ecologically valid settings (e.g., the classroom). Second, although the homogeneity of the samples increased our power to detect effects, it also limited generalizability of the findings. Although we are not aware of any research or theory suggesting that contrast effects may have emerged more readily in the current sample, future research may benefit by examining whether the same effects emerge in other populations. Finally, the current study examined the effects of only one stereotype against one group of people. Future studies may benefit from examining the effects of other gender stereotypes or negative stereotypes about other groups.

References

Abel, M.H., & Meltzer, A.L. (2007). Student ratings of a male and female professors' lecture on sex discrimination in the workforce. *Sex Roles, 57,* 173–180.

Ambert, A.-M. (1982). Differences in children's behavior toward custodial mothers and custodial fathers. *Journal of Marriage and the Family, 44,* 73–86.

Bem, S.L. (1974). The measurement of psychological androgyny. *Journal of Consulting and Clinical Psychology, 42,* 155–162.

Bennett, S.K. (1982). Student perceptions of and expectations for male and female instructors: Evidence relating to the question of gender bias in teaching evaluation. *Journal of Educational Psychology, 74,* 170–179.

Biernat, M. (2003). Toward a broader view of social stereotyping. *American Psychologist, 58,* 1019–1027.

Boulware, D.W., & Holmes, D.S. (1970). Preferences for therapists and related expectancies. *Journal of Counseling and Clinical Psychology, 35,* 269–277.

Broverman, I.K., Vogel, S.R., Broverman, D.M., Clarkson, F.E., & Rosenkrantz, P.S. (1972). Sex-role stereotypes: A current appraisal. *Journal of Social Issues, 28,* 59–78.

Bryan, L.R., Coleman, M., Ganong, L.H., & Bryan, S.H. (1986). Person perception: Family structure as a cue for stereotyping. *Journal of Marriage and the Family, 48,* 169–174.

Burgoon, J.K. (1986, February). *Expectancy violations: Theory, research, and critique.* Paper presented at the annual meeting of the Western States Communication Association.

Diekman, A.B., & Eagly, A.H. (2000). Stereotypes as dynamic constructs: Women and men of the past,

present, and future. *Personality and Social Psychology Bulletin, 26,* 1171–1188.

Eagly, A.H., & Crowley, M. (1986). Gender and helping behavior: A meta-analytic review of the social psychological literature. *Psychological Bulletin, 100,* 283–308.

Graham, T., & Ickes, W. (1997). When women's intuition isn't greater than men's. In W. Ickes (Ed.), *Empathic accuracy* (pp. 117–143). New York: Guilford.

Herr, P.M., Sherman, S.J., & Fazio, R.H. (1993). On the consequences of priming: Assimilation and contrast effects. *Journal of Experimental Social Psychology, 19,* 323–340.

Jussim, L., Coleman, L.M., & Lerch, L. (1987). The nature of stereotypes: A comparison and integration of three theories. *Journal of Personality and Social Psychology, 52,* 536–546.

Kahneman, D., & Miller, D.T. (1986). Norm theory: Comparing reality to its alternatives. *Psychological Review, 93,* 136–153.

Kerssens, J.J., Bensing, J.M., & Andela, M.G. (1997). Patient preference for genders of health professionals. *Social Science & Medicine, 44,* 1531–1540.

Kunda, Z., & Thagard, P. (1996). Forming impressions from stereotypes, traits, and behaviors: A parallell-constraint-satisfaction theory. *Psychological Review, 103,* 284–308.

Luthar, H.K. (1996). Gender differences in evaluation of performance and leadership ability: Autocratic vs. democratic managers. *Sex Roles, 35,* 337–361.

Miller, D.T., & Turnbull, W. (1986). Expectancies and interpersonal processes. *Annual Review of Psychology, 37,* 233–256.

Sekaquaptewa, D., & Espinoza, P. (2004). Biased processing of stereotype-incongruency is greater for low than high status group targets. *Journal of Experimental Social Psychology, 40,* 128–135.

Sprague, J., & Massoni, K. (2005). Student evaluations and gendered expectations: What we can't count can hurt us. *Sex Roles, 53,* 779–793.

Taynor, J., & Deaux, K. (1973). When women are more deserving than men: Equity, attribution, and perceived sex differences. *Journal of Personality and Social Psychology, 28,* 360–367.

Williams, C.L. (1992). The glass escalator: Hidden advantages for men in the "female" professions. *Social Problems, 39,* 253–267.

ANDREA L. MELTZER is an assistant professor of psychology at the University of Tennessee.

JAMES K. MCNULTY is an associate professor of psychology at the University of Tennessee.

Jennifer Senior  **NO**

Nurturer-in-Chief: Advice for Hillary Clinton from the Former Prime Minister of Pakistan

Benazir Bhutto, the former prime minister of Pakistan who has lived in self-imposed exile for eight years, has vowed to return to her country next month to lead her Pakistan Peoples Party in elections. If able to serve a third term as prime minister, she might be a different kind of leader: In August, she told the Council on Foreign Relations that she regretted not being more "nurturing" while in power. "The people wanted me to be there as a woman leader," she said. "I wish I had focused more on that than on the more militaristic notions." It's a dilemma familiar to a certain other woman running for chief executive. Bhutto spoke to Jennifer Senior.

Are there criticisms of Hillary you sometimes hear that you know are code for something else? One thing people often say to me is that Bill Clinton is a very warm leader and that Hillary is much colder. But I think that women leaders tend to be a little bit withdrawn, to protect themselves from unkind comments. When a male leader is warm, it's not misinterpreted. Whereas if a female leader is warm, it can have certain connotations. So a female leader has to be more restrained, in a sense. **When you were prime minister, were you scrutinized, as Hillary so often is, for trivial things, like the fashion choices you made?** Yes. I once had a male opposition leader get up in the assembly and say, "Oh, these white veils she wears, and how she brings them all the way from France!" Which was simply not true. I used to buy them in Pakistan. And then I looked at his shoes. He had bought Bally shoes! I couldn't believe the hypocrisy of it. He took it for granted that no one would scrutinize him! **Did you say anything?** I didn't. I didn't want to be that kind of leader. **Did you also have a hard time earning the trust of other women, at least at first?** I had a lot of support among ordinary women. But women in leadership positions could sometimes be competitive. Those who'd achieved a lot could be my sharpest critics. **Did being a woman influence your leadership in a more subtle way?** I was able to put iodine in salt. And I was able to do that because I shopped for salt. **Why do you think that the U.S. seems to have a harder time with women at the highest level of power than other countries?** In a country like Pakistan or India, when a charismatic leader dies, people are not sure that the traditions he symbolized will continue—there's a lot of illiteracy and there isn't the same access to information. So they tend to transfer allegiance from a male leader to a female descendant, in the hope that his policies will be continued. But in Westernized societies, it's a little different, because people have greater education and greater access to information—they don't have the same need to be sure of the message of the leader. **Any advice for Bill on the campaign trail?** All I can tell him is that either way, you won't win. Not if you disappear and not if you're there campaigning. He'll have to go by his instincts.

Jennifer Senior is contributing editor to *New York Magazine.*

EXPLORING THE ISSUE

Are Women "Hard-Wired" to Be Society's Nurturers?

Critical Thinking and Reflection

1. How do patriarchal notions of women's status in social stratification schemas impact social and cultural barriers that women face when entering arenas historically and traditionally held by men?
2. How do women's potential to become mothers also serve as a possible limitation or restriction to life opportunities?

Is There Common Ground?

The question of women, cultural expectations, and available opportunity can be the basis for unity as well as a source for division. Sheryl Sandberg is the chief operating officer of Facebook. She is also ranked on *Fortune*'s list of the 50 Most Powerful Women in Business and as one of *Time*'s 100 Most Influential People in the World. In her new book, *Lean In: Women, Work, and the Will to Lead*, Sandberg (2013) builds on her 2010 TEDTalk about women and the career barriers they continue to face in the workforce. The book ignited a firestorm among feminists, who reacted negatively to her advice due to what many characterized as Sandberg's relative privilege in the workforce (Chang, 2013). Despite criticism, Sandberg's work has ignited a national discussion about women, privilege, success, and the workplace.

Additional Resources

Chang, A. (2013, March 11). "Why You Should 'Lean In' to Sheryl Sandberg's New Book." *Wired*. Wired.com © 2013 Condé Nast. Retrieved from: www.wired.com/business/2013/03/lean-in-to-sheryl-sandbergs-book/

Kantor, J. (2013, February 21). "A Titan's How-To on Breaking the Glass Ceiling." *The New York Times*. © 2013 The New York Times Company. Retrieved from: www.nytimes.com/2013/02/22/us/sheryl-sandberg-lean-in-author-hopes-to-spur-movement.html?_r=0

Sandberg, S. (2013). *Lean In: Women, Work, and the Will to Lead*.

Create Central

www.mhhe.com/createcentral

Internet References . . .

Mother Jones

http://www.motherjones.com/slideshows/2010/06/female-heads-state-australia-gillard/gillard

Psychology Today

http://www.psychologytoday.com/blog/alpha-females/200809/can-woman-be-great-spouse-mother-and-leader

Women's eNews

http://womensenews.org/story/21-leaders-the-21st-century/121227/21-women-leaders-2013-seven-who-shake-the-status-quo#.UbEJ5_kSqO4

Working Mother

http://www.workingmother.com/nafe-top-companies/2010/03/women-leaders-of-nafes-top-companies

Lean in

http://leanin.org/

Unit 7

UNIT

Women as Objects: Subject to the Male Gaze

*I*s pornography for men different than pornography for women? Are preferences and personal tastes in erotica determined by gender? The popularity of British author E.L. James' erotic 50 Shades of Grey trilogy prompted media debate as women's response to the novels made the books a best-selling international sensation with a planned film franchise to follow.

Professor Gina Barreca (2012) wrote about the 50 Shades craze in her syndicated column. Barreca's take on the books was an indictment of the power dynamic represented in the narrative. In her estimation, the books were more about women's subjugation than women's sexuality. Other women writers across the blogosphere discussed the appeal of E.L. James' work. Blogger Kate Bartoletta (2012) compared the writings of Anais Nin to E.L. James and found 50 Shades pale in comparison. The furor over the novels provides insights to the issues that fuel the debate over what sort of pornography appeals to women.

The release of the Warner Brothers' film Magic Mike further exemplifies the uneasy relationship between pornography and women's sexuality (Carolin 2012). When women shift from erotic object to pornography consumer, a paradigm begins to transform. In one film review, Entertainment Weekly writer Owen Gleiberman (2012) examines an issue worth further consideration:

> Magic Mike *has a conventional structure, yet a teasing question percolates beneath: If selling yourself is as much fun as this movie makes it look, what could be wrong with it? The answer is that once you've sold yourself, losing yourself may not be far behind.*

The notion that pornography is ultimately about the creation and consumption of a product is one aspect of the issue. The flip side of the coin may be how pornography differs when creators or consumers transgress social norms regarding traditional sexual roles. How does pornography change when it is made for a female audience? How is pornography different when women write, direct, or produce the pornography?

Barreca, G. (2012, May 3). "Women Falling for 50 Shades of Degradation." *Hartford Courant*. Retrieved from: www.courant.com/news/opinion/hc-op-barreca-fifty-shades-op-grey-degrades-women--20120503,0,3932862.column

Bartoletta, K. (2012, May 23). "Fifty Shades of Anais Nin." *Elephant*. Waylon H. Lewis Enterprises © 2010. Retrieved from: www.elephantjournal.com/2012/05/fifty-shades-of-anais-nin/

Gleiberman, O. (2012, June 29). "Magic Mike: Movie Review." *Entertainment Weekly*. Retrieved from: www .ew.com/ew/article/0,,20483133_20588015,00.html

Carolin, R. (Producer) and Soderbergh, S. (Director). (2012). *Magic Mike*. [Motion Picture]. United States: Warner Brothers.

Selected, Edited, and with Issue Framing Material by:
Rachel Pienta, *Valdosta State University*

ISSUE

Is Pornography for Men Different Than Pornography for Women?

YES: Chyng Sun, Ana Bridges, Robert Wosnitzer, Erica Scharrer, and Rachael Liberman, from "A Comparison of Male and Female Directors in Popular Pornography: What Happens When Women Are at the Helm?" *Psychology of Women Quarterly* (September 2008)

NO: Jennifer L. Petersen and Janet Shibley Hyde, from "Gender Differences in Sexual Attitudes and Behaviors: A Review of Meta-Analytic Results and Large Datasets," *Journal of Sex Research* (vol. 136, no. 1, February 28, 2011)

Learning Outcomes

As you read the issue, focus on the following points:

- How do gender stereotypes influence perceptions about pornography?
- Can cultural norms influence sexual attitudes and behaviors?

ISSUE SUMMARY

YES: In "A Comparison of Male and Female Directors in Popular Pornography: What Happens When Women Are at the Helm?" Chyng Sun et al. suggest that women pornography directors vary the narrative to portray women as sexual agents rather than solely as sexual objects.

NO: In "Gender Differences in Sexual Attitudes and Behaviors: A Review of Meta-Analytic Results and Large Datasets," Jennifer L. Petersen and Janet Shibley Hyde examine the role of socialization in reifying gender norms and how cultural influences obscure gender similarities in sexuality.

The question of pornography and how gender differences play a role in its production and consumption is essentially a discussion about the complexities of sexuality. Research suggests that the tendency to categorize female and male sexuality as polar opposites has generated widely held beliefs that are largely myths. Exaggerated stereotypes about gender differences support misconceptions about sexuality and serve to perpetuate barriers to gender equality across multiple dimensions. In the pornography industry, research suggests that economic forces are more likely to drive the narrative as a steering influence than the gender identity of the pornographer.

In "A Comparison of Male and Female Directors in Popular Pornography: What Happens When Women Are at the Helm?" Sun et al. view the pornography industry through a comparative gender lens. Sun et al. conducted an empirical study of adult videos that employed a content analysis method to examine how the work of women pornographers diverges from the product of their male counterparts. The study focused on two units of analysis: scenes and primary characters.

Sun et al. hypothesized that male pornographers produce aggression-focused narratives that feature aggression between sexual partners as a key component of the narrative. The study results showed, however, that both men and women pornographers feature aggressive acts in their film narratives but the agent of aggression varied according to the sex of the director. Women directors were more likely to include narratives that included woman to woman sex acts as well as woman to woman aggression.

In "Gender Differences in Sexual Attitudes and Behaviors: A Review of Meta-Analytic Results and Large Datasets," Petersen and Shibley Hyde examine beliefs and behaviors about gender differences in sexuality. Petersen and Shibley Hyde suggest that shifting cultural norms that signal the relaxation of traditionally gender stereotypes and gendered norms for sexual behavior illustrate an evolution in sexuality for men and women. The literature meta-analyses conducted by the study authors show that differences in pornography consumption between men and women appear to result from cultural influences that assign negative connotations to female pornography use.

The stigma associated with pornography leads women to under-report behaviors such as masturbation and pornography consumption.

Petersen and Shibley Hyde suggest that social and cultural factors, rather than biological influences, account for gender differences in attitudes and behaviors. Furthermore, they assert, gender differences in power also seem to explain differences in sexual roles. Societies with higher levels of female equality may exhibit an inversely lower level of difference in expressions of sexuality.

Readers may want to consider the relationship between sexual aggression and pornography and how this relationship impacts the industry and the market, including how pornography is created and consumed.

YES

Chyng Sun et al.

A Comparison of Male and Female Directors in Popular Pornography: What Happens When Women Are at the Helm?

"**I**f you are somebody's sister, wife, or mother-in-law and picked us up by mistake, please pass us along to the man in your life and get back to the *Ladies' Home Companion*," Hugh Hefner announced in his first issue of *Playboy* published in 1953 (Johnson, 2003). Hefner was neither the first nor the last person to declare that pornography is a man's exclusive "secret club," but in the past two decades there have been signs of erosion of that club's walls. During the so-called "porn wars" in the 1980s, pornography was placed squarely and centrally as a feminist issue. Anti- and pro-pornography feminists engaged in heated ideological battles. The anti group argued that pornography is a form of violence against women (Dworkin, 1989; MacKinnon, 1984; Morgan, 1980) whereas the pro group stressed the dangers of censorship and/or pornography's benefit for women's sexual liberation (Berger, Searles, & Cottle, 1990; Duggan & Hunter, 1995; Strossen, 1993, 1995; Snitow, Stansell, & Thompson, 1983). Regardless of ideology, market forces have won: The pornography industry has grown from annual revenue of $75 million in 1985, the period when the porn wars occurred, to $12 billion in 2005, a 160-fold increase (AVN, 2006).

Even though women's roles in pornography historically have been relegated to that of sexual objects, it is only in recent years that some women have become consumers, directors, and producers (Dominus, 2004) of these products that remain largely made by men, for men[1] (Dines, Jensen, & Russo, 1998). So far, the research on pornography primarily has focused on how pornography consumption affects men's attitudes and behaviors (e.g., Donnerstein, Linz, & Penrod, 1987; Linz, Donnerstein, & Penrod, 1987; Mulac, Jansma, & Linz, 2002), with a comparatively small number of studies focusing on the content of pornography. This study asks a question regarding pornography content that has not been investigated previously: Does the content in popular pornographic videos and films created by female directors differ from that of their male counterparts? In previous content analytic studies of pornography, researchers have highlighted pornography's overrepresentation of aggression and degradation against women. In the current study we ask whether, when women are put at the helm of the production and direction of pornographic films, the content shifts in terms of its depiction of gender dynamics, aggression, and degradation? This question was addressed by a quantitative analysis of popular, mainstream adult videos directed by both men and women.

Literature Review

To our knowledge, no previous studies have directly addressed our research question regarding differences in media content between male and female pornography directors. Nonetheless, research from diverse disciplines informs our investigation. We broadly separate this research into two categories: (a) content analyses of pornography that examine gender-role depictions and aggression or degradation and (b) literature drawn from such areas as feminists' debates on pornography, the rise of female pornographers, and the relationship between media creators' gender (including those who create pornography) and the content created. . . .

Among the content analysis literature examined, a few patterns emerge. In pornography, women are frequently degraded (performing unusual sex acts or are ejaculated upon) and both physically (e.g., spanked, hair pulled, hit) and verbally (e.g., insulted) aggressed against by men. When sex is depicted in an interracial relationship, the violence occurs even more intensely than that among same-race couples. However, there are contradictory findings. For example, Prince (1990) argued that more dehumanization occurred to male characters than to female characters, and some indications of female and male equality was observered; Monk-Turner and Purcell (1999) found more vignettes depicting intimacy than violence; and Barron and Kimmel (2000) observed that most violence in videos occurred in consensual relationships. Because the operational definitions of aggression used in these studies are quite similar, one of the reasons for the inconsistent findings may be differences in sampling. That is, we cannot be certain that the studies analyzed the same type of materials or whether these materials were representative of pornography as a whole.

Even though most studies attempted to capture samples that are popular and widespread, almost all studies used sample methods of convenience, such as asking the store clerks to recommend titles (Yang & Linz, 1990), selecting lists from adult sections of a local video store (Monk-Turner & Purcell, 1999), or sampling from local stores (Barron & Kimmel, 2000). The selection process generally appears to be either subjective and unsystematic or lacking national representation, thus limiting the studies' generalizability. The selection process has become even more daunting in recent times. The pornography industry has gone through tremendous growth in the past decades and the number of videos produced yearly has increased from fewer than 2,000 titles in the early 1990s (most studies introduced in this section were conducted before or during this period) to 13,588 in 2005 (AVN, 2006). Thus, it is important to use a straightforward and reliable sampling process that can reflect the national trends. Such a process additionally can be repeated by other researchers so that we can trace the content change of pornography over time.

The current study is part of a larger study that analyzes the content of popular pornographic videos (Wosnitzer & Bridges, 2007) utilizing lists of the most frequently rented VHS and DVD titles from the leading trade journal *Adult Video News* (AVN, 2006) as the video material of interest. We randomly sampled a subset of titles from these lists for analysis. With a large, representative sample of mostconsumed pornographic films, this current study can address not only the patterns of the representations in pornography but also the ideological constructions that may have the most impact on the audience. In the following section, we introduce another body of literature that will help us delineate issues concerning female pornographers and the content they create.

Women Pornographers

Pro-pornography feminists have long argued that it is a mistake to assume that women are not as easily aroused by sexually explicit images as men (Caught Looking, 1986; McChesney, 2006). Such feminists have emphasized that pornography can be a vehicle for women's sexual liberation (Cody, 2001) and that women can and do enjoy pornography (Bower, 1986; Dunn, 1990; Strossen, 1993). At the same time, these pro-pornography feminists have acknowledged that male-dominated pornography ignores women's sexuality. As Williams (1989) observed, pornography has been a "myth of sexual pleasure told from the point of view of men with the power to exploit and objectify the sexuality of women" (p. 22). For many of these feminists, the solution is not to condemn or to abolish pornography, as advocated by anti-pornography feminists, but to have "better" pornography that addresses women's sexuality.

One of the most celebrated female pornographers is Candida Royalle, a former pornography performer. Royalle pioneered Femme Productions in 1984 to explore a potential female market for pornography (Cameron, 1990; Juffer, 1998; Williams, 1989). In addition to explicit sexual acts, Royalle claimed to emphasize "sexuality, caring and love" (Seger, 1996, p. 204). This softer vision of pornography is consistent with the principles for feminist pornography laid out by Marielle Nitoslawska, the filmmaker of *Bad Girl,* a documentary about female pornographers. Nitoslawska stated that degradation of another human being is unacceptable, regardless of his or her gender, race, and sexuality (West & West, 2002, p. 10). Instead, she advocates for an egalitarian sexual ideal.

Nitoslawska's vision is not shared by all female pornography consumers, directors, and advocates. Some pro-pornography feminists emphasize that not all women prefer "candles, lace, sunsets, and Harlequin romance" (West & West, 2002, p. 11) and argue that women may find that representation of sexuality to be too soft or "politically correct" (Agrell, 2006). A female consumer stated that women like her may prefer "low-brow, hardcore porn to feminine erotica" (Tisdale, 1992, para. 40) and a reviewer for pornographic videos claimed that women may like to watch depiction of male domination (Blue, 2005). These sentiments are echoed by some female pornographers who asserted that women may enjoy being dominated and may feel liberated when being degraded sexually (Mason, 2006). Joanna Angel, who is both a director and performer, gives feminist pornography this definition:

> You could do a porn where a girl is getting choked and hit and spit on, the guy's calling her a dirty slut and stuff and that's ok, that can still be feminist as long as everybody there is in control of what they're doing.[2]

Although there are wide disagreements over what constitutes feminist porn or what type of pornography women would enjoy, even among pro-pornography feminists and female pornographers, few have actually investigated women's responses to pornography. Nonetheless, the limited research that is available suggests that female viewers respond positively to sexually explicit images that depict egalitarian sex roles but respond negatively when women are dominated or degraded (Laan, Everaerd, van Bellen, & Hanewald, 1994; Senn, 1993; Mosher & Maclan, 1994). These findings and the debates over what type of pornography women may enjoy have significant relevance to our research questions regarding what type of content female directors may produce. First, the lack of consensus among the pro-pornography feminists and female pornographers regarding the appropriate content for women indicates that female-directed pornography may not represent sexuality in a way that is different from that already being expressed in popular, mainstream male-directed pornography. Second, although the research has shown that women viewers prefer egalitarian sex over aggression against women, the consumer base for pornography is not women, but remains dominated by men (Dines et al., 1998). Thus, we may ask if it is financially viable for female pornographers to produce content geared toward a small minority of consumers that may prefer intimacy over aggression. Taken together, the assertion that "what women need is women pornographers who can help create new images that will build a liberating feminist sexuality" (Berger, Searles, & Cottle, 1990, p. 33) has not been established.

Given the lack of previous studies in our area of inquiry, we now examine how and why women, when placed in decision-making positions, may affect stereotypical representations of gender roles and relationships in media other than pornography. Some researchers assert that women may try to produce more powerful images of women once they become the creators of media content (Seger, 1996).For example, Steenland (1995) describes how female mid-level managers in television production consciously create better representations, despite their lack of decision-making power, by reducing violence, verbal abuse, and offensive camera angles (Lauzen & Dozier, 1999). However, Lauzen and Dozier (1999) failed to find a consistent pattern of stronger female characters in their analysis of the top 65 prime-time series in the first 14 weeks of the 1995–96 television season. Lauzen and Dozier compared speech patterns of female characters portrayed in television series employing women working behind the scenes with those of male workers. They compared two possible theories to investigate the issue: (a) the auteur approach, favored by film scholars, which emphasizes the role of the directors and their personal vision, and (b) the structural approach, utilized mostly by sociologists, which stresses that, although directors may have a certain influence, business imperatives and market forces ultimately decide the content of a media product. The findings suggested that the structural approach received greater support: Despite higher numbers of female writers, creators, and producers of television shows, gender inequities continued to abound.

Lauzen and Dozier's (1999) research helps contextualize the experience of Tristan Taormino, a self-described feminist director and star of "The Ultimate Guide to Anal Sex for Women," featuring a 10-person "anal orgy." The film was financed by John Stagliano, a male director and producer who is credited with popularizing a type of pornography that contains nonstop explicit sex with minimal plot and set ("gonzo porn"). Even though Taormino did not want to include male actors' external ejaculation, she conceded to John Stagliano and to market forces: "John's loyal audience is primarily straight men," Taormino stated. Said differently, despite her own wish to avoid filming visible external ejaculation, she adhered to what "sells tapes" (Taormino, 2005, p. 91). Taormino's example illustrates how a female director's vision may be compromised by requiring the close following of a formula that the industry finds profitable.

Women directors of pornographic videos who seek to make profits may suffer social isolation and stereotyp-

ing in a male-dominated world (Yoder, 2002). Yoder argues that one way women can effectively overcome their lower status in such token conditions is by increasing their status in other ways, such as by adopting more masculine qualities. Examples of such adaptation are found in the case of women in the military (Timmons, 1992). When women displayed qualities that were conventionally classified as masculine, they had greater opportunities for career advancement (Wong, Kettlewell, & Sproule, 1985). Therefore, if a female pornographer wants to profit in the pornography industry, an industry where the majority of producers and consumers are men, would she adhere to the content or formula that has been well-established in that field so as to succeed? Or would she diverge from the formula, as some pro-pornography feminists have argued? If women do diverge from a traditional pornographic formula, how is this divergence exhibited? These questions were addressed in the present study. . . .

Discussion

The pornographic world constructed by popular mainstream female directors is not made up of "candles, lace, sunsets" (West & West, 2002, p. 11) or egalitarian gender relationships, as some have advocated (West & West, 2002). Instead, it is a world of violence and aggression, no different from the world portrayed by male directors, except that they portray significantly more woman-to-woman violence. In a typical scene, the female director's pornography comprises a variety of male and female oral sex acts as well as female vaginal and anal penetration. It has a high prevalence of nonnormative sexual acts such as anal sex and anal-to-mouth, and frequently portrays men ejaculating into women's mouths.

More than three quarters of scenes directed by both men and women contained either verbal or physical aggression: In an average segment, there were between 11 and 13 acts of aggression, with three times as many physical as verbal acts. This finding contradicts prior studies finding that pornographic films are generally more degrading than physically aggressive (Monk-Turner & Purcell, 1999; Cowan et al., 1988). The targets of aggression were overwhelmingly female and were aggressed by both men and women; they were often called "slut," "whore," or "bitch" and were frequently spanked and gagged. Furthermore, the female targets almost always exhibited pleasure or indifference toward the aggression inflicted on them. Thus, the world produced by female pornography directors portrayed sex as intertwined with violence: Frequently, sexual pleasure was contingent upon and derived from aggression. For both the perpetrators and the targets, aggression was intrinsic and integral for sexual excitement. In this regard, female-directed films did not offer an alternative construction of sexuality and gender roles from their male counterparts.

A major benefit of the current study was its revelation of the pornographic content created by female directors of top-renting films, a topic that had never been systematically researched before. To highlight the significance of the content created by female directors, we compared the films that they created with both the results from previous content analyses as well as with top-renting male-directed pornography films within our sample. Previous content analyses of pornography films have focused primarily on depictions of aggression and degradation, with an estimated 13.6% to 27.9% of all scenes containing aggression (Barron & Kimmel, 2000; Cowan et al., 1988; Duncan, 1991; Monk-Turner & Purcell, 1999). Our study found that best-renting pornography films, on the whole, contained nearly three times the rates of aggression than rates previously reported.

The significantly higher aggression rates in videos documented in this study, compared to aggression rates reported in previous studies, could be due to a number of factors. First, prior studies used different sampling methods. Video selection was often subjective, unsystematic, and unrepresentative of national trends. We argue for the usage of the industry's trade journal, *Adult Video News's* monthly *Top 250 Rented VHS & DVDs*, as a publication from which to compile the study sample (Wosnitzer & Bridges, 2007). If future studies on the content of pornography employ similar methodology, content changes over time can be tracked in a much more precise way.

The increase in aggression levels documented in the present study also may have been due, in part, to the detailed coding scheme used. For example, this study was the first, to our knowledge, that coded gagging as an aggressive act. Given that gagging appeared in 59% of female-directed and 54.1% of male-directed scenes, this coding category contributed to the high aggression levels in the current study compared to prior content analyses. It is possible that gagging was not a common sexual act in popular pornographic videos a decade ago, when most of the reviewed content analysis studies of pornography were conducted. Nevertheless, even without the inclusion of gagging, a full 77.9% of the films selected for this study contained physically aggressive acts such as hair pulling, choking, slapping, and other behaviors that have been coded in prior studies.

Taken together, we contend that the frequency of aggression in top-renting videos in 2005 that constituted our sample is, across-the-board, much higher than that of pornography produced a decade ago, despite differences in sampling techniques and coding schemes. Jensen's (2004, 2006) qualitative analyses of the current trends of pornographic content also suggest an escalation of aggression in recent years and a rise in the popularity of gonzo porn, characterized by the rough and brutal treatment of women.

The present study sought to examine how popular pornographic films differed regarding both sexual and aggressive content when directors were women versus men. In general, few gender differences were found. One important finding was that female directors were significantly more likely to direct woman-to-woman scenes. Therefore, female-directed scenes showed more woman-to-woman oral sex and less female-to-male oral sex compared to male-directed scenes. Female-directed scenes were also significantly more likely to portray positive behaviors, such as kissing, embracing, and verbal compliments.

An important analysis in the study at hand was that of female directors' depictions of sexual acts, particularly as they related to gender roles portrayed by the female characters. Sexual acts that suggest degradation were just as common in female-directed films as male-directed films. For example, ejaculation in a woman's mouth—a practice suggesting degradation (Cowan & Campbell, 1994)—was particularly prevalent (47.5% of female-directed scenes). Anal penetration was high (46.9% of female-directed scenes), as was anal to mouth (41.0% of female-directed scenes). (Anal to mouth is a sexual sequence comprising a penis or dildo being inserted into a woman's mouth immediately after it is penetrated in the anus of a woman. Male actors have jokingly referred to it as "eating her own shit"; Dines, 2006.)

When examining aggression in female- and male-directed scenes, verbal and physical aggression rates were similar, except that female directors were significantly more likely to show women as perpetrators of aggression. Regardless of director or perpetrator gender, women overwhelmingly were the targets of aggressive acts and almost always showed pleasure or indifference toward aggression. We suspected that the differences between female and male directors' depictions of sexual acts and aggression were due to female directors including significantly more female characters in each scene, so we repeated our analyses with a subsample of the original 122 coded scenes, but held the ratio of female to male characters constant across director gender. Even when matching for main character gender composition, female directors continued to depict significantly more woman-to-woman violence than did male directors.

Contrary to the hope and idealism expressed by some pro-pornography scholars and activists, who assumed and predicted that female directors would produce more sensual, egalitarian, and "women-centered" pornography, the present study found that directors of top-renting videos depicted a pornographic world in which some of the women, like most of the men in such films, were aggressive and dominant. Moreover, the majority of women were portrayed as masochists who enjoyed the degradation and violence that was inflicted upon them. Evidently, the ideals of some female pornographers, such as Candida Royalle, who are celebrated by pro-pornography scholars and are awarded for making feminist pornography (Agrell, 2006), have not been effective in changing popular mainstream pornography to be less misogynist. Female pornographers whose help compose top-rented video lists, such as Belladonna, appear to have learned the conventions of commercially successful adult films from male pornographers. Perhaps confined by the industry's formulas and market pressures (Taormino, 2006) and informed by their own sexual proclivity (Angel, 2006), these female directors have created a pornographic world that is remarkably similar to that of their male counterparts. Our findings are consistent with prior studies that have supported the structural approach to media development (Lauzen & Dozier, 1999): Money, rather than gender, dictates vision.

Even more alarming, it may be that female directors of top-renting pornographic videos were more willing to show extreme degradation and aggression. This is also consistent with studies of women who find success in male-dominated fields: While working in such jobs, some women display hyper-masculine traits to earn respect and gain favor from their male supervisors and peers (Wong et al., 1985). In total, female-directed films comprised only 4.4% of all best-renting films in the population of study. Such a small minority indicates that only a very small percentage of women have succeeded in this male-dominated profession. This phenomenon may help explain why female directors depicted significantly more woman-to-woman aggression. How best to demonstrate one's allegiance to patriarchy, thereby increasing one's status, than to exhibit one's masculinity by severely violating another woman?

Limitations

The current study, although providing a quantitative analysis of the world constructed by popular female pornographers, has its limitations. First, although this study presents a systematic method for mapping the content of popular pornographic films, by selecting only best-selling, best-renting videos it may not adequately describe the general patterns of most of female directors' work. It is possible that women who direct sexually explicit films are, in fact, more likely to produce materials that portray egalitarian sex than male directors. In fact, the variability seen in female-directed films, even in this best-renting sample, was greater than that of male-directed films. That is, women directors appeared to follow less of a rigid formula by both displaying more positive behaviors and more aggression among women. If combining sex and violence is the formula for market success, then egalitarian depictions of sex would not be represented in best-selling lists of pornography. Thus, our method of video selection can find only those female directors who appeal to the male-dominated consumer base and cannot offer insights into the content of female-directed films that aim to appeal to female audiences. What this study has done, however, is to provide support to the contention that in a capitalist economy where pornography is primarily consumed by men with specific sexual scripts and desires, if one wants to maximize profits, the gender of the pornography director may be irrelevant. Future studies may seek to compare the content of female-directed pornographic videos with varying levels of commercial success so as to better explore the relationship between director gender and market forces.

Even though there are conflicting results regarding whether gender affects how people code pornographic images (Cowan & Dunn, 1994; Glascock, 2005), the use of only female coders, trained by a male researcher, presents a second potential limitation to our study. Therefore, future studies may consider using both male and female coders. Additionally, inter-coder reliability was calculated only at the beginning of the analysis. It would have been beneficial to check reliability again as the analysis progressed.

There are limitations to how much a quantitative analysis that decontextualizes sexual and aggressive acts can help us understand images and decode meaning (Hall, 1989). Even though we found a great deal of woman-to-woman aggression in the videos of female pornographers, qualitative analyses can provide far more vivid and descriptive accounts of pornography than simple numbers can convey. Therefore, future studies may seek to examine best-selling and best-renting pornography using qualitative analyses as a complement to these findings. Similarly, understanding how female pornography directors view and manage the balance between artistic vision and market forces would enhance these quantitative findings. It would be immensely informative to interview female pornographers in order to understand the factors and considerations that went into their productions.

Conclusions

Despite its limitations, we believe that this study provides numerous important contributions to and furthering of our understanding of popular pornographic films directed by both men and women.[3] First, by grounding this analysis within feminist theoretical debates, it provides a model for future research wherein theoretical differences and points of contention are examined empirically. This analysis concerned itself with whether having more women make pornography would result in more egalitarian depictions of sexuality. We suggest that such simple directives miss important, complex structural constraints that guide pornography's production and consumption.

Second, by exploring the content of popular pornography, we take seriously the socio-economic forces that shape pornography's production. Prior analyses of pornography have generally ignored economic dictates, essential considerations given that pornography is primarily produced and consumed in a capitalist society. Although much attention has been paid to the patriarchal ideology manifested in pornography's production and consumption (e.g., Jensen & Dines, 1998), less frequently have economic forces been explored to examine how they shape the nature of the product. This study, therefore, brings an important, multidisciplinary, socio-political perspective to the discussion of the content of pornography directed by men and women.

Finally, this study provides an important update to the content of contemporary pornography. Because the industry has grown exponentially in the last two decades, much of our knowledge about its content is insufficient and outdated. Although pornographic products have increased significantly, in large part due to technological advances with the Internet, direct television, and home digital video equipment (Cooper, Putnam, Planchon, & Boies, 1999), scholarly work charting its content has declined. New themes and genres (such as gonzo porn) are not described in current academic texts. By utilizing an industry publication to select samples for investigation, this study and future research can chart changes in content among what is most representative of consumed pornography.

Notes

1. In an interview conducted by two of the authors of this article, *Adult Video News* senior editor Mark Kernes stated, "Our statistics show that 78% of the people that go into adult stores are men. They may have women with them, but it's men, and 22%, conversely, is women or women with other women or women alone." The interview took place at the Adult Entertainment Expo in Las Vegas, January 7, 2005.
2. After her pornography Web site "Burning Angel" (www.burningangel.com) became widely known and popular, Joanna Angel was hired by Hustler to perform and produce pornography videos for their distribution companies (VCA, Hustler Video). This quotation was based on an interview by two of the authors with Joanna Angel at the New York Erotica Expo on May 21, 2005.
3. The authors wish to thank an anonymous reviewer's insightful suggestions regarding the contributions of this research to the field of psychology.

References

Agrell, S. (2006, June 10). X-rated films for red-blooded feminists: New porn caters to female pleasure fantasies. *National Post (Toronto Edition)*, p. WP3.

Angel, J. (2006). On being a feminist with a porn site. In C. Milne (Ed.), *Naked ambition* (pp. 233–244). New York: Carroli & Graf Publishers.

AVN. (2006). Top 250 VHS & DVD rentals. Retrieved July 17, 2005, from http://www.avn.com/index. php_PrimaryNavigations=Charts

Barron, M., & Kimmel, M. (2000). Sexual violence in three pornographic media: Toward a sociological explanation. *Journal of Sex Research, 37*, 161–168.

Berger, J., Searles, P, & Cottle, C. (1990). Ideological contours of the contemporary pornography debate: Divisions and alliances. *Frontiers: A Journal of Women Studies, 11*(2/3), 30–38.

Blue, V. (2005). On experiencing boot camp on the road to becoming an adult video expert. In C. Milne (Ed.), *Naked ambition* (pp. 21–30). New York: Carroli & Graf Publishers.

Bower, M. (1986). Daring to speak its name: The relationship of women to pornography. *Feminist Review, 24*, 40–55.

Cameron, D. (1990). Discourses of desire: Liberals, feminists & the politics of pornography in the 1980s. *American Literary History, 2*, 784–798.

Caught Looking, Inc. (1986). *Caught looking: feminism, pornography & censorship*. Seattle, WA: The Real Comet Press.

Cody, G. (2001). *Hardcore from the heart: The pleasures, profits and politics of sex in performance*. New York: Continuum.

Cooper, A., Putnam, D. E., Planchon, L. A., & Boies, S. C. (1999). Online sexual compulsivity: Getting tangled in the net. *Sexual Addiction and Compulsivity, 6*, 79–104.

Cowan, G., & Campbell, R. R. (1994). Racism and sexism in interracial pornography: A content analysis. *Psychology of Women Quarterly, 18*, 323–338.

Cowan, G., & Dunn, K. F. (1994). What themes in pornography lead to perceptions of the degradation of women? *Journal of Sex Research, 31*, 11–21.

Cowan, G., Lee, C., Levy, D., & Snyder, D. (1988). Dominance and inequality in x-rated videocassettes. *Psychology of Women Quarterly, 12*, 299–311.

Dines, G. (2006). The white man's burden: Gonzo pornography and the construction of black masculinity. *Yale Journal of Law & Feminism, 18*, 293–297.

Dines, G., Jensen, R., & Russo, A. (1998). *Pornography: The production and consumption of inequality*. New York: Routledge.

Dominus, S. (2004, August 29). What women want to watch. *The New York Times*, p. 2.1.

Donnerstein, E., Linz, D. G., & Penrod, S. (1987). *The question of pornography*. New York: Free Press.

Duggan, L., & Hunter, N. (1995). *Sex wars: Sexual dissent and political culture*. New York: Routledge.

Duncan, D. F. (1991). Violence and degradation as themes in "adult" videos. *Psychological Reports, 69*, 239–240.

Dunn, S. (1990). "Voyages of the valkyries": Recent lesbian pornographic writing. *Feminist Review, 34*, 161–170.

Dworkin, A. (1989). *Pornography: Men possessing women* (rev. ed.). New York: Dutton.

Glascock, J. (2005). Degrading content and character sex: Accounting for men and women's differential reactions to pornography. *Communication Reports, 18*, 43–53.

Gossett, J. L., & Byrne, S. (2002). "Click here": A content analysis of internet rape sites. *Gender and Society, 16,* 689–709.

Hall, S. (1989). Ideology and communication theory. In B. Dervin, L. Grossberg, B. J. O'Keefe, & E. Wartella (Eds.), *Rethinking communication: Paradigm issues* (vol. 1; pp. 40–52). Newbury Park, CA: Sage.

Jensen, R. (2004, January/February). Cruel to be hard: Men and pornography. *Sexual Assault Report,* 33–48.

Jensen, R. (2006, February 23). The paradox of pornography. *ZNet.* Retrieved October 26, 2006, from http://lists.econ.utah.edu/pipermail/margins-to-centre/2006-February/000776.html

Jensen, R., & Dines, G. (1998). The content of mass-marketed pornography. In G. Dines, R. Jensen, & A. Russo (Eds.), *Pornography: The production and consumption of inequality* (pp. 65–100). New York: Routledge.

Johnson, R. (2003, November 28). Playboy at 50: A man's notes. *Los Angeles Times,* p. E1.

Juffer, J. (1998). *At home with pornography: Women, sex, and everyday life.* New York: New York University Press.

Laan, E., Everaerd, W., van Bellen, G., & Hanewald, G. (1994). Women's sexual and emotional responses to male- and female-produced erotica. *Archives of Sexual Behavior, 23,* 153–169.

Lauzen, M. M., & Dozier, D. M. (1999). Making a difference in prime time: Women on screen and behind the scenes in the 1995-96 television season. *Journal of Broadcasting & Electronic Media, 43,* 1–19.

Linz, D. G., Donnerstein, E., & Penrod, S. (1987). The findings and recommendations of the Attorney General's Commission on Pornography: Do the psychological facts fit the political fury? *American Psychologist, 42,* 946–953.

MacKinnon, C. A. (1984). *Feminism unmodified: Discourses on life and law.* Cambridge, MA: Harvard University Press.

Mason. (2006). On directing the hardest of hardcore. In C. Milne (Ed.), *Naked ambition* (pp. 125–138). New York: Carroli & Graf Publishers.

Matacin, M. L., & Burger, J. M. (1987). A content analysis of sexual themes in Playboy cartoons. *Sex Roles, 17,* 179–186.

McChesney, M. (2006, May 26). Visionary voicessing feminist porn's praises. *The Toronto Star,* p. D12.

Monk-Turner, E., & Purcell, H. C. (1999). Sexual violence in pornography: How prevalent is it? *Gender Issues, 17*(2), 58–67.

Morgan, R. (1980). Theory and practice: Pornography and rape. In L. Lederer (Ed.), *Take back the night: Women on pornography* (pp. 134–140). New York: William Morrow.

Mosher, D. L., & Maclan, P. (1994). College men and women respond to X-rated videos intended for male or female audiences: Gender and sexual scripts. *Journal of Sex Research, 31,* 99–113.

Mulac, A., Jansma, L. L., & Linz, D. G. (2002). Men's behavior toward women after viewing sexually-explicit films: Degradation makes a difference. *Communication Monographs, 69,* 311–329.

Prince, S. (1990). Power and pain: Content analysis and the ideology of pornography. *Journal of Film and Video, 42*(2), 31–41.

Seger, L. (1996). *When women call the shots.* New York: Henry Holt.

Senn, C. (1993). Women's multiple perspectives and experiences with pornography. *Psychology of Women Quarterly, 17,* 319–341.

Snitow, A., Stansell, C., & Thompson, S. (Eds.). (1983). *Powers of desire: The politics of sexuality.* New York: Monthly Review Press.

Steenland, S. (1995). Content analysis of the image of women on television. In C. M. Lont (Ed.), *Women and media: Content, careers, and criticism* (pp. 197–198). San Francisco: Wadsworth.

Strossen, N. (1993). The feminist critique of "the" feminist critique of pornography. *Virginia Law Review, 79,* 1099–1190.

Strossen, N. (1995). *Defending pornography: Free speech, sex and the fight for women's rights.* New York: New York University Press.

Taormino, T. (2005). On crossing the line to create feminist porn. In C. Milne (Ed.), *Naked ambition* (pp. 87–98). New York: Carroli & Graf Publishers.

Taormino, T. (2006). *Tristan Taormino's true lust: Adventures in sex, porn, and perversion.* San Francisco: Cleis Press.

Timmons, T. (1992). "We're looking for a few good men": The impact of gender stereotypes on women in the military. *Minerva, 10*(2), 20.

Tisdale, S. (1992, February). Talk dirty to me [Electronic version]. *Harper's Magazine, 284*(1701), 37–44.

West, D., & West, J. M. (2002). Women making porno: Feminism's final frontier? An interview with Marielle Nitoslawska. *Cineaste, 27*(3), 9–13.

Williams, L. (1989). *Hard core: Power, pleasure, and the "frenzy of the visible."* Berkeley, CA: University of California Press.

Wong, P. T. P., Kettlewell, G., & Sproule, C. F. (1985). On the importance of being masculine: Sex role, attribution, and women's career achievement. *Sex Roles, 12*, 757–769.

Wosnitzer, R. J., & Bridges, A. J. (2007, May). *Aggression and sexual behavior in best-selling pornography: A content analysis update*. Paper presented at the annual meeting of the International Communication Association, San Francisco.

Yang, N., & Linz, D. (1990). Movie ratings and the content of adult videos: The sex–violence ratio. *Journal of Communication, 40*(2), 28–42.

Yoder, J. D. (2002). Context matters: Understanding tokenism processes and their impact on women's work. *Psychology of Women Quarterly, 26*, 1–8.

CHYNG SUN is a clinical associate professor of media studies at New York University. Her research interests are in gender, sexuality, and race in the media.

Petersen and Hyde

Gender Differences in Sexual Attitudes and Behaviors: A Review of Meta-Analytic Results and Large Datasets

Men are different from women. They are equal only in their common membership of the same species, humankind.

—(Moir & Jessel, 1989, p. 5).

For decades, researchers have reported on the different mating strategies, sexual preferences, and sexual attitudes of men and women (Buss, 1994). In fact, Hyde's (2005) gender similarities hypothesis, which proposed that men and women are similar for the majority of psychological attributes, indicated that sexuality was one exception in which gender differences might be large. However, recent research suggests that men and women may not have such different sexual attitudes and behaviors as once thought (Petersen & Hyde, 2010). Here, we review research on gender differences in sexuality to evaluate the claim that men and women are different in terms of sexuality.

Gender differences in sexuality is a broad area of study that encompasses decades of research. This article is in no way an exhaustive review of all research in this field. Instead, we hope to provide the reader with a brief taste of general topics within the study of gender differences in sexuality. We begin by exploring theories that hypothesize gender differences in sexuality. Specifically, we review the accounts of evolutionary psychology, cognitive social learning theory, and social structural theory. We then review research on gender differences in sexuality including meta-analytic reviews and results from large, national datasets. Finally, we discuss biological and sociocultural explanations for gender differences and similarities in sexuality.

Theories of Gender Differences in Sexuality

It is beyond the scope of this article to give a complete account of evolutionary psychology, cognitive social learning theory, and social structural theory. However, we provide a brief review designed to cover the highlights of each theory as it pertains to gender differences in sexuality. For a more complete review of evolutionary psychology, cognitive

social learning theory, and social structural theory, see Buss (1994, 1995, 1998), Bussey and Bandura (1999), and Eagly and Wood (1999), respectively.

Sociobiology and Evolutionary Psychology

Perhaps the most well-known theories about gender differences in sexuality are based in evolutionary theory. Evolutionary psychology, in particular, proposes that psychological gender differences (not just gender differences in sexuality) are a product of men and women differing in their strategies for reproductive success. In other words, human gender differences in social behaviors, attitudes, and psychological mechanisms are evident because men and women have different strategies for maximizing the number of genes that are passed on to the next generation (Buss, 1998; Buss & Schmitt, 1993).

Evolutionary theorists invoke sexual selection, an evolutionary mechanism originally proposed by Darwin, as one force creating behavioral gender differences (Buss, 2009; Darwin, 1871; Gangestad & Thornhill, 1997). Sexual selection involves two processes: (a) members of one gender (usually males) compete among themselves to gain mating privileges with members of the other gender (usually females), and (b) members of the other gender (usually females) have preferences for certain members of the first gender (usually males) and decide which of them they are willing to mate with.

Evolutionary accounts invoke gender differences in parental investment as a second part of the explanation for gender differences in behavior (Trivers, 1972). This theory points to the fact that men have very little parental investment in a particular offspring because their sperm are plentiful and they are not responsible for gestation. In contrast, women invest a great deal in each sexual encounter and each offspring because their ova are much rarer than sperm are, and they must invest time and energy resources in pregnancy. This gender difference in parental investment leads to gender differences in sexual behavior. In particular, evolutionary psychology predicts that for men, who have little parental investment, the key to genetic success is to have as many children as possible with the hope that some of those children will survive to pass on their genes.

Petersen, Jennifer L. and Shibley Hyde, Janet. From *Journal of Sex Research*, February 28, 2011, pp. 149–150, 151, 153, 155–156, 157–160, 161, 162–165. Copyright © 2011 by Society for the Scientific Study of Sexuality. Reprinted by permission of Taylor & Francis via Rightslink.

Therefore, the best evolutionary strategy for men is to have many sexual partners and casual sexual relationships to increase the chances of having many offspring. In contrast, this theory proposes that women, who have more parental investment than men do, are most likely to achieve genetic success by having fewer children, being selective about their sexual partner, and caring for each of their offspring to insure their survival. Therefore, this theory proposes that women prefer long-term sexual relationships in which their partner helps them provide and care for their children to increase survival for each child.

Today, the majority of men and women invest time in raising their children and engage in both short-term and long-term sexual relationships; therefore, the actual gender difference in parental investment may be less than it was generations ago. However, evolutionary psychology proposes that sexual strategies and preferences have evolved over thousands of years because of differential parental investment.

Sexual strategies theory is one application of evolutionary psychology that distinguishes between short-term and long-term mating preferences (Buss, 1998; Buss & Schmitt, 1993). This theory suggests that both men and women engage in both short- and long-term mating, but that men devote a larger portion of their total mating to short-term partners because they have evolved to prefer sex frequently with many partners. For example, historically, men with power, such as kings, pharaohs, and nobles, typically chose to have several short-term partners such as concubines, as well as a long-term sexual relationship with a "queen" in order to maximize their genetic success (Betzig, 1986). According to this theory, men maximize their genetic success by preferring to mate with women who appear to be fertile, such as women who are young and physically attractive. In contrast, women prefer long-term mating over short-term mating because they have evolved to prefer a steady relationship in which both partners care for their offspring. According to this theory, women maximize their genetic success by preferring to mate with men who can provide resources for them and their children, such as men who are financially successful or those who have the potential for financial success (Buss & Schmitt, 1993).

Other research testing the predictions of evolutionary psychology suggests that contemporary gender differences in sexuality, particularly number of sex partners, may not be as large as sexual selection seems to predict. Although men typically report a greater ideal number of sex partners than women on average (Buss & Schmitt, 1993), other research suggests that this average difference is driven by a few extreme values for some men (Pedersen, Miller, Putcha-Bhagavatula, & Yang, 2002). The gender difference in the median ideal number of sex partners is actually very small (Pedersen et al., 2002). . . .

Summary of Theories

Although the various theories previously described propose distinct mechanisms for the creation of gender differences in sexuality, the theories—for the most part—

predict that men will have more sexual experience and hold more liberal attitudes toward sexuality than women. In particular, these theories propose that men prefer short-terms relationships with casual sex and multiple partners, whereas women prefer sex within the context of a committed relationship. The theories differ in some predictions, as well. Cognitive social learning theory predicts changes in patterns of gender differences over a short period of time as media images change, whereas evolutionary theories predict no change over short periods of time and change only over many generations of natural or sexual selection. Social structural theory focuses on variations in the magnitude of gender differences across cultures and proposes that these variations are correlated with the extent of gender inequality in the cultures, whereas evolutionary theories predict constancy across cultures in patterns of gender differences because humans share an evolutionary history.

Despite the multiple theories on gender and sexuality, some sexual behaviors remain largely unexplained. For example, same-gender sexual behavior has been neglected by many of these theories, which assume heterosexual relationships. In addition, modern aspects of sexuality such as contraception and concerns about HIV and AIDS and other sexually transmitted infections are not addressed by the theories. Finally, because the theories do not offer differential predictions on many points, supporting or rejecting one theory over another is difficult. . . .

Gender Differences in Sexual Behaviors

Heterosexual Intercourse

Prevalence rates. Perhaps the most commonly studied sexual behavior is heterosexual intercourse. All three of the meta-analyses that examined gender differences in heterosexual intercourse included over 100 studies in this category (Oliver & Hyde, 1993; Petersen & Hyde, 2010; Wells & Twenge, 2005). Oliver and Hyde found an effect size of $d = 0.33$, and Petersen and Hyde found an effect size of $d = 0.16$ for this behavior. These results suggest that men are somewhat more likely to engage in heterosexual intercourse than women are, but the gender difference is small and decreasing. This gender difference was larger among studies that included younger participants than it was for studies with older participants (Petersen & Hyde, 2010). Among adolescents, boys may be more likely to report being sexually active than girls are, but the prevalence of heterosexual intercourse among adults is comparable for men and women. Higher rates of reporting among adolescent boys might, in turn, be due to either or both of two factors: (a) a slightly earlier age of first intercourse for boys, particularly among Black and Hispanic Americans (Upchurch, Levy-Storms, Sucoff, & Aneshensel, 1998; see the more detailed discussion later); or (b) systematic reporting bias in which girls are more likely to deny their sexual experience (Alexander & Fisher, 2003).

Although these meta-analyses indicate that gender differences are decreasing across time, they give no information about whether men or women are changing at a faster rate. For example, this gender difference may be decreasing because women are engaging in heterosexual intercourse more in recent years, or it might be decreasing because men are engaging in heterosexual intercourse less in recent years. The Wells and Twenge (2005) cross-temporal meta-analysis provided more information about this trend. This analysis indicated that the prevalence of heterosexual intercourse increased over time, but the rate increased for women more dramatically than it did for men, thus decreasing the gender gap.

Large, national datasets provide further evidence that gender differences in the prevalence of heterosexual intercourse are small. Add Health ($d = 0.01$), the NHSLS ($d = 0.08$), the ASHR ($d = 0.07$), the NLSY ($d = -0.05$), and the YRBSS ($d = 0.13$) all indicate that men were only slightly more likely to report heterosexual intercourse than women were. The effect sizes from the large, national datasets were even smaller than those found in the meta-analyses of individual studies. This may reflect the inflated gender differences characteristic of publication bias in individual published studies. Alternatively, this could be a product of better sampling procedures in the large datasets than in the individual studies. Moreover, the nationally representative studies are all recent and their results may reflect the temporal trends toward smaller gender differences.

According to social structural theory, this small gender difference in intercourse prevalence would vary among different countries around the world depending on their level of gender equality. The Petersen and Hyde (2010) meta-analysis included data from over 80 countries and was able to test this hypothesis. For each country, the United Nations has calculated a gender empowerment measure (GEM; United Nations Development Programme, 1995, 2003) based on the ratio of men to women on the following characteristics: (a) percentage of parliamentary seats; (b) percentage of legislators, senior officials and managers, and professional and technical positions; and (c) estimates of income. GEM scores could potentially range from zero to one, with high scores indicating a greater degree of gender equality. For example, the United States has a GEM of 0.762, indicating relatively more gender equality when compared with Turkey, which has a GEM of 0.298. In support of social structural theory, the Petersen and Hyde meta-analysis found that nations with greater gender equality had smaller gender differences in intercourse prevalence than nations with less gender equality ($\beta = -0.41$), suggesting that gender differences in power affect gender differences in reported sexual behavior. . . .

Autoerotic Behaviors

Small gender differences in heterosexual behaviors should not be surprising given that both a man and a woman are required to engage in heterosexual activities. Perhaps men would prefer to have intercourse or oral sex more frequently, but they are limited by the preferences of their female partners. Therefore, it is important to consider other sexual behaviors that do not require a partner. In particular, the Oliver and Hyde (1993) and Petersen and Hyde (2010) meta-analyses examined gender differences in masturbation. The former meta-analysis reported a large gender difference in masturbation ($d = 0.96$), whereas the latter reported a medium-sized effect ($d = 0.53$). In both analyses, men were more likely to report masturbating than women were. Large, national datasets such as the NHSLS ($d = 0.44$) and ASHR ($d = 0.60$) also found medium-sized gender differences in masturbation. The NHSLS, for example, found prevalence rates for masturbation in the last year of 42% for women and 63% for men, among 18- to 59-year-old Americans (Laumann et al., 1994). Results also indicated that egalitarian countries had smaller gender differences in masturbation than less egalitarian countries, suggesting a sociocultural component to this gender difference (Petersen & Hyde, 2010).

Petersen and Hyde (2010) found a substantial gender difference in pornography use in which men were more likely than women to report using erotic materials such as magazines, videos, or the Internet ($d = 0.63$). This was the largest gender difference of any of the sexual attitudes and behaviors included in that meta-analysis. Large, national datasets, such as the NHSLS ($d = 0.32$), ASHR ($d = 0.50$), and the GSS ($d = 0.40$), found slightly smaller, but nonetheless substantial, gender differences in pornography use. Neither age of the sample, year of publication, nor gender empowerment of the country moderated the gender difference in pornography use.

Gender differences in masturbation may be due to gender differences in sex drive. Research suggests that men have a stronger sex drive than women do (Baumeister, Catanese, & Vohs, 2001). Men may prefer to have heterosexual intercourse, but if their partner is unwilling, they may masturbate instead. Women may masturbate less often than men because their sex partner is usually willing when they are interested in sex. One study indicated that the top reason women gave for not masturbating was lack of desire to do so (Arafat & Cotton, 1974). An alternative explanation for large gender differences in autoerotic behavior suggests that gender differences in reported rates of masturbation may be an artifact of socially desirable responding. Stigma continues to be associated with female autoerotic behavior (Hogarth & Ingham, 2009); therefore, women may underreport rates of masturbation or pornography use. For example, one study found that women, but not men, underreported rates of masturbation and pornography use, and that women's reported rates for these autoerotic behaviors were more distorted than their reports for any other sexual behavior (Alexander & Fisher, 2003).

Men may seek greater exposure to sexually explicit material than women because they are more aroused by it. A meta-analysis revealed that men self-reported more positive emotions in response to erotic material than women did (Murnen & Stockton, 1997). However, physiological responses to erotic material reveal much smaller gender differences (Allen et al., 2007). The type of erotic material may also contribute to gender differences in sexual arousal. Men and women are equally aroused by female-oriented erotic video clips, which focus on romance and center on female characters, but men are more aroused than women in response to male-oriented video clips, which center on sexual activity without romance (Janssen, Carpenter, & Graham, 2003; Rupp & Wallen, 2008). However, some research suggests that women may be sexually aroused by a wider variety of sexual images than are men (Chivers, Seto, & Blanchard, 2007). In one study, heterosexual and homosexual men and women watched video clips of sexual activity such as masturbation and intercourse for men, women, and nonhuman primates. Results suggested that male genital response and male and female subjective responses were consistent with their reported sexual orientation, but that female genital responses were not consistent with reported sexual orientation (Chivers et al., 2007). Instead, both heterosexual and homosexual women showed genital arousal in response to a variety of stimuli. For example, heterosexual men showed genital sexual arousal when watching heterosexual intercourse and female targets masturbate. Although heterosexual women showed subjective and genital arousal for those stimuli as well, they also showed genital arousal when watching sexual activity from both men and women and even showed genital arousal when watching *bonobo* intercourse (Chivers et al., 2007). Although women showed arousal to a greater number of stimuli, men generally reported more sexual arousal overall (Chivers et al., 2007).

Gender Differences in Sexual Attitudes
General Sexual Permissiveness

Although researchers often examine gender differences in specific sexual attitudes, in some research, a general scale of sexual permissiveness is used. An example is Hendrick and Hendrick's Sexual Attitudes Scale (Hendrick & Hendrick, 1987; Hendrick, Hendrick, & Reich, 2006), which examines sexual attitudes including attitudes toward casual sex and attitudes toward contraception. Oliver and Hyde (1993) reviewed gender differences in these general sexual permissiveness scales and found a medium-sized effect in which men were more sexually permissive than women were ($d = 0.57$), but Petersen and Hyde (2010) found a small gender difference ($d = 0.21$). Not only did gender differences decrease from the earlier meta-analysis to the later analysis, but Petersen and Hyde found that this gender difference was also moderated by year of publication, indicating that the gender difference in sexual permissiveness has decreased across time even

since the early 1990s. None of the large, national datasets administered a general measure of sexual attitudes. It is difficult to precisely interpret the meaning of this gender difference because the scales conflate attitudes about such a wide array of topics. . . .

Masturbation

Although gender differences in masturbation prevalence and frequency were one of the largest gender differences in both the Oliver and Hyde (1993) meta-analysis and the Petersen and Hyde (2010) meta-analysis, gender differences in attitudes toward masturbation were very small. The average effect size for attitudes toward masturbation was 0.09 in the Oliver and Hyde study, and was 0.02 in the Petersen and Hyde study. This gender difference was not moderated by year of assessment, age of the sample, gender equality of the nation, or race or ethnicity. It is unclear why men and women might have similar attitudes toward masturbation, but have very different rates of engaging in the behavior. Attitudes toward masturbation reflect approval or disapproval of the behavior for oneself and others, whereas masturbatory behavior reflects a willingness and desire to engage in autoerotic behaviors. Although men and women may be equally approving of the behavior, women may have less of a desire to masturbate than men do. This lack of desire may stem from gender differences in anatomy. When men are sexually aroused, their erect penis provides an obvious signal indicating to them that they are aroused. In contrast, women's sexual response to arousal is much less obvious, and they may not even be aware of their arousal (Baldwin & Baldwin, 1997). . . .

Homosexuality

Gender differences in attitudes toward homosexuals is perhaps the most studied sexual attitude. A crucial methodological issue is whether the primary empirical studies have inquired about attitudes toward homosexuality or homosexuals (gender unspecified, but perhaps assumed to be male), gay men, or lesbians. Oliver and Hyde (1993) reported no gender difference ($d = -0.01$) in attitudes toward homosexuals. However, Whitley and Kite (1995) argued that this statistic misrepresents gender differences in attitudes toward homosexuals because the authors did not include a search term about homosexual attitudes when they sampled the studies and they did not distinguish between attitudes toward gay men and attitudes toward lesbians. In response, they conducted their own meta-analysis on gender differences in attitudes toward homosexuals (Kite & Whitley, 1996). According to this study, men reported less accepting attitudes toward homosexuals than women did ($d = -0.38$). In particular, men were much less accepting of gay men than women were ($d = -0.52$), but there was no gender difference in attitudes toward lesbian women ($d = 0.00$). Women reported the same level of acceptance for gay men and for lesbian women, but men reported more accepting attitudes toward lesbian women than toward gay men. Gender differences were largest for college students and smallest for non-professional adults. There was no gender difference in attitudes toward homosexual civil liberties ($d = 0.04$). Petersen and Hyde (2010) found similar results, reporting that women had more accepting attitudes toward gay men ($d = -0.18$), but that there was no gender difference in attitudes toward lesbian women ($d = -0.02$). Kite and Whitley suggested that heterosexual men might have more negative attitudes toward gay men than toward lesbian women because society considers violations of gender roles more egregious for men than for women. Heterosexual men may also fear sexual advances from gay men. Alternatively, heterosexual men may have more positive attitudes toward lesbians, rather than more negative attitudes toward gay men. For example, heterosexual men enjoy lesbian pornography (Strager, 2003).

Agreement of Self-Report and Physiological Measures

Gender differences in sexual arousal are commonly measured with physiological assessments in the laboratory. Physiological sexual arousal may be measured with heart rate, pupil dilation, or galvanic skin response, but the most commonly used measures are those for genital arousal (Chivers et al., 2010). For example, a typical laboratory paradigm includes exposing participants to erotic material and measuring their genital sexual arousal. Genital arousal may be measured in men with a penile strain gauge—a flexible loop that is placed around the shaft of the penis and measures changes in penile circumference and volume. Genital arousal in women is measured using a vaginal photoplethysmograph. This instrument is a small probe that can be inserted into the vagina to measure vaginal pulse amplitude and vaginal blood volume. Female sexual arousal may also be measured using a labial thermometer to track temperature changes in the labia minora.

Because laboratory measures involve somewhat invasive procedures, it is often not possible for researchers to administer genital measures of sexual arousal, and they must rely on self-report measures. It is important to consider whether self-report measures are concordant with measures of genital sexual arousal. High correlations would suggest that self-report measures might be substituted for genital measures when the latter are not feasible. In contrast, a low correlation between psychological and physiological reports might indicate that self-report measures are distorted by social desirability, or that they are measuring a different aspect of sexual arousal that depends in part on cognitive processing (Rupp & Wallen, 2008).

A recent meta-analysis combined over 100 different studies to determine the correlation between self-report measures and laboratory measures of sexual arousal (Chivers et al., 2010). This study indicated that self-reports

and genital measures of sexual arousal were correlated, but that the correlations were higher for men ($r = .66$) than for women ($r = .26$). Visual or tactile perception of the penile erection may be a signal to the individual that one is sexually aroused. In contrast, genital blood flow is a less obvious signal that might not be consciously recognized by a woman; therefore, a woman may be less conscious of her arousal and, therefore, less likely to report it (Rowland, 2006). Another explanation for the gender difference in correlations may be socially desirable responding in women's self-reports. The sexual double standard holds that expression of sexual desire is more appropriate for men than for women (Crawford & Popp, 2003). Therefore, women may underreport their sexual arousal in self-report measures to conform to the sexual double standard (Alexander & Fisher, 2003). Finally, gender differences in concordance rates might be explained by experience with self-identifying sexual arousal. Because men engage in more masturbation and pornography use than women do, they may be more experienced with identifying their own sexual arousal, especially in the absence of a sexual partner. Women might rely on the presence of a sexual partner to convey the message that it is appropriate to be sexually aroused. In support of this hypothesis, women who masturbate have higher correlations between vaginal and self-reported arousal than women who do not masturbate (Stock & Geer, 1982).

Overall, then, there is moderate concordance between physiological and self-report measures of arousal. However, the concordance is lower for women than for men. It is unclear which of several factors accounts for the lower concordance for women.

Gender Differences in Same-Gender Sexuality

Traditionally, researchers have believed that male homosexuality was more common than female homosexuality, and the 1993 meta-analysis confirmed that view ($d = 0.33$). However, the Petersen and Hyde (2010) meta-analysis found no gender difference ($d = -0.05$). Therefore, it may be the case that the long-standing gender gap has disappeared. The studies reviewed in these meta-analyses, however, typically used simple, categorical measures of sexual orientation.

Alfred Kinsey was the first researcher to suggest that sexual orientation is not dichotomous, but rather a complex system including sexual identity, sexual attraction, and sexual behaviors (Kinsey, Pomeroy, & Martin, 1948). According to Kinsey, sexual orientation should not be conceptualized as two categories, heterosexuals and homosexuals, but instead should be considered as a continuum between exclusive same-gender attraction to exclusive other-gender attraction. In his famous survey of sexual behaviors and attitudes, he asked participants to rate their sexual attraction on a scale from zero to six in which zero represented exclusive attraction to individuals of the other gender, and six represented exclusive attraction to same-gender individuals. Later, Kinsey et al. (1948) allowed participants to use this scale to identify their sexual identity and sexual behaviors as well. This pioneering research, as well as current studies, suggests that, although sexual attraction, sexual behavior, and sexual identity are closely related constructs, they are not always concordant (e.g., Pathela et al., 2006). For example, a man may identify as heterosexual, but may be attracted to men and may have sexual relationships with both men and women. Moreover, patterns of attraction, identity, and behavior may change across time and context (Diamond, 2008). Although the majority of research continues to exclusively focus on sexual identity and typically categorizes sexual identity instead of using a continuum, Kinsey's efforts to characterize the complexity of same-gender sexuality have had a profound impact on the understanding of gender differences in sexuality.

A variety of studies suggest that same-gender sexuality may be different for men and for women. In terms of sexual identity, women are more likely to identify as bisexual than as homosexual, whereas men are more likely to identify as homosexual than as bisexual (Mosher, Chandra, & Jones, 2005). Gay and bisexual men often report that they felt different from heterosexual men at a very young age, whereas lesbian and bisexual women often report later recognition of their "differentness" (Savin-Williams & Diamond, 2000). In terms of sexual attraction, women report their first same-gender attraction at a variety of ages, and report a great deal of fluidity in their attraction to men and to women (Diamond, 1998; Rosario, Schrimshaw, Hunter, & Braun, 2006; Savin-Williams & Diamond, 2000). For example, it is not uncommon for a woman who was exclusively attracted to men throughout adolescence to develop attractions toward women in adulthood. Similarly, it is not uncommon for a woman who reported a lifetime of exclusive sexual attraction toward women to become attracted to men later in life. In addition, bisexual and lesbian women often report that an emotional attraction toward women (or one woman in particular) developed into a sexual attraction, whereas men typically report that they felt a same-gender sexual attraction before an emotional attraction (Weinberg, Williams, & Pryor, 1994). In terms of sexual behaviors, men are more likely than women to report both same-gender sexual attractions and same-gender sexual behaviors, whereas women commonly report that they have same-gender attractions, but do not act on them (Weinberg et al., 1994).

Essentialists argue that sexual orientation is formed early in life and is not changeable (Kitzinger & Wilkinson, 1995). They suggest that women who identify as lesbians but have sexual relationships with men are not "true" lesbians. However, Diamond (2008) believed that sexual orientation is fluid, and that women's sexuality is fundamentally more fluid than men's sexuality. She argued for "detailed, longitudinal data on the multifaceted expression of same-sex and other-sex sexuality" in order to fully comprehend the nature of sexual development across the lifespan (p. 53).

Explaining Gender Differences in Sexuality

In general, the available evidence indicates substantial gender differences in sexuality in some domains but not others. Men generally report more sexual activity, more liberal sexual attitudes, higher correlations between reported arousal and physiological measures, and a more stable sexual identity than women do. However, many of these gender differences are small and appear to be decreasing across time. The most substantial gender differences appear to be in the use of pornography and masturbation. Researchers have proposed a variety of explanations for existing gender differences in sexuality. These explanations include biological factors, sociocultural factors, and methodological factors, among others. . . .

Brain differences. Brain activation in response to arousal is similar for both men and women. However, the areas of the hypothalamus that are activated during sexual arousal are somewhat differentiated by gender. In particular, the ventromedial hypothalamus is activated during women's sexual response, whereas the medial preoptic area is highlighted during men's sexual response (Graziottin, 2004). Activation of the hypothalamus and the amygdala during sexual arousal is greater among men than among women (Canli & Gabrieli, 2004). Men's cingulate gyrus and thalamus also are activated during sexual arousal (Hamann, Herman, & Nolan, 2004; Park et al., 2001). Research on these areas of the brain during women's sexual arousal has not yet been conducted.

Anatomical brain differences may also contribute to sexual orientation. LeVay (1991, 1993) found that the anterior portion of the hypothalamus in gay men was more similar to that of women than to that of straight men. However, this postmortem study focused almost exclusively on men who had died from AIDS, ignored lesbian women, and presumed heterosexuality for all participants not explicitly known to be homosexual (Wilson, 2000).

A recent review of gender differences in the brain suggested that there are very few differences, and differences that do exist are small (Eliot, 2009). In addition, these small gender differences generally have insignificant effects on gender differences in behavior. In terms of brain anatomical differences, there seems to be more variation within gender than between gender. . . .

Sociocultural Factors

Simone de Beauvoir (1968) proposed that "one is not born a woman, but rather becomes one" (p. 283). This famous dictum suggests that social factors, not biological factors, are responsible for psychological gender differences. For example, the sexual double standard states that premarital sex and sexual activity outside the context of marriage are acceptable for men, but not acceptable for women (Crawford & Popp, 2003). Although this double standard is not enforced to the same degree today that it was 50 years ago, the general belief in most cultures is that it is more acceptable for men to engage in casual sexual relationships and have more sex partners than it is for women to do the same (Milhausen & Herold, 1999). According to cognitive social learning theory, girls learn to avoid casual relationships and multiple sex partners in order to avoid punishment, whereas men learn to engage in the same behaviors without negative social consequences. Gender differences in sexuality such as differences in casual sex and multiple partners may be a product of the influences of the sexual double standard, which reduces female sexual expression.

Cognitive social learning theory also suggests that gender differences in sexuality may decrease across time to the extent that female models in the media become more sexually permissive (Oliver & Hyde, 1993). In accordance with this theory, meta-analytic results suggest that gender differences for many sexual attitudes and behaviors decreased across time as women became more sexually permissive and their reports of their sexual attitudes and behaviors grew closer to men's reports. Gender differences in sexual behaviors and attitudes can be expected to continue to decrease in the future if role models in the media become increasingly sexually liberal.

Social structural theory proposes that gender differences in sexuality are a product of gender differences in power (Eagly & Wood, 1999). As predicted by this theory, nations with greater gender equality had smaller gender differences for many sexual behaviors, including intercourse prevalence and the prevalence and frequency of oral sex, anal sex, casual sex, and masturbation (Petersen & Hyde, 2010). Societies with a large gender difference in power often devalue women, allowing men to treat women as sexual objects for their pleasure. Male sexuality is less regulated in such societies and men are often encouraged to engage in casual sex with many partners. In contrast, these societies often place strict regulations on women's sexuality, discouraging sex in any context outside of marriage. Therefore, it is not surprising that these societies would have larger gender differences in sexuality than societies with greater female equality. . . .

Conclusion

The research reviewed here indicates that many gender differences in sexuality are smaller than researchers once thought. The majority of gender differences in sexual behaviors and attitudes are small, indicating that within-gender variation is larger than between-gender variation in reported sexual behaviors and attitudes. When gender differences do exist, research suggests that they are a product of gender differences in biological factors, societal power differentials, and social pressures to respond according to assigned gender roles.

Despite the research suggesting that men and women are similar in many aspects of their sexual expression, researchers continue to emphasize gender differences, rather than similarities, in sexuality. Exaggerating gender differences may lead to a number of social and sexual problems. Conforming to strict gender roles limits one's sexual expression. For example, women who have a strong sexual desire may be derogated for having multiple sex partners or engaging in casual sex. In contrast, men who have low sexual desire do not fit the cultural stereotype and may be accused of being less masculine and not virile. These strict gender roles do not allow for variability within genders and may inhibit sexual expression in men and women.

In addition, strict gender roles may lead to increased sexual disorders. Women who are sexually inhibited may not explore their sexuality, they may feel guilt or shame for having sex, and this emotional suppression may lead to sexual disorders, such as reduced sexual desire. For example, research suggests that women who masturbate tend to be more satisfied with their sex lives than women who do not masturbate (Hurlbert & Whittaker, 1991). Masturbation may be a healthy way for a woman to explore her body and become comfortable with her sexuality, but women who feel guilt or shame about their sexuality are unlikely to become comfortable with their sexuality and may have unsatisfying sex lives. Culturally imposed gender roles may also increase sexual disorders among men. Men who feel as though they must use their sexuality as an expression of their masculinity may feel unnecessary pressure to perform sexually, thus increasing performance anxiety (Zilbergeld, 1999).

Recognizing gender similarities in sexuality where they exist is essential for challenging the double standard and gaining equality of sexual expression. If societies become more sexually liberal and gender differences continue to narrow, equal opportunities for sexual expression become more realistic. Trends in various cultures toward or away from societal gender equality, in turn, are likely to have implications for gender differences in sexuality.

References

Alexander, M. G., & Fisher, T. D. (2003). Truth and consequences: Using the bogus pipeline to examine sex differences in self-reported sexuality. *Journal of Sex Research, 40,* 27–35.

Allen, M., Emmers-Sommer, T., DeAlessio, D., Timmerman, L., Hanzal, A., & Korus, J. (2007). The connection between the physiological and psychological reactions to sexually explicit materials: A literature summary using meta-analysis. *Communication Monographs, 74,* 541–560.

Arafat, I. S., & Cotton, W. L. (1974). Masturbation practices of males and females. *Journal of Sex Research, 10,* 293–307.

Baldwin, J. D., & Baldwin, J. I. (1997). Gender differences in sexual interest. *Archives of Sexual Behavior, 26*, 181–210.

Baumeister, R. F., Catanese, K. R., & Vohs, K. D. (2001). Is there a gender difference in strength of sex drive? Theoretical views, conceptual distinctions, and a review of relevant evidence. *Personality and Social Psychology Review, 5*, 242–273.

Betzig, L. L. (1986). *Despostism and differential reproduction: A Darwinian view of history*. New York, NY: Aldine.

Buss, D. M. (1994). *The evolution of desire: Strategies for human mating*. New York, NY: Basic Books.

Buss, D. M. (1995). Evolutionary psychology: A new paradigm for psychological science. *Psychological Inquiry, 6*, 1–30.

Buss, D. M. (1998). Sexual strategies theory: Historical origins and current status. *Journal of Sex Research, 35*, 19–31.

Buss, D.M. (2009). The great struggles of life: Darwin and the emergence of evolutionary psychology. *American Psychologist, 64*, 140–148.

Buss, D. M., & Schmitt, D. P. (1993). Sexual strategies theory: An evolutionary perspective on human mating. *Psychological Review, 100*, 204–232.

Bussey,K.,&Bandura,A. (1999). Social cognitive theory of gender development and differentiation. *Psychological Review, 106*, 676–713.

Canli, T., & Gabrieli, J. D. (2004). Imaging gender differences in sexual arousal. *Nature Neuroscience, 7*, 325–326.

Chivers, M. L., Seto, M. C., & Blanchard, R. (2007). Gender and sexual orientation differences in sexual response to activities versus gender of actor in sexual films. *Journal of Personality and Social Psychology, 6*, 1108–1121.

Chivers, M. L., Seto, M. C., Lalumiere, M. L., Laan, E., & Grimbos, T. (2010). Agreement of self-report and genital measures of sexual arousal in men and women: A meta-analysis. *Archives of Sexual Behavior, 39*, 5–56.

Crawford, M., & Popp, D. (2003). Sexual double standards: A review and methodological critique of two decades of research. *Journal of Sex Research, 40*, 13–26.

Darwin, C. (1871). *The descent of man, and selection in relation to sex*. London, England: John Murray.

De Beauvoir, S. (1968). *The second sex*. New York, NY: Modern Library.

Diamond, L. (1998). Development of sexual orientation among adolescent and young adult women. *Developmental Psychology, 34*, 1085–1095.

Diamond, L. (2008). *Sexual fluidity: Understanding women's love and desire*. Cambridge, MA: Harvard University Press.

Eagly, A. H., & Wood, W. (1999). The origins of sex differences in human behavior: Evolved dispositions versus social roles. *American Psychologist, 54*, 408–423.

Eliot, L. (2009). *Pink brain, blue brain: How small differences grow into troublesome gaps—and what we can do about it*. Boston, MA: Houghton Mifflin/Harcourt.

Gangestad, S. W., & Thornhill, R. (1997). Human sexual selection and developmental stability. In J. A. Simpson & D. T. Kenrick (Eds.), *Evolutionary social psychology* (pp. 169–195). Mahwah, NJ: Lawrence Erlbaum Associates, Inc.

Graziottin, A. (2004). Sexual arousal: Similarities and differences between men and women. *Journal of Men's Health and Gender, 1*, 215–223.

Hamann, S., Herman, R., & Nolan, C. (2004). Men and women differ in amygdala response to visual sexual stimuli. *Nature Neuroscience, 7*, 411–416.

Hendrick, C., Hendrick, S. S., & Reich, D. A. (2006). The Brief Sexual Attitudes Scale. *Journal of Sex Research, 43*, 76–86.

Hendrick, S., & Hendrick, C. (1987). Multidimensionality of sexual attitudes. *Journal of Sex Research, 23*, 502–526.

Hurlbert, D. F., & Whittaker, K. E. (1991). The role of marital and sexual satisfaction: A comparison study of female masturbators and nonmasturbators. *Journal of Sex Education and Therapy, 17*, 272–282.

Hyde, J. S. (2005). The gender similarities hypothesis. *American Psychologist, 60*, 158–192.

Janssen, E., Carpenter, D., & Graham, C. (2003). Selecting films for sex research: Gender differences in erotic film preferences. *Archives of Sexual Behavior, 32*, 243–251.

Kinsey, A., Pomeroy, W., & Martin, C. (1948). *Sexual behavior in the human male*. Philadelphia, PA: Saunders.

Kite, M. E., & Whitley, B. E. (1996). Sex differences in attitudes toward homosexual persons, behaviors, and civil rights: A meta-analysis. *Personality and Social Psychology Bulletin, 22*, 336–353.

Kitzinger, C., & Wilkinson, S. (1995). Transitions from heterosexuality to lesbianism: The discursive production of lesbian identities. *Developmental Psychology, 31*, 95–104.

Laumann, E. O., Gagnon, J. H., Michael, R. T., & Michaels, S. (1994). *The social organization of sexuality. Sexual practices in the U.S.* Chicago, IL: University of Chicago Press.

LeVay, S. (1991). A difference in hypothalamic structure between heterosexual and homosexual men. *Science, 30,* 1034–1037.

LeVay, S. (1993). *The sexual brain.* Cambridge, MA: MIT Press.

Milhausen, R. R., & Herold, E. S. (1999). Does the sexual double standard still exist? Perceptions of university women. *Journal of Sex Research, 36,* 361–368.

Moir, A., & Jessel, D. (1989). *Brain sex: The real difference between men and women.* New York, NY: Dell.

Mosher, W. D., Chandra, A., & Jones, J. (2005). Sexual behavior and selected health measures: Men and women 15–44 years of age, United States, 2002. *Vital and Health Statistics, 362.* Washington, DC: Centers for Disease Control and Prevention.

Murnen, S. K., & Stockton, M. (1997). Gender and self-reported sexual arousal in response to sexual stimuli: A meta-analytic review. *Sex Roles, 37,* 135–153.

Oliver, M. B., & Hyde, J. S. (1993). Gender differences in sexuality: A meta-analysis. *Psychological Bulletin, 114,* 29–51.

Park, K., Seo, J. J., Kang, H. K., Ryu, S. B., Kim, H. J., & Jeong, G. W. (2001). A new potential of blood oxygenation level dependent (BOLD) functional MRI for evaluating cerebral centers for penile erection. *International Journal of Impotence Research, 13,* 73–81.

Pedersen, W., Miller, L. C., Putcha-Bhagavatula, A. D., & Yang, Y. (2002). Evolved sex differences in the number of partners desired? The long and the short of it. *Psychological Science, 13,* 157–161.

Petersen, J. L., & Hyde, J. S. (2010). A meta-analytic review of research on gender differences in sexuality: 1993 to 2007. *Psychological Bulletin, 136,* 21–38.

Rosario, M., Schrimshaw, E. W., Hunter, J., & Braun, L. (2006). Sexual identity development among lesbian, gay, and bisexual youth: Consistency and change over time. *Journal of Sex Research, 43,* 46–58.

Rowland, D. L. (2006). The psychobiology of sexual arousal and response: Physical and psychological factors that control our sexual response. In R. D. McAnulty & M. M. Burnette (Eds.), *Sex and sexuality, Vol 2: Sexual function and dysfunction* (pp. 37–66). Westport, CT: Praeger.

Rupp, H. A., & Wallen, K. (2008). Sex differences in response to visual sexual stimuli: A review. *Archives of Sexual Behavior, 37,* 206–218.

Savin-Williams, R. C., & Diamond, L. M. (2000). Sexual identity trajectories among sexual-minority youths: Gender comparisons. *Archives of Sexual Behavior, 29,* 607–627.

Stock, W. E., & Geer, J. H. (1982). A study of fantasy-based sexual arousal in women. *Archives of Sexual Behaviors, 11,* 33–47.

Strager, S. (2003). What men watch when they watch pornography. *Sexuality and Culture: An Interdisciplinary Quarterly, 7,* 50–61.

Trivers, R. L. (1972). Parental investment and sexual selection. In B. Campbell (Ed.), *Sexual selection and the descent of man, 1871–1971* (pp. 136–179). Chicago, IL: Aldine.

Udry, J. R. (1988). Biological predisposition and social control in adolescent sexual behavior. *American Sociological Review, 53,* 709–722.

United Nations Development Programme. (1995). *Human development report 1995.* New York, NY: Oxford University Press.

United Nations Development Programme. (2003). *Human development report 2003.* New York, NY: Oxford University Press.

Upchurch, D., Levy-Storms, L., Sucoff, C. A., & Aneshensel, C. A. (1998). Gender and ethnic differences in the timing of first sexual intercourse. *Family Planning Perspectives, 30,* 121–127.

Weinberg, M. S. C., Williams, C. J., & Pryor, D. W. (1994). *Dual attraction: Understanding bisexuality.* New York, NY: Oxford University Press.

Wells, B. E., & Twenge, J. M. (2005). Changes in young people's sexual behavior and attitudes: A cross-temporal meta-analysis. *Review of General Psychology, 9,* 249–261.

Whitley, B. E., & Kite, M. E. (1995). Sex differences in attitudes toward homosexuality: A response to Oliver & Hyde (1993). *Psychological Bulletin, 117,* 146–154.

Wilson, E. A. (2000). Neurological preferences LeVay's study of sexual orientation. *Substance, 91,* 23–38.

Zilbergeld, B. (1999). *The new male sexuality* (Rev. ed.). New York, NY: Bantam.

JENNIFER L. PETERSEN is a doctoral candidate at the University of Wisconsin-Madison.

JANET SHIBLEY HYDE is a professor of psychology and women's studies at the University of Wisconsin-Madison.

EXPLORING THE ISSUE

Is Pornography for Men Different Than Pornography for Women?

Critical Thinking and Reflection

1. What factors determine when sexually explicit narratives in film become categorized as pornographic images?
2. How does the consumption of pornography influence sexual attitudes and behaviors?

Is There Common Ground?

University of Connecticut professor of English and feminist theory Gina Barreca examined women's relationship with pornography in a series of responses to the E. L. James' erotic *50 Shades of Grey* trilogy. Barreca argued that women do enjoy pornography when it is written and enacted as an art form and cited the works of Anaïs Nin as an example of recommended erotic literature.

Poulsen, Busby, and Galovan (2013) conducted research that suggests pornography use has different implications for men and women. The data of their study showed a negative impact on men's sexual relationships when men engaged in solitary pornography use. Women who used pornography in the context of a relationship with a male partner reported positive impacts on the quality of their sexual relationship. Their research also noted that the meaning attached to pornography may differ and that this difference in perception impacts how men and women experience pornography consumption.

Additional Resources

Barreca, G. (2012, May 3). "Women Falling for Fifty Shades of Degradation." *Hartford Courant.* Retrieved from: http://articles.courant.com/2012-05-03/news/hc-op-barreca-fifty-shades-op-grey-degrades-women--20120503_1_women-powerful-man-actual-men

Barreca, G. (2012, July 14). "Hot Summer Reading: Good Dirty Books vs. Bad Dirty Books." *Huffington Post.* Retrieved from: www.huffingtonpost.com/gina-barreca/hot-summer-reads-good-dir_b_1671806.html

Poulsen, F., Busby, D., and Galovan, A. (2013). "Pornography Use: Who Uses It and How It Is Associated with Couple Outcomes." *Journal of Sex Research, 50*(1), 72–83.

Create Central

www.mhhe.com/createcentral

Internet References . . .

The Half the Sky Movement

http://www.halftheskymovement.org/

Girl Rising film

http://girlrising.com/

Salon

http://www.salon.com/2013/06/02/the_truth_about_female_desire_its_base_animalistic_and_ravenous/

The Atlantic

http://www.theatlantic.com/sexes/archive/2013/06/turns-out-women-have-really-really-strong-sex-drives-can-men-handle-it/276598/